Marvel Comics into Film

Marvel Comics into Film

*Essays on Adaptations
Since the 1940s*

Edited by
MATTHEW J. MCENIRY,
ROBERT MOSES PEASLEE *and*
ROBERT G. WEINER

McFarland & Company, Inc., Publishers
Jefferson, North Carolina

LIBRARY OF CONGRESS CATALOGUING-IN-PUBLICATION DATA

Names: McEniry, Matthew J., 1988– editor. | Peaslee, Robert Moses, 1973– editor. | Weiner, Robert G., 1966– editor.
Title: Marvel Comics into film : essays on adaptations since the 1940s / edited by Matthew J. McEniry, Robert Moses Peaslee, and Robert G. Weiner.
Description: Jefferson, North Carolina : McFarland & Company, Inc., Publishers, 2016 | Includes bibliographical references and index.
Identifiers: LCCN 2016009375 | ISBN 9780786443048 (softcover : acid free paper) ∞
Subjects: LCSH: Comic strip characters in motion pictures. | Comic books, strips, etc.—United States—Adaptations. | Marvel Comics Group—History.
Classification: LCC PN1995.9.C36 M375 2016 | DDC 791.43/652—dc23
LC record available at https://lccn.loc.gov/2016009375
Includes bibliographical references and index.

BRITISH LIBRARY CATALOGUING DATA ARE AVAILABLE

ISBN (print) 978-0-7864-4304-8
ISBN (ebook) 978-1-4766-2411-2

© 2016 Matthew J. McEniry, Robert Moses Peasleee and Robert G. Weiner. All rights reserved

No part of this book may be reproduced or transmitted in any form or by any means, electronic or mechanical, including photocopying or recording, or by any information storage and retrieval system, without permission in writing from the publisher.

Manufactured in the United States of America

*McFarland & Company, Inc., Publishers
Box 611, Jefferson, North Carolina 28640
www.mcfarlandpub.com*

Acknowledgments

The editors would like to thank Alicia Goodman and Naomi Joelle Glover, and Derrick Holland for their help with this project.

Matthew J. McEniry: Thank you to my co-editors, Robert Moses Peaslee and Robert G. Weiner, for allowing me to contribute in the journey of this volume. Thanks to my colleagues Ryan Litsey, Ryan Cassidy, and Le Yang for academically challenging me every day. Much love to my parents, Allen and Deborah McEniry, sister, Cortney McEniry, and grandparents, George and Naomi White. Thanks to my two great friends of twenty years, Matthew Gille and David Killian; you guys are the best, and I thank you for all the encouragement. A special thanks to the community of AJB; you all are awesome. Finally, thanks to my close gaming cadre of Spectear, Tesserae, Shadowed, and Boozy. What leisure I did have during this project you all certainly made special.

Robert Moses Peaslee: I would like to thank my co-editors, Matthew J. McEniry and Robert G. Weiner, for their tireless efforts in bringing this volume to fruition. Thanks also to my colleagues in the College of Media & Communication at Texas Tech University, who provide unyielding support, friendship, and mentorship at every turn. To my students, who inspire me every day to continue thinking and writing about things that "don't matter," I offer a hearty word of appreciation. Loving thanks finally to Kate, Coen, Hazel and Nora: my collective North Star, the first and last chapter of everything.

Robert G. Weiner: Love to Tom A. Gonzales, Joe L. Ferrer, John Oyerbides, Sara Dulin, my lovely mother, Marilyn Weiner, and Larry and Vicki. Special thoughts to my late father, Dr. Len Weiner.

Thanks to Felicity Smoak, Harrison Wells, Chuck Chandler, Phil Grayfield, Ryan Litsey, R. Cassidy, my colleagues in the Research, Instruction, and Outreach Department, Laura Heinz (for always having an open ear), Sheila Hoover, the Dean of Libraries, Dr. Bella Gerlich (you rock!), the Document Delivery Department at Texas Tech, Dr. Mark Charney, Dr. Erin Collopy, my library colleagues for their support and understanding, and Dr. Aliza Wong (for your energy, suggestions, and support). Special thanks to all my critters especially my buddy Murphey, my pal Miss Tess, and my girl Rocket. Dedicated to the memory of Little Spike.

Thanks to Matthew J. McEniry for your friendship and for keeping me in line all the time.

Thanks to Robert Moses Peaslee; it is always a pleasure to work with you. Your insights are always appreciated.

Special dedication to the architects of the original Marvel Universe, Martin Goodman, Carl Burgos, Bill Everett, Alex Schomburg, Allen Bellmen (a true gentleman if there ever was one), and all of the artists and writers who created and worked on all the amazing characters at Timely.

Special dedication to Stan Lee, Jack Kirby, Steve Ditko, Wally Wood, John Buscema, Roy Thomas, Larry Leiber, Don Heck, Jim Steranko, and everyone else at the original Marvel Bullpen who created the fantastic universe we all know today. Thanks to Avi Arad and Kevin Feige for bringing to life those wonderful characters on film.

Special thanks also to Miss Hanna Sawka, Mr. Brett Brock, Mr. Morgan Hyman, Dr. Gary Elbow, Mr. Spike Spiegal, Jack Russell, Frank Castle, Mr. Mason West, Dr. Paul Reinsch, Dr. Brad Duran, Dr. Darren Hudson Hick, Dr. Wyatt Phillips, Mrs. Shelley Barba, Professor Ghislaine Fremaux, Miss Stephani Shagula, Jamie Maberry (love you Dr. J.), the folks at the Southwst Popular Culture Association (Lynnea, Tammy, Kelli, Anna) and the Associate Deans of the TTU Libraries (Bob, Jennifer, Earnstein, Sheila—thank you for your support). Thanks to all my Honors students, past and present, who teach me every day the importance of education and how to think about popular culture topics in new and unique ways. You are the leaders of the future: Go forth and make the world a better place!

Table of Contents

Acknowledgments — ix

Introduction
    Robert G. Weiner, Robert Moses Peaslee,
    and Matthew J. McEniry — 1

Part 1: Myth

"Yeah? Well, MY god has a HAMMER!": Myth-Taken Identity in the
Marvel Cinematic Universe
    Brian Cogan *and* Jeff Massey — 10

"The terms of the contract have changed": How *Ghost Rider* Carries
on Goethe's Faustian Tradition
    Jacob Garner *and* Thomas Simko — 20

Transformers: The Movie: Making Modern Mythology the Marvel Way
    Jason Bainbridge — 27

You Can't Stop Her: *Elektra* Re-Configured
    Daniel Binns — 39

Part 2: Licensed Properties

Dare to Be Stupid: The Fetishization of Heavy Metal and the New
in *Transformers: The Movie*
    Eric Garneau — 52

Science Fiction in *G.I. Joe: The Movie*: Its Influence, Origin, Introduction
and Development
    Liam T. Webb — 60

Conan the Destroyer of a Franchise? Analyzing and Evaluating the Adaptive
and Narrative Features of *Conan the Barbarian, Conan the Destroyer*
and *The Horn of Azoth*
    Rodney Donahue — 72

Part 3: The Japanese Connection

Marvel and Toei
    Jesus Jimenez-Varea *and* Miguel Ángel Pérez-Gómez — 84

viii Table of Contents

Japanese Characters and Culture in Marvel's American Films
    STEPHEN MILLER   94

Part 4: Setting Up the Marvel Cinematic Universe

Sowing the Seeds: How 1990s Marvel Animation Facilitated Today's Cinematic Universe
    LIAM BURKE   106

The Death of the First Marvel Television Universe
    ARNOLD T. BLUMBERG   118

Frozen in Ice: Captain America's Arduous Journey to the Silver Screen
    DAVID RAY CARTER   129

The Primetime Heroics of Small Screen Avengers: Finding Sociopolitical Value in Marvel TV Movies
    JEF BURNHAM   138

Part 5: The Attempt of Progressivism in the Marvel Universe

Damsels in Transgress: The Empowerment of the Damsel in the Marvel Cinematic Universe
    JOSEPH WALDERZAK   150

Elektra: Critical Reception, Postfeminism and the Marvel Superheroine on Screen
    MIRIAM KENT   165

Gods and Freaks, Soldiers and Men: Gender, Technologies and Marvel's *The Avengers*
    JEREMIAH FAVARA   177

An Archetype or a Token? The Challenge of the Black Panther
    JULIAN C. CHAMBLISS   189

Part 6: Genre Studies

The Daywalker: Reading *Blade* as Genre Hybridity
    NAJA LATER   200

Body vs. Technology: *Iron Man: The Rise of Technovore* and Cyberpunk Culture
    VANESSA GERHARDS   212

On Your Stupid Earth: The De-Gerberized Duck
    RICK HUDSON   224

Part 7: The Anti-Hero

Punishing the Punisher: Can Hollywood Ever Capture the Essence of the Character?
    CORD A. SCOTT   232

Hulk Smash Binaries
 D. Stokes Piercy *and* Ron Von Burg   241

From Comic Book Anti-Hero to Cinematic Supervillain: The Transmedia
 Extension of Magneto
 Joshua Wucher   250

About the Contributors   261

Index   263

Introduction

ROBERT G. WEINER, ROBERT MOSES PEASLEE
and MATTHEW J. MCENIRY

Beginning with *Iron Man* (2008), the Marvel Cinematic Universe (MCU) films have established themselves as the template for the contemporary blockbuster movie. Audiences now expect and look forward to new MCU movies each year. Fox's reboot of *Fantastic Four* (2015), however, which bombed during its first weekend ($62,000,000) with a plethora of scathing reviews and the director distancing himself from the project,[1] provides a rare opportunity for substantial speculation about the future of the MCU. Could it make audiences reluctant to see future Marvel property films? Will it encourage Marvel Studios to reincorporate its First Family by reaching a rights deal with Fox (as Sony has done with regard to Spider-Man), moving it from what we'll call the "Cinematic Marvel Universe" into the MCU proper? Moving into its so-called "Phase Three," Marvel Studios hopes it can continue to maintain its successful momentum. In fact, the studio is betting big on this success—with Disney's backing—having planned releases all the way up to 2028.[2] The MCU has made itself a prominent part of the popular culture landscape and there are now college classes being taught featuring the MCU.[3] As one commentator pointed out recently, "Today the Marvel Cinematic Universe is the blueprint for every studio hoping to follow their path to the box office."[4] Contributor Liam Burke discusses in *The Comic Book Film Adaptation* (in his detailed chapter "How to Adapt Comics the Marvel Way") that many of the successful comic-related films take a page out of Stan Lee and John Buscema's 1978 *How to Draw Comics the Marvel Way*. The films use the principles outlined in Lee and Buscema's text (composition and framing of shots, layout, etc.) and translate them to the screen. Sometimes this is intentional (especially in Marvel-related films), but not always.[5]

When Marvel decided to form its own film studio in 2005, it was tremendously risky—many went so far as suggest it was ill-advised. For example, the man who brought other Marvel properties to the big screen, Avi Arad, resigned and the risk fell to Kevin Feige, who became president of the studio in 2007. It did seem like a tremendous gamble, since Fox owned the adaptation rights to the X-Men and Sony owned similar rights to Spider-Man, the two major Marvel franchises. Could Feige bring to worldwide box office success characters like Iron Man, Captain America, Thor and others? Those fears were put to rest when *Iron Man* (2008) was successful at the box office and the films that followed started gaining momentum. In 2012, Marvel's *The Avengers* became the third largest box office success of all time until 2015, when *Jurassic World* pushed it into fourth. The studio was also able to adapt z-grade characters like the *Guardians of the Galaxy* (2014), who had almost no name recognition outside diehard comic fans, and create a successful, smart, and funny movie that through word of mouth was a worldwide sensation. *Big Hero 6* (2014) met with similar success and was loosely based on Marvel characters. Following all of these moves, Feige has become one of the most influential producers in Hollywood.[6]

Much like the comic universe that Stan Lee, Jack Kirby, Steve Ditko, et al., created with the MCU, the studio has developed a shared universe that could potentially feature any of the 3,000 characters for which it continues to retain the movie rights.[7] MCU films are increasingly cross pollenated with MCU television programs like *Agent Carter* (2015), *Daredevil* (2015), *Agents of S.H.I.E.L.D.* (2013), and other future endeavors. In fact, with the reboot of Marvel Universe comic books—marked by the *Secret Wars* series in 2015—Marvel is trying to make the comics mirror the MCU in order to bring in new readers and make the comics more commercially viable. Those characters that are outside the MCU and are owned by other studios, like the Fantastic Four or Deadpool, have either been given the axe or new origins (e.g., Quicksilver as a "hero," not a mutant). Since Marvel Studios can now utilize Spider-Man, one could speculate that eventually they will reacquire all their characters, from the X-Men and the Fantastic Four to the Sub-Mariner, the Silver Surfer, or the Man Thing. Certainly with Disney owning Marvel, they could afford to buy back the rights to such characters.

Although technically one could argue it was New Line's *Blade* (1998) (see Naja Later's essay) that started the current wave of feature films featuring Marvel characters, it was really Fox's *X-Men* in 2000 that began the superhero film as a juggernaut industry. Sony's 2002 *Spider-Man* was even more successful in terms of box office sales, with both fan and critical acclaim. *X-Men* and *Spider-Man* showed that it was possible to bring superhero characters to the screen and not be "cheesy" (although 1989's *Batman* did this, the franchise ended up in a downward spiral until 2006's *Batman Begins*). There were, however, duds along the way in terms of box office success (or lack thereof), critical evaluation, and fan reception.

This volume addresses all aspects of the Marvel Cinematic Universe's history from a wide variety of perspectives and ideas. It is as comprehensive as we could make it, covering animated films, Marvel characters in non–U.S. settings, films produced when characters were properties controlled by Marvel (such as Conan and Transformers), television films, and even the current MCU. On the *Internet Movie Database*, an enterprising fan put together a list of Marvel-related films and series before 2000.[8] It is fairly complete, including television programs and series featuring the usual suspects like Spider-Man, Hulk, Captain America, X-Men, and the Silver Surfer. Some of the oddities listed include *Power Pack* (1991), *Solarman* (1986), *The Electric Company* (1971),[9] *Battle Fever J* (1979), *Fred and Barney Meet the Thing* (1979), *Ultraforce* (1995) and even the *Men in Black* movies and series (1997).[10] Missing from the list, however, are films and series produced by Marvel Productions like *Transformers: The Movie* (1986), *My Little Pony* (1986), *InHumanoids: The Movie* (1986), *Muppet Babies* (1984–1991), *Attack of the Killer Tomatoes* (animated series 1990–1991) and others.[11] Though many of the films discussed in this volume are critical and box office failures, or could be considered horrible movies by today's standards, that does not mean they are not worthy of study. It does not make them any less interesting from a historical, scholarly or analytical perspective.

As David Ray Carter discusses, Marvel characters first appeared on the cinema screens as early as 1944 in the 15-part Republic serial *Return of Captain America* (although Cap barely resembles the character as we know him today). It was not until 1986's *Howard the Duck* (Universal/LucasFilm) that another film featuring a Marvel character would have a major release in theaters. Although it was heavily hyped at the time (produced by George Lucas with a budget of $35,000,000), it was a box office disaster only grossing around $16,000,000 (see Rick Hudson's essay for the reasons behind this, although the film does have its fans). There were other ill-fated attempts to bring Marvel characters to the big screen: 1989's *Punisher* (see Cord A. Scott's essay) or 1990's *Captain America* (see Carter) and other films went straight to video or had a limited release in non-U.S markets (a practice that continued even as late as 2005's *Man-Thing* from Lions Gate).[12] On a budget of around $1,500,000, Roger Corman produced the 1994 *Fantastic Four* movie. It proved to be such an embarrassment that Avi Arad bought back the rights and reportedly "destroyed every print of the film."[13] Over the years the film has grown in cult status, even generating a feature documentary exploring the story behind the film (*Doomed: The Untold Story of Roger Corman's Fantastic Four*).[14] It would take another eleven years for a big screen version of *The Fantastic Four* (2005) to come to fruition.

Lee always believed that Marvel characters could be brought to the big and small screen successfully. He tried for years to get studios and Hollywood executives to buy into the commercial potential of Marvel's stock of characters. It was a difficult proposition and very little ever came of it, even though there was a rich history with the characters. The success of 1978's *Superman* film should have shown Hollywood executives that comic characters could be profitable if done right. In the early 1980s, according to Sean Howe, there was talk of both big- and small-screen Marvel film projects, including the *X-Men*, *Doctor Strange*, *Daredevil*, *Power Man*, and *The Human Torch* (and with big-name actors like Carl Weathers and Tom Selleck).[15] Part of the problem was not only the technological difficulties in making these characters believable, but as Liam Burke points out, rights issues were difficult: "Attempts were made to adapt Marvel Comics characters, but without the shelter of a parent company, the rights became increasingly diluted and complicated."[16] Spider-Man was one of biggest offenders in this category, and although there was a feature film scheduled to be produced in 1986,[17] it was not until 2002 that the big screen version of Spider-Man would be realized.

Oddly enough, there were television movies that made it to the big screen in non–U. S. markets. Episodes of *The Amazing Spider-Man* (1978) television series were cobbled together, released as *Spider-Man the Dragon's Challenge* (1981), and saw theatrical release in Ireland, Spain, Australia and other international markets. *Captain America* (1979) saw theatrical release in Columbia in 1981, while *Captain America Death II Soon* (1979) was released on the big screen in France in 1980 and even had a special film festival screening in Finland in 2014.[18] This shows that, in at least some selected markets, there was a desire to see MCU superheroes on the big screen despite the quality of the films. On television there was a more success with *The Incredible Hulk* (1978–1982) series and various animated programs. Official adaptations of Marvel characters like *Spider-Man* and the animated *Tomb of Dracula* (1980) were popular in Japan (as Jesus Jimenez-Varea and Miguel Ángel Pérez-Gómez discuss). With reference to *Supaidaman* (1978), Rayna Denison points out the unique hybridization of the Spider-Man character in the context of traditional Japanese television and film, characterizing *Supaidaman* as "Japanese reimaginings of the U.S. superhero character for a *tokusatsu* (special effects) genre diegesis."[19]

Unauthorized adaptations of Marvel characters worldwide provide an equally fascinating look at non–Western superheroics on film. It's no surprise that Spider-Man is one of the most popular to imitate. For example, the Turkish Spider-Man or *3 Dev Adam* (*Three Angry Men*, 1973) is the most notorious of all unauthorized Marvel related films featuring Captain America, the Mexican superhero Santo, and an evil Spider-Man who has a green costume.[20] A musical sequence from the Bollywood film *Daria Dil* (1988) called *Tu Mera Superman* ("You are my Superman") features Superman and Spider-Woman. Spider-Woman's costume looks very similar to that of a certain wall crawler right down to the colors, and the short sequence has over ten million views on YouTube.[21] The *Italian Spiderman* (2007) was originally released in short mini-episodes on YouTube and has more in common with anti-heroes like The Punisher or Italy's anti-hero/thief Diabolik. *Italian Spiderman* was created as a comedic parody of 1960s Italian adventure movies, even though the filmmakers were Australian.[22] Although the above have little in common with their official Marvel counterparts, they would not exist if were it not for Marvel's inspiration. This shows, among other things, how important cultural icons like Captain America, Spider-Man and others can be to the international filmmaking process.

Fan films also provide a unique glimpse into how ordinary people interpret these characters beyond the Hollywood system. Fan films have an interesting history and go as far back as 1963, when teenage director Donald Glut was making movies featuring his favorite comic, monster, and pulp characters, including the Marvel characters Captain America, Human Torch, and Spider-Man.[23] With the ease of digital film technology and the rise of advanced cosplay techniques, it is increasingly possible for anyone to create their own fan film starring their favorite popular culture character—films, moreover, that have decent production values and look good.[24] Fanfilms.net, Vimeo, and YouTube provide an easy way for fans to have their productions seen or noticed. A brief glance at fanfilms.net shows dozens of films for an assortment of Marvel characters, with Spider Man having the most adaptations at 71.[25] In fact, fan films like director Dan Poole's *The Green Goblin's Last Stand* (1992) have become famous by virtue of their stand-alone quality.[26]

In this volume, then, we have attempted to account for as much as possible of the diverse and ubiquitous MCU presence within and influence upon popular culture. This is an inherently losing battle, of course, since a truly comprehensive report would take up volumes, if indeed it were possible at all. Our stab at it begins in Part 1, which relates to myth. We start off with Brian Cogan and Jeff Massey's contextualization of the modern MCU in traditional mythical storytelling through explanation of how Stan Lee and Jack Kirby, in creating the Marvel Universe, created modern folklore. Jacob Garner and Thomas Simko look at the Faustian tradition in the *Ghost Rider* (2007/2011) films while Jason Bainbridge discusses how the seeds of the *Transformers* (1986) movie were set up in the Marvel Universe proper. Daniel Binns, finally, examines how *Elektra* (2005) portrayed the central character with some of the traditional characteristics of heroic women from ancient Greek culture.

Part 2 deals with licensed properties, starting with Eric Garneau's discussion of the various musical styles in *Transformers* (1986). Liam T. Webb takes us through the history and development of the direct-to-video *G.I. Joe* (1987), while Rodney Donahue digs into the difficulties the *Conan* (1982) franchise has encountered in its various adaptations. In particular, Donahue looks at the difficulties *Conan* scribe Roy Thomas had in bringing his vision to *Conan the Destroyer* (1984).

Part 3 engages the complex relationship between Marvel and Japanese producers and audiences. Jesus Jimenez-Varea and Miguel Ángel Pérez-Gómez examine the studio Toei and its adaptation of Marvel properties, while Stephen Miller looks at Japanese characters within Marvel-related films.

Part 4 concerns itself with nascent Marvel influences present in today's Marvel Cinematic Universe. Liam Burke describes, for example, how the original Marvel animated programs (particularly the Fox Kids programs) set up the trappings that we recognize today in the MCU. Arnold T. Blumberg describes how, through the *Incredible Hulk* (1988–1989) television films, there was a first effort to create a coherent Marvel Television Universe. David Ray Carter gives us a detailed history behind Captain America's cinematic adventures, while Jef Burnham looks at the original Marvel television movies and finds the American monomyth.

Part 5 focuses on progressive tendencies (social justice, race and gender equality) in Marvel-related films. Joseph Walderzak writes on the women in MCU's "Phase One" and how they can be seen as powerful. Miriam Kent discusses the critical reception of *Elektra* (2005) and how the character could be seen in a positive feminist context. Jeremiah Favara analyzes how "superbodies" function and are represented in *The Avengers* (2012), while Julian C. Chambliss investigates the history of the Black Panther—particularly in relation to the *Marvel Knights* (2010) animated series and *Ultimate Avengers II* (2004)—and the apparent difficulties with bringing this character to the big screen.

Part 6 deals with what we are calling genre studies starting with Naja Later's piece on hybridity in *Blade* (1998–2004) and how the filmic version of the character is difficult to pigeonhole. Vanessa Gerhards discusses the animated feature *Iron Man: Rise of Technovore* (2013) and the interconnection of the biological (flesh) and the technological as it relates to cyberpunk, while Rick Hudson argues that the reason *Howard the Duck* (1986) was a failure was that there was very little of creator Steve Gerber's version of Howard left in the film.

Finally, Part 7 looks at anti-heroes, beginning with Cord A. Scott's discussion of why it's been so difficult to bring a successful version of the Punisher to the big screen. D. Stokes Piercy and Ron Von Burg discuss the Hulk as a morally ambiguous but heroic figure in the animated film *Planet Hulk* (2010). Our last essay, by Joshua Wucher, addresses the character of Magneto in the *X-Men* (2000–2014) films and why his experiences with the Nazis as a child disturb his status as hero or villain (as do his transmedia and transcorporate characterizations).

As this volume shows, there is a "Cinematic Marvel Universe" that exceeds the boundaries of the so-called Marvel Cinematic Universe. Regardless of some of these movies' poor overall quality, they provide a unique glimpse not only into the history of Marvel on film, but also the ways superheroes and other sequential art and literary characters have been portrayed in different historical times. The essays in this volume show us that there is something of cultural value in taking a closer look at these films, no matter how excellent or dreadful they may be. Obviously, one of the biggest problems with many of these films is the lack of understanding among the producers and writers of the original source material. The other obvious problem is special effects. In the last twenty years of filmmaking, CGI filmmaking technologies have made the realistic portrayal of most superheroes and sequential art characters easier (which doesn't always mean a good movie if the storytelling is bad).

With so many MCU films in the pipeline as of this writing, it's highly probable that some of the forthcoming films will perform below expectations, perhaps causing producer anxiety and/or audience fatigue. While *Ant Man* (2015) was not the huge success that perhaps Marvel/Disney was hoping for, the film was certainly not a dud. The film made over $300,000,000 worldwide and was not the economic disappointment that DC's *Green Lantern* (2011) was (which made a little over $215,000,000). Both *Green Lantern* and *Fantastic Four* show that not every superhero related movie is going to do well if there is not a good story, no matter how good the special effects are. Disney, for their part, is not worried about the future of Marvel, as CEO Robert Iger is quoted as saying "the possibilities are endless."[27]

Notes

1. The monetary figures for the films taken from Boxofficemojo.com. See Keith Simanton, "Weekend Report-Fantastic Four Gets Clobbered," Boxofficemojo.com (August 9, 2015), last modified 8/10/15, http://www.boxofficemojo.com/news/?id=4094&p=.htm; Variety Staff, "Fantastic Four Director Josh Trank Disses His Movie, Implies Studio Screwed It Up," Yahoo.com (August 6, 2015), last modified 8/10/15, https://www.yahoo.com/movies/fantastic-four-director-josh-trank-disses-his-126062867512.html.

2. Devin Leonard, "The Master of the Marvel Universe: How Kevin Feige Became One of the Most Powerful Producers in Hollywood," *Bloomberg Businessweek*, no. 4373 (April 7–13, 2014): 64.

3. For example, the University of Baltimore offers a class on the MCU (taught by one of this volumes' contributors, Arnold T. Blumberg). See Eric Alt, "Why Marvel Works: A Scholarly Investigation: Studying the Impact of the Marvel Cinematic University on Pop Culture Warts and All," *Fast Company*, last modified 8/2/15, http://www.fastcompany.com/3036710/why-marvel-works-a-scholarly-investigation.

4. Devin Faraci, "Come Together: Marvel, the Avengers and the History of Shared Universes," *Birth. Movies. Death*, no. 23 (May 2015), 39.

5. Liam Burke, *The Comic Book Film Adapation* (Jackson: University of Mississippi Press, 2015), 228–262.

6. See Leonard 62–68.

7. DC is following in Marvel's footsteps with its films, but not always in its television programs.

8. See Mallorca-Moon, "Marvel Comics Films Before 2000 (in Chronological Order)," IMDB.com, last modified 8/7/15, http://www.imdb.com/list/ls000732305?ref_=tt_rls_1.

9. A children's variety program featuring a live action mute Spider-Man in short skits. The show also featured a young Morgan Freeman.

10. The *Men in Black* comic was at one time published by Marvel.

11. For a much fuller list see "Marvel Productions," IMDB.com, last modified 8/7/15, http://www.imdb.com/company/co0106768/?ref_=tt_dt_co.

12. *Man-Thing* was released as an Sci Fi channel original movie before it went to video.

13. Sean Howe, *Marvel Comics: The Untold Story* (New York: Harper, 2012), 356.

14. See "Doomed the Untold Story of Roger Corman's *Fantastic Four*," DoomedtheMovie.com, last modified 8/515, http://doomedthemovie.com/. Note at one time Marvel Comics was owned by Roger Corman's New World Pictures.

15. Howe, 261.

16. Burke, 58.

17. Burke, 58. Director James Cameron was involved with making a big screen version of *Spider-Man* even writing a script treatment.

18. This information about non–U.S. release dates comes from the *Internet Movie Database*, imdb.com.

19. Rayna Denison, "American Superheroes in Japanese Hands: Supaidaman," in *Superheroes on World Screens*, edited by Rayna Denison and Rachel Mizsei-Ward (Jackson: University of Mississippi Press, 2015), 59.

20. A version of *3 Dev Adam* is available on YouTube, https://www.youtube.com/watch?v=qKstTGjOjMw.

21. See "Indian Superman," YouTube.com, last modified 8/6/15, https://www.youtube.com/

watch?v=f5Pjo0WjBcs. See also Ian Robert Smith, "Tu Mera Superman: Globalization, Cultural Exchange and the Indian Superhero," in *Superheroes on World Screens*, edited by Rayna Denison and Rachel Mizsei-Ward (Jackson: University of Mississippi Press, 2015), 113–130.

22. A full version of the *Italian Spiderman* episodes can be seen on YouTube, https://www.youtube.com/watch?v=zVpJnGCwlMA.

23. These include *Captain America vs the Mutant* (1964), *The Human Torch* (1963), *Captain America Battles the Red Skull* (1964) and *Spider-Man* (1969). These are available on *I Was a Teen Age Movie Maker: Don Glut's Amateur Movies*, directed by Don Glut (Frontline Entertainment, 2006), DVD.

24. One caveat to this, however, is that the relative ease of making films also increases the number of low-quality productions.

25. See *fanfilms.net*, last modified 8/8/15, http://www.fanfilms.net/.

26. So much so that there was demand for the director to create a documentary on the making of the fan film which is not unheard of as *Batman Dead End* also had a documentary made about it. You can see *The Green Goblin's Last Stand* on YouTube, https://www.youtube.com/watch?v=bddH-GCYWMw, and the documentary *The Real Spider-Man: The Making of The Green Goblin's Last Stand*, https://www.youtube.com/watch?v=BE0gummUhtw.

27. Leonard, 68.

PART 1
Myth

"Yeah? Well, MY god has a HAMMER!"
Myth-Taken Identity in the Marvel Cinematic Universe

BRIAN COGAN *and* JEFF MASSEY

With box office returns of well over a billion dollars worldwide, *The Avengers* (2012) clearly struck a chord with audiences beyond Marvel's loyal comic book fan-base. The script is tight, the action intense, the production values high, and the casting stellar, but are these elements enough to warrant the insane popularity of one superhero film amidst a Hollywood landscape already saturated with spandex-clad do-gooders and four-color villainy? As many a film critic has lamented of late, we currently live in an age of superhero cinema. Combined, the "Big Two," Marvel and DC, have overseen more than 30 live-action superhero films featuring their properties in the last decade alone. And while some have been more successful than others (the gamut runs from *Green Lantern* and *Elektra* to *Iron Man* and *The Dark Knight*), none has generated fandom, buzz or box-office revenue to match *The Avengers*.[1]

What, then, does *The Avengers* have that other contemporary superhero films do not? Is it simply—as Tony Stark says to Loki—that "we have a Hulk"? Or could it be that the *Avengers* film franchise finally tapped into a mode of storytelling that has permeated popular culture for millennia and comic books for decades? Hollywood has long been fond of touting summer blockbuster films as "epic" (an overt nod to a classical works of massive scope such as the *Iliad* and the *Odyssey*), but is *The Avengers* the first truly "mythological" superhero film ever made? Or at least the first franchise to fully articulate and codify its own mythology?

The Avengers certainly profits from its own high production values and the current cultural predilection for costumed heroes, but it ultimately succeeds as a narrative because it is the culmination of a coherent, integrative film mythology that paints a world far greater than that shown on screen for 143 minutes. It represents, in the parlance of myth studies, a holistic cultural narrative; in the jargon of comics studies, it shows strong integrative continuity. Hollywood often talks of "tent-pole" films, big-splash events that are designed to support secondary and tertiary retail streams (toys, Happy Meals, t-shirts, video games, sequels, etc.) and *The Avengers* is certainly that. But the holistic continuity of *The Avengers*—the erection of the tent-pole itself—would not have been possible without the preceding films that tied into and presaged the meta-referential superhero universe about to unfold. Each of the *Avengers* "prequels"—*Iron Man* (2008), *Iron Man II* (2010), *Thor* (2011), and *Captain America: The First Avenger* (2011)—tapped into particular world mythologies (Greek, American, and Germanic), recalled universal heroic archetypes (the Selfish Intellect, the Good Soldier, and the Hubristic Warrior), and through sly Easter eggs and post-credits teasers suggested that these particular and universal themes were an integrated part of a greater narrative whole.[2] Marvel Studios president Kevin Feige branded these films the "Marvel Cinematic Universe": multiple heroes in multiple films operating within a singular continuity. While such continuity in traditional comics had been *de rigueur* for decades, for film fans accustomed to strings of "stand-alone" superhero films and constant reboots, this was an unexpected revelation. Or, as Nick Fury tells Tony Stark at the conclusion of the first *Iron Man* film, "You think you're the only superhero in the world? Mr. Stark, you've become part of a bigger universe. You just don't know it yet."

Marvel's cinematic "Avengers Initiative" resonated with modern audiences by offering a new and exceedingly rich form of intercultural and intertextual movie mythology rather than a single, stand-alone myth. *Avengers* director (and comic book fanboy/writer) Joss Whedon noted in the 2012 "Assemble the Ultimate Protection" featurette (an odd promo piece sponsored by Norton Antivirus) that "Marvel is taking the characters that they are putting into their movies and bringing them all together in a team franchise experience, which really has never been done before." Of course, as Whedon knew full well, this type of "team franchise experience" has been done before often and successfully in comic books and cultural mythologies, from Jason and the Argonauts to the Fantastic Four. Whedon's own Buffyverse (which links a film, multiple television series, and various comic titles) remains a model of successful integration across media: the adroit on-screen crossovers of two television series (*Buffy* and *Angel*) alone proved Whedon's capacity for fantasy-based continuity. And so, under his direction, the "Avengers Initiative"—and eventually the larger Marvel Cinematic Universe—became the first synergistic mythology effectively orchestrated by Hollywood. Unlike so many of the more recent superhero films that are, in the view of critics like Derek Thompson, "average on purpose," the results of this cross-cinematic narrative are spectacular (in a way the Spider-Man films could only dream).[3] The Marvel Cinematic Universe is now, in nearly every sense, mythology.

Indeed, while the pre–*Avengers* films owe much archetypically and structurally to ancient mythology, they also continue Stan Lee and Jack Kirby's reimagination of costumed superheroes stories as modern day mythology. Both Lee and Kirby looked at superhero stories not as black-and-white morality plays about good and evil (as their objectivist peer Steve Ditko often did), but instead tried to create new worlds with modern myths appropriate for the twentieth century.[4] In an Atomic Age that saw bombs with enough power to destroy the world many times over, many twentieth century writers, including Lee and Kirby (both of whom had served during World War II), felt that the modern world needed its own monsters and abominations, its own gods and heroes, rather than simple retellings of ancient myths. Historically speaking, the Marvel Comics Universe was rife with its own self-consistent mythology long before the current Marvel Cinematic Universe was a gleam in Hollywood's eyes.

To please several generations of comic fans, the Marvel Cinematic Universe had to take the canonical adventures of almost five decades and distill them into something commercially viable, while simultaneously employing mythological elements familiar to a general, or non–comics savvy, audience. Hence the older mythological frameworks adapted by Lee and Kirby, as well as their post–World War II re-imaginations of the hero, had to be adapted a third time to create a movie-friendly modern mythos, one that would lead to an epic film that could incorporate all the major Marvel characters (or at least the ones not licensed to other studios). Unlike many earlier superhero films, which too often required viewers to be well-versed in comics continuity for any sense of scope (vague references to other heroic properties and sly "in-jokes" designed to reward the nerd-core), the pre–*Avengers* MCU films slowly built up a series of mythic films that could reference one another. As a result, Marvel has created a cinematic universe with its own continuity, one that stands apart from the (often convoluted) continuity of comics, a continuity that rewards cinema-goers for being cinema-goers, rather than just rewarding comic fans for going to the movies.

Beginning with *Iron Man* in 2008, elements of a larger Marvel mythology would be integrated into almost every pre–*Avengers* MCU film. Book-ending *Avengers* both before (*Iron Man* [2008], *Iron Man 2* [2010], *Thor* [2011], and *Captain America: The First Avenger* [2011]) and after (*Iron Man 3* [2013], *Thor: The Dark World* [2013], and *Captain America: The Winter Soldier* [2014]) the "solo" Avengers films initiate and maintain a consistent narrative that builds towards and builds upon the actions of the contiguous films. This carefully planned mélange of mythologies within the films not only set up the canon for the *Avengers* franchise, but also successfully referenced ancient and modern mythology to create universally appealing heroes for a modern movie-going audience.[5] In the pre–*Avengers* films, familiar echoes of Greco-Roman demigods, Norse gods, Celtic heroes, and Arthurian legends commingle with Lee and Kirby's post-atomic superheroes: as in the comics, our gods wear spandex on screen.[6] *The Avengers* succeeds where other mythologically-inspired one-shot films (the many Beowulfian warriors, Arthurian kings, and Grecian earners that have paraded across the marquees of late) comparatively fail, because Marvel managed to integrate ancient (Western) and modern (American) mythologies throughout the pre–*Avengers* solo films. Iron Man, Thor, and Captain America individually paved the way for their own communal success. Superman and Batman, who had held the cinematic advantage for decades prior, had to wonder: where did we go wrong?

Crisis on Multiple Earths: The MCU vs. the DCU

Given the early history of narrative structures and superheroic models employed by DC and Marvel, it is perhaps surprising that, in the last decade, DC has been mythologically beaten to the punch by Marvel on the big screen. One long-standing view of comics' history posits that DC founded their superheroic universe in the 1930s on Ancient Mythic Archetypes, while Marvel—some thirty years later—seized the market share by portraying Everyman rather than Superman, in essence trading high-flying mythic heroes for more identifiable, grounded heroes. And so on the DC side of the equation we have Superman, the embodiment of LIGHT, a hero whose godly powers are derived from our yellow sun; he is the four-color avatar of the ancient Sun God. Grant Morrison, one of the most prolific and celebrated comic book writers of the last twenty years, noted in his book on superheroes and modern mythology, *Supergods*, that "Superman was Christ, an unkillable Champion sent down by his heavenly father (Jor-El) to redeem us by example and teach us how to solve our problems without killing one another."[7] Batman, conversely, is the DARK Knight, a legendary creature of shadow, forged from murder, a man who preys upon the fears of criminals while operating almost exclusively under cover of darkness; he is the monochromatic God of Death. Rounding out the divine DC "Trinity" is Wonder Woman, a being straight out of Greek mythology: she is the GODDESS Incarnate. Other heroic avatars with deep roots in mythology (the Flash [Greco-Roman], Shazam [Hebraic and Greco-Roman], Hawkman [Egyptian], Aquaman [Atlantean], among others) show that DC has long relied on Western mythology for narrative inspiration.[8] With the notable exception of Thor (more on him below), Marvel's early heroes—a teenage arachnid, a stretchy genius, an invisible woman, a rock-like brute, a fiery hot-rodder, an iron-clad technophile, a Jekyll-and-Hyde rage monster—are harder to identify as part of the ancient Western mythological tradition. Marvel's key properties, in other words, are less obviously mythic than those of DC.

It is important to emphasize (especially as most film viewers and modern comics readers are not comic book historians) that DC heroes were, in their earliest presentation, superhuman first and human second if at all. Superman's alter ego is Clark Kent, but that is, as Quentin Tarantino opines through his eponymous antagonist in *Kill Bill: Vol. 2* (2004), a construct, a false identity adopted by an alien god walking about on Earth among humans:

> BILL: Superman didn't become Superman. Superman was born Superman. When Superman wakes up in the morning, he's Superman. His alter ego is Clark Kent. His outfit with the big red "S," that's the blanket he was wrapped in as a baby when the Kent's found him. Those are his clothes. What Kent wears—the glasses, the business suit—that's the costume. That's the costume Superman wears to blend in with us. Clark Kent is how Superman views us. And what are the characteristics of Clark Kent. He's weak ... he's unsure of himself ... he's a coward. Clark Kent is Superman's critique on the whole human race.[9]

In other words, Superman is *always* Superman, just as Zeus (Jove) is always God, no matter what name he may offer the mundane nymphs and human maidens he seduces while "vacationing" on Earth. Humanity is a pose for these celestial beings, these sky-kings.[10]

Marvel heroes, by contrast, were often reluctant to take up the mantle of superhero at all. When Stan Lee, Jack Kirby, and Steve Ditko reinvigorated Marvel Comics in the early '60s (beginning with the Fantastic Four and Spider-Man), they quickly established the Marvel Comics Universe as distinct from the DC model. The art at Marvel was both crisp and evocative, the colors really popped, and the dialogue sounded closer to realistic speech than ever before "heard" in a comic. By most accounts, Stan Lee's dialogue actually sounded like it was coming from human beings, rather than proselytizing moral compasses (Thor, once again, being a notable [and quasi–Shakespearean] exception). But the greatest difference between the DC and Marvel Comics was in Marvel's presentation of the human hero.

Spider-Man is a teen who is bitten by a radioactive spider, sure, but one who—as he swings along the steel corridors of NYC—is as likely to be worrying about his beloved Aunt May, paying his rent, finishing his homework, and meeting girls as he is about the impending brouhaha with Doc Ock. Peter Parker is always Peter Parker, even when he's self-consciously wearing his "web-pits" or displaying the proportionate strength of a spider. Meanwhile, as citizens of Metropolis routinely "Look! Up in the sky!" for their sky-god to save them, Spider-Man, regardless of the fact he is a superhero, is far more likely to be labeled a "costumed menace" than a god. And although the Fantastic Four can be read as a quartet of superheroic archetypes—the Brains, the Brawn, the Hothead, the "behind-every-good-man-is-a-protective-1960s-mother"—they are, first and foremost, a human family. They bicker, they argue, they love, they marry, they feel guilty, and so on. The "normal" interpersonal dynamics between Reed, Ben, Johnny, and Sue remain largely unchanged even after their life-altering cosmic-ray–enhanced journey into space. Perhaps most significantly, the Fantastic Four do *not* have secret identities—they are always, simultaneously, Reed Richards/Mr. Fantastic, Sue Storm/the Invisible Girl (Woman), Johnny Storm/the Human Torch, and Ben Grimm/the Thing. There is no separation of identity, no god-pretending-to-be-human ruse as in the DCU. Marvel traditionally presents human beings dealing with being super, not superbeings dealing with being human.

Thor, of course, is a bit of an exception to this model, but even he breaks the DCU model of "caped god on Earth." In his earliest Marvel incarnation (solidified by the outstanding 1980s run by Walt Simonson), Thor is truly the ancient Norse God of Thunder, not a superheroic approximation, avatar, or archetypal doppelganger (however much the modern films take a step back on this, replacing "magical science" for "magical belief"). But if the brash superhero was a god, he was nevertheless exiled to Midgard by his father, Odin, as a lesson in humility, his godly identity hidden even from himself. In fact, *Journey into Mystery* #83 suggests that Thor has no memory of being Thor at all, until mild-mannered (and physically disabled) physician Don Blake—on the run from space invaders—finds the mighty hammer Mjolnir in a cave and is apparently judged worthy of wielding the mantle of Thor. As Blake/Thor exclaims: "**Thor**!! The legendary God of **Thunder**!! The mightiest warrior of all mythology!! This is **his** hammer!! And I—**I am Thor**!!!" Thor and Blake would, just like the Hulk and Bruce Banner,[11] body swap periodically over the years until Blake finally discovers (in issue #159) that he never really existed at all, that Donald Blake was just a skinny human parody of Thor with amnesia and a limp. As Thor wonders aloud, "But what happens now? Do I walk amidst the civilized world as a mythological god?? Or—? It is too bewildering!"[12] Thor (in the early comics, at least) is not a god pretending to be a human, but alternately a god and a human, then a god and a human version of himself, then only god.

So, on the whole, Marvel responded to the DC model of flat, often one-dimensional mythic avatars by showcasing the humanity of their spandex-clad heroes. Spider-Man and the Fantastic Four are "superhuman" and the X-Men literally "homo superior," but they are all humans first, godlings second. The cinematic Avengers—a playboy in a tech suit, an unfrozen soldier, a quasi-godling, a rage monster, and two spies—hardly seemed to come of a pedigree destined for modern mythology.

I'm a Marvel and I'm a DC: The Rise of the Cosmic Marvel Film

Of course, such reductive views of superheroes have been in print and on screen for—in some cases—nearly a century now. But these broad stroke definitions encapsulate the models and reflections of superheroes that the average consumer knows and which (therefore) Modern Hollywood draws upon most frequently: Superman is a god-like do-gooder, Batman is a frightening dark "knight," the Fantastic Four is a sci-fi family, and Spider-Man is an angsty teen.[13]

In all fairness, producing a successful super-hero film, getting the nuances (costumes!) right, placating the comics fan-base, and playing to the core strengths of long term characters with lengthy story arcs is not easy. Tapping into the cultural zeitgeist never is. But overall, the creators of the Marvel Cinematic Universe have taken more time and care to balance the mythological with the mundane than their Distinguished Competitor. Even the films outside of the current MCU continuity (due to ownership disputes between Marvel and Sony) focus on the human within the cosmic. The recent Spider-Man films have invariably concentrated on Peter Parker's human problems over his sometimes comically portrayed "super" problems ("How do I use my webs again?" and "Why is Peter's room all sticky?"). Likewise, the non–MCU *Fantastic Four* films, although often dismissed by critics and fans,[14] really lean into the humanity of the main characters. As in the early comics, Mr. Fantastic's nemesis, Dr. Doom, is introduced as Reed Richards' foil long before superpowers entered the picture. Ben Grimm still longs to be human rather than "super." And despite the global threat of Galactus the World-Devourer looming ominously, *Fantastic Four: Rise of the Silver Surfer* (2007) is really about Sue and Reed getting married. Their stories remain super personal, not superhuman. So again, on the face of it, the god-like DC heroes should, by all rights, have given rise to the most mythological cinematic narratives. But there's more to mythology than predictable heroic archetypes.

Successful mythologies—from the Homeric to the Whedonesque—need not be entirely predictable, or even logical. In *Works and Days* and *Theogony*, the ancient Greek mythographer Hesiod presents two versions of the "Pandora's Box" myth, for example, and the Christian Bible offers two versions of the creation of Adam and Eve in Genesis. Yet narrative inconsistency has not detracted from the popularity, power, or persistence of these myths. Paradoxes abound in "mythic reality." One of the most perplexing "mythic time" moments of Western culture is the Birth of Athena/Birth of Hephaestus paradox. According to Hesiod, Athena is born parthenogenically from Zeus' head. That is, Zeus (ever the philandering husband) woos and beds the goddess Metis, who becomes pregnant with his child. But jealous Zeus, citing a prophecy that stated Metis' child would overshadow the father, consumes Metis entirely. Soon after internalizing the pregnant goddess (whose name translates as "thought"), Zeus experiences excruciating headaches, so Hephaestus (the god of craft and metallurgy) splits open his step-father's head with a giant axe. Out pops Athena, a fully-grown and armor-clad warrior woman: the new Goddess of Wisdom (and clear precursor to Wonder Woman and Xena).

This is a wonderful myth, full of weirdness and supernatural allegory. But there's a mundane problem with Hephaestus in the scene. For, according to Hesiod, Hephaestus is the son of Hera, Zeus' long-suffering wife, who parthenogenically gives birth to her son without the "help" of Zeus or any other male donor. As his myth goes, Hera initiates his unusual birth as a rebellious reaction to Zeus' solo-birth of Athena. Narratively, then, Hera gives birth to Hephaestus *after* Zeus gives birth to Athena—a birth that Hephaestus midwifes.

Yet like all of Hesiod's *Theogony*, the individual myths of Athena and Hephaestus are interconnected, forming a grand narrative relevant to Greek society at the time. That's what mythology is, at its core: an interconnected set of stories embraced by a culture. In other Greek myths, we see the Olympian gods interact with various "local" Greek and Trojan heroes; in the often-retold tales of Hercules and his labors, the hero runs into creatures who interact with other heroes in their own subsequent tales; Virgil's *Aeneid*— mythological propaganda at its finest—recycles the various monsters and heroes of

Homer's *Iliad* and *Odyssey*. Thus old myths serve new cultures, linking people through shared narratives beyond the constraints of time and space (and sometimes, logic).[15]

Despite the paradoxes characteristic of mythological storytelling, there is an interconnectivity and continuity to the individual "mythic" tales of Ancient Greek heroes that results in a grand "mythology." By this standard, comic books can be—and have long been—considered "modern mythology." The heroes of the DC comics universe, the heroes of the Marvel comics universe, traditionally interact with one another, operate within a consistent world, and even refer to one another. There are highly literate editors—envied by Hesiod, no doubt—who now patrol for "narrative continuity." At various points in comic history, companies have "rebooted" their entire universes in the name of self-consistent narrative. In many ways, the comic book model of mythology is more mythological, thanks to continuity controls, than classical mythology. And its fans, as the ultimate worshipers, embrace (sales!), emulate (cosplay!), critique (spoiler alert!), retell (fanfic!), and thus ultimately help shape the future of their new cultural mythology. The current interconnected films of the Marvel Cinematic Universe warrant the "mythology" label not simply because they recall ancient myths, or tap into cultural archetypes, but because they present a cohesive and epic universe: the MCU presents a deep mythology rather than a simple series of singular myths.

Behold True Believers! The Mighty Marvel Movie Era Marches On

Just as the post–*Avengers* MCU films continue to expand the universe established in *Avengers* through post-credits teasers (meta-theatrically voiced by folks as diverse as Baron Strucker), the pre–*Avengers* appearances of Nick Fury (in Campbell's mythology who can be seen as the archetypal elder who ushers the heroes along on their quest) served to herald an expanding cinematic future that pleased fans, but also acknowledged its ancient narrative heritage.

There are many differences between the DC films and the Marvel films. Some fans have argued that the recent Marvel films are simply better produced; they are certainly more consistent than the DC films (*Green Lantern* [2011] is often trotted out as evidence in such debates). But one key difference is that the recent Marvel films have tapped into undercurrents of mythology that DC films have seemingly abandoned in an effort at shaking off their own staid—even inflexible—mythic archetypes. That is, the DCU of late, and in stark contrast to its earlier success in the 1970s with *Superman*, has portrayed its cinematic heroes in increasingly dark and dour "realistic" tones. Witness the relentless greyscale of Gotham in the *Dark Knight Trilogy*, or the toned-down palette dominating *Man of Steel*; these are sky-kings made mundane on the big screen. Meanwhile, the MCU has been expanding their increasingly fantastic mythology with more and more super beings as the *Avengers* mythology leads towards a cosmic conflict against Thanos and the Infinity Gauntlet storyline. It's a trend towards more and more fantastic, super, and potentially hopeful myths that seems likely to continue past the current *Avengers* films. If we are to believe what villainous Baron Wolfgang von Strucker says at the end of *Captain America: The Winter Soldier*, the ever-expanding MCU will soon include the twin "miracles" Scarlet Witch and Quicksilver. This proved to be prophetic with the release of *Avengers: Age of Ultron* (2015). In an interview for his book, *Supergods*, Morrison suggested that we "can look at *Dark Knight Rises* as the conclusion of a trend and the *Avengers* as the beginning of one."[16] The MCU is riding a wave of fantastic storytelling and universe expansion that has successfully drawn new fans to the Mighty Marvel Marching Banner.

With the teaser at the end of the first *Iron Man* film, the MCU began to herald a grandeur that, while perhaps unfamiliar to film-goers, was refreshingly familiar to card-carrying members of FOOM (Friends of Old Marvel). When Nick Fury appears unexpectedly in Tony Stark's apartment to announce that Stark is not "the only superhero in the world," but is now a "part of a bigger universe," Stark's immediate reaction is to ask, "Who the hell are you?" Comic fans in the audience already knew, of course, that Samuel L. Jackson is "Nick Fury. Director of S.H.I.E.L.D.," but at this moment Stark stands for traditional film structure: one wherein the hero's (his!) story is all that matters, as if Iron Man's superheroics exist within a narrative bubble. But from this moment on, Marvel's cinematic myth become cinematic mythology.

The interconnectivity of the films, and of the MCU, is reinforced by character cameos and name-drops, as well as a conspicuous prop, the Tesseract, an otherworldly energy source that acts as a grail item throughout the pre–*Avengers* MCU films. Fury is a central, and active, linking figure throughout many of the films, but so too is Agent Coulson, who acts as Fury's proxy and eventual impetus for the "Avengers" unification: their common reason for vengeance. Coulson lends his wry humanity to *Iron Man*, *Iron Man II*, and *Thor*, before dying in *Avengers* (never fear: he subsequently appears on the small screen in Marvel's *Agents of S.H.I.E.L.D.* [2013]). Black Widow simultaneously kicks ass and unifies the narratives of *Iron Man II*, *Avengers*, and *Captain America: The Winter Soldier*. Minor "recurring villains" also occupy this celluloid universe: in *Iron Man II*, Tony Stark battles not only physical threats, but political ones, including the governmental control of his armor, spearheaded by Senator Stern (Gary Shandling). In the course of governmental hearings over Stark's possession of the "nuclear deterrent" that is the Iron Man armor, Stark suggests that Stern is an "ass-clown"; by the end of the film, Stern suggests that Stark is a "little prick." This mildly homosocial badinage serves as a side-conflict to Iron Man's physical battles against Whiplash and Tony's corporate battles against Justin Hammer. But the Stern flyting gains further depth when, in *Captain America: The Winter Soldier*, Stern subtly whispers to Jasper Sitwell's character: "Hail HYDRA." We suddenly realize that Stern is not just Stark's personal enemy, but the enemy of all heroes in this universe. The interconnectivity of the MCU is, in this one short line, highlighted to the viewer: what happens in the Captain America universe matters in the Iron Man universe, because they are—lest we forget—the same place and the same epic cycle.[17]

Conclusion: To Infinity (Gauntlet) and Beyond!

Superheroes in Hollywood have not, historically, succeeded in maintaining a continuity that would enable mythology, only mythic moments. The cinematic world of the *Dark Knight*, for example, has not, as far as the viewer can tell, also been the world of the *Man of Steel*. Gotham City and Metropolis have long "known of one another" in their shared comics universe (in that mythology, replete with crossovers and "World's Finest" team-ups), but Superman and Batman films have never successfully synergized; Batman never calls for Superman to back him up, and Superman never does a fly-by over Gotham on screen. Their worlds and their myths are discrete. Likewise, as far as non–MCU films are concerned, the X-Mansion may exist fifty miles north of the Baxter Building, but since their inhabitants have never crossed paths on screen, we may never know unless we bring our own comics-based mythology to the cinema with us.

Yet like the chapters in the *Theogony*, the Norse *Eddas*, the Bible, or the *Mahabharata*, the myths of the MCU are now interconnected, forming a grand mythology: an interconnected set of stories embraced by a culture. By this standard, superhero comic books can be and have been considered "modern mythology" for geek culture. Within the four-color page, the heroes of the Marvel Comics Universe, like their counterparts in the DCU, interact with one another via team-ups and smack-downs, occupy the same consistent geography, and operate within a self-consistent world (what JRR Tolkien would call a true "sub-creation"). Overseeing these universes are editors who patrol for "continuity."[18] And at various points in history, comics companies have rebooted their entire universes in the name of self-consistent universal narrative: in the name of mythology. Superheroes have even died for the sake of such continuity. It is perhaps fitting, then, that Coulson died to unite the Avengers and catalyze their continuity on screen.

Grant Morrison once opined that superheroes "fill in the gap in a secular culture because they open up dimensions of the cosmic and the transcendent, which is the stuff legends usually have to deal with. [...] What superheroes have done is give these ancient qualities a new dress so we can recognize ourselves again."[19] Jack Kirby created the "New Gods" as a continuation of his old comic heroes, which were, in turn, a continuation of ancient mythological heroes; the MCU is a coherent continuation of the Marvel Comics Universe: a new cosmic mythology that offers cinemagoers an enduring new, but familiar meaning system.

The ancients had Gilgamesh, Samson, Achilles, and Hercules. What about us in the modern world? Our god has a hammer. And we have a Hulk.

Notes

1. Compare relative takes—*Superman* (1978) garnered more critical acclaim at the time, Oscar-nods. See http://www.boxofficemojo.com/genres/chart/?id=superhero.htm.

2. Claude Lévi-Strauss brought the term "mytheme"—the smallest core narrative element in a mythic story—into vogue as part of "La Structure des mythes" in his *Anthropologie Structurale* (Paris: Plon, 1968) 227–255.

3. Derek Thompson, "The Reason Why Hollywood Makes So Many Boring Superhero Movies," *The Atlantic* (13 May 2015), http://www.theatlantic.com/entertainment/archive/2014/05/hollywoods-real-superhero-problem/370785/.

4. Kirby evidenced this particular drive later in his career as well, when he created the aptly named New Gods for DC Comics.

5. For brevity's sake, and since, for the most part, they were not intentionally used to set up the Avengers, we exclude the first two Hulk movies from this analysis. But note the deleted scenes in Hulk with the Cap cameo.

6. Christopher Knowles and Joseph Michael Linsner, *Our Gods Wear Spandex: The Secret History of Comic Book Heroes* (San Francisco: Weiser Books, 2007).

7. Grant Morrison, *Supergods* (New York: Spiegel and Grau, 2011), 16.

8. For in-depth analyses of the "archetypal patterns" underlying DC's "mythological super-heroes," see Don LoCicero, *Superheroes and Gods: A Comparative Study from Babylonia to Batman* (Jefferson, NC: McFarland, 2007). And for a dismissal of "structural mythology" as a valuable critical lens through which to view comic book heroes, see Geoff Klock, *How to Read Superhero Comics and Why* (New York: Continuum, 2006).

9. *Kill Bill: Vol. 2*, directed by Quentin Tarantino (2004; Burbank: Miramax Lionsgate, 2011), DVD.

10. Likewise, the Amazon princess Diana (daughter of Queen Hippolyte) is always Wonder

Woman, even when she is pretending to be the bespectacled Army nurse, Diana Prince (a human whose identity she *literally* buys in *Sensation Comics* #1). It's an identity of convenience at the basest level, brought about by a weird coincidence suddenly noticed by the self-exiled Amazonian who spies a weeping nurse: "I just noticed—with these glasses off, you look a lot like me! I have an idea! If I gave you money, would you sell me your credentials?" The weeping nurse agrees (happily going AWOL to join her fiancé in South America), saying, "I'm Diana too! Diana Prince! And you'd better remember that last name—because it'll be yours from now on." In the early comics, Wonder Woman's human identity isn't even a self-creation, but that of another. As for Batman, although he was born Bruce Wayne, a real human boy, hasn't been a boy (or a fully functional human being) since the night his parents were murdered and he took up the mantle of the Dark Knight. Despite Bill's assurance in *Kill Bill II*, Bruce's "playboy billionaire" routine (sleep all day, collect investment checks, disappear into the night) is only a guise to keep Batman funded and well-rested. The cape and cowl are Batman's "real" face and the suit and cravat are his disguise. When these three Golden Age DC heroes are in their "civilian" guises, they are all still on the clock, heroically speaking. The DC Universe is predicated upon gods wearing human masks essentially being superheroes 24/7.

11. The Hulk, of course, isn't a god-disguised-as-human, but a metamorphic human who loses his humanity/godhood depending on his mood. But in his early representations (before the modern comics introduced "Smart Hulk," "Mr. Fixit," and "Gladiator Hulk"), Bruce Banner provides most of the emotive, human hook that drives the narrative. The Hulk simply exists to, well, smash.

12. See Paul O'Connor's excellent history of Thor's "muddled" secret identity in "Who Is Don Blake?" in *Sequart* (http://sequart.org/magazine/30757/who-is-don-blake/).

13. Superman, in particular, has suffered a good deal on the big screen because of cultural expectations of his godhood. That is, his films have succeeded most when he has been portrayed as the Sun God—the morally righteous, one-dimensional Boy Scout—and not when he has been allowed an excess of humanity or personal desire. Witness, on the one hand, the much-lauded first *Superman* film (1978), wherein a happily four-color Superman makes the "hard choice" between saving his beloved Lois Lane (and California) or saving Hackensack, New Jersey; spoiler alert: he saves Hackensack ... first. The early Superman films repeatedly delighted in drawing the "you are a god, not a man" dichotomy rather large: when Superman gives up his powers for "human love" in *Superman II* (1980), the world suffers, including his personal world, and so he gives up his humanity to be "super," or an aloof god once again. On the other hand, note the derision heaped upon the recent *Man of Steel* (2013), in which a grey-spandexed Superman exacts personal vengeance upon his familial nemesis, Zod. There is not room in Superman's cinematic world for human and god to co-exist. Aeneas would sympathize. Batman has had a greater variety of on-screen incarnations, but as the recent allegory-heavy *Dark Knight Trilogy* attests, what Batman stands for is far more important to fans than who wears the Batsuit. And Wonder Woman is still looking for her modern Hollywood moment.

14. *The Fantastic Four* (2005), for example, is often unfavorably compared to Pixar's *The Incredibles* (2004) which is touted as the best "Fantastic Four" film ever made, much as *Galaxy Quest* has been ranked the best "Star Trek" film ever made.

15. This can also be true with comics. As Morrison has noted, "one of the most amazing things about those [comic] universes is that they exist, there's a paper continuum that reflects the history, but people don't die, it's like the Simpsons, people don't age, they just change" (Brian Hiatt, "Grant Morrison on the Death of Comics," RollingStone.com, 8/22/11, retrieved 2/20/15).

16. Ifanboy, "Interview: Grant Morrison on *Supergods*," www.ifanboy.com, 8/9/12, retrieved 2/20/2015.

17. Likewise, S.H.I.E.L.D. Agent Jasper Sitwell appears alongside Coulson in *Thor* and *The Avengers*, only to be revealed as a HYDRA Operative in *Captain America: The Winter Soldier*. There, Sitwell confesses to Captain America and Black Widow that Arnim Zola's targeting algorithm enables the Insight Protocol to target and eliminate anyone on the planet, including "a TV anchor in Cairo, the Undersecretary of Defense, a high school valedictorian in Iowa City. Bruce Banner, Stephen Strange, anyone who's a threat to HYDRA!" Sitwell name-drops not only the Hulk, but also Marvel's Sorcerer Supreme, Dr. Strange, a character whose film will not be released until 2016. Clearly, Marvel has the "long con" in mind here, or, a universe in which everything is connected going forward.

18. See "Jonni DC: Continuity Cop" who appeared in the outstanding *Ambush Bug* series.

19. Scott Thill, "Meet the New Gods: Better Than the Old Gods," *Wired Magazine*, 2011, Wired.com, retrieved 2/20/15.

"The terms of the contract have changed":
How Ghost Rider *Carries on Goethe's Faustian Tradition*

JACOB GARNER *and* THOMAS SIMKO

Characters in myth and story have been making deals with demons and devils, sprites and spirits, and all manner of other supernatural entities since the ancient Sumerians spread myths of soliciting the aid of their own personal deities using prayer, service, and ritual sacrifice. Invoking the name *Faust*, however, is to speak to a solicitor of a decidedly specific sort, and it is a sort that is itself not without transmutation. Since the popularization of the Faust myth in the 16th century, to Marlowe's Faustus in the 17th, to Goethe's retelling two hundred years later, popular culture has seen a plethora of mortals soliciting devils for favors. One such mortal who, to this writing, has seen very little exploration on this topic is Johnny Blaze of Marvel's *Ghost Rider* (2007), and there are many parallel facets between Blaze and Faust, which we should put to consideration.

An essential aspect of this comparison to note, however, is *which* Faust we are talking about. As stated, the Faust legend has been told and retold and, like many other tales, been transformed and adapted to suit the sensibilities of a changing audience. To compare the Ghost Rider to the Faustus of Marlowe would be a wasted labor. Ultimately, the two are at best dissimilar and at worst directly at odds, the devilish deal being the only remaining link between the two. Conversely, Goethe's version of Faust shares a number of significant correlations with Blaze, not only in terms of the deal itself, but also of their internal conflicts, the women they love, and their ultimate redemption. Prior to Goethe, the Faust character was irredeemable. He served as a frightening cautionary tale of the dangers of forsaking the divine for earthly pleasure (unless you were a Calvinist; in that case you were just doomed). He was a boogeyman to the overly ambitious. Goethe applied to Faust the allegorical equivalent of a comic book retcon. Goethe's Faust spoke to the morals and understanding of an audience hundreds of years displaced from the original tales, and Blaze's story speaks to an audience with especially similar inclinations.

While the deal in and of itself is an act shared across all the Faustian mediums, Goethe took a particularly divergent path in terms of the motivations to make said deal. Goethe's Faust is a scholar at the apex of human knowledge. He is learned in every subject, an expert in every field, and still, he is unhappy. He is immersed in an existential crisis, a lack of any sense of fulfillment in his life, and his ever-increasing knowledge base simply reinforces his certainty that he will never find lifelong fulfillment. Thus, the contract he makes in lines 1660–70 seems a simple one: his own eternal soul for the means by which he may attain a single moment of complete, edifying satisfaction:

> **Faust.** Beyond to me makes little matter;
> If once this earthly world you shatter,
> The next day may rise when this has passed.
> It is from out this earth my pleasures spring,
> It is this sun shines on my suffering;
> If once from these I draw asunder,
> Then come to pass what will and must.
> I do not further choose to wonder
> If hate may then be felt or love,
> Or whether in those regions yonder
> They still know nether or above.[1]

For Blaze in *Ghost Rider*, the deal is equally simple. Mephistopheles takes possession of Blaze's soul, and, in return, heals his father of terminal cancer. Blaze is of course a fool for taking this deal—while his father is cured of the cancer in his body, he dies the next day during a stunt show performance. Additionally, both deals are part of a greater power play. In the film, Mephistopheles is a Satanic analog that makes the deal to establish the avatar of the Ghost Rider on Earth, protecting himself from whatever may come to disrupt his plans. In the case of *Ghost Rider* (2007) it is the evil intentions of Mephistopheles' son, Blackheart. Getting rid of anything Johnny Blaze might care about in the world helps him achieve this, as Mephistopheles tells him: "I cured his cancer. That was the deal. But I couldn't let him come between … us."[2] In the sequel, *Ghost Rider: Spirit of Vengeance* (2011), the reasoning behind these deals is expanded to explain that Mephistopheles (now called Roarke) has far less power when he is not in his normal domain—Hell:

> Why does the devil walk in human form anyway? I have no idea. Maybe he doesn't know either. Maybe he passes on from body to body, down through history, waiting for the perfect fit. But I know one thing—on Earth, he's weak. His powers are limited. He needs emissaries to do his dirty work, so he finds them or makes them, using his greatest power—the power of the deal.[3]

In lines 307–15 of *Faust*, Mephistopheles is recognized as a devil of Hell trying to win in his own Jobian wager with God Himself:

> **The Lord.** Though now he serve me but in clouded ways,
> Soon I shall guide him so his spirit clears.
> The gardener knows by the young tree's green haze
> That bloom and fruit will grace it down the years.
> Mephistopheles. You'll lose him yet! I offer bet and tally,
> Provided that your Honor give
> Me leave to lead him gently up my alley![4]

Further, Faust's desire is a metaphysical one. He does not seek base pleasure or power like his Faustian predecessors. He seeks basic, unfettered fulfillment, and just a single moment of it at that, which makes him something of a moral anomaly in Faustian lore. Carter Slade, one of the earlier bearers of the Ghost Rider's power, notes a similar anomaly with Johnny Blaze's version of the rider:

Any man that's got the guts to sell his soul for love has got the power to change the world. You didn't do it for greed; you did it for the right reason. Maybe that puts God on your side. To them that makes you dangerous, makes you unpredictable. That's the best thing you can be right now.[5]

This analog creates the greater conflict between the protagonists and their devils. The distinction between base desire and a higher calling is lost on both versions of Mephistopheles. Goethe's Mephistopheles tries to win Faust his moment by imposing a glut of sensual pleasure that may well have worked on the previous Faust characters, but is anathema to the wishes of this one. Blaze is similarly underestimated—Mephistopheles assumes that Blaze will want to be rid of the Ghost Rider and have a "normal" life once again.

> MEPHISTOPHELES: Congratulations, Johnny. You upheld your end of the bargain. It's time I take back the power of the Ghost Rider. You get your life back. The love you've always wanted. You can start a family of your own. There are more deals to be made. More people willing to give their souls for what they desire. Let someone else carry the curse. You're free now. After all … a deal's a deal.
> JOHNNY BLAZE: No. I'm gonna own this curse … and I'm gonna use it against you. Whenever innocent blood is spilt, it'll be my father's blood. And you'll find me there. A spirit of vengeance—fighting fire with fire.
> MEPHISTOPHELES: I will make you pay for this.
> JOHNNY BLAZE: You can't live in fear.
> MEPHISTOPHELES: NO![6]

Mephistopheles cannot comprehend that someone would turn away the chance at having their life back, much less turning down one of his own offers. Mephistopheles is not used to being told "no" by lesser beings and will continue to plague Johnny Blaze into the next film. However, Mephistopheles should have understood why something like this would have occurred—the spirit that is within Johnny seeks similar things—this instance being a form of justice to be spread throughout the world:

> MOREAU: Zarathos was an angel, a Spirit of Justice. Sent to protect the world of men. But he was tricked, captured, brought down to Hell. Corrupted. Driven insane. [laughs]. His mission to protect the innocent was perverted into a lust to punish the guilty. He became the Spirit of Vengeance.
> JOHNNY BLAZE: Yeah, but the angel, the Spirit of Justice, he's alive in there? Somewhere?[7]

Johnny Blaze wanted to ensure that no one else would have to go through the same pain and loneliness that he has endured, but also realized the good that the powers could bring to the world. No longer the servant of Mephistopheles, he could use this power to rid evil wherever he felt it.

So, in both cases, what appears on the surface to be the typical trope—man makes deal with devil, man misses important detail, man gives in to hubris, man is tricked and ultimately loses soul—becomes instead a commentary on the deeper, more complicated aspects of human life and an allegory for the value of greater psychological fulfillment that simple worldly pleasures cannot provide. Further, the inability of the long-lived, immortal demons to foresee and compensate for these needs gives us insight into society's own developing ideas about what is valuable in life. As the Fausts of previous centuries were lured to base desire, they become foils to Goethe's Faust, and this social development is echoed in Johnny Blaze, whose kneejerk, emotional reaction becomes amended and tempered by his higher calling to love and justice. The devils of Hell, to our social mind, cannot comprehend these callings, and justifiably so. It is their own inherent lack of empathy, their own inability to grow and change, which keeps them damned. This idea was solidified by Dante seven centuries ago and has seen little change. As Virgil noted:

> And he to me, as one experienced:
> "Here all suspicion needs must be abandoned,
> All cowardice must needs be here extinct.
>
> We to the place have come, where I have told thee
> Thou shalt behold the people dolorous
> Who have foregone the good of intellect."[8]

This is later reinforced by Brother Guido:

> For who repents not cannot be absolved,
> Nor can one both repent and will at once,
> Because of the contradiction which consents not.[9]

In this light, the shortcomings of the devilish malefactors seem reasonable, and they become an Achilles' heel that mere mortals can use, even unwittingly, to avoid their own damnation. In both cases, however, this proves to be temporary.

In this way, we are brought to the women of these tales, both of whom, though they are marginalized in the fashion typical of so many other narratives, are essential. Without them, no matter how transcendent the yearnings of our protagonists, they would have been damned. The ideals of the protagonists managed to confuse their devils, and they put off the terminal consequences of their contracts, but they only serve as a temporary fix. Something more is needed to fully redeem them. That "something more" is provided in the stories' female counterparts. In Goethe's *Faust,* this role is played by young Gretchen, alternatively called "Margarete" (Gretchen is the diminutive form of Margarete). Gretchen embodies absolute purity. Even Mephistopheles admits in lines 2621–26, on seeing her leaving a church, she has no sins to confess:

> **Mephistopheles**. Her? I just so happened by the curtain
> At her confession; she's just been
> Pronounced absolved of any sin;
> She's a right innocent young lass
> Who brought mere nothings to confess
> On her I have no hold at all![10]

Faust is irrevocably drawn to her, likely because her essential purity is tantamount to the kind of personal meaning he himself seeks. He fights with his conflicting feelings to the derision of Mephistopheles, but, as were a symptom of the times and with the unhelpful goading of Mephistopheles, he eventually mistreats her, impregnates her, and abandons her. However, the love she develops for him is absolute, and whether or not he knows it, Faust loves her deeply as well. As she awaits execution for the infanticide she committed in lieu of any other options, Faust, using the powers granted by Mephistopheles, makes to rescue her from her cell and her impending death. He cannot see her punished, though he omits personal responsibility while he struggles with his feelings. To Faust's chagrin, Gretchen refuses escape. Though mad with grief, she takes personal responsibility for her actions, even within the confines of so many unjust circumstances, and she cringes away from the demonic presence of Mephistopheles. Upon her death at the end of the first part of *Faust,* Mephistopheles states her condemnation, but because of her purity and absolute repentance, a voice from the heavens contradicts Mephistopheles, assuring that she is saved.

It is her purity and love that eventually save Faust when, in the play's second part, he finally experiences that single moment of fulfillment, completing the terms of his contract. Mephistopheles believes he's won, but instead, his soul is carried to the heavens, leaving Mephistopheles at a loss until it is explained by the angels in lines 11933–40:

> **Angels.** [*floating in the higher atmosphere, bearing FAUST'S IMMORTAL ESSENCE*]
> Pure spirits' peer, from evil coil
> He was vouchsafed exemption;
> "Whoever strives in ceaseless toil,
> Him we may grant redemption."
> And when on high, transfigured love
> Has added intercession,
> The blest will throng to him above
> With welcoming compassion.[11]

Faust's own actions are not enough. It's only through the redemptive power of Gretchen's love in tandem with Faust's "ceaseless toil" that he is saved; this concept is echoed by Roxanne in the *Ghost Rider* comics as well as, to a lesser extent, in the film version.

In the first *Ghost Rider* film, Roxanne provides a redemptive moment at the end by reminding Johnny Blaze of his own humanity. After having defeated Blackheart at San Venganza, Johnny Blaze (still in his Ghost Rider form) tries to turn away from Roxanne, simply calling himself "a monster." Reminding Johnny that she is not afraid of this side of him, the two share a brief moment before Mephistopheles interrupts them. Unfortunately, the character of Roxanne is completely written out of *Ghost Rider: Spirit of Vengeance*, eliminating the need for a pure female counterpart. If we are to turn to the comics instead, we see that it is her love for Johnny that seems to be the only thing keeping him from being dragged to Hell for all eternity. Johnny Blaze recounts the events in *Marvel Spotlight* #6:

> Later that same night, the master appeared to claim my soul ... but I defied him, hurling forth epithets which would have singed the ears of gods....
> But my mere words were no match for his demoniac powers, until the pure innocence of Roxanne entered into the fray....
> No sooner did she appear ... than the master fled, since the presence of one pure in heart is to the devil as a cross is to a vampire....
> Thus I was saved ... or at least partially saved, for the arrival of my beloved had come too late to spare me half the master's curse....
> And I am thus doomed to suffer the dark houses in this ungodly form ... until I totally defeat the master, or become his slave....[12]

Not only is Satan (later retconned to a demon named "Mephisto" near the end of the original *Ghost Rider* comic series[13]) unable to harm Johnny Blaze due to Roxanne's purity, he is also unable to cause harm to her,[14] as seen later issues. The need for Roxanne to be there for protection would be a constant plot device through early issues of *Ghost Rider*, as would Satan constantly going after Johnny. This is especially true with the introduction of "the friend"—a Jesus-like character that intervenes just when it seems like all hope is lost for the title character. First appearing in Ghost Rider #9, "the friend" reminds Johnny that despite Satan having his soul, there would always be a chance for his redemption:

> As long as there are people of good will on this world, Satan, they shall always stand between you and your innocent victims. Johnny Blaze's only sin was despair—and that is not sin enough

to condemn him to your domain. [...] Johnny Blaze's soul is beyond you, Satan. He has earned his second chance. [...] No man lives his life without contending with you several times, Satan. Johnny Blaze won his first battle. The future is up to him. For now, remember that he is free—that you have no claim to his soul.[15]

Of aesthetic note is the fact that Faust and Ghost Rider seem to have little explicit similarity in terms of the powers granted them by Mephistopheles: while Faust looks human, Ghost Rider becomes a leather-clad, chain whip-wielding monster with a flaming skull for a head. At their core, however, the powers are identical. Both are granted a level of protection from harm. The first *Ghost Rider* film makes this clear in the beginning, as we see Johnny Blaze in his human form survive a bad landing during a stunt that should have killed him. Both can change their forms, but what they metamorphose into is different. Faust chooses to become young, eschewing any potential option for flame-headedness in favor of regaining a full head youthful of locks. Blaze describes his own transformation as terrifying not only for him, but those around him:

> I was possessed by an ancient demon. In the presence of evil, I change into a monster, and I prey on the wicked, and I suck out their souls. And you don't want to be around when that happens. See, there's good and bad in all of us, and maybe you're not a murderer, but you did something that you didn't want the Rider to see—a white lie, an illegal download. [...] I've tried to fight it, to hold it back, but the darkness inside me only gets stronger.[16]

Most importantly, both gain the ability to conjure items, seemingly from nowhere. Faust conjures up expensive jewelry, potions, and methods of transportation. Ghost Rider can conjure his own form of transportation, transforming any motorcycle that he touches to turn into his special Hell Cycle. It should be noted that the Hell Cycle has a far more unique look in the first *Ghost Rider* movie, while the Hell Cycle for *Ghost Rider: Spirit of Vengeance* is more subdued (but in line with look of the original comics). This power carries over to other vehicles, as seen with the Bagger 288 excavator in *Ghost Rider: Spirit of Vengeance*. Faust may have a seemingly infinite amount of knowledge, but Ghost Rider's "Penance Stare" allows him not only to gain the information he needs by seeing into someone's soul, but also to punish them by making them experience all of the pain that they have ever caused to others all at once.

Ultimately, what we've discovered in comparing these two seemingly disparate characters is a valuable understanding of the shift in the human narrative concerning how we view our interactions with malevolent supernatural beings and what we would expect in return for our souls. Where once it was assumed we would ask for commodities or pleasures of the flesh or the power to impress, we now ask for what fulfills us existentially—we ask for the emotional fullness granted by love or by helping those we love. And while once we would be dragged to hell for the asking, now the asking itself is enough to mire those devils and keep us from their reach. Last, as illustrated by Gretchen and Roxanne, we see that striving for peace, or justice, or meaning is not enough. It is the love of another, their ability to see through us into the core of our being and to love us because of (or perhaps in spite of) what they see there, that finally redeems us. As humans, as long as we "[strive] in ceaseless toil" for transcendent purpose, our souls will remain our own.

Notes

1. Johann Wolfgang von Goethe, *Faust,* ed. Cyrus Hamlin, trans. Walter Arndt, 2d ed (New York: W.W. Norton, 2001), 45.

2. *Ghost Rider*, directed by Mark Steven Johnson (2007, Sony Pictures, United States, DVD, 2007).

3. *Ghost Rider: Spirit of Vengeance*, directed by Mark Neveldine and Brian Taylor (2011, United States, Sony Pictures, Blu-ray, 2012).

4. Goethe, *Faust*, 10.

5. *Ghost Rider*.

6. *Ghost Rider*.

7. *Ghost Rider: Spirit of Vengeance*.

8. Dante Alighieri, *Divine Comedy, Longfellow's Translation, Hell* (1997; Project Gutenberg, 2009), canto 3, http://www.gutenberg.org/files/1001/1001-h/1001-h.htm.

9. Alighieri, *Divine Comedy, Longfellow's Translation, Hell*, canto 27.

10. Goethe, *Faust*, 71.

11. Goethe, *Faust*, 339.

12. Gary Friedrich, Mike Ploog, and Frank Monte, *Marvel Spotlight* #6, October 1972 (New York: Marvel), 8.

13. J.M. DeMatteis, Don Perlin, Dave Simons, *Ghost Rider* #76, January 1982 (New York: Marvel), 6.

14. Tony Isabella, Jim Mooney, Sal Trapani, *Ghost Rider* #8, October 1974 (New York: Marvel), 10.

15. Tony Isabella, Jim Mooney, Sal Trapani, *Ghost Rider* #9, December 1974 (New York: Marvel), 15–16.

16. *Ghost Rider: Spirit of Vengeance*.

Transformers: The Movie
Making Modern Mythology the Marvel Way

Jason Bainbridge

"Beyond good. Beyond evil. Beyond your wildest imagination."—Original tagline, *Transformers: The Movie*[1]

"It was an ass kicker.... I'm friggin' dying. What the hell's all this about? I guess I'm not coming back next year."—Peter Cullen, voice actor for Optimus Prime, on reading the script for *Transformers: The Movie* and discovering Optimus Prime was to be killed[2]

In the 2013 ABC sitcom *The Goldbergs*, a program set in the 1980s based on the showrunner's own family and experiences, child protagonist Adam Goldberg (Sean Giambrone) is a massive fan of the *Transformers* toy line and its Saturday morning cartoon series. So in Season 2, Episode 11, "The Darryl Dawkins Dance," when *Transformers: The Movie* (hereinafter *TTM*) has its theatrical release, his grandfather Albert "Pops" Solomon (George Segal) offers to take him to "the talking car movie." But while Adam goes to the movie expecting to see the heroic Autobots kick (evil) "Decepticon butt," he is alarmed by what actually occurs:

> Narrator: "They killed all the good guys ... even Optimus Prime was killed. In cold blood. And along with it my innocence."
> Pops: "Do the good guys always die like this?"
> Adam: "They're not dead. It's probably a plot twist. They'll come back and save the day."
> Narrator: "But they didn't."
> *Cut to Adam and Pops sitting in an empty theatre.*
> Pops: "Are you ready to go?"
> Adam: "No. Optimus will be back."
> Pops: "I don't think he's coming back."
> Adam: "Oh, he's coming back, bigger and better and not dead."
> The Cinema Usher: "He's dead, dude."

With the death of Optimus Prime in *TTM*, the *Transformers* franchise came to represent not only the final stage in the evolution of the action figure, a figure whose action is to turn into another toy entirely, but also a major change in the transmedia strategies used to market them. Using *TTM* as a case study, this chapter analyses Marvel's role in franchise development and how this complex web of paratexts (to borrow Jonathan Gray's term, defined in more detail below) centered around *TTM* became more than just another exercise in world-building. Rather, these paratexts became the building blocks of a rich and complex modern mythology that itself "transformed" the *Transformers*, in many ways prefiguring the strategies that Marvel would use throughout the 1990s and 2000s around their own characters under the emergent Marvel Studios brand.

Transformers: The Movie

Released in 1986, *TTM* was a co-production between Marvel Productions (an animation subsidiary of the Marvel Entertainment Group, formerly DePatie-Freleng Enterprises), Sunbow Productions (an animation studio, owned by Griffin-Bacal Advertising, who represented Hasbro), Toei Animation (a Japanese animation studio), and Hasbro (a contraction of Hassenfeld Brothers, the toy company responsible for the production, marketing and release of *Transformers* toys). Set twenty years after Seasons One and Two of the cartoon, in the then future of 2005, the movie's characters and storylines continue into Series Three of the television series and the subsequent *Transformers: Headmasters* three-part miniseries.

As Adam Goldberg discovered, the movie advances the Autobot/Decepticon war on an epic scale. It kills off multiple characters and introduces several new ones (including new leaders Ultra Magnus, Rodimus Prime, and Galvatron, along with the first female *Transformer*, Arcee). It develops and deepens the *Transformers* mythology by introducing the Matrix of Leadership, the Quintessons (subsequently revealed to be the creators of the Transformers, at least in the animated series) and Unicron, a giant robot that consumes planets. It also features a celebrity voice cast (including Leonard Nimoy, Robert Stack, Judd Nelson, Eric Idle, Lionel Stander and, strangely appropriately as the voice of the giant robot that eats planets, Orson Welles), a pounding 80s rock sound track, and a much stronger anime look and adult sensibility (including limited violence and swearing that gave the film a PG rating). A box office failure on release (making U.S. $5.8 million on a budget of U.S. $6 million), the film has subsequently developed a cult following (particularly among the now adult fans of the franchise).

Most importantly, *TTM* provides one of the best examples of how canny marketing decisions can give rise to complex transmedia narratives. *TTM* literally killed off characters from the 1984/1985 toy lines as these toys were being phased out of retail assortments in favor of all-new characters. In this way the death of Optimus Prime—and by extension a number of Generation 1 Transformers—serves as perhaps the perfect blend of creativity and commerce, simultaneously dramatic and providing narrative momentum while also encouraging children to seek out toys of the new Autobots and Decepticons. Indeed, story consultant Flint Dille suggests that an earlier draft of *TTM* was even more explicit, with the discontinued 1984 line of Autobots being eliminated as they ran a gauntlet of Decepticons, so children "would have seen their entire toy line wiped out."[3]

In truth, the strategy was not *that* successful. As *The Goldbergs* episode demonstrates Adam is deeply distressed by Prime's death:

> ADAM: "I mean who murders Optimus Prime. It's like killing Superman or Knight Rider or Lassie."
> POPS: "You've been ranting about this for two days kiddo. Come on, he's just a cartoon robot."
> ADAM: "To you. To me he's a hero. If I made that movie Optimus would live forever and he would bring peace to Cybertron."

According to the *TTM* Special Edition DVD Commentary by Chris McFeely, many children shared Adam's feelings and were reportedly deeply distressed when Optimus Prime (not to mention characters such as Ironside, Brawn, Prowl, Ratchet, Wheeljack, Bluestreak and Starscream) were killed, leading to Prime's return in Series Three of the cartoon (which was set after the events of *TTM*). A similar plan to kill the heroic leader Duke in the *G.I. Joe* movie (that had been in development before *TTM* but was released straight to video thanks to *TTM*'s poor box office returns) was also quashed in post-production as a result of the negative feedback. Commenting on *The Goldbergs* reference to the death of Prime, creator/showrunner (the real) Adam Goldberg notes:

> [our] episode came out and got all this attention, and everyone was stunned it got this much attention … it's Bambi for a lot of people. And it's a lesson—never underestimate the power of nostalgia, and memory, and what you experienced as a kid. We got so many Tweets! And it was because so many people had the same experience I had, which was going to the theater and sitting there and saying, "What the hell did I just watch?"[4]

But *TTM*'s marketing failure also points to the franchise's even greater success; children like Adam were so distressed because Prime had been so well developed as *a character*. As story consultant Flint Dille explains: "the real answer [as to why we killed Optimus Prime] is that we didn't know he was an icon … it was a toy show. We just thought we were killing off the old product line and introducing a new product."[5] The film had underestimated the effectiveness of the transmedia strategies the franchise had used to make the audience care for and believe in Prime. In trying to reduce Prime back to a commodity that could be replaced, they had failed to consider the individual appeal of the character they had created.

Origins

Transformers were very much early products of convergence culture and, more particularly, one of Hasbro's international licensing deals for the 12-inch *G.I. Joe* figure to the Japanese toy company Takara in 1970. When Japanese consumers failed to embrace *Combat Joe*, he was subsequently retooled as the 12-inch *Henshin Cyborg* (until 1974) and then shrunk to the 3½-inch *Microman*. The line evolved again in 1980 into *Diaclone*, a range of robots and vehicles with inch-tall action figures that fitted into their cockpits. By 1982 the *CosmoContak* Lamborghini was transforming into a robot figure, launching a *Diaclone* sub-line inventively called *Car Robots*, comprised of cars and trucks that transformed into robots. This subsequently gave rise to the *Real and Robo* line (1983) that expanded the offerings to include jets, trains and construction vehicles as well as living creatures like dinosaurs and insects. Ultimately, the *Microman* line itself developed the *Microchange* sub-line with normal household items like cassettes, a microscope, a cassette player and a gun that all similarly converted into robots.[6]

A Hasbro representative attending the 1983 Tokyo Toy Fair discovered these transforming figures and they were presented to Hasbro's head of R&D, George Dunsay—who suggested using the *Microchange* and *Diaclone* figures to create a single toy line for the West. The Griffin-Bacal ad agency in the employ of Hasbro (who had previously created the "Real American Hero!" tag line for the 1982 relaunch of *G.I. Joe*) also created the concept that brought the *Microchange* and *Diaclone* toy lines together, the line creative director, Joe Bacal, dubbed *Transformers*. Two tag lines were created—"More than meets the eye" and "Robots in Disguise"—and certain cosmetic changes were made, replacing many of the metal parts with plastic and recoloring the heroic leaders Optimus Prime (and later *TTM*'s Ultra Magnus) a patriotic red, white and blue.[7]

The Marvel Way

Hasbro went to Marvel to employ the three-pronged marketing scheme that had worked so well with their 1980s *G.I. Joe* relaunch: their toy line, coupled with Marvel comics and a Marvel Productions/Sunbow animated series. When relaunching *G.I. Joe*, Hasbro had looked to the success of *Star Wars* and more particularly the high visibility and character recognition the franchise had derived from a regular monthly (Marvel) comic. As *G.I. Joe* writer Larry Hama describes it:

> [Hasbro] wanted an angle on being able to advertise it [*G.I. Joe*], which is how the Marvel [comics] connection came in…. There were only a few seconds of animation you could have in a toy commercial, and you had to show the toy, so people wouldn't get totally deluded…. [Hasbro's] Bob Prupish [*sic*] realized that a comic book was protected under the first amendment and there couldn't be restrictions based on how you advertised for a publication.[8]

Hasbro's strategy was this: they went to Marvel comics to create a *G.I. Joe* comic book and develop the characters and storylines around these action figures. In exchange Hasbro would provide fully animated commercials for the comics that would also advertise the toys (and later this became a Marvel/Sunbow animated series in its own right).[9] In so doing, Hasbro put forward a marketing plan that was to become an industry standard, "a model for non-film properties to survive in other mediums."[10]

As they did with the *Joes*, Marvel similarly provided the robots of the *Transformers* line with personalities, storylines, a comic (commencing with the cover date of September 1984), and, through Marvel Productions/Sunbow, a cartoon series (also commencing in 1984). As Flint Dille explains, the mandate was to make the *Transformers* series more adult, particularly as the franchise's major competition was younger.[11] (This was *Challenge of the Gobots*, a Hanna Barbera series similarly about transforming robots, in this case the Tonka toy line adapted from the Japanese Popy/Bandai *Machine Robo*.) Dille derived the world-building aspect of *Transformers* from his experience working for TSR on role-playing games.[12] While the storylines differed between the cartoon and the comics (the latter was originally set in the Marvel Universe, thanks to an appearance by Spider-Man in Issue #3, and provided different origins for some of the characters), Marvel editor and writer Bob Budiansky provided the basic source material of Autobots and Decepticons, as well as the rivalry between Optimus Prime and Megatron that informed both narratives and continued to resonate through later adaptations, including the Michael Bay live action/CGI franchise of the mid 2000s.

However, it would be another comic book writer, Simon Furman, famous on the UK edition of the comic and transferring over to the American version with *Transformers* #61 in mid–December 1989, who would be most linked to the *Transformers*. He used the characters and situations of *TTM* to provide an epic sweep to the comic narrative, commencing with Ultra Magnus and Galvatron time travelling from 2006 to the then present day[13] (in the *Target: 2006* storyline in issues #78–88), drawing in *TTM*'s use of Optimus Prime's death and Megatron's transformation into the megalomaniacal Galvatron, reviving Unicron (in *The Legacy of Unicron* storyline in issues #146–151), and ending with a mythology that linked the *Transformers* to order and chaos as personified by the space gods Primus and Unicron (in issue #150), very much in the spirit of Marvel's cosmic storylines. As Furman explains, his original idea was

> "Let's do an origin story and see if Hasbro objects"... Stan Lee had had this grand cosmic otherworldly thing going on with a lot of early Marvel stuff, and so the idea of turning Unicron into this time-and-dimension-spanning entity, like Galactus, and then having another character, Primus, to be the Yin to that Yang ... it felt like a no brainer.... It's one of the biggest things that Hasbro adopted that I layered in ... the biggest thing in terms of my little mark on the brand.[14]

It was under Furman and with the folding of Furman's work into the larger *Transformers* brand that *Transformers*' paratexts became more mythological than world building, involving time travel, destiny and the cyclical nature of death and rebirth.

But as with the death of Optimus Prime, Furman's work was motivated by a similar blend of creativity and commerce, particularly the launch story, *Target: 2006*. It was designed as a prolonged advert not for *TTM*, but for the new toys Galvatron and Ultra Magnus. "Hasbro basically said we needed to have Galvatron and Magnus in a story because they were planning a big marketing push on the toys and billing it as The New Leaders and everything," says Furman. "It was definitely a case of, 'They're going to be featured on the cover, they're going to be promoted as a toy and you're going to get your TV advertising,' and so we needed a story to match the promotional push."[15] Furman's response was to develop *Target: 2006* as a prequel to the movie (albeit one involving time travel), providing greater depth as well as brand awareness around the characters *Transformers* comic readers would then go and see on the screen. It was a similar strategy Marvel would later adopt in relation to their own cinema properties, providing comic book prequels to the movies in the lead up to their box office release that were in-continuity with the movie (and therefore outside the general Marvel Comic Universe).

Target: 2006 and Furman's later series also served a more pragmatic purpose. Marvel's weekly UK *Transformers* comic consisted of 32 pages, of which 11 pages were comic strip material either reprinted from the American comics or originated in the UK. As then editor Ian Rimmer explains, "[w]e wanted to run a long UK story to build up a backlog of U.S. material [we could then reprint] ... we needed the additional breathing space."[16] Furman adds that being asked to introduce the New Leaders "felt like the biggest invitation to do our own big storyline because we were going to use characters without having to worry about what the Americans were going to do with them."[17]

In a similar way to the comic, *TTM* also rebooted the cartoon series into more of a science fiction show, as Season 3 (set after the events of the film) featured darker and more complicated storylines provided by a host of comic book and science fiction writers. *TTM* is therefore relatively unique in that it became a central narrative in two transmedia story lines.[18] As Eric Clark notes, "in the two decades since *Transformers* was born, the tie between toys and entertainment and total marketing has grown ever more solid.... Now it's really just one business.... Toy-led programming ... has become part of mainstream marketing."[19] But at the time *TTM* represented a big step forward in this process, with such an approach shifting the *Transformers* franchise away from "toy as object. Now it was defined characters [Galvatron, Ultra Magnus] in a preplotted scenario [the prequel comic, the movie, the sequel cartoon]."[20] The success of this approach was best demonstrated by the death of Optimus, as it was the death of the character that children mourned, not the replacement of one object with another.

Toyesis

Media properties suitable to be merchandised across a range of licensed tie-ins, including toys, games and novelties, are generally referred to as *toyetic*. While the word toyetic suggests a reductionist view of merchandising related only to toys in practice, toyetics include merchandise that has some element of play value thereby extending to items like clothing and food. As such, toyetics are also examples of paratextuality: that web of intertexts such as posters, trailers, merchandise, reviews and interviews that frequently surround, inform and extend screen (and literary) texts. In this instance it can be used to describe the relationship between *Transformers* action figures and the screen text *TTM*. As Gerard Genette explains "a text is rarely presented in an unadorned state, unreinforced and unaccompanied by a certain number of verbal or other [in this case visual or material] productions.... These accompanying productions, which vary in extent and appearance, constitute what I have called elsewhere the work's paratext."[21] Indeed, the producers of these paratexts often and quite deliberately make it very difficult to separate any memory of a text from its accompanying paratexts; for example, a child playing with the Galvatron action figure may replicate Leonard Nimoy's delivery of lines from *TTM* or elements of time-travel from Furman's comic narratives. In this sense Marvel comics, Hasbro toys and Marvel/Sunbow/Toei cartoons all work together to create this sense of Galvatron's "character."

If we can define merchandising as the materiality of licensing (an extension of virtual screen texts into physical paratexts), then toyetics is the interactive "make-and-do" aspect of merchandising, encouraging audiences to engage and play with aspects of the screen text: acting out episodes or creating new adventures or stories. Dan Fleming refers to this as "textual phenomenology"[22] where he suggests "a great deal [is] going on when a child plays with the toy, for which a TV programme cannot be held responsible."[23] Here, the materiality of the Galvatron figure provides this potential for play in a way that the scripted/acted/circumscribed virtually mediated Galvatron of *TTM*, the television series or the comic cannot. Whereas the mediated Galavatron can only be rewatched, reread or revisited, the material Galvatron figure can be redeployed, rewritten and reimagined; Galvatron is an *action* figure precisely because he carries within him the possibility for new stories and situations through imaginative play. Indeed, Henry Jenkins explicitly imbues toyetics with the qualities of digital culture when he notes that "action figures provided this generation with some of their earliest avatars, encouraging them to assume the role of a Jedi Knight or an intergalactic bounty hunter, enabling them to physically manipulate the characters to construct their own stories."[24]

Like any number of '80s toy lines, *Transformers* inverts this notion of toyetics and paratexts because it is the toy line that is the content industry, meaning that the paratexts are in fact the cartoons, the comics, the books, even *TTM*. The animation model designs by Takara's Shohei Kohara, for example, are based on the toy designs and illustrations on the *Transformers* packaging; it is the toys that provide the source for transmedia adaptation.

To complicate it further, *TTM* introduced characters who were subsequently made into toys (Hot Rod/Rodimus Prime, Wreck-Gar, Springer, Blur, Arcee, and Kup). As such it marks Hasbro's transition from "toys licensed from Japanese companies to toys they were producing themselves"[25]; that is, original toys based on Floro Dery's animation designs or making the film toyetic in the traditional sense. To describe these complex textual relationships I have previously referred to the notion of "toyesis,"[26] a kind of reverse toyetics where these paratextual relays erase a text's origins to the point that they cultivate multiple origins across multiple media platforms, generating the production of more media texts around them. The word is modeled on the relationship between kinetic (relating to or resulting from motion) and kinesis (motion itself). Whereas "toyetic" implies a one-way adaptation from screen/literary text to physical paratext (through merchandising), "toyesis" implies movement both ways across platforms to the point that the distinction between different texts becomes obscured and therefore less important.

Marvel's involvement in the development of both the *GI Joe* and *Transformers* franchises clearly assists in this erasure, making the *Transformers* characters simultaneously familiar (if subtly different) across a number of different textual sites. For example, the *Diaclone* Ultra Magnus action figure is recognizable as the same Ultra Magnus designed by Floro Dery, voiced by Robert Stack in *TTM*[27] and appearing in Marvel comics, but he is also subtly different in appearance, motivation and characterization across these different platforms.

Such ambiguity around the *Transformers*' textual origins is itself important, as it would be a strategy Marvel would later adopt in developing recognition of their suite of characters. Media theorist Jonathan Gray argues that "a proper study of paratexts … challenge(s) the logic of 'primary' and 'secondary' texts, originals and spinoffs, shows and 'peripherals'… [rather] they often play a constitutive role in the production, development, and expansion of a text."[28] In the example of the *TTM* Transformers, their textual origins are erased to the point that Hot Rod, Blurr or Galvatron can be constructed across any number of paratexts without any clear sense of which one is primary. For example, while created for the movie, all three of these characters first appear in the *Transformers UK* comic in the *Target: 2006* storyline and then on toy shelves well before they are ever seen on the screen.

The materiality of *Star Wars* merchandise (action figures, space craft, and playsets) allowed audiences to pass what Gray terms "the barrier of *spectatorship* into the *Star Wars* universe, thereby complicating established dichotomies of the authentic text and the hollow, cash-grab paratext."[29] In this way these paratexts, again according to Gray, are involved in "refining and accentuating certain meanings, multiplying them and carrying them beyond the film into the child's play world."[30] The *Transformers UK* comic operates as just such a paratext for *TTM* in a similar way. Taking a gap 35 minutes into the film (where Galvatron commands his "Decepticons to Earth"), Furman developed his time travel storyline in *Target: 2006* that brought both the *TTM* and original *Transformers* casts together. Here Furman is quite literally "playing" in the gaps of both the timeline and the narrative of the film in a way that children could similarly play with the film using the toys from *TTM* advertised within those same comic pages. This is toyesis at work, paratextual relays that obscure the textual origins of the product, instead giving them multiple origins across transmedia stories that flow from screen to material media and back again, capturing audiences across each platform of delivery.

What marks out the *Transformers* franchise, then, is that while the toy remains the content provider, the complex web of paratexts responsible for creating narrative content means that the textual origins are continually obscured, making it hard for consumers to know which came first: the toy, the cartoon or the comic series. Similarly, the *Transformers* origins are obscured still further by the toys originating in Japan and being adapted across media channels for Western audiences. In part this is how Optimus Prime becomes iconic (and his death so significant)—because he simultaneously becomes a cartoon/comic/toy *character* rather than a mere toy.

Multiple Origins

The three-pronged strategy developed between Marvel and Hasbro around *G.I. Joe* and *Transformers* started being replicated by Marvel itself in the 1990s largely as a result of the influence of Avi Arad (who had himself adopted a similar strategy with *Transformers'* rivals the *Gobots*). Here, the combination of Marvel comics, Fox Cartoon television series and Toy Biz action figures marked Marvel's move toward Marvel Studios. Indeed, to a large extent the latter Marvel Cinematic Universe (commencing with *Iron Man* in 2008) is bounded by this series of licensing decisions Marvel made in the mid–90s, including licensing the X-Men and Fantastic Four to Fox and Spider-Man to Sony (in 1999). This meant that when Marvel Studios moved from character licensing to self-financing their own films (commencing under David Maisel in 2004), they had a greatly reduced slate of characters with which to work, mostly comprised of character rights that had reverted back to them because of non-production, *Avengers*-related characters (as with Iron Man and Captain America) or characters deep in their back catalogue who had never been optioned before (as with the Guardians of the Galaxy).

With some of their most successful (and recognizable) characters excluded from the Marvel Cinematic Universe, Marvel Studios relied on the same strategies they had used in relation to *Transformers* and their own properties in the 90s to make their characters recognizable through a triage of comics, associated cartoons and toy lines (produced by Hasbro). In this way, when the relatively obscure *Guardians of the Galaxy* (2014) was being made into a movie, a new comic book series (written by Brian Michael Bendis and drawn by Steve McNiven) and a boxed set of action figures from Hasbro were released in the lead-up; the characters also guest starred on the cartoon series *Avengers Assemble* on Disney XD. While Guardians' character Rocket Raccoon first appeared in 1976, this three-pronged strategy means that audiences may come to Rocket through the comics, the toys, the film or television appearances. Like the *Transformers* before him, Rocket therefore becomes textually ambiguous, with multiple origins that make him at home across multiple media platforms. Most importantly he becomes *known*. He becomes *familiar*.

TTM then confirmed what Forster and Sorenson note, that "[t]he name Optimus Prime has truly transcended its origins to become a part of the pop culture landscape."[31] Where Prime went, so many of Marvel's characters followed, deliberately cultivating multiple origins so as to transcend their textual origins, whatever they might be. No longer were Marvel's characters simply comic book superheroes; they were familiar from cartoons, fast food tie-ins, action figures, theme park attractions and, ultimately, films.

The Junkions

Introduced in *TTM*, the Junkions are a race of transforming robots lead by Wreck-Gar who, as their name implies, reassemble and repurpose "junk." They speak "TV," in that their speech is littered with phrases and sounds sampled and repeated from television series and commercials. Appropriately, Monty Python's Eric Idle-voiced Wreck-Gar and the Junkions first appear to the strains of Weird Al Yankovic's "Dare to Be Stupid" (both artists known for parodying and sampling other's material). Their talents extend to rebuilding Ultra Magnus and constructing a spacecraft that carries the characters to their final battle with Unicron.

The Junkions are important characters because in many ways they speak to the culture of adaptation at the heart of the *Transformers* franchise: control, creation and transformation (recreating one set of materials as another). Gray viewed toys as important paratexts because, as in the example of *Star Wars*, they "represented to many that media worlds could and should be somewhat *inhabitable*."[32] While it is the *Transformers* toys that originate these media worlds they also allow consumers to play with how these worlds operate, in the spaces of their bedrooms and playrooms.

In this way, the action figure itself becomes a metaphor for the active child, a wanting, desiring child that is "an active participant in that process of defining their identit[y]."[33] Following Jean Piaget,[34] Zago argues that "children translate images and sounds from their mental imagination to the physical with skits and productions they perform with their action figures."[35] This is borne out in *The Goldbergs*, where Adam's trauma at seeing Optimus Prime die (his consumption) is remade into the activity of a home movie (his production) to, in Pop's terms, "right the wrongs of those Hollywood bastards." With a $75 budget, Adam makes a movie with Pops starring as Optimus (in a replica cardboard suit) proudly stating: "I literally cannot die." Over the end credits we see the real Adam Goldberg's home movie from that period similarly depicting Optimus' triumphant return from the dead (as acted out with his toys and the handwritten sign "Optimis [sic] Lives"). In both instances, fictional and factual, the tools of consumption become the tools of production.

Much like the Junkions' repurposing of materials, as the child matures, action figures become the tools of prosumption (where consumption leads to further production), or elements used to construct new narratives and fantasies. Here too, the "action" of the "action figure" comes to refer more broadly to the momentum that transforms the toy itself into an "intertextual commodity" (a central part of world-building), then collectible and then object of desire, that point at which children's entertainment and adult entertainment becomes virtually indistinguishable.

Toys have similarly become an important cornerstone of the Marvel Cinematic Universe, through Marvel's licensing deals with Hasbro and Diamond Direct. Lines such as *Marvel Legends* are deliberately targeted to older consumers (through both price point and detail) while *Marvel Infinity* features a broader range of 3¾-inch characters. These ranges serve to create toyetic representations of Marvel's current movie stars (Ant-Man, Rocket Raccoon, the Chris Evans Captain America) while also creating brand awareness for Marvel comic book characters (Hellcat, Wasp, Baron Zemo) who are yet to be, or are currently being, adapted into cinematic and televisual characters. As such they too encourage a space for creation and control, giving consumers the ability to mix and match the various characters (and worlds of Marvel) before they come together in the MCU.

Unicron

The major antagonist of *TTM* is the planet-eating Unicron (as previously noted, in many respects a robotic version of the Marvel comics character Galactus). Just as Unicron opens up the universe of the *Transformers* (introducing us to the worlds of Quintessa, Junkion and Lithone) as he rampages across the stars, his recurrence throughout subsequent elements of the franchise (particularly the 2002–2003 *Transformers Armada* cartoon and Marvel's 1980s *Transformers* comics) suggests a *multi*verse of different *Transformers* universes and, indirectly, the future of the franchise. While *TTM* becomes an important aspect of both the cartoon and comic narratives (and therefore a major point of *convergence*), the franchise would subsequently evolve more through *adaptation* than convergence.

Like myths, Cybertron, Unicron and the war between Optimus and Megatron would be retold in different formats as the *Transformers* franchise itself became a series of "intertextual commodities"[36] leading to countless convergent media spin-offs, from Japanese-specific cartoons that continued the storyline from *TTM* (*The Headmasters, Super-God Masterforce*), to Canadian animation (*Beast Wars*), and to British comics (*The Legacy of Unicron, Time Wars*). Like a modern myth, *Transformers* becomes a story to be repeated, taken apart, rebuilt and repeated again for generations of fans for over twenty-five years across alternative media. Indeed, its longevity and complexity becomes a source of pride, as in this caption that appears on the packaging for the 25th anniversary re-release of the original Optimus Prime figure:

> In 1984, the Transformers robots stormed into televisions, comic shops, and toy aisles worldwide, and changed forever how we thought about action figures. It created a craze that has lasted for a quarter of a century, through dozens of permutations. Our world was expanded beyond the mundane fantasies of action heroes and fashion idols to include an endless universe populated by unstoppable metal giants, vicious alien tyrants, and monstrous planet-eaters from the beginning of time. From then on, we lived in a world that was *More than Meets the Eye*!

In truth, *Transformers* really only ended in the United States in 1991. They continued to be marketed internationally and were relaunched as "Generation Two" in the States (along with the rest of the world) in 1993, swiftly followed by *Transformers: Beast Wars* in 1996 and continuing uninterrupted up until the present day, supported by a selection of high-end statues and collectibles, the *Transformers Collector's Club*,[37] and comic-books, together with attendant toy lines for Dream Works/Paramount's live-action *Transformers* franchise and new cartoon series (2007–2009's *Transformers Animated*). As Clark describes it, "Toys have become part of kid culture, coveted for reasons divorced from play."[38] But the toys go beyond children: with *Transformers*' transformation into adult collectibles, the toys have become objects of desire for *all* members of the family. The adult audience that *TTM* reached for with its PG rating now makes up a significant part of Transformers fan community.

The most recent iteration of the franchise, Dream Works/Paramount's four-film franchise (directed by Michael Bay, commencing in 2007) has a combined box office of U.S. $3,761,212,649, meaning that *Transformers* are the content industry for a billion-dollar franchise. Just as the *Transformers* prefigured the trend towards convergence culture engendered by digital technology, so too has digital technology prolonged the life of the *Transformers* through digital special effects, digital technologies and digital recording. In doing so, *Transformers* has made the action figure an integral part of children's entertainment for the foreseeable future.

Marvel similarly evolves through adaptation rather than convergence. The Marvel Cinematic Universe exists quite apart from the Marvel (Comic) Universe, which in turn is quite distinct from the various animated iterations of Marvel. Yet, like the *Transformers* franchise, certain mythic elements (Captain America being frozen after World War II, Tony Stark becoming Iron Man, Bruce Banner struggling to control the Hulk) remain the same, tropes that recur again and again across these adaptations, providing a sense of familiarity and recognition to each of these iterations.[39]

Conclusion

"The funny thing about killing Optimus Prime is that it probably gave the movie its resonance," says Flint Dille.[40] It pointed to how much investment audiences could have in franchise characters. But even more importantly, I would argue that it was *TTM* that was one of the first points of intersection for adult pleasures and childish fantasies, structured narratives and free-ranging play, material culture and virtual culture that is so much a part of franchise culture today.

Through this breaking down of barriers, it was *TTM* that indicated not only how the *Transformers* franchise would become one of the most potent (if overlooked) symbols of media convergence and adaptation, but also how the Marvel Cinematic Universe would itself develop: the multiple origins of characters cultivated through paratextual relays to the point that their true textual origins are erased and they simply become "familiar"; a culture that encourages fan production and extension (often through toy lines); and storylines that are capable of adaptation and re-adaptation across multiple platforms (while retaining some recurrent mythic elements).

Marvel was an important part of the *Transformers* franchise's origins, giving names (Optimus Prime, Megatron) and conflict (the heroic Autobots, the evil Decepticons) to Hasbro's repurposed Japanese robots. With *TTM* and its attendant comic prequels and sequels, they enriched the story with time-travel, tragedy (the death of Prime) and wonder (the Chaos God Unicron). It is little wonder then that these same strategies currently underpin the expansion of the Marvel Cinematic Universe and the franchise's own building toward the *Infinity War* films in 2019.

Notes

1. *Transformers: The Movie,* directed by Nelson Shin (1986; *Special Edition* Madman DVD, 2009), DVD.
2. *Transformers: The Movie: Special Edition*, DVD, Disc Two.
3. Ibid.
4. Zack Smith, "Adam F. Goldberg, Part 2: The Death of Optimus Prime, Breaking in and Gobots," *Newsarama*, last modified March 18, 2015, http://www.newsarama.com/23839-adam-f-goldberg-pt-2-breaking-in-and-optimus-prime.html.
5. *Transformers: The Movie: Special Edition*, DVD, Disc Two.
6. For more detail on the history of the Transformers toy line see *Transformers Wiki* (http://tfwiki.net), Transformers.com (http://www.transformers.com) and Transformers Toys (http://www.transformerstoysonline.com). TakaraTomy's Official Transformers Web Site provides information on the original Japanese lines (http://www.takaratomy.co.jp/products/TF) while Chris McFeely's commentary on the two-disc *Transformers: The Movie Special Edition* (Madman Entertainment, 2008) provides an all-inclusive overview.
7. Eric Clark, *The Real Toy Story: Inside the Ruthless Battle for Britain's Youngest Consumers* (London: Random House, 2007), 213–214.
8. Hama qtd. Christopher Irving, "The Swivel-Arm Battle-Grip Revolution: How G.I. Joe Recruited a New Generation of Comic-Book Readers," *Back Issue: The Ultimate Comics Experience* 16 (June 2006): 15–16.
9. Clark, *The Real Toy Story*, 215–216.

Part 1: Myth

10. Irving, "The Swivel-Arm Battle-Grip Revolution," 15.
11. *Transformers: The Movie: Special Edition*, DVD, Disc Two.
12. Ibid.
13. Originally the film was to be set in 2006. It was later revised to 2005 but the error remained in the comic book storyline's title *Target: 2006* as it had prepared earlier.
14. Furman qtd. in James Roberts, "The Legacy of Furman," in *Transformers Classics UK Volume 5*, edited by James Roberts (San Diego: IDW, 2014), 37–38.
15. Furman qtd. in *Transformers Classics UK Volume 3*, edited by James Roberts (San Diego: IDW, 2012), 19–20.
16. Rimmer qtd. in *Transformers Classics UK Volume 3*, 6.
17. Furman qtd. in *Transformers Classics UK Volume 3*, 6–7.
18. Relatively unique in that the only other example would the Budiansky penned *Transformers* origin story mentioned earlier, that appeared in the cartoon, comic and CGI *Beast Wars* series.
19. Clark, *The Real Toy Story*, 220.
20. Ibid., 214.
21. Gerard Genette, *Paratexts: The Thresholds of Interpretation*, trans. Jane E. Lewin (Cambridge: Cambridge University Press, 1997), 1.
22. Dan Fleming, *Powerplay: Toys as Popular Culture* (Manchester: Manchester University Press, 1996), 11.
23. Ibid., 15.
24. Henry Jenkins, *Convergence Culture* (New York: New York University Press, 2006), 147.
25. Bill Forster and Jim Sorenson, *Transformers Legacy: The Art of Transformers Packaging* (San Diego: IDW, 2014), 8.
26. Jason Bainbridge, "From *Toyetic* to *Toyesis*: The Cultural Value of Merchandising," in *Entertainment Values*, edited by Stephen Harrington and Christy Collis (New York: Palgrave Macmillan, 2015).
27. Ultra Magnus is an exception to the general rule that characters in *TTM* originated in the movie. He was in fact based on a *Diaclone* toy.
28. Jonathan Gray, *Show Sold Separately: Promos, Spoilers and Other Media Paratexts* (New York: New York University Press, 2010), 175.
29. Ibid., 176.
30. Ibid., 181.
31. Forster and Sorenson, *Transformers Legacy*, 8.
32. Gray, *Show Sold Separately*, 187.
33. Jenkins, *Convergence Culture*, 2.
34. See Melvin Konner, *Childhood* (Boston: Little Brown, 1991).
35. Vera Zago, "Action Figures: Props of Performance," in *Performing the Force: Essays on Immersion into Science Fiction, Fantasy and Horror Environments*, edited by Kurt Lancaster and Tom Mikotowicz (Jefferson, NC: McFarland, 2001), 146.
36. David Marshall qtd. Jenkins, *Covergence Culture*, 287.
37. *Transformers Collector's Club*, last modified August 11, 2015, http://www.transformersclub.com.
38. Clark, *The Real Toy Story*, 212.
39. For more on comic book adaptation see Liam Burke, *The Comic Book Adaptation* (Jackson: University of Mississippi Press, 2015).
40. *Transformers: The Movie: Special Edition*, DVD, Disc Two.

You Can't Stop Her
Elektra *Re-Configured*

Daniel Binns

On May 15, 2006, the group Equality Now presented writer and director Joss Whedon with a "Men on the Front Lines" Award. The award was given in recognition of his outstanding contributions to gender equality on screen, through his television shows *Buffy the Vampire Slayer* and *Firefly*, and *Firefly*'s follow-up film *Serenity*. In his acceptance speech, Whedon assumed the persona of a reporter, repeatedly asking himself variations on a single question: "Why do you write these strong women characters?" Each answer took a slightly different tack. In one response, he spoke about his mother: that she was a tough, independent, sexy woman, of a kind that he wanted to surround himself with for the rest of his life. Another answer was about the empowering effect that stories can have. Still another discussed the concept of equality as something that should just exist, rather than be fought and striven for. At the conclusion of his speech, he asks himself the question one last time:

> So, why do you write these strong female characters?
> Because you're still asking me that question.[1]

In the line-up for Whedon's *The Avengers* (2012) were three leading women: Scarlett Johansson as Black Widow, Cobie Smulders as Agent Maria Hill, and Gwyneth Paltrow as Pepper Potts. Male characters dominate the first and second phases of the Marvel Cinematic Universe (from *Iron Man* to 2015's *Ant-Man*), but feminist critiques have pointed to an improvement in terms of portraying women neither as damsels-in-distress, nor as decoration for male heroes. There is a growing tendency, at least in the Marvel franchise, to present even minor female characters as more than equal to their male counterparts. This is of course embodied by the major characters Black Widow, Agent Hill, and Peggy Carter, love interest of Captain America, whose own spin-off television series started in 2015. But looking beyond the sanctioned Cinematic Universe, there are quite a few Marvel properties deserving of further scrutiny. One such character is Elektra Natchios, frequently known only by her first name. A lesser-known yet well-liked female superhero from the Marvel universe, Elektra was created by Frank Miller, and has appeared in a number of comic book series, beginning with an appearance in Daredevil #168 in 1981.[2] This chapter begins with an examination of the character's origins in Greek tragedy, specifically the tragedy written by Sophocles, before looking at the character in the comic books. We then move to the focus of the essay: Rob Bowman's 2005 film adaptation, starring Jennifer Garner in the title role. I argue that the character's connection with strong females from antiquity, and her complex development through the comic books as interpreted in Bowman's film, paved the way for the contemporary Marvel women mentioned above. Furthermore, I examine the performance of the character in key fight sequences of Bowman's film and argue it is through the action-image, rather than the affect-image, that these strong characters are configured. Put simply, what role do fight sequences play in terms of the narrative of superhero films, and how have they allowed more nuanced representations of women in roles of strength and complexity?

Elektra: Origin Story

In Sophocles' tragedy, written circa 400 BCE, Electra is presented as a strong-willed and principled woman. She has one brother, Orestes, who has returned from many years away, swearing bloody vengeance for the murder of their father Agamemnon at the hands of their mother, Clytemnestra. Clytemnestra has taken Agamemnon's cousin Aegisthus as a lover, and Orestes plots to kill them both. Through the course of the play it is Orestes who schemes and works for revenge, while Electra is Orestes' elder, and remains torn between sharing her brother's desire for justice, and wanting to keep the peace among her family and society at large. Electra clearly despises Clytemnestra. In one notable exchange, mother and daughter circle each other, slinging venom:

Electra	Let me assure you, however it looks to you, I *am* ashamed of my actions and very aware Of being untrue to myself. But your hostility And cruel treatment force this behavior on me. Shameful ways are learned by shameful example.
Clytemnestra	You impudent creature! *I'm* to blame, I suppose. *My* words and actions inspire your long tirades.
Electra	The speeches are yours, not mine. It's you Who perform the actions, and they discover the words.[3]

This seething hatred is palpable, and certainly justified given Clytemnestra's role in her former husband's death.

Scholars generally agree that Sophocles was the first playwright to present the figure of the "tragic hero," i.e., "a single, central character, whose action and suffering are the focal point of the play."[4] Sophocles' archetype might be taken further and combined with the Aristotelian notion of hubris. Shakespeare was known for doing this, but also for making it almost compulsory for the tragic protagonist to die before the play's end. Electra suffers no such fate, and, with Orestes' help, justice is done. Clytemnestra and her lover Aegisthus are both killed, and order is seemingly restored. The character of Electra, at least in Sophocles' rendering, seems driven not simply by a pure desire for vengeance. Rather Electra seems inspired by the need to right the universe, and at one point invokes divine aid to do so. She says:

> O Lord Apollo, graciously hear their prayers
> And mine besides. Many a time I have stood
> In supplication before your holy altar
> And offered there such gifts as I could afford.
> So now, Lycean Apollo, with what I have,

> I pray, beseech and supplicate your godhead.
> Vouchsafe to aid us in this enterprise
> And show to all mankind what recompense
> The gods bestow on sinful wickedness.[5]

It seems strange that Electra is the focal point of the play, given that she does not engage in Orestes' plot. As Raeburn notes, however, *Electra* seems to be much more a play about how her brother's plot affects her.[6] As her brother has been away for some time, Electra does not recognize him at first. A key part of the revenge plot is to convince his family that Orestes has died, and Electra is fooled by the deception. While overjoyed at the realization that the death is fake, a sense of emotional turmoil pervades the remainder of the drama: her characterization to this point is shattered, and she seems to transition into a bloody rage. For instance, Raeburn notes the shockingness of Electra's plea for Orestes to strike their mother a second time.[7] A female as a central protagonist, though, is not as unusual as one might think in ancient theatre. The role of women in antiquity is known to be multifaceted. Blundell states quite categorically that, at least in a legal capacity, "an Athenian woman had no independent existence."[8] Further, the women of Athens could only act legally through their male guardian, or *kyrios*; the *kyrios* could be her father, her husband or, if widowed, her sons. However, the part women played in terms of marriage and lineage—the provision of sons and the control she and her family retained over any dowry provided to her husband—resulted in an element of power unseen almost anywhere else in the ancient world.[9] Similarly, while women were unable to own large amounts of property, they could certainly manage property; this was often that of their husbands, managed in business and transactions conducted in and around the home.[10] As in Italy, it is probable that the women of Ancient Greece, while certainly not in public life themselves, were never far from the halls of political power, exerting influence through their connections to men. However, Blundell points out that the spread of democracy throughout Greece was irrevocably tied "to the subordination of women, in that both were linked in some degree to the emphasis placed on the economic independence of the *oikoi* [translated loosely as 'household,' in the sense of the family unit]."[11] In theatre, female characters often held prominent supporting roles, if they were not the protagonists themselves. Three of the most revered ancient plays, *Medea*, *Antigone*, and *Electra*, feature women as their main characters. This is not a token gesture, either. These women are strong, independent, and complicated figures. Despite their relative subordination in a legal and political sense, their strong reliance on their familial connections—largely, but not always to males—make women complex figures in ancient Greek life. This is certainly reflected in ancient Greek theatre. Where female characters were often occupied with affairs of the heart, they were also active, engaged citizens. Here can be observed the emergence of a character configuration based on emotion *and* action, rather than just pure affect. The comic book version of Elektra, however, demonstrates that such complexity is not easily translated between media.

Elektra Inked

In the world of comics, the character of Elektra Natchios lacks the concrete, or at least, universally or corporately agreed upon history of many Marvel superheroes. She has an older brother named Orestez, who, in one storyline, hires assassins to kill their mother.¹² In an alternate series, Christina Natchios is killed during the Greek Civil War.¹³ In both series, Christina prematurely gives birth to Elektra just before her death. In differing stories, Elektra and her father, Hugo, are alternately close or estranged. There are rumors of sexual abuse between father and daughter, though these are later proved to be false memories.¹⁴ Throughout different manifestations of the story, the character of Elektra has a complex relationship with all of her blood relatives.

The most important character beside Elektra herself is her on-and-off partner and boyfriend, Matt Murdock, otherwise known as Daredevil. Matt and Elektra meet at university in New York City, but fate intervenes when a terrorist group kidnaps Elektra and her father. Matt tries to rescue them, but Hugo is killed in the process. Elektra is desolate and flees to China to learn martial arts under the guidance of Stick, head of the benevolent "Chaste." Daredevil and Elektra cross paths sporadically beyond this chain of events, but Elektra's pain at the loss of her family does not allow her to fall into any kind of loving relationship again. This pain forms the basis for the 2014 Blackman and Del Mundo reboot of Elektra, wherein Elektra takes a contract to capture the mysterious Cape Crow. Competing for the same mark is the bizarre Australian assassin named Bloody Lips, who has the capacity to take on the characteristics and emotions of those whose flesh he eats.¹⁵ Where Elektra's contract is to capture, Bloody Lips has been tasked with the kill. Elektra must also face Cape Crow's son, Kento, who steps in to defend his father's life. Elektra soon realizes it was Kento who took out the capture contract. She defeats Bloody Lips, then moves on with Kento and his father, vowing to protect them until they are truly safe. Cape Crow sums up the first five issues thus: "By helping me, you just made yourself the Assassins' Guild's next target. They'll never stop hunting us."¹⁶

Elektra's family features prominently in this new storyline, but, as they are all dead, appear only as spectral figures: memories, ghosts, and visions of the past. Bloody Lips and Elektra end up sharing memories, and Bloody Lips manipulates Elektra's perception such that when she incapacitates Cape Crow and takes off his protective helmet, it is Hugo's face she sees.¹⁷ Similarly, in the netherworld where Elektra and Bloody Lips' minds meet, Elektra is confronted by the specter of her mother, who accuses Elektra of her death.¹⁸

From the original comics to the reboot, Elektra's role is reactionary: she does not function in the absence of other characters. This would often make for a weak character, one that does not exist independently. But we learn enough of Elektra's history—however contradictory it may be between series—to know that she is a complicated character. Indeed, in this latest comic series, her familial connections drive the action, inspiring her to feats of endurance and physical and emotional toughness that would defeat lesser heroes. Rather than keep images of action and affect separate, we see in Blackman and Del Mundo a blending of the two. The leap, then, to feature film, would seem the perfect opportunity to develop the character and reconcile more completely these disparate aspects of her configuration.

Elektra Empowered

Both the character of Elektra and the stories that feature her can be interpreted as mash-ups of a number of different tropes and storylines. In many ways, Marvel's Elektra perpetuates the ancient myth that she is based on. In the process, the 2005 film paved the way for similarly strong female characters in the Marvel Cinematic Universe, such as Black Widow and Peggy Carter. Director Rob Bowman makes a conscious attempt to move the "comic book movie" away from the alpha masculine hero, instead presenting Elektra as a strong, if troubled, heroic female lead.

In reading the character of Elektra, I see apt comparisons between Elektra and another grand superheroine who has certainly had much more time in the spotlight: Wonder Woman. Like Elektra, Wonder Woman has conflicting origin stories, but they both present a woman torn between a powerful, strong, Amazonian heritage and the troubled patriarchal society she chooses to protect. Emad's reading of Wonder Woman's body as the site of social and national tensions presents a way of examining those same tensions in Elektra's character. The differences between these two characters are also relevant in how Elektra, in particular, laid the foundations for strong female characters in later Marvel films. Emad identifies a number of tropes that present Wonder Woman as a strong character, refusing, rather than perpetuating, a typically patriarchal view of the nation. For example, in numerous Wonder Woman comic book covers between 1942 and 1995, Wonder Woman is depicted carrying an unconscious, uniformed male.[19] This trope, along with a setting change to World War II, shifted the target audience of most comics from young children to adults (both male and female), "largely through rhetorics of nationalism."[20] Wonder Woman was used as a propaganda machine for the war effort, frequently seen raising morale among the infantry, and suggesting ways in which women might do their part on the home front.[21] Emad draws on the work of Lori Landay, who writes "that Wonder Woman operates in wartime popular culture as a metaphor for the movement of femininity out of the garden and into the war."[22] Wonder Woman struggled with consistency through the Women's Liberation movement of the 1960s and 1970s. One magazine cover shows a giant Wonder Woman, panicked, running over the tiny townspeople, carrying one of the scales of justice. "Wonder Woman's enlarged and dangerous body," writes Emad, "attempting to straddle the masculine realm of war and politics with the feminine realm of peace and justice, echoed the discourses of danger surrounding the women's movement in the 1970s."[23]

The Wonder Woman of the 1980s and 1990s became hyper-sexualized, targeted predominantly at young men. After the September 11 terror attacks, where a reboot, or reorientation, may have legitimized her character,[24] Wonder Woman's writers instead perpetuate the "othering" of non–Americans, and the overt sexualization of the character. This is most notable in one scene in 2001's *Spirit of Truth*, where, having been disguised under a traditional Islamic hijab, Wonder Woman tears it away, emerging as the conventional American hero and, simultaneously, a conventionally curvaceous, desirable, and near-naked, woman.[25] Emad establishes Wonder Woman as a character torn between polarities: mother figure and paragon of sexual power and attractiveness; symbol of justice and fearsome warrior; icon of the empowerment of both nation and individual. Interestingly, the character of Elektra has no such lofty tensions in her character. Her tensions and complexity come from her past and from within, such that her stories feel more personal. Elektra is not projecting ideas or ideals about the nation; rather she is presenting nothing but herself in her stories. That being said, her inevitable "conversion" from fearsome assassin to guardian of justice speaks in some sense to the character arcs of the various incarnations of Wonder Woman. The strength of the character, whatever independence she possesses, must be reigned in.[26] This is generally achieved through the hyper-sexualization of the female body. There are a number of parallels to be drawn between the characters, particularly Bowman's rendition of Elektra, which will be visited shortly.

The story of Elektra largely reflects the "monomyth" inscribed by Joseph Campbell, wherein the hero sets off on a journey, encounters strong and powerful forces, overcomes them, and re-engages with society newly enlightened.[27] Certainly in Bowman's film, Elektra journeys far from home to discover her new targets, Mark and Abby Miller. She goes on to encounter strong opposition, in the form of the assassins of "The Hand," and she must singlehandedly complete her training in "The Way," *kimagure*, the capacity to predict the future and even resurrect people from death, in order to overpower them. She thus returns from her travels "newly enlightened," in that she has learnt compassion and completed her training. The mythological origin of the character of Elektra (transmitted in part via Greek tragedy) lends a gravitas to her story. The nature of tragedy, indeed, lends the name and any associated character universality. As Campbell writes:

> Tragedy is the shattering of the forms and of our attachment to the forms; comedy, the wild and careless, inexhaustible joy of life invincible. Thus the two are the terms of a single mythological theme and experience which includes them both and which they bound: the down-going and up-coming ... which together constitute the totality of the revelation that is life."[28]

Cinema, by its nature, is particularly suited to present mythological themes and characters. Singer writes that the techniques of film—those of camera angles and movement, zooming, editing—automatically distance the viewer from the everyday. "This distancing puts the spectators of the finished product into a receptive attitude toward narratives that are unlike life itself precisely *because* they are mythic or include mythic aspects."[29] Similarly, the use of slow-motion estranges the audience, drawing out time, making movement unnatural and lending power and emphasis to whatever is in the frame; slow-motion leads the viewer "straight into 'the reality of another dimension.'"[30] These techniques will be returned to later in the discussion, but there are a number of elements in the Elektra comics and 2005 film that link her and her story to a much larger mythological oeuvre. The Chaste and The Hand represent, at their most basic, the forces of light and dark, good and bad, respectively. *Kimagure,* the mysterious force that gives Stick and Elektra the capacity to see the future and resurrect the dead, echoes similar powers from other superheroes, other universes, and other mythologies. For this author, the most prominent analogue is the Force from the *Star Wars* films (1977–present). The Marvel character Thor possesses superhuman strength and draws power from his homeworld of Asgard—this leads many humans to believe that he is a god, as showcased in *Thor* (2011). In *The Matrix* (1999), Neo learns to manipulate the code of the titular software, and thus become incredibly powerful. Many of these powers find their inspiration in mythology or mysticism. The Force, for instance, has its origins in Eastern mythology. Wetmore states quite succinctly that "[t]he theology and cosmology of *Star Wars* constructs an ultimate reality much closer to Taoism than to any Western religious philosophy."[31] As for the philosophy of Bowman's film, *kimagure* certainly seems Asian in nature and nomenclature. Very little is explained about how *kimagure* works; the voiceover of the opening sequence suggests that the power has existed for all of time, but goes no further than stating what its masters can do. Elektra is proficient in a system of martial arts incorporating elements of karate, kendo, krav maga and, obviously, knife combat. *Kimagure* seems to be a cohering factor between these disparate disciplines, allowing Elektra to tailor her attacks or defensive maneuvers according to what her opponent is about to do. The timelessness and universality of the battle at the heart of the story of *Elektra* seems to point to its creators hoping to establish a modern myth with ancient origins, seamlessly tying the character of Elektra into an endless chronology. Eastern mysticism is a suitably vague and exotic way of tying a character into such an enormous world. Further, the naming of the character is another attempt to invoke otherworldly connotations. As Mark Miller notes in a quiet moment of the film: "Elektra, like the tragedy. Your parents had a sense of humor."

Two scenes from the film *Elektra* demonstrate how the character's mythic origins, and the hero's journey itself, have been reconfigured to present a layered, complex character. This character, regardless of gender, *performs* the superhero genre through fight sequences. Elektra, thus, appears to the audience more often in terms of action rather than affect images. The first scene occurs very early in the film, as Elektra hunts down an old enemy, DeMarco. The scene is crucial because it establishes Elektra as the feared and deadly assassin we will get to unravel for the remainder of the film. The second scene is the final confrontation between Elektra and Kirigi, the lead assassin of The Hand. This latter battle takes place at Elektra's childhood home, now abandoned and overgrown with vines and weeds. Both of these scenes are fight sequences. *Elektra* was widely panned by critics for its dialogue, structure, and clichéd storyline.[32] Less divisive was Garner's performance, which turned some critics around.[33] The fight sequences, though, were rarely questioned or critiqued, which begs the question: what role do fight sequences play in terms of the narrative of superhero films? For this analysis, fight sequences form a key part of the superhero film genre. The relentless action-image of the superhero film imparts information about the characters, the narrative, and necessarily progresses the plot.

Elektra is introduced as a whisper, a barely-audible whip of material past the camera. It is clear that DeMarco has been expecting a visit from Elektra for some time. He sits by the fire with a drink, talking to his skeptical head of security, Bauer, about the legend of Elektra the assassin and, by extension, setting up the character for the audience, before she even appears in full on screen:

> My private security detail: the best money could buy. This non-existent woman killed fourteen of them in half an hour. I barely got away. Spent the next two days in Monte Carlo wondering why she let me go. Then she came for me. I was under the protection of The Hand itself, who sent their best, although they seemed more interested in killing Elektra than protecting me. She cut 'em down like wheat.

As DeMarco talks, Bauer keeps track of the sensors and security cameras of DeMarco's compound and soon, one by one, the monitors go dead. Bauer cannot contact any members of his team, and soon there is movement outside the door of DeMarco's office. As DeMarco tells Bauer that Elektra often whispers in your ear just before she kills you, DeMarco's earpiece purrs, "It's too late for your boss, Bauer, but you still have a chance." Bauer sprays the door with bullets, then exits the office, gun at the ready. He spins right, then left, just as the ring of a knife signals Elektra's presence. We see the point making an indentation on the back of Bauer's neck, and that sultry voice once more: "You can't fight a ghost." Bauer tries to resist, and is dispatched. The cinematography here plays with light and movement, working in conjunction with the sound design. The whole scene, from Bauer's office out into the hallway, is lit very sparsely, with only small points of light piercing the blackness. In this way, DeMarco's conversation with Bauer simmers, and the pulsing, building score underneath adds to the tension. When Bauer emerges into the hallway, the tension nearly peaks, and when Bauer and Elektra are fighting, big drums highlight Elektra's strength and speed. After Bauer is killed, we see a medium close up of Elektra's back, and the straps of her signature red corset. Time slows as she spins around, the draft whipping her long brown hair about her face and neck. She then steps forward and we can see her face, locked in determination. She steps into the office, and the tension rises once again—with cinematography, lighting, and music working in concert—as DeMarco engages Elektra in conversation while readying a concealed pistol. "Here we are, at last," he says, and when Elektra realizes DeMarco knows she is there, we cut as she briefly exhales. This could indicate a modicum of surprise, but also that Elektra, too, is aware of the significance of the completion of this pursuit. DeMarco, though, does not stand a chance. Elektra releases one of her *sai* from across the room, piercing the back of DeMarco's chair, and emerging through his chest. A shot of the hilt of Elektra's *sai*—perfectly illuminated in the flickering light of the fire—is held for a few seconds, before Elektra grasps it, and slowly removes it such that the audience is made aware of its length and its engravings. The final few centimeters of the *sai* are followed by a small trickle of blood, glinting red in the firelight. We then see DeMarco's bowed head, lower right of frame and out of focus, and the camera looks up to Elektra standing over her kill. She turns; we cut back to the point of view of the door as she marches purposefully out of the room, her *sai* sheathed with the same eerie ringing sound.

The character of Elektra here is established as a strong and fearless assassin, with the speed and dexterity to move across great distances almost instantaneously. She works as much by stealth as by strength, moving in the shadows to break her opponents psychologically as well as physically. She is presented in this sequence as near-invulnerable, with none of her opponents laying as much as a hand on her, let alone wounding her. Elektra thus "performs" the superhero genre single-handedly in her action-images in this fight sequence, in much the same way as Bruce Lee performs the martial arts genre, or Clint Eastwood the Western.

The succeeding scenes continue in this way, but with the introduction of Mark and Abby Miller, images of affect are blended with those of action. In these scenes, featuring the Millers as friends, then targets, then wards, the characterization of Elektra as invulnerable becomes problematic. Thus, when we see her return to her family home to face the Hand once again, her view of herself, and ours of her, has been changed. We now know Elektra is constantly haunted by the death of her family, and has completed her training for the Chaste; regaining her capacity for compassion was the final lesson. It is also revealed that Abby Miller is the Treasure, a young martial arts prodigy in need of either protection or exploitation. Crucially, this scene demonstrates the harnessing of affect and emotion as strength: a motivation further developed in later female Marvel characters.

As Elektra enters the house, we see it being surrounded by warriors of the Hand. Elektra ignites gas in the kitchen, dispatching a number of these agents. A wide shot of the house, tracking right, reveals Kirigi. He is wearing a white cloak, and its folds and layers are billowing in slow-motion. Elektra enters the entrance hall of the house, where all her family's belongings are covered in white sheets. She hears a sound and stops for a long time in the center of frame: the fluttering of the white sheets almost physically represents the audience being given a space to breathe. There are cuts to a close-up of Elektra's face, back to the staircase, a lateral tracking shot of Elektra's whole body: the whole time, similarly to the earlier sequence with DeMarco, the orchestra is swirling in the score underneath. There is, however, a complexity and deeper meaning in the music here. Where Elektra was in control before, now she is at the whim of her opponent.

The volume of the score builds, and we see the uncertainty inscribed in another close-up of Elektra's face. Suddenly, the white sheets fly up into the air, swirling and billowing around the enormous space. Kirigi appears for the first time on a walkway above Elektra, unsheathing his swords and saying, "We meet again." Elektra raises her *sai* in readiness, and Kirigi launches himself over the balustrade. Elektra's face is once more the definition of determination, but Kirigi's sorcery sends the sheets into her face and wrapping around her body, disorienting her. The audience too, is confused, as the sheets alternately cover and reveal parts of the scene. At one point Elektra's face, wild and panicked, struggling to get her bearings; at another moment, the confident visage of Kirigi, stalking his prey. Elektra also has flashbacks to her mother's murder, and realizes it was Kirigi who was responsible. The entire sequence is shot in something just short of full slow-motion: every movement is accentuated, emphasized. Just as Kirigi brings Elektra to her knees, his sword at her neck, Abby appears, and the scene of battle shifts to the hedge maze in the grounds outside the house. The maze setting further disorients Elektra, Abby, and the audience, as another agent of the Hand sends spectral snakes throughout the maze. Elektra dispatches this agent, saving Abby from the snakes. Elektra and Kirigi meet in the center of the maze, where the upper hand shifts between them. Elektra soon kills Kirigi, spearing him with a *sai* and tossing him down a well. Elektra senses another member of the Hand in the maze—one with the power to kill with a kiss. As Elektra searches for Abby, Abby too is lost, and is found and killed by the Hand agent. The maze sequence is dark, and the normally secure spatial logic of the frame is rendered incomprehensible by the sudden turns, red herrings, and dead ends. The characters seem as adrift in the camera as they are in the maze, and this is designed to further disorient the viewer. Elektra's development as a mother figure, or at least a sister-like connection, to Abby underscores this entire scene, as their connection fuels the affect of every shot. The action-image that was so pure in the scene with DeMarco is now re-figured as an affect-image, and the prevalence of close-ups throughout this sequence clearly shows the emotion inscribed on Elektra's face, and the stakes of the situation in which she finds herself. The hero's journey nears its end with this sequence; indeed, Elektra uses her new powers over *kimagure* to resurrect Abby. She then leaves, presumably to find a new path, to re-engage with society newly enlightened.

Conclusion

In Rob Bowman's film, Elektra's character is complex: on her face are inscribed mythologies old and new, and histories specific to her character and some more universal, dated to antiquity or even earlier. She also is undoubtedly a female character, torn between a fierce independence and a connection to those she encounters. In learning compassion, Bowman's Elektra distances herself from her comic book origins, making her a mother figure, drawing on inner strength, as well as physical prowess, to defend her young ward. Elektra's progression in this film, though, weakens her character, and reduces the options for any sequel. Much like Wonder Woman, frequently put into the role of mother and caretaker rather than punisher, Elektra here has more to experience than just the dispensation of justice. Indeed, no sequel has been made, and it is unlikely that Elektra, or even Daredevil, will be revived in feature film form any time soon.[34] It is not the development of the character in the film, though, that is the key problem drawn from this analysis. The problem with Bowman's *Elektra* is the sheer complexity of the character, and the need to distil that for an audience. Elektra suffers from obsessive-compulsive disorder; she has the name of a mythological Greek princess; she has complicated relationships with her family, and has almost no friends. Few of these character traits can be explored in any real depth in the length of a feature film. What is truly inscribed about Elektra's character can be read—as we have seen—in her face and actions during the key fight scenes of the film. She is without doubt a fearsome force, and elements of her treatment by Bowman and by his cinematographer, editor, and composer are echoed in the films of the Marvel Cinematic Universe. The introduction of Black Widow in 2012's *The Avengers*, for example, sees her taking a phone call while freeing herself from being tied to a chair and overpowering a gang of strong men. Peggy Carter takes aim at Captain America in the 2011 film: believing him to be cheating on her, she fires a round into his new vibranium shield, irrespective of potential danger. There is a new history being written of female characters in comic book film adaptations that are figured not just as strong and independent, but also complex and multifaceted. This researcher suggests that regardless of the film's critical treatment, this history's entries should certainly include Bowman's *Elektra*.

Notes

1. Joss Whedon, "Equality Now Tribute Address," *American Rhetoric: Online Speech Bank*, accessed February 22, 2015, http://www.americanrhetoric.com/speeches/josswhedonequalitynow.html.
2. Frank Miller, Klaus Janson, and D. R. Martin, *Daredevil* #1, January 1981 (New York: Marvel).
3. Sophocles, "Electra," in *Electra and Other Plays*, edited by David Raeburn (London: Penguin, 2008), 155.
4. B. M. W. Knox, *The Heroic Temper: Studies in Sophoclean Tragedy* (Berkeley: University of California Press, 1964), 1.
5. Sophocles, 183.
6. David Raeburn, "Preface to *Electra*," in *Electra and other Plays*, Sophocles (London: Penguin, 2008), 130.
7. Ibid., 132.
8. Sue Blundell, *Women in Ancient Greece* (London: British Museum Press, 1995), 114.
9. Ibid., 118¬–19.
10. Ibid., 114–15.
11. Ibid., 129.
12. D. G. Chichester, Scott McDaniel, and Hector Collazo, *Elektra: Root of Evil* #1–4, March 1995 (New York: Marvel).
13. Greg Rucka, Carlo Pagulayan, and Danny Miki, *Elektra* vol. 2 #18, February 2003 (New York: Marvel).
14. Frank Miller and Bill Sienkiewicz, *Elektra: Assassin* vol. 1 #1, August 1986 (New York: Marvel).
15. W. Haden Blackman and Michael Del Mundo, *Elektra* #2, May 2014 (New York: Marvel).
16. W. Haden Blackman and Michael Del Mundo, *Elektra* #5, October 2014 (New York: Marvel).
17. Ibid.
18. W. Haden Blackman and Michael Del Mundo, *Elektra* #4, September 2014 (New York: Marvel).
19. Mitra C. Emad, "Reading Wonder Woman's Body: Mythologies of Gender and Nation," *The Journal of Popular Culture* 39, no. 6 (2006): 958–59.
20. Ibid., 960.
21. Ibid., 962.
22. Ibid., 964.

23. Ibid., 968.

24. Captain America, for example, found the politics of September 11 troubling, and asked questions even politicians of the time refused to consider. See John Ney Reiber and John Cassaday, *Captain America: The New Deal* vol. 1, February 2003 (New York: Marvel).

25. Emad, 978–79.

26. Ibid., 982.

27. Joseph Campbell, *The Hero with a Thousand Faces* (London: Fontana Press, 1993), 30.

28. Ibid., 28.

29. Irving Singer, *Cinematic Mythmaking: Philosophy in Film* (Cambridge: MIT Press, 2008), 9–10.

30. Siegfried Kracauer, *Theory of Film: The Redemption of Physical Reality* (Princeton: Princeton University Press, 1960), 52.

31. Kevin J. Wetmore, Jr., "The Tao of 'Star Wars,' or, Cultural Appropriation in a Galaxy Far, Far Away," *Studies in Popular Culture* 23, no. 1 (2000): 94.

32. Manohla Dargis, "Moral Conflict Plus a Hot Bod: What More Does a Girl Need?" *New York Times*, last modified January 14, 2005, http://www.nytimes.com/2005/01/14/movies/14elek.html?ex=1137214800&en=d5b2a56a95e7701d&ei=5083&partner=Rotten%20Tomatoes&_r=0; Lisa Schwarzbaum, "Elektra," *Entertainment Weekly*, last modified January 12, 2005, http://www.ew.com/article/2005/01/12/elektra; Andrew L. Urban, "Elektra," *Urban Cinefile*, n.d., http://www.urbancinefile.com.au/home/view.asp?a=9849&s=Reviews_Archives.

33. Christy Lemire, "Elektra," *Deseret News*, last modified January 13, 2005, http://www.deseretnews.com/article/700003736/Elektra.html?pg=all; Helen O'Hara, "Elektra," *Empire*, n.d., http://www.empireonline.com/reviews/ReviewComplete.asp?FID=9967.

34. At the time of writing, however, Elektra has just been announced as a featured cast member in the second season of the Netflix revival of *Daredevil*. See Marc Strom, "Elodie Young Cast as Elektra in the Netflix Original Series *Daredevil*," *Marvel*, July 7, 2015, http://marvel.com/news/tv/24840/elodie_yung_cast_as_elektra_in_the_netflix_original_series_marvels_daredevil.

Part 2
Licensed Properties

Dare to Be Stupid
The Fetishization of Heavy Metal and the New in Transformers: The Movie

Eric Garneau

A Planet Devoured: A Theme Turned Up to 11

"Arblus, look! It's Unicron!"
"The ships! Get to the ships! It's our only chance!"

The above lines are the only pieces of dialogue (not counting random screams and sound effects) spoken within the first four minutes of the 1986 Marvel Productions[1]/Sunbow film *Transformers: The Movie*.[2] Yet, in those four minutes, viewers are asked to digest an immense amount of information. First, an ethereal synthesizer produces a treble-like, haunting sound, that is eventually accompanied by booming bass notes as danger looms closer, announcing a giant yellow and gray planet we're told is called "Unicron." For those who'd seen the film's promotional material, we might assume this to be the villain of the piece. We're briefly introduced to another planet (later referred to as "Lithone") populated by a different robotic race, presumably not the eponymous Transformers, then, in a two-minute sequence, flush with metallic violence, that planet is torn asunder—its inhabitants turned into fuel for Unicron's gorging mass. The detail with which we're shown this carnage is impressive and, again, mostly not commented upon.

Then, as Unicron leaves nothing of his victim except some outer-space flotsam, we abandon the synthesizers for something relatively foreign to *Transformers*: a 4/4 kick-snare rock beat. The opening credits of *Transformers* roll, heralding something familiar—a recognizable television show theme song we've been subjected to since 1984, but also something new—a hard rock arrangement. *Where have these screeching vocals and commanding guitar riffs come from? What is their purpose? What kind of movie are we about to see?*

For this author, the key to understanding the 1986 *Transformers* movie presented itself in the form of a DVD special feature containing some of the film's original trailers.[3] In these trailers, the movie is frequently referred to as "an incredible rock and roll adventure," a phrase that certainly challenges how one is encouraged to view the film. Animated cinema of the 1980s set a precedent for incorporating rock and roll, for example, segments of *Pink Floyd—The Wall,* or Columbia Pictures' *Heavy Metal*. But *Transformers* was a licensed property for children, to some no more than a feature-length commercial. However, that analysis feels all too dismissive. This essay will argue that, analyzed through a certain lens, we can view *Transformers* less as a typical narrative film than an extended music video, a *Heavy Metal* for all ages.

Concomitant with that, *Transformers* is a film obsessed with the *new*. Its narrative structure recalls an art form that had really only come into mainstream ubiquity five years prior with the 1981 launch of MTV. Its soundtrack buoys itself with one of the two titanics of the musical genres of the day, picking the edgier heavy metal[4] over the more pop-friendly, new-wave metal (though the film certainly nods to the other dominant '80s genre with its Devo sound-alike "Dare to Be Stupid" courtesy of "Weird Al" Yankovic).

It's not just a fascination with metal *music* that fuels *Transformers*. A sharp 2002 review from *The A.V. Club*'s Nathan Rabin brings insight: "Crucial to the film's cult appeal is its fetishization of metal."[5] This movie takes joy in the steely bodies within it—in scenes of mechanical violence and drawn-out transformation sequences. Science fiction fans might compare this film's fascination with metal bodies to director Robert Wise's fixation with starships in the 1979 *Star Trek: The Motion Picture*.[6]

Heavy metal, living machines, this was a world of the mid–1980s when Van Halen topped the charts and personal computers (intelligent machines) were becoming a reality for the middle class of the West—these were the facets of the new modern man. But even *within* the world of *Transformers*, this movie wants you to feel its newness. Consider that almost all familiar Transformers characters meet their demise within 20 minutes of screen time, leaving only an unfamiliar crew to propel this story forward.

This essay will closely examine the ways that *Transformers: The Movie* combines its use of heavy metal and a focus on the "new" to attempt to create an edgy, modern viewing experience that recalls predecessors such as *Heavy Metal*, even while remaining essentially a children's film.

A Brief Synopsis

For readers unfamiliar with *Transformers* or who need a quick reminder, we'll run down the plot of the film briefly. The aforementioned "Unicron," a hulking, robotic planet, runs amok through the galaxy, consuming other planets for sustenance. Meanwhile, the evil Transformers, known as Decepticons, have all but driven the heroic Transformers, known as "Autobots," from their home of Cybertron. The Autobots have only two strongholds left: Cybertron's moons and on Earth, where the Decepticons are determined to wipe them out. Decepticon leader, Megatron, leads a siege on Earth's so-called "Autobot City" and almost succeeds in exterminating our heroes, but a last-minute intervention from Autobot leader "Optimus Prime" staves off the Decepticon attack, though with a fatal cost to both leaders.

As a result, both sides in the Transformers' conflict find themselves scrambling for leadership. A dying Optimus appoints the stiff "Ultra Magnus" as his side's steward, while conniving character, Starscream, attempts to take over for Megatron. Unicron has other plans and turns Megatron into "Galvatron," a more ruthless killing machine than the Decepticons have ever seen. Galvatron tracks down the remaining Autobots and strikes again, seemingly killing Ultra Magnus in the process.

Fortunately, a few Autobots, led by the plucky Hot Rod, manage to turn our heroes' luck around and mount a last-ditch assault on the Decepticons. Meanwhile, Galvatron, resentful of his forced obeisance to Unicron, attempts to destroy his master. Enraged, Unicron turns on his servant and threatens to feed on the Transformers' home world. Fortunately, Hot Rod is able to unlock the power hidden within the Autobot Matrix of Leadership and become the new Autobot standard-bearer, "Rodimus Prime." Rodimus and his remaining soldiers destroy Unicron and retake Cybertron for themselves, ushering in an era of peace at last for the robotic race.

The Top-Billed Talent in Transformers

There are, maybe, two minutes of *Transformers: The Movie* that aren't backed by soundtrack. More than the writing, the directing, or any of the acting (and Sunbow's rounding up of an impressive array of talent for the film), composer Vince DiCola's synth-rock score (occasionally interrupted by single power-metal songs) drives the film, commanding our attention and supplying the emotion we're meant to feel at that given point. The sequencing of the film's credits almost concedes this point; immediately after listing the (again, stunning) voice talent for the film, the screen reads "Music Composed by Vince DiCola," giving the keyboard player primacy over writers and producers.

In a typical film, even an animated one, a musical score supports dialogue or directing choices, underlying a scene to amplify the emotional content present. In *Transformers*, the exact opposite happens. In a DVD interview, DiCola notes that he scored *Transformers* exclusively to storyboards.[7] He couldn't time out the music to fit the individual moments of a scene; he could work only with broad beats and hope to match the general tone a segment was meant to convey. "There are some things that I probably would change if I had seen it on video in the first place rather than storyboards," DiCola remarked in 2000.[8]

As it stands, DiCola's score provides the most present cue we have to access the film's emotions (if you'll accept that a movie about giant warring robots indeed contains emotions). It's relatively easy to see how this works; in numerous scenes, the score powers right on through incidents that one might imagine a typical soundtrack would play up. Consider Hot Rod and his companion Kup's trial by the alien Quintessons, for instance; one might guess a normal score would make way for the eventual verdict, slowing down and building suspense for a line of dialogue that determines our heroes' fate. Instead, the dialogue ends up being almost incidental to the overall development of the scene, as though there's no doubt what outcome Kup and Hot Rod will meet.

Besides Vince DiCola's omnipresent synthesizer score, several moments in the *Transformers* film set themselves against individual hard rock songs. If you accept the idea that *Transformers* is a feature-length music video, then these segments make themselves videos-within-videos—more digestible bits of action (frequently very destructive) that serve to progress the plot while supplying viewers with an abundance of material for their senses.

In this regard, *Transformers*' most obvious structural predecessor is the aforementioned 1981 picture *Heavy Metal*,[9] which, incidentally, also has its roots in the comics medium. Like *Transformers*, *Heavy Metal* is a sub-90 minute sci-fi/fantasy romp with a relentless soundtrack punctuated by set pieces determined by the start and stopping of a pop-metal song. Of course, *Heavy Metal* aims for a decidedly adult audience, much like the comic that birthed it, whereas *Transformers* (again like its comic) primarily targets a younger viewer base, at least ostensibly.

Still, the similarities cannot be denied. Consider the *Transformers* sequences set on the alien landscapes of the Quintesson planet, particularly the scenes accompanying two Spectre General songs, "Nothing's Gonna Stand in Our Way" and "Hunger." Here, the stranded Hot Rod and Kup have to fight for their life against hordes of hostile alien creatures. Clanging power chords and strident vocals carry us through segments involving a metallic gold octopus, an onslaught of shark-robots, and our heroes almost drowning in alien waters, twice. With its emphasis on familiar creatures twisted into out-of-this-world abominations that incite fantastical action, this section of the movie best recalls its edgier relative, though with less scantily clad outer-space women.

Transformers relies on a number of lesser known artists than did *Heavy Metal*, however, whose score featured a who's-who of rock and metal acts at the time, including Black Sabbath, Blue Oyster Cult, and Sammy Hagar; The *Transformers* soundtrack mostly uses artists signed to the Scotti Bros. record company (which released the film's soundtrack, naturally). One almost-crossover does exist—the above-mentioned "Weird Al" Yankovic's "Dare to Be Stupid," which features prominently in the scenes on the planet Junk, is written as a style parody of the band Devo, which has one of its songs "Working in a Coal Mine" on the *Heavy Metal* soundtrack. This makes a potentially tenuous connection, sure, but the producers' motivations to use a Devo sound-alike reads as a tip of the hat to their motion picture forbear, while the message "dare to be stupid" nicely characterizes the bizarre Junkion robots, headed up in voice talent by *Monty Python* alum Eric Idle.

Transformers also recalls *Heavy Metal* in that, even in these rock song sequences, the movie doesn't shy away from including lots of dialogue—despite the fact that it has to compete with lyrics, a rarity in film almost certainly because a film's creators generally don't want their dialogue obscured. In *Transformers,* robots happily converse over the belted vocals of glammed-up lead singers, lending their conversation to the sound mix instead of standing apart from it. Again, plot subordinates to music. In fact, there are times when it feels like the plot *is* the music, or at least the plot takes on musical qualities. Much of the dialogue in *Transformers* feels like sound bites instead of conversation. The film is endlessly quotable, something in which fans can delight.

"The Insecticons are in our way," says Kup. "Wrong! They're our way in!" replies Hot Rod. Other phrases include "I've got better things to do tonight than die," "I can't deal with that now!" and "One shall stand; one shall fall." The bits of speech that stand out from *Transformers* are not discussions but incisive clips—short, declarative sentences that almost find a musical quality in their punctual brevity.[10]

Further, notice how many characters in the film have off-kilter, often melodic, speech patterns. The easiest example here is "Wheelie," the young Autobot stranded on the Quintesson world that speaks purely in rhyme (e.g., "You get ship if I get trip"). There's Grimlock, the comic relief, whose broken speech recalls a robotic Lennie from *Of Mice and Men*: "Tell Grimlock about the petro-rabbits again." There's a planet full of Junkions who speak only in television tropes ("Offer expires while you wait. Operators are standing by"), and then, of course, there's Unicron, the final role played by film legend Orson Welles, whose bass-like voice booms through processors to channel the feel of a planet-devouring giant. Unicron's dialogue is mixed so low and has had so many effects applied to it that it's almost unintelligible at points, as though he's not really speaking at all but just adding to the on-screen ambiance (further supported by the fact that, whenever we actually hear him talk, we never see his lips move—even when he's in robot form). All of these dimensions of the soundtrack—the quip-filled dialogue, the unique vocal tones and styling—merge together to make a film more concerned with the *form* of audio you're experiencing than the *content*.

In fact, the film prizes form over content so much that it seems to hope you'll get so caught up in its soundscape you won't notice the many gaps in its narrative. Anyone looking to poke holes in this film's logic is shooting Sharkticons in a Quintesson torture chamber; *Transformers* plays fast and loose with the sensibility of its scenarios as well as basic narrative techniques. *Why is the Cybertronian Wheelie stranded alone on the Quintesson planet when the Dinobots, Kup, and Hot Rod arrive? How does everyone know who Unicron is but the Transformers, who are apparently the only race in the galaxy that can bring his rampage to a halt? Why is Unicron's interior structured like some kind of demented, hellish maze? Why does it seemingly take no time for Decepticon forces to travel from Earth to Cybertron and back?* Certainly these are all questions that *can* be answered (and certainly devoted groups on the Internet have given it the old college try), but they're not things to which the film itself wants us to pay too much attention. This is not necessarily a *fault* with the movie; after all, music videos often don't obey linear storytelling logic in favor of more impressionistic narrative techniques.

Alien Encounter

Intentional or not, the story gaps that make *Transformers* a potentially frustrating viewing experience serve a function. Besides the soundtrack, another facet of *Transformers* that demands its audience's attention is how alien, how new, it all seems. The film does nothing to hold the hand of its viewers, perhaps a strange choice for something based on a popular children's series. Parents probably assumed the film to be impenetrable simply for lack of familiarity with the Transformers concept, but even if you'd seen every episode of the television show, a lot here would feel very unfamiliar to you. The movie's promotional poster even exemplifies this. It features not even one character who existed on-screen prior to the film itself—no Optimus Prime, no Megatron, no Starscream, no Grimlock. And it features the tagline: "Beyond good. Beyond evil. Beyond your wildest imagination." Translation: "You've never thought of anything like this before!"

Of course, most of the marquee characters of the Transformers franchise do make their way into the movie anyway. Many are slaughtered, some unceremoniously, in the film's first act. *Transformers* is surprisingly violent toward, and unsentimental about, its familiar heroes; the edgy soundtrack (specifically NRG's "Instruments of Destruction") certainly assists here in the murder of a good dozen or so Autobots about ten minutes into the film.

As if this weren't a traumatic enough introduction to a new status quo, even familiar faces who escape mass execution tend not to fare well in the rest of the movie. To many young fans, *Transformers* is notable for featuring the death of Optimus Prime, the franchise's flagship character. While certainly his death receives more noble treatment than say, Ironhide's (there's even a soundtrack piece called "The Death of Optimus Prime" and this scene is its own video, if you accept the analysis above), it's still brutal. Prime's nemesis and murderer, Megatron, is also killed and replaced by the sleeker-looking, more angular Galvatron, replete with an army of spaceship soldiers.

Even children who completely bought in to the Transformers concept, then, would have almost no familiar heroes or villains to follow as the movie's second act gets underway. The only preexisting characters featured prominently are "Perceptor," who made his debut in the 1985 second season of the television show (every crew needs a scientist, I guess), and four-fifths of the Dinobots who are powerhouse, intellectually stunted heroes from early in the show's run, repurposed here for comic relief (not ineffectually, in this writer's opinion). The rest of the stars—Hot Rod, Ultra Magnus, Kup, Springer, Arcee, Blurr—would have had no prior relationship to Transformers viewers, except perhaps as a toy purchased in the months leading up to the movie.

What is the effect of this? It actively and forcefully disorients viewers, making them buy into a world that bears only faint resemblance to something they've seen before. It pushes the notion that *Transformers* is a *new* product, a modern narrative representing a cool, edgy sci-fi world with a rockin' soundtrack and serious action with serious consequences. This is a movie that tries hard to convince you of its freshness.

To further buffer this point, we can look back to Nathan Rabin's statement that *Transformers* is a film that "[fetishizes] metal." In the technology-obsessed 1980s, this seems like a fair way to convince audiences of your timeliness. This no doubt played into some of the original appeal of the Transformers series (it seems like a product that could only have launched in 1984, the year of Orwell and of Apple computers), but the movie embraces the literal metal of its titular stars in a way the cartoon never did.

This is apparent from the very opening scene, where we spend an unexpected amount of time watching as Unicron (in planet mode) flies past the camera. We become intimately acquainted with his outline, his contours and his appendages. The trend continues throughout the whole film, especially in sequences that feature transformations. How long does Autobot City take to reconfigure into its battle mode, for instance? How many shots are we shown of ramps retracting, guns deploying, walls fortifying? And again when Unicron reformats Megatron into Galvatron—the animation for this sequence incorporates something like wire-frame models for the characters that Unicron updates, as though he's writing new code onto Megatron and his lackeys to upgrade them, channeling a bit of techno-jargon for no real reason other than that the movie's creators probably felt they looked cool.

The obvious rebuttal here is to answer that *Transformers* had toys to sell, and featuring characters in extended transformation sequences essentially plays like an overlong commercial. Undoubtedly, there's some truth to that, but it's not the entire truth. The film takes equal joy in the transformations of "Metroplex" (available at all fine retailers in 1986!) and Unicron, for instance, even though Hasbro had no Unicron toy to market; the imbiber of worlds never officially received a place on toy store shelves until 2003, in the *Armada* toyline based on a much later Transformers series.[11]

The easiest comparison here, one made earlier in this essay, is to Robert Wise's directing style in 1979's *Star Trek: The Motion Picture*, a movie that simply *delights* in panning shots of starships almost to the point of pornographic exploitation. One gets the impression that Wise, a titan of cinema who'd contributed to such films as *Citizen Kane* (editor), *West Side Story*, and *Sound of Music* (both as a director) was simply fascinated with the new, futuristic genre to which he'd been given the reins. Either that or he just felt like starships were what people went to *Star Trek* to see, so why not give it to them? Although, unlike Wise, *Transformers* was not director Nelson Shin's first exposure to the source material (he'd worked on the television show as well), one imagines a similar thought process in place: "People came to this movie for robots. Let's show them robots."

And so, in a roundabout way, we come upon an answer for one of the seemingly nonsensical plot holes mentioned above. Why do Unicron's insides look like a hellish funhouse maze? Because of this fetishization of metal, because it lets us explore an alien, futuristic robot's insides in a visually compelling way. It doesn't have to make sense beyond that. It's a rock and roll adventure that embraces heavy metal in all its forms. What more do you need?

Till All Are One

Perhaps positioning *Transformers* as a "rock and roll adventure," and a music video for kids who like action toys, feels like a cop-out—it's certainly a way to salvage a piece of nostalgia for critics and other viewers who want to do so. But, importantly, it also clues us in to the way *Transformers* situates itself as a product of its time. Heavy metal robots clashing set against heavy metal songs—this seems like a movie that could only exist in the 1980s. It's easy to write off *Transformers: The Movie* as a toy commercial, but as this essay has argued, the creators seem to have been going for *something* more. Whether intentionally or not, similar comic-based adult animation like *Heavy Metal* plays a huge part in the construction of *Transformers,* and even though its critics don't see a lot of narrative logic in the film, it would be almost incomprehensible were it not situated in the music video-saturated MTV era of pop culture that was 1986. (It's worth noting that MTV's 1986 Video of the Year, Dire Straits' "Money for Nothing," features a merging of live-action performance footage with crude computer animation; surely the Megatron-to-Galvatron transformation at least looked *a little* better.)

And to return to *Transformers*' comic roots for a moment, in comparison to the other four (so far) Transformers films that have received a major theatrical release, *Transformers: The Movie* feels the most genuinely connected to its four-color source material; it's a snappy, vivid, action-packed film that even inspired comic writers who later followed in the franchise, like the UK's Simon Furman, who spent years at Marvel UK and then Marvel U.S. following up on Galvatron, Rodimus Prime, and the rest. The film is certainly highly stylized and highly confusing, but for fans of rock and roll robots, there's entertainment value to be had. Sometimes a rock and roll adventure is the most fun kind.

Notes

1. To address the Marvel Comics connection, in 1983 Transformers creator Hasbro sought out Marvel comics to create the world in which their toys would live. The work mostly fell to then-Marvel editor Bob Budiansky, who created many of the names and personalities fans love today. In that sense, Transformers has always had a gigantic connection to Marvel Comics, albeit at some points a surreptitious one. For more information, an archived interview with Budiansky about the creation process can be found here: http://web.archive.org/web/20070309223445/http://transfans.net/interviews_budiansky.php.

2. *Transformers: The Movie 20th Anniversary Special Edition,* directed by Nelson Shin (1986; New York: Sony BMG Music Home Entertainment, 2006), DVD.

3. An example of such a trailer can be accessed here: https://www.youtube.com/watch?v=QP9kzG-YEI0.

4. This essay will essentially conflate the genre terms heavy metal, hard rock, metal, and power metal. Certainly one could split hairs at distinctions in connotation there, but they all belong to the same sort of family and are similar enough for our purposes.

5. Nathan Rabin, "Transformers: The Movie," *The A.V. Club,* last modified March 29, 2002, http://www.avclub.com/review/transformers-the-movie-19682.

6. *Star Trek: The Motion Picture*, directed by Robert Wise (1979; Hollywood: Paramount, 2009), Blu Ray.

7. This interview can be accessed here: https://www.youtube.com/watch?v=sjnmQoY8oo8.

8. Interesting digression given the topic of this book: DiCola's method of scoring the *Transformers* film was not unlike the traditional "Marvel style" of writing a comic, where an artist storyboards his pages before a writer comes in to supply dialogue.

9. *Heavy Metal*, directed by Gerald Potterton (1981); viewed at www.netflix.com.

10. One potential exception is Kup, the "old war hero" trope voiced by Lionel Stander. He delights in telling lengthy stories, though mostly these, like the Dinobots, are played in the film for comedy; he and the slow-witted Dinobot Grimlock even form something of a jokey duo. Of course, Kup's also often the subject of ridicule from the young protagonist Hot Rod, voiced by *Breakfast Club* alum and paragon of '80s cool Judd Nelson.

11. TFWiki contributors, "Unicron/Toys," *Transformers Wiki*, http://tfwiki.net/wiki/Unicron/toys (accessed March 8, 2015).

Science Fiction in *G.I. Joe: The Movie*
Its Influence, Origin, Introduction and Development

Liam T. Webb

Science Fiction's Background Presence in the Creation of the 1980's Reboot of G.I. Joe

By the time *G.I. Joe: The Movie* came out in 1987, Hasbro's G.I. Joe property was already 23 years old.[1] Conceived as a toy line based on the American armed forces, and later expanding that idea to include anti-terrorist military task forces, it only makes sense that their adversaries in their first feature film were ... wait a minute ... underground alien snake people and giant bug monsters?

Yes, that's right: underground alien snake people and giant bug monsters. Not exactly the first thing many thought of when envisioning the bad guy targets for Joe's Kung Fu grip. So why did this happen? Was it because Marvel Comics, a company whose general stock in trade was science fiction and fantasy stories, was the company producing the comic and cartoon? Did Marvel direct or influence the introduction of these new wildly fanciful elements? Or was it because Hasbro wanted to go in that direction? This article will address where these thoroughly science fiction ideas came from, why they were included in what started as a relatively normal military toy/cartoon property, and why science fiction elements grew in the property over time.

To begin with, the answer to whether Marvel or Hasbro wanted *G.I. Joe: The Movie* to become a science fiction film is "both and neither." It wasn't so much policy or direction from either company; rather, science fiction was introduced into the property (and okayed by Hasbro) because the people hired to do the job were science fiction fans, in combination with both companies' hands-off approach to the actual work. However, the creative staff on the film were influenced by Marvel's products even when they may have been unaware of it, as was the likely case in *Alien*, as shall be shown. In fact, it is more proper to say that science fiction was "reintroduced" to the G.I. Joe property in the film than "introduced." To begin this examination, and to see science fiction's initial soft influence on the property, we must look at the 1980s version of G.I. Joe, which owed the initial form of its existence to *Star Wars* (1977) and Marvel's Larry Hama.

The *G.I. Joe* toy line was originally made of 11.5-inch figures that could wear cloth clothes. In the 1980s, the toy was revived as 3.75-inch plastic figures with the clothes molded on in plastic. The main reason the size of the toy was reduced was to mimic the success of the *Star Wars* action figures and to save on production costs.[2] Once Hasbro made this decision, but possibly before making any others,[3] Hasbro's then–CEO had an accidental meeting with Marvel's then-editor-in-chief at a charity function,[4] which led to representatives of the two companies meeting. Archie Goodwin, a comics and science fiction writer with two decades of experience, came up with the idea of Cobra Commander, but more importantly, Marvel provided the impetus for the existence of Cobra.[5] As former Marvel editor-in-chief Jim Shooter explains:

> They showed me what they had. A logo: "G.I. JOE, a Real American Hero." That was about it. They didn't want to revive the big doll…. And they wanted a line of figures, not just one. Someone said, "So, besides G.I. JOE, do we have G.I. George, G.I. Fred…? I said ["H]ow about if 'G.I. JOE' is the code name for the unit? Call in G.I. JOE?" They liked that. I also said it should be an anti-terrorist team. Not a "war" toy. That was obvious to everyone, I guess.
>
> [Hasbro] explained the rollout. They didn't plan to have any villains in the launch. We protested. "Who are they going to fight? They need bad guys!" Archie pitched his bad guy concept. The Hasbro people resisted on the grounds that villain action figures "don't sell." We persisted. Finally, they caved in and included one Cobra figure…. Later, by the way, villains became 40% of their volume.

Then Marvel's Larry Hama took Hasbro's plan and fleshed out the *Joe* team:

> My job was to write a comic book based on the figures. All I had were black and white drawings of the figures and job titles, like "infantry," "mortar-man," etc. I had to figure out names and personalities for them, but I also knew that there was going to be many more figures down the pike, so I needed a way to keep track of them all. That's why I created the file cards, which I originally called "dossiers." When the guys at Hasbro saw these first dossiers, they said, "These would be cool on the back of the blister pack!"[6]

When building up the *Joe* property, Hama drew from his military background, so the stories in the *G.I. Joe* comic (called *Action Force* in the UK) were all more or less military action adventures. However, when building the refurbished Joe property, Marvel had Hama include elements from his unused science fiction military adventure pitch called "Fury Force." The "Fury Force" concept was an update of Marvel's Sgt. Fury and S.H.I.E.L.D. group, whose opponent was a "ruthless, terrorist organization determined to rule the world" named Hydra.[7] According to Hama:

> [T]here were a lot of holdovers from the "Fury Force" concept that I had been developing for Marvel at the time. The whole idea of a secret base under a motor pool, for instance. I even had a "Snake-Eyes" type character, who didn't speak, had his face covered with a cowl and was a mysterious assassin type. He carried a pump shotgun and a commando knife in his boot and was actually inspired by the Pahoo-Ka-Ta-Wah (Wolf Who Stands in Water) character in the old "Yancy Derringer" TV show.

While the "Fury Force" idea updated a different property than originally intended, it kept the same general ideas of high technology with normal people (like S.H.I.E.L.D.). Then Hasbro, or, Hasbro together with Marvel, decided to keep the *Joe* property separate from other Marvel properties, even within the comic. This made sense, given that this specialized military unit was made to combat terrorists, and the *Joe* force would make no sense if the U.S. government could just call in "Thor" or the "Hulk" on an off weekend to beat Cobra into submission.

So, while the new form of the *G.I. Joe* toy was inspired by a science fiction source (*Star Wars*) and another property that dallied with science fiction extensively (S.H.I.E.L.D. often encountered superheroes and supervillains), it was quickly diverted into the military action subgenre due to Hama's background and decisions, and stayed there on the comics page. Of course, from the many accounts which show Hasbro very open to new ideas for their *Joe* property,[8] it seems that if Hama had a different idea—say, giving each soldier a piece of equipment to make him or her a "super-soldier," like Hasbro's "Bullet Man Joe" idea[9] or like the exosuits shown in the live action *G.I. Joe: The Rise of Cobra* (2013)—the 1980s G.I. Joe would have been more science fiction from the start. This "laissez-faire" attitude of Hasbro's regarding the property would prove to be the main reason science fiction came into the property so easily at a later time. Since Hama created all the character concepts and names,[10] he set the parameters of what the show runners started with; the show producers did indeed use this same layout for the first season of the show, with Joes fighting Cobras over Weather Dominators, M.A.S.S. devices, and various government overthrow plots. Hasbro's requests for the second season of the show, combined with the latitude they gave the show writers (who were science fiction fans) in filling those requests, eliminated the book and show's original synchronicity. While the book remained grounded in real world military action, the second season of the show introduced science fiction elements, and these elements led to the complete and immediate genre change seen in the movie.

"Arise, Science Fiction, Arise!" or the Re-Introduction of Science Fiction with Season 2

The science fiction elements were re-introduced to the property and emphasized in the second season of the television show, which set the stage for the film becoming a complete science fiction film. Hasbro ultimately expanded the line, without seeming to care greatly about the way in which it was done. Story editor and writer Buzz Dixon explains,[11] in a written interview personally conducted by this writer, that the science fiction elements (or at least the groundwork for them) were initiated due to Hasbro's desire to introduce the Serpentor character to the *G.I. Joe* universe:

> When I took over as story editor for *GI Joe* in season two, I wanted to do a story about the origin of Cobra (since the TV series had a different continuity than the comic book, this would have been our version, not Larry Hama's). My idea was that Cobra was based on the philosophy of an obscure professor who had gone so far afield of what he taught that when he threatened to denounce them, they had to kidnap him and throw him in a secret prison. When he escaped, Cobra [and the Joes would vie to find him first] would drop everything to hunt him down, and the Joes, realizing that whoever this unknown prisoner was must be important, would be trying to find him first.
>
> Hasbro approved of the idea and told me to start working on it, then said, "Oh, and by the way, start adding the Cobra Emperor (his original designation) to your scripts."
>
> I said, "The Cobra what?"
>
> "The Cobra Emperor."
>
> "Un-huh. And just where has the Cobra Emperor been all this time?"
>
> "Oh, he's always been there."
>
> "No, he hasn't," I said.
>
> [So then Hasbro gave us the default task of explaining how the Cobra Emperor got there.]
>
> "Cobra Commander has been the leader of Cobra all this time. If you had wanted us to hint at

some leadership level above him, you should have told us last year. We could have dropped hints so this wouldn't come as a surprise. Now we've got to explain how the Cobra Emperor got there."

"Okay, well, come up with some ideas."

So I came up with two ideas: The first one (the good one) was that Cobra, dissatisfied with Cobra Commander's leadership, creates a new leader using super-science. The second idea (the one I wasn't fond of) was that Cobra was the front organization for a shadowy group that had been secretly funding them all this time.

I preferred the first version because that would let me do "The Most Dangerous Man in The World," which was my Cobra philosopher story.

Well, Hasbro come back with, "We like your idea." So I ask, "Which one?" and they said, "Both of 'em!"

[Hasbro said they liked and wanted both ideas, s]o I put the two together, first writing "Arise, Serpentor, Arise!" in which Dr. Mindbender, frustrated at their lack of success, comes up with the idea of creating Serpentor as a replacement for Cobra Commander. This was followed with *G.I. Joe: The Movie* in which it's learned that there's a secret hidden civilization behind Cobra and they are the ones who implanted the idea in Dr. Mindbender's head.[12]

The Serpentor character, while perhaps not a science fiction-based character in Hasbro's initial idea, allowed the writers to introduce straight science fiction into the property, and Serpentor became the key to fully opening up related possibilities for the film.

Unlike all other previous Joe and Cobra characters, which were set up at the beginning, Serpentor was the first fully science fiction–bred character instead of a one-off plot device. Unlike other science fiction–heavy ideas that were created and disposed of in one twenty-two-minute episode,[13] his was a recurring character whose continual existence changed the genre of the show, the film, and ultimately changed the background of Cobra Commander from a person as he was in the comics (and arguably could have been in the television show's first season) into the film's hooded, disfigured, alien, snake-person hailing from a hidden society. In fact, in what could have been a "wink-and-nod" in the second season (and briefly in the film), there is even a character codenamed "Sci Fi" who wore neon-green. Serpentor's status as the gateway to turning the Joe movie into a full-on science fiction film was due to two things: who the writers were, and what they were told they couldn't do.

First, one rule put in place by Hasbro was that the film and show writers were not to tie themselves into the Marvel Comic: "[O]ur explicit instructions were not to tie ourselves to what was being done in the comics but to create our own continuity. Basically Hasbro was giving the same character and vehicle concepts to Hama & co[mpany] and to us and telling us to build from them."[14] Note that since Hama came up with most, if not all, names, code names, backgrounds and vehicles, the show writers based themselves on Hama's concepts more than Hasbro's. Because the show's stories could not be similar to Hama's more "real-world" tack, the writers took the show in a new direction via science fiction conventions (shrinking troops, teleportation, synthetic people, mechanically amplified psychic phenomena, and a parallel universe). The show's season one writers, however, kept the science fiction influences mainly to outlandish science and machinery overall at first, but drew from it immediately when Hasbro wanted changes made. Their inclination to draw from science fiction and not another genre when confronted with Hasbro's unannounced changes was, of course, a result both of their viewing and creative backgrounds and of sci-fi culture at the time.

Writer Flint Dille, for example, was the grandson of John F. Dille, the man who commissioned and influenced the creation of Buck Rogers and whose family-trust still holds the copyright. Dille is therefore no stranger to science fiction. Dixon also has a thorough background in the science fiction genre. Among other things, he was a reader of *Rip Hunter, Time Master*; *Superboy* (preferring him to Superman because "the plots were wilder"[15]); *Kona, Monarch of Monster Isle* and *Closer Than We Think* (a comic strip projecting what 21st century life will be like). He is also quoted as saying that "the *Buck Rogers* strip was a major influencer in my life,"[16] and was active in science fiction fandom and a frequent writer to fanzines.[17] Dixon also says that fellow show writer Steve Gerber "read anything and everything" and remembers that he was "heavily into Carlos Castaneda and other mystic writers."[18] It would be these mystical and science fiction influences on the film's creators that would contribute to the science fiction emphasis in the film and show—if Hama had written the film, he likely wouldn't have used such a fantastic idea as a snake society to explain away Cobra's underpinnings. Hama might have made the secret group more "realistic," like a secret government or the mob or a dirty corporation, since, after all, his version of Cobra Commander was a married father and former used-car salesman who decided to take over the world.

With this shared background, it was natural that Dixon, Dille, Gerber, and the other writers relied on it when Hasbro wanted to make what could have looked at first glance like "non-sequitur" changes to the property that they had to accommodate. They relied on their science fiction background for inspiration, to "fill the gaps" getting from point A to B (like working in a Cobra Emperor from nowhere), and to flesh out these story ideas. Regarding the feature film, when creating Cobra-La Dixon says they took from a variety of classic and contemporary science fiction and dramatic sources:

> To give this hidden civilization a place holder name, I dubbed it Cobra-la, … clearly based on the most famous of all literary lost civilizations, Shangri-la in James Hilton's novel *Lost Horizon*.
>
> The insect/organic/biological component of Cobra-la came from a myriad of sources: The late Richard E. Geis had written a series of stories set in a far future where genetic engineering had replaced chemical and electronic research; H.R. Giger's various biometric designs; Hayao Miyazaki's *Nausicaa of the Valley of the Wind*; and a host of other sources including the old sci-fi movies *Rodan* and *The Black Scorpion*. The old Marvel monster comics were part of that mix [I asked about these books specifically for this article], but not really a conscious influence.

In effect, it was Hasbro's desire to expand the toy line—without providing any information about the products to the people who were to write either series—that eventually turned the *G.I. Joe* feature film into a heavily science fiction-influenced product. If Hasbro hadn't wanted a Serpentor character, there would never have been a reason to create the Cobra-La society to begin with.

The Cobra-La society is the first element that Marvel's other work may have contributed to *G.I. Joe: The Movie*, but the film writers likely didn't know that at the time. This is because the Marvel product in question, Jack Kirby's *Eternals*, passed through the science fiction film *Alien* before coming to the film writers' attention. Though the main visuals of *Alien* were designed by H.R. Giger, the cockpit of the derelict alien ship that *Alien*'s monster eggs are found on looks strikingly like the "Chamber of the Gods" on pages 2 and 3 of the first issue of Kirby's *The Eternals* comic,[19] which preceded *Alien*'s production by two years.[20] There are two people who could have seen and used Kirby's images for *Alien*. The first is Ron Cobb, conceptual artist for *Alien*, and a cartoonist since 1965[21]; the second is comic artist Jean Giraud, better known as Moebius, who also worked on *Alien* and by that point had a long comics career himself.[22] And though the on-screen visuals of the *Alien* franchise were clearly Giger's, there almost certainly was some comic influence in the *Alien* property, through Cobb and Giraud, which later was used by the *G.I. Joe* writers. Later, James Cameron would admit in an interview that Kirby's work did influence the *Alien* franchise. Cameron said about his 1986 sequel, *Aliens*: "It's not intentional in the sense I sat down and looked at all my favorite comics and studied them for this film ... but yeah, Kirby's work was definitely in my subconscious programming. The guy was a visionary. Absolutely. And he could draw machines like nobody's business."[23]

By the time *G.I. Joe: The Movie* came out, it was a full-on science fiction film. It features a Kirby-influenced, Giger-esque alien secret society that uses xenobiological methods of underwater and air travel, weaponry, and other uses, in part just to be different than other secret societies:

> When Hasbro went for both ideas [for the secret society behind Cobra], we retrofitted Cobra-La into "Arise, Serpentor, Arise" by explaining that they [the Cobra-La people] had implanted the knowledge to create Serpentor in Dr. Mindbender's brain. We went big re: sci-fi ending because I felt there was little point of just doing another secret organization wanting to take over the world. That's what Cobra was (and Thrush and Spectre and so many other super villain leagues). To give them the level of technology necessary to create Serpentor via mind manipulation, we had to postulate a super science society, and if they were so super, why didn't they just run the planet from the get go? So they had to come from space (because if they originated on Earth they would have been the dominant species, not us), assumed humans would never amount to anything, and when we did [amount to something, the La society] decided to do something about it by sending Cobra Commander out to create Cobra.[24]

With this new society structure in place, Ron Friedman began writing the first draft of the film, which was ultimately discarded. But there was one thing Hasbro wanted kept from Friedman's first draft: Nemesis Enforcer, who went on to become one of the three main villains in the final film.[25] Nemesis Enforcer was a silent giant with bat wings and large sharp bones that extended from his wrists. Nemesis Enforcer looked more like a science fiction character, which, combined with the *Aliens*-inspired look of Cobra-La, is what encouraged Dixon to go in a more science fiction direction for the film's story.[26] This inclination then led to Dixon's creation of the second of the film's three main villains, Golobulus.

Golobulus is a humanoid from the waist up, who hovers/flies slowly about in a large green ball with bright blue portions (which could be eyes considering everything is organic) and a few tentacles trailing below. Golobulus's left arm is green, but the rest of him appears Caucasian. He wears a chest and arm piece, also organic, with coloring like that of a boiled-lobster. He has a conspicuous oversized, yellow, right eye and some support structure for it, which draws our attention to the "alien-ness" of his face. Later in the film we will find he rides this green shell transport to hide his lower half, which is that of a gray snake, like something out of Greek mythology. However, this was a far cry from Dixon's original conception of Golobulus:

> Golobulus was originally supposed to be an obese Charles Laughton-as-Nero character who looked human but would be revealed to have astonishingly fast reflexes and strength. My idea was that he would be portrayed as an indolent fat emperor until his fight w/Sgt. Slaughter & then he would astonish us w/lighting quick moves. Hasbro thought that approach was too effeminate (!) and [Hasbro] came up w/the design used in the film.[27]

So in this instance, Golobulus's original conception was more normal than the final product would have us believe, but here it was Hasbro's desires, and not Marvel's or the writers,' that took it into the realm of the fantastic.

The third main Cobra-La character is Pythona, who has acrobatic fighting skills and an ability to emit venom from her nail beds, but is otherwise a "standard" snake person. Curiously enough, she is the only female seen in the Cobra-La society, unless wearing the biological armor of their rank and file soldiers, which makes females appear male.

Though all of these things were much more the result of interactions between the writing staff and Hasbro, and not directly the result of Marvel's tendency to make products using science fiction or fantastic genres, there was one more background Marvel influence on *G.I. Joe*: Marvel's old monster comics. *G.I. Joe*'s general plot of a non-human alien force's desires to take over the Earth (and, naturally for the genre, begin with America) was such a constant in the Marvel monster genre—from Xemnu the Titan,[28] to the four-armed unnamed alien society,[29] to so many other stories—that Stan Lee stated his exhaustion in writing them was what made him buck his publisher by writing *Fantastic Four* #1 the way *he* wanted.[30] The idea that the Cobra-La society was on Earth for 40,000 years[31] had precedent in Marvel's Gorgolla,[32] the original concept of Fin Fang Foom,[33] and others. While no idea is truly new (and there were likely other monster movie reruns on television that the writing staff could have seen that had the same general idea of aliens hiding on Earth for centuries), none were particularly memorable enough to be mentioned by Dixon. Monster movies with mindless monsters, like *Rodan* and *The Black Scorpion*, were cited for their inspiration[34]; however, those mindless monster films' influences are seen more in the large mind*less* bugs and worms used by Cobra-La society than by the society members themselves—the society members seem to have a stronger resemblance to the Marvel monsters/aliens in intellect and motivation. One other factor which corroborates this theory is that, like films that reflected the nervous Cold War zeitgeist, Marvel monster comics of the 1950s and early 1960s used aliens as allegories for Soviet Russians. Cobra-La could easily be seen this way—a foreign society in central Eurasia that takes steps (i.e., creates the Cobra organization) to conquer America.

With Cobra-La and its inhabitants made into fantastic creatures by the various participants, the film's plot naturally became a science fiction plot, which finally pushed the property completely away from even an exaggerated real-world military adventure. The plot revolves around the Cobra-La group contacting Serpentor to get him, and in turn use him to get Cobra, in order to steal the Broadcast Energy Transmitter (BET), a machine that provides free-flowing electrical power. This plot point is more in the "traditional" Joe plots of both groups (made of normal people) fighting over who possesses a super weapon; however, the reasons for the theft, the theft itself, and all that follows are purely science fiction. The reason they want Cobra to steal the machine is so that the Cobra-La society can use it to mutate the world's human population into "mindless beasts," which would then allow the Cobra-La society to rule the Earth. This new ruling status, the film says, is actually a return to the status quo in Golobulus' eyes, as the film reveals that before mankind evolved, the Cobra-La people did rule Earth. The film also reveals/retcons Cobra Commander into a mutated Cobra-La nobleman, who is then punished with mutating spores (apparently, de-evolved into a snake by these spores) by Golobulus for failing to conquer Earth (i.e., America) for Golobulus. Cobra's forces and Cobra-La's forces, including their organic guns and their large worm and moth monsters, combine to steal the BET and use it to heat the mutagenic spores they previously fired into a sub-orbital pattern above the Earth. The Joe team, with a mutated Cobra Commander's help, track down the site of Cobra-La in the Himalayas (which is of course near the same locale as Shangri-La), invade it, fight the new and familiar bad guys of the series, and stop their plan, completely destroying the Cobra-La site (but likely not Golobulus) in the process.

Strangely enough, however, the film treats the science fiction introduction as almost "natural" through the reactions, or rather lack of reactions, of the Joe characters. None of the Joe characters express more than mild surprise when first encountering the bizarre, new enemy of Cobra-La. The Joes' initial contact with Cobra-La is seeing Cobra-La's strange plant life followed very quickly by an ambush. While the Joes express surprise at the attack, they do not comment or seem to react to the fact that those attacking them are not human beings. When the Joes first see Cobra-La's bizarre plants and environment, the Quick-Kick character is awed and says, "What is this, the Twilight Zone?" However, he is quickly cut off by the Roadblock character who says, "Forget those redwood toadstools, it's battle time!"[35] This first exchange points out to the young audience that this new enemy is bizarre and science fiction-based in a way that their previous television episodes were not, and more than that, it shows a critical audience that with this film, the Joe property is literally and figuratively walking into full-on science fiction territory, yet treats it as fait accompli. Even when the Joes stop fighting after being fought to a standstill, the film doesn't show the Joes reacting to the fact that it was alien-looking creatures who defeated them. This lack of reaction in the characters shows that, to the characters, science fiction, on this scale an unknown before this moment, is a "given" in the Joe universe. While this is a strange way to introduce a paradigm shift for the franchise, it makes sense when considering that the show and film creators were trending this way for a long time, and that the property's revival was based in science fiction. In fact, later in the film, it is unclear whether the Scarlett character's horrified reaction is to the fact that she was just cut off and almost killed, or that what had attacked was a "100-foot spiked worm." Just prior to this moment, in the Joe's second meeting with Cobra-La's forces in combat (and the first for the Joe characters in this scene), Duke says, "What the—?" And quickly follows up with "Shoot them down, whatever they are!"[36] He doesn't stop in horror or even wonder about what in the world the Cobra-La airpower even is. Furthermore, at the end of the film, the Joes are heard laughing and talking as they walk away from the smoking crater, which was just recently the site of Cobra-La; no one is even slightly bothered (or shell-shocked) to have just fought ten-foot spiders, centipedes the size of bridges, and a bunch of xenomorphic animals that defy classification. This final portrayal of the Joes' reactions now thoroughly solidifies the world of *G.I. Joe* as a science fiction property, because only characters in a science fiction universe *can* react this way.

Literarily speaking, if a character lives in a science fiction world, he or she knows things like this are possible, so it isn't as traumatizing if one day it happens to him or her. This unspoken assumption is why, when the Tunnel Rat character is eaten by a giant slug, he simply shoots his way out as if it's just "a typical move during a fight." If a person in a non–science fiction universe (like a Joe character from season one) was confronted with a giant, man-eating slug they would likely be immediately traumatized and might not even be able to function—military training be damned. Characters in science fiction worlds perceive those bizarre things the way that we, in the real world, perceive plane crashes or hostage situations; they might be rare occurrences, but the shock to the person is that it is happening to *them*, not that the event itself can happen.

The Final Solidifying of G.I. Joe *as a Science Fiction Property in a Science Fiction World*

The writing of the Joes and their reactions as science fiction world inhabitants includes them in a larger, fantastical universe that is referred to as the "Hasbroverse." The writing staff had this idea earlier in production, but not seriously, at first. In his interview, Dixon noted, "[a]fter we completed 'Once Upon a Joe,' we realized we should have made the Joe characters ponies so we could have linked that episode to *My Little Pony*. We kicked around the idea of Jem and the Holograms doing a USO show for the Joes, but that was always a background gag, not a main story point." When later, the G.I. Joe movie established that G.I. Joe's world included science fiction occurrences as a normal part of life, the writing team took the final step and combined all of Hasbro's properties into one science fiction world. In a prior interview with Joeheadquarters.com, Dixon said they had a particular character linking all the properties:

> [Reporter] Hector [Ramirez] first appeared in [G.I. Joe cartoon episode] "Twenty Questions" as a parody of Geraldo Rivera, but soon became a semi-regular whenever we needed a recognizable news anchor (for example, instead of the usual "In our last episode…" recap for "The Traitor," we began part two with Hector reporting the events of part one as if they were a news story). I think he's in two or three other G.I. Joe episodes and may have even been briefly in the movie in a cutaway scene. While writing "One Jem Too Many" [a Jem cartoon episode], I had a scene at a televised gala premiere and, since Hector needed the work, wrote him in.… [Writer] Flint [Dille] needed a newscaster for Inhumanoids, so he wrote Hector in. I even think he made an appearance or two in *Transformers*.[37]

This, as the unnamed writer of Joeheadquarters.com established, places *Transformers*, *G.I. Joe*, *Jem* and *Inhumanoids* all in the same sub-universe of Marvel/Hasbro productions,[38] which only makes sense given that most of the same creative personnel were working on all these shows more or less simultaneously.[39] Finally, Hasbro passively, if not actively, adopted the idea of the properties functioning in one science fiction world when they allowed characters to be killed. As Dixon states:

> I finally got permission from Hasbro to do something we had never done in the series: kill off a character. Since Duke … was being phased out of the toy line, I decided to kill Duke off as the final impetus that turns Lt. Falcon into a real Joe. The scene was animated and, if you watch the visuals and don't listen to the soundtrack, it's obvious Duke dies.
> However, Hasbro decided if killing off a major character was good for G.I. Joe, it would be even better for *Transformers*, so they ordered Optimus Prime to be bumped off in the *Transformers Movie* even though that had never been the intent in the original script. The audience for Transformers was about 3–4 years younger on average than the Joe fans. The Joes fans at least made *some* acknowledgment that War Is Not Fun and People Get Hurt.
> The younger Transformer fans freaked when Optimus Prime went to that big junkyard in the sky; there had been nothing in the tone of the story that indicated it could take such an ominous turn (yeah, Orson Welles was going to eat the galaxy, but that was all a fun *Star Wars*–ish romp; it wasn't like somebody you knew and liked was going to bite it). Parents howled in protest to Hasbro, and Hasbro decreed *G.I. Joe: The Movie* be slightly re-edited and re-dubbed to indicate Duke survived (that clunky "We just heard Duke's going to be all right—yea!" ending).[40]

Going forward, the Joe and Transformer universes continued to be intertwined in comics and on television. Captain Marissa Fairborne appeared in later episodes of *Transformers*; she was intended to be the daughter of G.I. Joe character "Flint."[41] The property universes were later "officially" put completely together in Marvel's 1987 miniseries *G.I. Joe and the Transformers*.

"And now you know..."

All of this shows us that, at this point in Marvel's film efforts, their fantastic and heroic stock in trade had (consciously) extraordinarily little to do with the *G.I. Joe: The Movie*'s science fiction turn. The film became a science fiction film because of the writers' and Hasbro's decisions, which started out small then grew and grew until the G.I. Joe franchise was in a thoroughly science fiction world. The only influences that Marvel's fantastic products had were indirect, as a part of the film writers,' or *Alien*'s, backgrounds. The Marvel comic remained relatively more "normal" than the show and film throughout its lifespan, even while accommodating Hasbro's requirement to start adding in characters like Serpentor. In fact, in the comics (and a year after the film came out), Serpentor is killed by a simple arrow to the eye[42] with nary a snake man or large insect to be found.

While at first glance the film seems to fit the more familiar Marvel science fiction product, it only does so because of Hasbro's orders and nothing that Marvel ordered or required at all. While the idea of Cobra-La as a hidden alien society trying to take over America is strikingly similar to the bulk of Marvel's monster comics products in the 1950s to early 1960s (and the look of Cobra-La was based on *Alien*, which was in turn based on work Jack Kirby did for Marvel), the similarities are either subconscious, or supported, but not fully confirmed as of today. Even later, when the *Jem*, *G.I. Joe*, *Transformer* and *Inhumanoid* properties condensed and solidified into the Hasbroverse, Marvel had nothing to do with it. This came from natural progressions made by Hasbro and the properties' writers. While Marvel would go on to make other films that were increasingly, and then directly, taken from their superheroic and science fiction genres, *G.I. Joe: The Movie* was not one of them.

Notes

1. Dan Fletcher, "A Brief History of G.I. Joe," Time.com, last modified August 7, 2009, http://content.time.com/time/nation/article/0,8599,1915120,00.html; Bathroom Readers Institute, "The Facts About G.I. Joe" in *Uncle John's Second Bathroom Reader* (New York: St. Martin's Press, 1988), 117.
2. Jimmy Stamp, "Now You Know the History of G.I. Joe. And Knowing Is Half the Battle: The Evolution of the All American Hero from Artist's Mannequin to Action Figure," Smithsonian.com, last modified March 29, 2013, http://www.smithsonianmag.com/arts-culture/now-you-know-the-history-of-gi-joe-and-knowing-is-half-the-battle-11506463/?no-ist.
3. Kurt Anthony Krug, "G.I. JOE Generalissimo Larry Hama: Comics Scribe Talks Toys, Comics and Movies Exclusively with Mania.com," mania.com, last modified July 1, 2009, http://www.mania.com/gi-joe-generalissimo-larry-hama_article_115801.html; Jim Shooter, "The Secret Parts of the Origin of G.I. JOE," jimshooter.com, last modified July 6, 2011, http://www.jimshooter.com/2011/07/secret-parts-of-origin-of-gi-joe.html.
4. http://www.jimshooter.com/2011/07/secret-parts-of-origin-of-gi-joe.html.
5. Ibid.
6. http://www.mania.com/gi-joe-generalissimo-larry-hama_article_115801.html.
7. Ibid.
8. "G.I. Joe: A Real American Hero (Marvel Comics)," wikipedia.com, last modified February

18, 2015, http://en.wikipedia.org/wiki/G.I._Joe:_A_Real_American_Hero_%28Marvel_Comics%29 #cite_note-30th. Vincent Santelmo, *The Official 30th Anniversary Salute To G.I. Joe 1964–1994* (Iola, WI: Krause Publications, 1994), p. 159.

    9. Brian Heiler, "1976 Hasbro GI Joe Selection," plaidstallions.com, last modified January 29, 2015, http://www.plaidstallions.com/hasbro/gijoe.html.

    10. http://www.mania.com/gi-joe-generalissimo-larry-hama_article_115801.html.

    11. Liam Webb, Buzz Dixon interview conducted via FB Messenger, January 13, 2015.

    12. Liam Webb, Buzz Dixon interview conducted via FB Messenger and via email, January 13, 2014 and February 28, 2015.

    13. Marvel/Sunbow Animation, *G.I. Joe: A Real American Hero*, G.I. Joe and the Golden Fleece, 21:50. http://www.watchcartoononline.com/g-i-joe-a-real-american-hero-season-2-episode-22-g-i-joe-and-the-golden-fleece.

    14. Liam Webb, Buzz Dixon interview conducted via FB Messenger, January 13, 2015.

    15. Ibid.

    16. Ibid.

    17. Ibid.

    18. Ibid.

    19. Jack Kirby, *The Eternals* #1, July 1976 (New York: Marvel Comics), 2–3.

    20. No name given, "Alien Unseen: Part Two—Production Storyboards," Weyland-Yutani Archives, last modified January 30, 2013, http://weyland-yutaniarchives.blogspot.com/2013/01/alien-unseen-part-two-production.html.

    21. Woody Anders, "Ron Cobb Biography," IMDB.com, accessed July 10, 2015, http://www.imdb.com/name/nm0167803/bio?ref_=nm_ov_bio_sm.

    22. Cyriaque Lamar, "Legendary French Artist Moebius, the Man Who Made *The Abyss, Alien*, and Tron Even Weirder, Is Dead at 73", io9, accessed July 13, 2009, http://io9.com/5892148/legendary-french-artist-moebius-the-man-who-made-the-abyss-alien-and-tron-even-weirder-is-dead-at-73; No name given, "How Moebius Revolutionised Comic Art," creativebloq.com, accessed July 13, 2009, http://www.creativebloq.com/illustration/how-moebius-revolutionised-comic-art-21514203 and http://www.creativebloq.com/illustration/how-moebius-revolutionised-comic-art-21514203?page=1 and http://marvel.com/news/comics/18278/marvel_remembers_moebius.

    23. Frank Lovece, "'Aliens' Arrives on Video This Week," repost nationally syndicated newspaper column (United Media, February 26, 1987) on scribd.com, accessed February 20, 2015, http://www.scribd.com/doc/146229501/Aliens-Arrives-on-Video-This-Week-James-Cameron-interview.

    24. Liam Webb, Buzz Dixon interview conducted via FB Messenger, February 25, 2015.

    25. Ibid.

    26. Ibid.

    27. Ibid.

    28. Stan Lee, Jack Kirby and Dick Ayers, *Journey into Mystery* Vol 1 #66, March 1961, reprinted in *Monsters on the Prowl* Vol. 1 #14, December 1971 (New York: Marvel).

    29. Stan Lee, Jack Kirby and Dick Ayers, *Tales to Astonish* Vol. 1 #26, December 1961, reprinted in *Where Monsters Dwell* Vol 1. #8, March 1971 (New York: Marvel).

    30. Stan Lee and George Mair, *Excelsior! The Amazing Life of Stan Lee* (New York: Fireside, 2002), 111–15.

    31. *G.I. Joe: The Movie*, directed by Don Jurwich (1987, accessed via https://www.youtube.com/watch?v=EKzayGo6NaE).

    32. Stan Lee, Jack Kirby and Dick Ayers, *Strange Tales* Vol. 1 #74, April 1960, reprinted in *Where Monsters Dwell* Vol. 1 #35, May 1975 (New York: Marvel).

    33. Stan Lee, Jack Kirby and Dick Ayers, *Strange Tales* Vol. 1 #89, October 1961 (New York: Marvel).

    34. Liam Webb, Buzz Dixon interview conducted via FB Messenger, January 13, 2015.

    35. *G.I. Joe: The Movie*, directed by Don Jurwich (1987, accessed via http://www.dailymotion.com/video/x8lr9n_g-i-joe-the-movie-part-2_shortfilms).

    36. *G.I. Joe: The Movie*, directed by Don Jurwich (1987, accessed via http://www.dailymotion.com/video/x8lun2_g-i-joe-the-movie-part-5_shortfilms).

    37. No name given, "Interviews," joeheadquarters.com, last updated May 27, 2005, http://www.joeheadquarters.com/interviews_dixon.shtml.

    38. Ibid.

39. G.I. Joe movie aired 4/87, the series 9/83 to 11/86; Transformers aired 9/84 to 11/87; Jem aired 10/85 to 5/88; and Inhumanoids aired 9/86 to 12/86.

40. No name given, "Interviews," joeheadquarters.com, last updated May 27, 2005, http://www.joeheadquarters.com/interviews_dixon.shtml.

41. No name given, "Interviews," joeheadquarters.com, last updated May 27, 2005, http://www.joeheadquarters.com/interviews_dille.shtml.

42. Larry Hama, Ron Wagner, and Fred Fredericks, *G.I. Joe A Real American Hero* #76, September 1988 (New York: Marvel Comics).

Conan the Destroyer of a Franchise?

Analyzing and Evaluating the Adaptive and Narrative Features of Conan the Barbarian, Conan the Destroyer *and* The Horn of Azoth

RODNEY DONAHUE

Conan the Barbarian was an iconic film featuring the world's most well-known sword-and-sorcery character. The film was a critical and commercial success, leading to the 1984 sequel *Conan the Destroyer*, a moderate commercial success. Why not a critical success? By all accounts, *Conan the Destroyer* contained an array of positives that assured a critical success as well: Schwarzenegger returning as the hulking, sword-wielding hero; *Tora! Tora! Tora!* and *Soylent Green* director Richard Fleischer at the helm; and a story by Roy Thomas, author of the first 115 issues of the *Conan the Barbarian* Marvel comic series and a man now synonymous with Conan mythology. And yet, while *Conan the Barbarian* scores a "certified fresh" 72 percent on Rotten Tomatoes with an audience score of 74 percent,[1] *Conan the Destroyer* remains "rotten" in the ratings with 27 percent and an audience score of 39 percent.[2]

The goal of this essay is to examine the feature films *Conan the Barbarian* and *Conan the Destroyer* from an academic standpoint, when Conan was still a property that Marvel licensed. The first part of the essay analyzes and evaluates *Conan the Barbarian* as an adaptation and as a film, as well as how the film was adapted into comic form. The second part of this essay analyzes and evaluates *Conan the Destroyer* and the curious history surrounding its creation; an exploration of interviews, recollections, and comics answers questions surrounding the three-decade gap between *Conan the Destroyer* and *The Legend of Conan*, a prospective film at the time of this writing. The third part of this essay examines Marvel Graphic Novel #59, *Conan the Barbarian in The Horn of Azoth*; this graphic novel by Roy Thomas and Gerry Conway was devised six years following the theatrical premiere of *Conan the Destroyer* and was inspired by the original screenplay penned for that film.

The Creation of Conan

In *How to Adapt Anything into a Screenplay*, Richard Krevolin provides his chief rule regarding adaptations: "*You owe nothing to the original text!*"[3] He instructs the adaptor "not to do a verbatim and faithful transcription, which is in many ways impossible anyway, but to capture the truth of the original work and convey that onscreen."[4] While these statements appear contradictory, adapting across media is indeed a difficult process. Each project is fresh and requires delicate handling. Once Hollywood began to split the final installments of series like *Harry Potter* and *Twilight* into multiple films, adaptation theory queried: should individual books like *The Hobbit* or *Mockingjay* receive multiple installments? According to Krevolin, all bets are off the table and anything is conceivable, so long as the truth of the work is conveyed. Of course, whether or not the truth of each individual adaptation was conveyed is often in the eye of the beholder, and Krevolin's principles serve as an important instrument for measuring the adaptations of *Conan the Barbarian* and *Conan the Destroyer*.

The long-running Marvel comic series *Conan the Barbarian* was created by Roy Thomas. During his tenure, Thomas generated more than 200 issues of *Conan the Barbarian*, *Savage Sword of Conan*, and *King Conan* comic books and graphic novels, devoted two years to a Conan newspaper strip, created TV cartoons, worked as a paid consultant on the movie *Conan the Barbarian*, and co-wrote the first five drafts of its sequel *Conan the Destroyer*.[5] Not only is Thomas' Conan resume extensive, but his standing in comics community is indisputable: Thomas is the fifth-ranked comic-book writer of the twentieth century.[6]

The series, however, was not an original concept; it was adapted from Robert E. Howard's collections of short stories on the Conan the Cimmerian, Cimmeria being the culture from which Conan derives. For Thomas, "the *Conan* of the two dozen or so Robert E. Howard stories will always be the only one that really matters."[7] From the beginning, Marvel's version of the hero adhered to the scrutiny of Krevolin's system. Thomas, by his own admission, sought to draw from original source material on Conan as his primary inspiration: "By the time I had left in 1980 we had adapted almost everything that anybody had ever written about Conan in prose up to that point."[8] In this manner, Thomas worked to capture the truth of the original work by attempting to create a Howard-built Conan for comics. "I believe it was [artist Barry Windsor-Smith's] idea to have Conan walk amongst the mammoths and establish an almost symbiotic relationship with them; I doubted Robert E. Howard's Conan would've done such a thing, but I wasn't 100% sure he *wouldn't*."[9] What would Howard's Conan do? It is from this scale that Thomas's Conan emerged.

Thomas's reverence for Robert E. Howard is apparent from very early in the *Conan the Barbarian* comics run. On the first and second issue of *Conan the Barbarian*, "Based on the Character Created by Robert E. Howard" appears in the lower right-hand corner of the cover page; these first issues simply credit the author of the original source material. Issues 3 and 4 point out that stories belonging to Robert E. Howard are adapted; instead of relegation to a list of names, the Howard reference receives its own stylized banner at the bottom-center of the cover. The most pointed expression comes on the cover of issue #5, "Zukala's Daughter." The designation is clear: "Robert E. Howard, Creator of Conan." Howard's name is stylized and emboldened in a manner linking him directly to the comic in a fashion the names of the editors, writers, and artists do not. "Creator of Conan" is often applied hereafter to indicate Robert E. Howard's importance to those involved in the adaptation process and the progression of the series.[10]

Marvel championed multiple Conan titles: *The Savage Sword of Conan*, *King Conan*, and, of course, *Conan the Barbarian*. But the adaptation journey of Howard's sword-and-sorcery hero did not stop at the illustrated page. After more than a decade of comics, Conan was primed for Hollywood. In a film era teeming with heroes like Luke Skywalker and Indiana Jones, the arresting form of Conan stood apart as the Cimmerian burst to life on the big screen.

Conan the Barbarian: *A Treasure Worth Plundering*

Conan the Barbarian is a revenge tragedy that arises from the murder of Conan's parents in his adolescence. As the Cimmerian matures, he spends more than a decade as a slave and gladiator, finally receiving his freedom after much butchery. Conan hunts for his god and his parents' murderers, the image of snakes and a moon residing in his mind. He creates a band of thieves, one of whom is Conan's love Valeria. Earning reputations as great thieves, Conan's party is recruited by King Osric to rescue his daughter from Thulsa Doom, who is coincidentally the perpetrator for whom Conan searches. Conan's thirst for vengeance deepens when Thulsa Doom slays Valeria as they liberate the princess. In the end, Conan eradicates Thulsa Doom's army and beheads him before his supporters. The faction disbands, and Conan returns the princess to Osric.

For the most part, critics exploring the cinematic narrative of *Conan the Barbarian* recognize it as a fine film. It possesses exemplary visual storytelling, unrepentant violence portrayed in a cautious manner, and circumstances are at stake in every scene. I will focus on three major reasons *Conan the Barbarian* stands out as a good movie: the religious subject matter, honest emotional development inherent in what could easily become an adventure film, and well-crafted production standards.

Conan the Barbarian is a film steeped in religious thinking and allegory. Prior to the film's climactic battle sequence, Conan prays: "Crom, I have never prayed to you before."[11] Though he cites Crom as his god, this is new for him, the prayer sanctioning Conan to display his true beliefs in a moment of tension. He needs help in the coming battle. His belief is only sealed in victory, though, as he damns his own god if the battle is lost. The spirit of Valeria salvages success at the opportune time, and Conan's faith journey is complete. Certainly Conan's crucifixion bears religious symbolism; the initial image of the Tree of Woe is a startling one. Many films display the death of the hero, such as the bullets momentarily killing Neo until he is revived by Trinity in *The Matrix*, but what non–Passion-based film totes the literal crucifixion and resurrection of its hero in the brazen style of *Barbarian*? Even at the end of the film, Thulsa Doom's flames are extinguished in a pool; the cult disbands with overwhelming shades of Judges 9, when Abimelech is killed, and all of his followers simply walk away. Even into the last shot of the film, when heavenly light beams down on the path of Conan, *Barbarian* extends a religious experience.

Conan the Barbarian shies away from neither the horror of violence nor its integral drama. The film contains an emotional awareness that the audience experiences with the characters. The earliest example of this comes from the medium close-up of the boy Conan holding the hand of his mother. She is decapitated off-screen, her head plummeting through the shot as though dropped from above. Her entire body falls to the side, and Conan only recognizes his mother's demise when her hand pulls away from his, a boy's strength unable to manage the weight of her unresponsive body. There are numerous examples of the audience being allowed the experience of feeling: the fear Valeria displays when she sees she may have to combat two opponents instead of one; the literal and figurative disarmaments of Conan and Valeria prior to lovemaking; the remorse apparent in Osric's tone when he realizes "all that is left is a father's love for his child."[12] Even the raw emotion from the antagonists is honest: when the mustached captain mourns the death of his brother by Conan's hand, he attacks the Cimmerian with a yearning for vengeance, and the music aids in his expressive attack. The most climactic emotional outpouring comes from the ill-fated death of Valeria, desperately clinging to Conan as she realizes the sacrifice she made, permitting him to live. The scene is unequivocally melodramatic, but the score, the shot, and the actors work as one to create a passionate, heart-wrenching summit.

Conan the Barbarian features well-executed production values. From Thulsa Doom's soldiers carrying a cauldron of human stew in step with the resounding beat of the musical score to Conan slaying Doom with the same sword the villain used to murder Conan's mother, every moment of the film demonstrates meticulous exactitude. The most dynamic highlight takes place in the cavern of Mount Doom. When Conan, Valeria, and Subatoi gain entry to the mountain fortress, the interior is saturated with red. They find a chamber of headless corpses hanging in various positions, their lifeless skins ripped to drain blood from the meat. The horror of split bodies amassed for carving and consumption is masked by glowing red light that hides the open cadavers. The presence of the corpses is unnerving, the advent of the cavern reminiscent of a scene in Rob Zombie's *House of 1000 Corpses*. *Barbarian* avoids trespassing into the audience-appalling torture horror genre by presenting this sequence with a technical finesse that displays artistic awareness of Thulsa Doom's cult representing the worst humanity offers.

Despite the film's successes, Roy Thomas "unabashedly believes the Conan comics he did ... to be superior to anything Hollywood did with the Cimmerian."[13] He does not care for the film *Conan the Barbarian*.[14] Thomas considers the film a poor substitute for his and certainly Howard's Cimmerian, the source for his adaptation barometer. Concerning his work as a consultant on the film, Thomas remarks that he was responsible for labeling: "Was this Conan or wasn't it Conan? And he didn't have to heed what I said." While he expressed that the origin story was dissimilar to Conan's actual (read: Howard's) origin, he thought the origin portion of the film leading up to Mount Doom was interesting. Of basically everything else in the film he said, "I really hate this a lot,"[15] particularly referencing *Barbarian* director John Milius's story as a parable on the dangers of cults and the casting of James Earl Jones as Thulsa Doom. He calls Jones a fine actor, but comments that Thulsa Doom has a skull head, another Howard/Thomas principle. "As a result, there's almost nothing in the final movie that reflects anything that I had anything to do with. It was all John's movie."[16]

Thomas's opinion is well-documented; fans appreciate the openness, honesty, and willingness to educate them on his work and sentiments. His estimation of *Barbarian* comes from a highly subjective base where the measure of a good adaptation, or at the very least a good Conan-based adaptation, comes from a faithful transcription of Howard's Cimmerian. This is the opposite not only of how Richard Krevolin views adaptation, but film critics as well. *Conan the Barbarian* is a well-constructed motion picture and an excellent example of adaptation based on Krevolin's principles, particularly that of owing nothing to the original. In the case of *Conan the Barbarian*, director John Milius and company owe nothing to the works of Robert E. Howard, a premise to which Thomas does not adhere.

There are two versions of the comic book adaptation of the movie: a Marvel Illustrated Book and a two-issue *Conan the Barbarian* movie special, though both contain basically the same comics, neither written by Thomas. The Conan of this tale is a cross between Marvel's Cimmerian and Schwarzenegger. The account follows the film very closely, skipping the sex scenes and reducing the gore. In so doing, the comic version is undoubtedly rated PG by movie standards, a treat for Conan fans too young to view the R-rated film in theatres. For example, the impalement of Thulsa Doom that leads to his demise in the comic is vastly different from the hacking butchery with which the film's Conan decapitates Doom; this is also relatively benign compared to even the earliest imaginings of the Cimmerian.[17] The "Red Nails" saga by Thomas presents a Conan of PG-13 material just outside the realm of an R rating in terms of sex and violence. In several instances, only shadows cover bare breasts, and the amount of rendered gore soaks the panels in blood. *The Chronicles of Conan* edition of this storyline playfully pairs the action with red-bordered pages. In one frame, the boundaries of sex and violence are pushed to the brink when a ray of fire enters a woman's back and exits her chest, causing one of the armored circles covering only her breasts to pop off.[18] Roy Thomas is notably absent from the credits of the comics adaptation of the film.

Conan the Destroyer: *What Happened (Not a Question)*

Conan the Destroyer is an adventure tale in which Conan embarks on a quest with a princess to track down a horn. Conan does not know that the horn will reincarnate Dagoth, nor that the princess' bodyguard is commissioned by Queen Taramis to kill Conan once the horn is safely recovered. Unfortunately for the bodyguard, Conan employs three comrades to help. En route, the princess is captured by a wizard, and Conan and crew storm his castle and rescue her. Returning to the quest, they find the horn deep in an ancient tomb, where the group is separated—the princess and her bodyguard on one side, Conan and his companions on the other. Conan reasons the deception of Taramis, and he storms another castle, the queen's, where the group kills the queen, the bodyguard, and Dagoth, restoring the princess to her rightful place on the throne.

Can criticism of *Conan the Destroyer* occur independent of *Conan the Barbarian*? Certainly not. While each individual film should receive its own criticism, *Destroyer* as a sequel naturally follows and is structurally connected to its predecessor. It is *Destroyer* that presents the reason for this. The end of *Conan the Barbarian* reveals the Cimmerian with a crown while the wizard concludes his narration: "In time, he became a king by his own hand.... And this story shall also be told." But not next, apparently. *Destroyer* is not the story of how Conan earns his kingdom; rather, it is a tale of a man who searches for and will continue searching for his kingdom. It is not a sequel but the second installment of a trilogy that has no end. It is a bridge removed from the second landmass, and the audience crosses this bridge, tumbling into raging waters, awash of a complete ending. As an independent venture, critics panned *Conan the Destroyer* for a plethora of shortcomings, the most notable of which are celebrity ushering, poor writing, meager production values, uncomfortable subject matter, and the dislodging emotional association.

Perhaps the most detrimental aspect of *Conan the Destroyer* concerns the primary character. Where *Barbarian* is about the hero Conan, *Destroyer* is designed to feature the actor Arnold Schwarzenegger. In "Arnold at the Gates: Subverting Star Persona in *Conan the Barbarian*," Nicky Falkof draws the conclusion that *Conan the Barbarian* "fails to conform to any of the standard behavioral traits of the Schwarzeneggarian universe.... Even the Terminator, another iconic character defined by body, learns humor and humanity in *T2*. Conan stands alone within the Schwarzenegger cosmos."[19] The essay surmises that Schwarzenegger films after *Conan the Barbarian* all emphasize a particular heroic structure that purposefully coincide with his meteoric rise into the American political atmosphere. Most interesting is that Falkof's essay ignores mention of *Conan the Destroyer*. This is intriguing as *Barbarian*'s sequel is not immune to the persona-pedaling mentioned of the movies in the rest of the article and suffers from it as much as any post–*Barbarian* film in the aforementioned cosmos. The most likely reason is that the Conan of *Destroyer* is analogous to the Terminator of *T2* and unhinges the argument from a seemingly impermeable frame.

Falkof's dismissal of *Conan the Destroyer* is not a rare practice. *Conan the Destroyer* is mentioned twice in *Conan Meets the Academy: Multidisciplinary Essays on the Enduring Barbarian*. The introduction comments that Roy Thomas worked on the initial screenplay.[20] The second instance mentions a *Conan the Destroyer* custom action figure in a chapter footnote.[21] In a book of academic essays on Conan, misplacing the second of only two major motion pictures featuring the barbarian is a glaring omission of the relevance of the character in his most public display. Two possibilities exist: Either the omission is accidental and a large oversight took place, or the omission is purposeful and the film that nearly destroyed the franchise is despised in academic circles where Conan is concerned. While *Conan the Destroyer* is not a good film and certainly damaged the franchise for three decades, this should not excuse it from the critical eye of objective observation. Only by being aware of its existence can audiences understand the whole history surrounding the Cimmerian, including the mistakes.

Incompatible production values plague *Conan the Destroyer*. Where *Destroyer* is clean, *Barbarian* is dirty; where *Destroyer* is colorful, *Barbarian* is earthy; where *Destroyer* appears unnatural, *Barbarian* appears natural. The winged creature *Destroyer*'s wizard summons to capture the princess is a primitive display of animation the film had yet to earn and never does; the demons Valeria fights in *Barbarian* look primitive as well, but by the time they enter the film, the audience can forgive their appearance in a way the sequel's audience never could the dragon. The entrance to the castle and the castle interior appear unnatural; everything has the look of a constructed Hollywood set, a far cry from Osric's throne room in *Barbarian*. The gorilla "mask" under the wizard's hood is cheap and unrealistic, as is the entire sequence surrounding Dagoth; there is nothing in *Barbarian* with which these appalling gimmicks compare. The most egregious violation comes in the form of a Grace Jones costume malfunction that reveals a large portion of her rear, which she corrects mid-shot as the band ascends a staircase. While one could argue that this could really happen to a warrior like Zula, such an argument would be better served if captured by a camera in front of her instead of capturing her from behind.

From the evil queen revealing her plan very early in the film to a reliance on humor due to little driving action, the writing of *Conan the Destroyer* leaves much to be desired. The example that best suits this notion is the campfire scene starring a drunken Cimmerian. The sequence is over-extended in a film already rife with protracted passages. Conan delivers a difficult tongue-twister, "Instead of thanks: threats," but moments later he is unable to form the simple sentences "the kingdom I was promised" and "not on your life"; Schwarzenegger is, however, able to clearly annunciate the mismatched phrases without the traditional drunken accompaniment of slurred speech.[22] Conan's sophomoric reveries may never have ended, as no clear exit for the scene emerged aside from a well-placed tree for Conan to ram his head, the unfunny climax in an entirely unamusing scene.

The preoccupying sex talk in *Conan the Destroyer* is uncomfortable. Though it may seem realistic that a girl bestowed the title of kingdom ruler pursues the sexual pleasures available to her in Conan, there is an uneasy tension to the surrounding dialogue. This is not as much with the natural impulses of a teenage girl as it is with the potential entertainment of these ideas in a grown man. Each character curiously tackles the topic but lacks the objective awareness to recognize the potential audience's perception of the discussion. The subject is not handled with the care and sensitivity realized in Stanley Kubrick's *Lolita*; rather, the topic is broached in a carefree and casual manner that disregards a general audience, both in the 1980s and today. Stranger still is that the issue is pitched as an ordinary subject in a PG-rated film, where any unaccompanied minor could very well take to heart a relationship with an unlawfully older individual in a society that would widely regard such an act as statutory rape. The irony is that while *Destroyer's* Conan resists the advances of the princess, the Howard/Thomas Cimmerian would probably not and might feel free to entertain them because such edicts in society do not concern him.

Another major issue in *Conan the Destroyer* evolves from neither the story nor the dialogue but from the cinematography and editing choices. From a formalist perspective *Destroyer* has intriguing moments, but these moments are ruined by overly long takes. The mirror pieces revealed under the cloak of the dead wizard and the interior shot of the opening of the temple door are examples of spectacular camerawork; however, both last too long to remain stimulating. The shot revealing the mirror pieces under the robe is superb—for a time. But the camera lingers, and the shot becomes unnecessarily elongated. Likewise, the entry of the crypt containing the horn is fantastic; the entire party marvels at the interior. Again, though, insistence on a one-shot ruins an otherwise fine moment; the director is more concerned with ensuring that every character remains in the shot as they descend to a lower level, and this negates the sense of awe initially created. Moments of wonder cannot be taken for granted in any film, but especially when so few occur in a film like *Destroyer*. The two best visual moments of the film are ruined by a lack of editing choices.

Worse still, audience members of *Conan the Destroyer* are denied an emotional experience because of formalist decisions to remove the audience from danger. The most compelling example occurs on the stairway leading into the wizard's castle. The stairway winds up and around like a road on a mountainside. Malik slips and tumbles down the steep staircase, just barely rescued from peril. But Malik's fall transpires in an extreme longshot, which keeps the audience a great distance from the drama. This one moment is representative of the entire film: *Conan the Destroyer* is objective and a great distance from the drama.

It is not unusual for producers of a large-budget Hollywood picture to parade numerous writers through the development of a sequel. It is somewhat unusual to rely on a subject expert like Roy Thomas to compose five screenplays and then dismiss these almost entirely. Ponder the notion of an executive asking Stan Lee to serve on a Marvel film as a writer, having him work through five screenplays, and then dismissing him for the remainder of the process. "Who's to say who was right and who was wrong in a given situation? No one—producer, director, writer, or audience—can ever be quite certain whether 'his way' would have worked out better than what was actually filmed."[23] This statement penned by Roy Thomas in "Conan the Screenplay," his introduction to *The Horn of Azoth*, provides insight into the complications arising throughout the production of *Conan the Destroyer*.

Thomas's opinion on collaborating with Dino DeLaurentiis solidifies a sense of unevenness: "He didn't know what Conan was. He'd never read any of the Conan books, and he wasn't interested in it.... He just had his own vague idea of what it might be. He didn't listen to our ideas of what Conan was really like. He didn't like the first movie very much. So we just kept getting further and further away from what we wanted to do."[24] Based on this, Roy Thomas would undoubtedly maintain that *Conan the Destroyer*'s Cimmerian should at the very least resemble a Conan indicative of the work of Robert E. Howard, if not a particular story by Howard.

Based on Richard Krevolin's criteria, *Conan the Destroyer* is not only a poor adaptation; it is also a poor film and sequel. Thomas's astute observations indicate all of these. It is a poor adaptation because the film did not work to find Krevolin's sought-after spirit; it is a poor film because there is an open-ended question concerning who's "way" was right or wrong; most notably, it is a poor sequel because the executive in charge of production did not like the first movie, a critically-acclaimed commercial success.

It is not surprising that Roy Thomas bears no affiliation with the official comics adaptation of *Conan the Destroyer*; in fact, the only mention of Thomas comes from an on-set story deeming the first five screenplays as efforts that were deemed unacceptable.[25] A prime example of his non-involvement is the "KRACK" noise when Conan snaps the neck of an elite guard.[26] According to Thomas, his Conan comics "would not have any non-verbal sound effects.... No non-verbals."[27] This not only differentiates the work from Thomas, it usurps the control Thomas held over Conan during the 1970s in the same way DeLaurentiis removed control from him as the film's initial screenwriter.

Most striking in the comics adaptation is the return to a more mature rating. *Conan the Destroyer* was rated PG in an attempt to appeal to a broader audience, the audience reached in the comic adaptation of the *Barbarian* movie. The comics adaptation contains a rating akin to at least PG-13. In her palace, Queen Taramis wears only a gold-plated bikini and a hanging skirt similar to Princess Leia's prison outfit in *Return of the Jedi*. The violence carries more weight as well, such as the aforementioned neck-breaking. Also, the princess Jehnna looks older than she does in the film, probably because the artists sought to avoid the uncomfortable sexual material clearly present in the latter. Interestingly, the comics adaptation skips two of the most preposterous parts of the film, the drunken scene and the fall down the staircase. For this reason, the comics adaptation comprises a far better narrative construction of *Destroyer* than the film.

Conan, King of Thieves *and* The Horn of Azoth: Full Circle for Roy Thomas

The Horn of Azoth is an adventure tale in which Conan embarks on a quest with a priestess to track down a horn. While Conan fights in an arena, he is informed of the execution of his friend Gambinus. This drives him to eliminate the city magistrate. After a night with a prostitute, the woman betrays him to the men of the city. During the imprisonment, Conan is rescued by Natari, a woman who seeks the Eye of Ibis. This woman is actually the daughter of a priest seeking to resurrect Azoth, a winged demon destroyed before the dawn of man. Conan infiltrates a fortress in order to obtain the gem; in the process, he kills the wizard guarding it. Conan escapes, tracked by a group of Kezankian warriors and the wizard's son, Rammon. Eventually Conan, Natari, and her protector find an ancient tomb, the Crypt of Shadows. They fix the artifact and are allowed to remove the horn of Azoth. The protector renders Conan unconscious. Left for dead, Conan escapes the tomb only to be confronted once more by Rammon. In fact, Rammon is the new guardian of the horn, replacing his father. If the horn is placed on Azoth, an age of apocalypse will transpire. Conan, Rammon, and their Kezankian companions storm the labyrinth of Azoth, but they are too late. The horn is placed on the god, who springs to life and immediately terminates the priest responsible for bringing him to life. Locked in combat, Rammon conveys to Conan that he must tear the horn from Azoth. Conan does so, and the winged demon dissolves. Conan asks Rammon and Natari to remain together, as they are believers. The tale ends with Conan considering a return to the fighting arena, but instead he rides off, the perpetual loner.

Conan the Barbarian in *The Horn of Azoth* is essentially the original, to use Sammon's word, "effort" Roy Thomas concocted for *Conan the Destroyer*. In "Conan the Screenplay," Thomas explains that he and fellow writer Gerry Conway shared the script to obtain writing jobs, and everyone who read the script enjoyed it. Marvel editor Craig Anderson had the same reaction and asked the two to create a Marvel graphic novel. The names were changed to avoid confusion with *Destroyer*, but Thomas and Conway reconstructed the first screenplay, *Conan, King of Thieves*, into *The Horn of Azoth*.[28]

With creative control of *The Horn of Azoth*, Thomas predictably returns Conan to the realm of the comics and the ideals of Robert E. Howard. The Cimmerian is inherently non-religious, stating, "All gods are cruel. What do they care about men?"[29] He does not pine for Valeria as he does in *Destroyer*; this man continues sexual conquests, procuring a prostitute very early in the story. The maturity rating of this graphic novel is in line with the comics, a deep PG-13, perhaps closer to an R rating. *The Horn of Azoth* contains partial nudity and an overabundance of graphic violence; the climax of the story combines both the naked body of Natari and the gory impalement of the priest. Most important, *The Horn of Azoth* was the movie Thomas wanted made, and through the graphic novel, Thomas's movie vision for Conan was adapted into an ideal form, unchained by the constrictive and demanding fetters of Hollywood. "So now things have come full circle."[30]

And they continue to come full circle. Even now Arnold Schwarzenegger is slated to reprise his role of Conan the Cimmerian for a potential return in the tentatively-titled *The Legend of Conan*. This is probably the case, as Schwarzenegger stars in his fourth *Terminator* film, *Terminator: Genisys*, released in the summer of 2015. The hope is that the *Legend* filmmakers complete the aforementioned bridge absent in *Conan the Destroyer*, that they allow the journey of Conan to come full circle and give him his kingdom. The beginning of the bridge, *Conan the Barbarian* and *Conan the Destroyer*, may remain, but the end, *The Legend of Conan*, should allow the audience to completely cross its thoroughfare and end the journey. It does not have to utilize the entire bridge; Krevolin would point to the spirit of the first two films as inspiration rather than history. I am more than certain that the creators will work heavily with the story of *Conan the Barbarian* and attempt to dismiss that of *Conan the Destroyer* in much the same way mention of the film was omitted from *Conan Meets the Academy*. This remains to be seen at the time of this writing. The structural completion is of utmost significance: Conan's acquisition of his kingdom. As the attempted reboot of *Conan the Barbarian* starring Jason Mamoa indicated in 2011, *Destroyer* is not the end of the franchise. It serves as a reminder to individuals extending their reaches too quickly, tightening their grasps on films that require collaborative artistic excellence rather than the fortune of simply attaining a dream team like Schwarzenegger, Fleischer, and Thomas. *Conan the Destroyer* was a misstep reoriented with two course corrections: *The Horn of Azoth* and *The Legend of Conan*.

Notes

1. "Conan the Barbarian," *Rotten Tomatoes*, last modified March 26, 2015, http://www.rottentomatoes.com/m/conan_the_barbarian/?search=conan th.
2. "Conan the Destroyer," *Rotten Tomatoes*, last modified March 26, 2015, http://www.rottentomatoes.com/m/conan_the_destroyer/?search=Conan the d.
3. Richard Krevolin, *How to Adapt Anything into a Screenplay* (Hoboken: John Wiley & Sons, 2003), 10.
4. Ibid.
5. Roy Thomas and Barry Windsor-Smith, *The Chronicles of Conan*, Vol. 1 (Milwaukie: Dark Horse Books), 163. (Originally published in *Conan the Barbarian* #1–8, 1970–1971.)
6. Ibid., 166.
7. Roy Thomas, Barry Windsor-Smith, and Gil Kane, *The Chronicles of Conan*, Vol. 3 (Milwaukie: Dark Horse Books), 166. (Originally published in *Conan the Barbarian* #14–15, 17–22, 1972–1973.)
8. Komixmaster, "CONAN The Making of COMIC BOOK Legend [Part 1]," *YouTube*, Last Modified April 2, 2010, https://www.youtube.com/watch?v=qMA5FAbTHuY.
9. Roy Thomas and Barry Windsor-Smith, *The Chronicles of Conan*, Vol. 2 (Milwaukie: Dark Horse Books), 144. (Originally published in *Conan the Barbarian* #9–13, 16, 1971–1972.)
10. Roy Thomas and Barry Windsor-Smith, *The Chronicles of Conan*, Vol. 1 (Milwaukie: Dark Horse Books). (Originally published in Conan the Barbarian #1–8, 1970–1971.)
11. *Conan the Barbarian*, directed by John Milius (1981; Universal City: Universal Studios, 2003), DVD.
12. Ibid.
13. Roy Thomas, Barry Windsor-Smith, and Gil Kane, *The Chronicles of Conan*, Vol. 3 (Milwaukie: Dark Horse Books), 166. (Originally published in *Conan the Barbarian* #14–15, 17–22, 1972–1973.)
14. Michael Marsden, "Roy Thomas on Conan—Part 1," *YouTube*, last modified March 4, 2012, https://www.youtube.com/watch?v=Xzp1FmBjlKg.
15. Michael Marsden, "Roy Thomas on Conan —Part 2," *YouTube*, last modified March 4, 2012, https://www.youtube.com/watch?v=DIaCbLbl8T8.
16. Ibid.
17. Michael Fleisher, *Conan the Barbarian Movie Special* #2, November 1982 (New York, Marvel), n.p.
18. Roy Thomas, Barry Windsor-Smith, and John Buscema, *The Chronicles of Conan*, Vol. 4 (Milwaukie: Dark Horse Books), 148. (Originally published in *Savage Tales of Conan the Barbarian* #2–3.)
19. Nicky Falkov, "Arnold at the Gates: Subverting Star Persona in *Conan the Barbarian*" in *Conan Meets the Academy: Multidisciplinary Essays on the Enduring Barbarian*, edited by Jonas Prida (Jefferson, NC: McFarland, 2013), 140.
20. Jonas Prida, *Conan Meets the Academy: Multidisciplinary Essays on the Enduring Barbarian* (Jefferson, NC: McFarland, 2013), 6.
21. James Kelley, "'Hot Avatars' in 'Gay Gear': The Virtual Male Body as Site of Conflicting Desires in *Age of Conan: Hyborian Adventures*" in *Conan Meets the Academy: Multidisciplinary Essays on the Enduring Barbarian*, edited by Jonas Prida (Jefferson, NC: McFarland, 2013), 172.
22. *Conan the Destroyer*, directed by Richard Fleischer (1984; Universal City: Universal Studios, 2003), DVD.
23. Roy Thomas, Gerry Conway, Mike Docherty, Tony DeZuniga, and Tom Vincent, *Conan the Barbarian in the Horn of Azoth* (New York: Marvel Comics, 1990), 2.

24. Michael Marsden, "Roy Thomas on Conan—Part 3," *YouTube*, last modified March 4, 2012, https://www.youtube.com/watch?v=Et9CbvE5BpU.

25. Paul M. Sammon, "Celluloid Deltoids: Behind the Scenes at Conan II" in *Conan the Destroyer* by Michael Fleisher, *Marvel Super Special* Vol. 1 #35, December 1984 (New York: Marvel), n.p.

26. Michael Fleisher, *Conan the Destroyer*, *Marvel Super Special* Vol. 1 #35, December 1984 (New York: Marvel), n.p.

27. Komixmaster, "CONAN The Making of COMIC BOOK Legend [Part 1]," *YouTube*, last modified April 2, 2010, https://www.youtube.com/watch?v=qMA5FAbTHuY.

28. Roy Thomas, Gerry Conway, Mike Docherty, Tony DeZuniga, and Tom Vincent, *Conan the Barbarian in the Horn of Azoth* (New York: Marvel Comics, 1990), 2.

29. Ibid., 17.

30. Ibid., 2.

PART 3

The Japanese Connection

Marvel and Toei

JESUS JIMENEZ-VAREA *and*
MIGUEL ÁNGEL PÉREZ-GÓMEZ

In 1997, Marvel Comics' editor Tom Brevoort signed a text accompanying the American edition of the first "manga" based on Spider-Man. Brevoort contrasted the state of things as he was writing the words within—when the properties of the company he worked for were "known and beloved around the globe […] translated and circulated in dozens of countries worldwide"—to the difficult beginning of that process of internationalization, particularly "when we attempted to expand into the lucrative Japanese comics market in the mid–1970s."[1] While it is hard to conceive such difficulties from the perspective of the second decade of the 21st century, with the phenomenal success of the MCU, Marvel characters were not welcome by Japan in their original forms. Even so, it was the Japanese industry that produced several milestones in the expansion of Marvel Comics into audiovisual media, and, in turn, these products exerted a crucial influence on the evolution of Japanese popular culture.

This little known episode in the history of Marvel Comics illustrates the challenges faced when passing not only from one medium to another, but also to a different language and another cultural context. Within their possibilities in the 1970s, Marvel's project of globalization tried to follow the example of much more powerful companies in their aim to "maximize [standardized] production methods by subtly adapting them so as to retain overall continuity while at the same time fitting the specific market requirements (primarily linguistic) of different cultural milieus."[2] In Japan, this resulted in a phenomenon called "Japanization": "the adaptation of […] products, customs, and idea systems to a Japanese cultural landscape. […] Japanese popular culture illustrates a response to American influences. With an inundation of American cultural icons, Japan responds defensively with the global going local or the global in the local."[3] In that regard, the theoretical foundations of this chapter include the notions of "interlingual transposition—from one language into another" and "intersemiotic transposition–from one system of signs into another."[4] But even more important to this case study are the intercultural dimensions of transposition, which are determined by "the choices linked to the logistics of production and audience captivation, which directly depend on the producers and the receivers in the target cultural system."[5]

Spider-Man *in Japan*

The first incursion of Marvel in the Japanese cultural market resulted in comics like the abovementioned manga version of the arachnid superhero. It was most probably a part of the Cadence Industries Corporation's plans to capitalize on the popularity of these properties they had acquired along with the publishing company from founder Martin Goodman in 1968. Instead of translating material already published in the United States, Japanese giant publisher Kodansha commissioned native *mangaka*—Japanese comics artists—to produce new stories based upon Spider-Man and Hulk. Japanization affected names and settings, and the events depicted diverged from those experienced by their American counterparts. Yet, both series retained the appearances and premises of their respective models: Yu Komori is a shy bookish student who gains arachnid abilities after being bitten by a radioactive spider[6]; since he was exposed to a nuclear explosion, Dr. Araki is tormented with the curse of transforming into a green-skinned brute whenever he gets excited.[7] By contrast, an earlier transposition of another American superhero, Batman, to Japan in the midst of the Bat-Mania provoked by the television series had followed the American original more closely regarding the setting and the names of secret identities, even though the stories were completely new.[8] Apparently, Japanization accentuated with time, since the appropriation of Spider-Man by Japanese television a few years later would differ radically from its model: the drastic modifications imposed on the Marvel property may seem purely arbitrary to non–Japanese viewers even today, but were actually calculated in accordance with formulas of proven success within the popular culture industry of that country.

The venture that resulted in the first *Spider-Man* film for theatrical exhibition started as a newly frustrated attempt to commercialize direct translations of Marvel comics in the Japanese market. In 1976, the licensing department of Cadence Industries sent to Japan a representative, Gene Pelc, "with the basic commitment to put Marvel Comics in the Orient."[9] According to Pelc, after a few installments of translated American Spider-Man stories in "a very popular magazine" of the publishing company Shueisha, who had agreed to include them only reluctantly, he finally realized "the cultural gap that existed [...] something was missing." Pelc had also become aware of the proliferation of television, "shows for very young people [...] ages twelve and under," featuring what he could best describe as "Japanese super-heroes."[10] Thus, in his desperation to find some way to introduce the Marvel characters to Japan, he decided to contact the studios from which many of those shows seemed to come: the Toei Company.

Toei was the most important producer of film and television content in Japan, either animation or live action, and the shows that had drawn Pelc's attention corresponded to the latter category, in particular *tokusatsu* (special effects filming). This term encompasses genres like science fiction, fantasy, and horror, which in the Japan of the 1970s had evolved into several specific subgenres including *daikaiju*, about huge monsters, initiated and best represented by Toho Studios' *Godzilla*, directed by Ishiro Honda (1954); and *mecha*, featuring colossal robots or vehicles controlled by human pilots, like *Mazinger Z*.[11] The first boom of television *tokusatsu* in the 1960s was characterized by another subgenre: the protagonist of each *kyodai hero* show could grow to giant size in order to fight the *daikaiju* of the week. In the following decade, the predominant subgenre was the *henshin hero*, where the main character remained human-sized but experienced a transformation (*henshin*) into a *kaizo ningen*, i.e., an artificially "remodeled human," often a cyborg. The first television *henshin hero* series was Toei's *Kamen Rider*,[12] about a biker on a mission against the same malevolent organization, SHOCKER, which had manipulated his body in order to endow him with extraordinary abilities. Reaching a certain speed on his motorcycle triggers his *henshin* into a superhuman fighter wearing a grasshopper mask, while the vehicle becomes the Cyclone Superbike. *Kamen Rider* had been created by artist Shotaro Ishinomori, whose manga *Cyborg 009* (1964) already advanced such plot elements—such as an evil society that enhances humans, who in turn, begin to rebel against them. After *Kamen Rider*, Ishinomori's next important contribution to Toei's shows was *Himitsu Sentai Gorenger*,[13] which incorporated the idea of the *sentai*: a squadron whose members wear color variations of the same basic uniform and combat evil. Ishinomori employed this formula again in the less successful *J.A.K.Q. Dengekitai*.[14] *Sentai* would prove to be one of the most important developments in the history of *tokusatsu*, but there was still a factor lacking in the equation that was to revolutionize Japanese popular culture: the live-action Spider-Man show and its related theatrical film.

The first thing Pelc learned when he contacted Toei was that Marvel characters had potential, but they had to be reinterpreted for Japan: "A comic is a product of a culture. Spider-Man and Captain America are American super-heroes. They have their roots in the people."[15] In addition, Pelc was convinced that the right medium to popularize Marvel properties, in that country, was television; he reached a licensing agreement with Toei that would allow the company to work with them for the next several years. The first project would be a television series based on a Marvel superhero, but completely produced in Japan for a Japanese audience. The chosen superhero was Spider-Man. The heads of Toei decided to keep the costume and the basic powers, but they would "expand on the character from a Japanese viewpoint."[16] In charge of such expansion was none other than Ishinomori,[17] which explains many of the peculiarities of his version of Spider-Man. Given the success of *Kamen Rider*, it was simply natural that Ishinomori would include some of the most attractive attributes of his previous bug-themed hero in Toei's Japanization of Spider-Man: motor bikes, artificial enhancement of human abilities, *henshin*, and the ongoing menace of a secret organization. He combined this formula with a fresh twist on a couple of infallible staples of the Japanese fantastic genre: *daikaiju* and *mecha*.

The origin of the Nippon webhead, Supaidaman, differed from that of its American counterpart: young motorcycle racer Takuya Yamashiro (actor Kosuke Yakama) senses a strange call in his mind and finds himself in the middle of an intergalactic conflict between the evil Iron Cross Army and Garia, the last survivor of the Spider Planet, devastated by the former. Takuya is mentally summoned to the cave where Garia is trapped; he has been chosen to continue the struggle against the Iron Cross Army, whose next target is the Earth itself. Takuya has been fatally wounded and forced to take shelter in that cave by an advance party of the alien army; once there, Garia saves him from certain death by locking around one of his wrists the Spider-Bracelet, a device that injects the youth with a "Spider-Extract," which heals him immediately. After explaining to Takuya the vital role he is to play in this ancient war, Garia undergoes a metamorphosis into a common spider and goes on mentoring his successor telepathically in that form. Besides curing him, the Spider-Extract has endowed Takuya with arachnid powers similar to those of the American Spider-Man. The Spider-Bracelet, meanwhile, is identical to the classic web shooter, but it has many other functions as well, including its ability to contain the so-called "Spider-Protector." This "Spider Protector" is a costume, identical to that of the comic-book original, which shoots out of this gadget whenever the hero needs to suit up—"much like the Flash's costume would come out of his ring in comic books."[18] The bracelet also enables Tayuka to control a flying fortress known as the Marveller— an obvious nod to Stan Lee's so-called "House of Ideas." In addition, his equipment includes another colorful vehicle: the Spider-Machine GP7. When the character, Supaida- man, drives this fantastic car into the Marveller, the aircraft transforms into the *mecha* called "Leopardon." On the other hand, this version of the arachnid hero does not lack his own dose of pathos due to the tragic loss of a paternal figure: Peter Parker suffered the murder of his Uncle Ben, while Takuya loses is his own father—a scientist, who dies while researching the alien invaders in the very first episode of the series. The young hero is left with his little brother and sister, and a girlfriend, all of them unaware of his double identity, but appearing in every adventure. On the villainous side, the Iron Cross Army consists of an indefinite number of undistinguishable henchmen, the Ninders, led by Professor Monster and his right hand, the female commander Amazoness. Occasionally there are two other amazons, Rita and Bella, but the great attraction of every episode is whatever new, extravagant creature the sinister professor throws against Supaidaman. These ingredients granted the television show *Supadaiman* huge popularity during its run of forty-one half-hour episodes between May 17, 1978, and March 14, 1979.

The *Supaidaman* film, directed by Koichi Takemoto and written by Susumu Takaku, was to be exhibited in Toei Manga Matsuri, the yearly festival of animation, on July 22, 1978. In fact, it is no different from any other episode of the television series and illustrates perfectly its formula, but for the fact that it introduces a new character who would appear again in later installments of the show: Interpol agent Juzo Mamiya.[19] This intelligence agency solicits the assistance of Supaidaman to put an end to a chain of sabotages against oil tankers perpetrated by the Iron Cross Army, in particular by their "monster-of-the-week," the Sea Devil, a semi-mechanical, anthropomorphic swordfish with the ability to shoot torpedoes from its mouth. Like almost every episode of the series, the film includes a lengthy dose of climbing up and down buildings, along with fighting legions of Ninders, as a pretext for a succession of acrobatic exploits performed by members of the Japan Action Club (JAC) stunt team. Then, the Marveller, which the hero can control remotely through his Spider-Bracelet, prevents the Sea Devil from bombing an industrial complex by making the monster's missiles explode in the air. Enraged, the Amazoness orders the amphibian creature to grow to Godzilla-size by shouting, "Machine BEM Sea Devil!" so that it can crush the complex under its feet. To oppose this giant, Supaidaman calls his Spider-Machine GP7 and drives it into the Marveller, activating its transformation into *mecha* Leopardon, which, after an exchange of blows, uses its huge sword to disintegrate the Sea Devil.

As exemplified in the film, *Supaidaman* added a fresh twist to *tokusatsu* conventions: initially, the monster of the episodes approximately human-sized, like the creatures in *Kamen Rider*, but in the final act it grows to the colossal scale of the *daikaiju* in *kyodai hero* shows like *Ultraman*; on the other hand, *Supaidaman* has the eponymous hero pilot a *mecha* instead of becoming a giant himself.[20] This formula would prove to be very successful, especially when combined with the abovementioned *sentai* concept in the following television show born of the deal between Marvel and Toei: *Battle Fever J*.[21] According to Gene Pelc, the original idea was "a concept based on The Avengers,"[22] but the process of Japanization turned the "World's Mightiest Heroes" into a quintet of costumed fighters, akin to the one Ishinomori had already worked with a few years earlier. In this case, variations were nationality-themed, as the each hero represented a different country: "Captains France, Kenya, Russia and Japan—and Miss America. Originally, we wanted Miss America leading the team, but we couldn't do that in Japan, so Captain Japan became the leader."[23] *Battle Fever J* inaugurated the *super sentai* subgenre within television *tokusatsu* by basically replicating the *Supaidaman* formula but multiplying the individual superhero into a super-team. Marvel was also involved in the next two *super sentai* shows that Toei produced, *Denshi Sentai Denziman*[24] and *Taiyo Sentai Sun Vulcan*,[25] though there is no apparent relationship with any of the American publisher's characters. As Pelc explained: "I found that it was much easier, once we had done a lot of Japanese programs, to come up with new concepts based more closely on what Japanese are viewing, rather than just taking Marvel characters and redoing them."[26] Actually, Toei would go on to produce one series after another in this successful *super sentai* line without further involvement of Marvel, and these shows would later provide the materials for the hugely popular franchise *Mighty Morphin Power Rangers*,[27] which were heavily re-edited to match the tastes of Western audiences, just as Spider-Man had been reinvented for the Japanese market some years earlier.

Animating the Undead

Shortly after the *Supaidaman* television series and related movie, Toei marked another milestone in the history of Marvel transposition to moving-image media in the form of two feature-length, animated television movies. Toei had entered the field of animation in 1956, when they bought the prestigious Nihon Doga studio and transformed it into Toei Doga (later, Toei Animation), with the explicit goal of becoming "The Disney of the East."[28] Following that model, the new animation department of Toei focused on producing art-film adaptations of folkloric and literary tales, very often of western origins.[29] Since the 1960s, they dedicated increasingly to animation for the equally growing demand of the television market, but these adaptations were not abandoned and they went on being produced either in the form of television series or as feature films. This tradition may well be one of the factors contributing to the apparent paradox that, despite having the whole Marvel universe of superheroes at their disposal, Toei preferred to adapt Marvel versions of the two most popular icons of western horror: Dracula and Frankenstein.

In 1971, the Comics Code of the Comics Magazine Association of America relaxed some of the strict standards this industry had self-imposed in 1954. One of these modifications established that "vampires, ghouls and werewolves shall be permitted to be used when handled in the classic tradition such as Frankenstein, Dracula and other high caliber literary works."[30] Almost immediately, Marvel started a new line of comic books starring the monsters popularized by the Universal Studios in the 1930s and 1940s: the Werewolf, Dracula, the monster of Frankenstein, and the Mummy. The most successful of them all, both critically and commercially, was writer Marv Wolfman and artist Gene Colan's *The Tomb of Dracula* (#1–70, April 1972–August 1979), which has been considered "the first true comics' novel, with an overarching theme, supporting cast, a beginning and, most importantly, an ending marked by a central character that changed and evolved from what he started out as in the opening chapters to what he finally became in the last."[31] Actually, Wolfman joined the creative team of the title in the seventh issue, after writers Gerry Conway, Archie Goodwin, and Gardner Fox had written a couple of issues each in that same order. He worked from the premise of Dracula being accidentally revived by a group of American tourists including Frank Drake, a descendant of the vampire, along with a little group of antagonists consisting of Rachel van Helsing, the granddaughter of Bram Stoker's master vampire hunter, the mute Hindi giant TajNital, and the tormented Drake. Wolfman rapidly added to this cast the wheelchair-bound Quincy Harker—the baby born to Jonathan and Mina at the end of the classic novel and now an elderly man—and his German Shepherd dog, Saint, especially trained to combat vampires (*The Tomb of Dracula* #7). Later Wolfman and Colan would add such memorable characters as the "blaxploitative" vampire slayer Blade (#10), the benign hard-boiled detective vampire Hannibal King (#25), and the comic-relief-wannabe, horror novelist Harold H. Harold (#37), to name just a few.

The television anime *Dracula: Sovereign of the Dead*[32] opens with a narrator's voiceover that presents the film as the story of Dracula, thus misleading viewers ignorant of the Marvel comic book to frame the film as a direct adaptation of Stoker's canonical text. Actually, the bulk of this *anime* is a relatively faithful adaptation of the lengthy final story arc of *The Tomb of Dracula* (#45–70), with the added introduction of the vampire hunters, who are reduced to Quincy Harker, Rachel van Helsing, Frank Drake, and the dog Saint, transmuted into a Great Dane. Remarkable absences include allies Taj—who by the time of this plot had already disappeared from the comic book series—and the charismatic Blade—whose presence in that run of issues was limited to subplots and parallel stories that were not adapted into the film's screenplay. The basic story is a mostly orthodox condensation of the main plotline in the abovementioned story arc: eager to gain a cult of his own, Dracula supplants Satan during a ceremony in the Church of the Damned, where a group of Satanists led by Anton Lupeski are offering a bride to their worshipped demon. Instead, it is Dracula who marries the young woman, called Domini, and they fall in love with each other. On the next Christmas Eve, Domini gives birth to their son, Janus; meanwhile, Satanist leader Lupesky has discovered Dracula's true identity and plans to kill the vampire with a silver bullet. Janus is accidentally shot, and dies in the arms of his mother—then, an enraged Dracula hideously murders Lupeski. Thus ends the first act of the film, which also includes the parallel recruitment of a reticent Frank Drake by Quincy Harker and Rachel van Helsing. The following segment depicts how God resurrects Janus as an angel-like adult—wingless, but with the ability to transform into a golden eagle—to use him as Dracula's nemesis. After some confrontations between father and son, a sort of divine light emanating from Janus's eyes turns Dracula into a mere human, deposed of his vampire powers. The rest of the act develops around Dracula coping with such circumstances as stealing money to buy food—a hamburger, instead of human blood—while looking for a way to become a vampire again. This permits a brief appearance of Marvel original character Lilith, Dracula's first daughter and a vampire herself: the desperate Dracula asks her to bite him so that he can get back to his undead status. Lilith, who holds a centuries-old grudge against her father, refuses to do so and humiliates him instead. The last act of the film portrays Dracula's return to Transylvania with the vain hope that some of his former subordinates will agree to turn him into a vampire. However, he finds out that they are now following a new Lord of Vampires, Torgo, and he has to fight against a legion of these beings for his own life. In the process he also defends a few children who give him shelter in their house, and Dracula even holds a crucifix to repel the vampires. Even though he is human now, this holy object burns Dracula's hand, and the resulting cross-shaped scar enables him to defeat

Torgo in a singular duel, thus recovering his title as Lord of Vampires, and becoming himself a vampire again. But Dracula does not enjoy his restored status very long, as Quincy Harker reappears for their final showdown in the vampire's castle, where the old man succeeds in stabbing his archenemy with a silver spoke and subsequently sacrifices himself in an explosion that destroys the whole building. In the epilogue of the film, Janus returns to his mother, Domini, with the news of Dracula's annihilation; his mission accomplished, God turns him back into a baby and leaves him with the happy mother.

This production has gained a terrible reputation among Dracula and *anime* fans, framed as "a good example of when one culture adapts something from another without a true understanding of what it is they are translating."[33] However, most of the elements these critics find laughable are not the result of Japanization, but are directly taken from Wolfman and Colan's particular elaboration on the Dracula myth in the comic books. In this case, Japanization is mostly limited to audiovisual choices in the process of animation, which involve glowing fangs and weird accompanying sound effects, as well as a tendency toward "frozen tableaux" that is characteristic of Japanese performances.[34] Regarding characters, the one most evidently Japanized is Frank Drake, a red-haired adult in the comics who becomes a teenage-looking, dark-haired martial artist, interchangeable with the male protagonists of countless other Toei animations.[35] Actually, when news of this film got to the American fan press of the time, some reviews praised its fidelity: "Does the Dracula of Toei's TOMB OF DRACULA movie look like Gene Colan's version for Marvel, you ask? Yes, astonishingly and unmistakably so. [...] We have endured many disastrous adaptations of Marvel and DC material. The TOMB OF DRACULA film stands as a sign of what is possible."[36] Even Wolfman expressed himself along those lines and highlighted its significance: "it is pretty much a faithful adaptation of the comic [...], the first time a major series of stories from an American comic has been adapted into a two-hour movie, (albeit) animation."[37] On the other hand, this film was also a milestone in the landscape of Japanese popular culture because it initiated the horror genre in anime,[38] and was succeeded by productions that consolidated the Japanized version of the western vampire.[39]

The other Marvel horror comic book that somehow inspired a Toei animated film was a logical next step: *The Monster of Frankenstein*, started by writer Gary Friedrich and artist Mike Ploog, who had already created the Ghost Rider together. However, the Frankenstein title lacked the consistency of *The Tomb of Dracula*, insofar as the creative team changed several times over the comparatively shorter run of issues the series lasted.[40] Friedrich and Ploog used the first four issues to adapt the central story of Mary Shelley's novel quite faithfully, though they framed it in an original narrative set about a century after the end of the classic tale. In this frame narrative, a descendant of the ship captain who met both Frankenstein and his creature leads an expedition to the Arctic in order to find the frozen body of the monster, which subsequently revives and continues his misadventures up to the twentieth century. In Friedrich's words, "the stories that followed the novel adaptation felt like a sequel to the novel."[41] Yet, Toei's 1981 television special *Frankenstein*[42] seems more indebted to the films directed by James Whale[43] insofar as it portrays an inarticulate monster reminiscent of Boris Karloff's characterization. Very few Marvel ingredients made it to the final screenplay—most importantly, a spectacular fight between the creature and a bear. To sum up, and compared to the Dracula *anime*, *Frankenstein* holds much less relevance regarding film transpositions of Marvel Comics since its relationship with Friedrich and Ploog's interpretation of the corpse-reanimating doctor and his monster is tenuous in the best of cases.

Conclusion

After their original deal had expired, the collaboration between Marvel and Toei entered a wholly new phase in the mid–1980s, when the former was already working directly within the field of animated cartoons as Marvel Productions and the latter would provide the animation for a number of shows based on superheroes. With regard to feature films, their most important collaboration—with the intervention of American animation studios Sunbow Productions—was what may be called the Hasbro Trilogy: *G.I. Joe: The Movie* (1987), *Transformers: The Movie* (1986), and *My Little Pony: The Movie* (1986).[44] These deserve a study of their own (see elsewhere in this volume for discussions of *Transformers* and *G.I. Joe*), especially given the synergy Hasbro established with Marvel in both its publishing and animating capacities. But Toei's role in these ventures was limited to assuming the work of animation, outsourced to cheapen the costs of production as well as to take advantage of the efficient infrastructure of this Japanese giant. They were productions written and directed by Americans for American viewers, so they are not pertinent to the current discussion about the films that resulted from the attempts to adjust Marvel properties to Japanese tastes.

The Japanization of Marvel is a phenomenon that finished over thirty years ago, but its legacy still extends today, especially with regard to *Supaidaman*: not only did it lead to the development of the Super Sentai franchise—and its version for global audiences in the form of the *Mighty Morphin Power Rangers*—but also, throughout the years, it has achieved a sort of cult status among fans. Ultimately, this popularity has resulted in the great expectation generated when the character, along with his *mecha*, Leopardon, has appeared in Marvel comic books at last.[45] In conclusion, this chapter has described the accommodation of Marvel properties to Japanese tastes and the relationship of the resulting products with their American models.

Notes

1. Tom Brevoort, "On the Origins of Spider-Man the Manga," *Spiderman: The Manga* #1, December 1997 (New York: Marvel Comics), n.p.
2. Peter Sedgwick, "Globalisation," in *Cultural Theory: The Key Concepts*, edited by Andrew Edgar and Peter Sedgwick (New York: Routledge, 2007), 146.
3. Jay Gould, "Globalization: Asia," in *New Dictionary of the History of Ideas*, vol. 3, edited by Maryanne Cline Horowitz (Farmington Hills: Thomson Gale, 2005), 945.
4. Roman Jakobson, *Selected Writings: Word and Language* (The Hague: Mouton, 1968), 266.
5. Nicola Dusi, "Translating, Adapting, Transposing," *Applied Semiotics. Special Issue (Translating Culture)*, no. 24 (2012): 82.
6. The Spider-Man manga (*Supaidaman*), by writers Kosei Ono and Kazumasa Hirai with artist Ryoichi Ikegami, was serialized in *Weekly ShonenMagazine* between 1970 and 1971. For an overview of the successive manga interpretations of Spider-Man, see Daniel Stein, "Of Transcreation and Transpacific Adaptations: Investigating Manga Versions of Spider-Man," in *Transnational Perspectives on Graphic Narratives: Comics at the Crossroads*, edited by Shane Denson, Christina Meyer and Daniel Stein (London: Bloomsbury, 2013), 145–162.
7. The Hulk manga (*Haruku*), by writers Kazuo Koike and Yukio Togawa with artists Kosei Saigo and Yoshihiro Morito, was serialized in *Weekly Bokura Magazine* between 1970 and 1971.
8. The Batman manga (*Battoman*), by Jiro Kuwata, was serialized between 1966 and 1967 in the magazine *Shonen King*, published by Shonen Gahosha.

9. Gene Pelc in "Marvel's Man in Japan: Gene Pelc," *FOOM*, no. 22 (January 1978): n.p.
10. Ibid.
11. Fuji Television, 92 episodes from December 3, 1972, to September 1, 1974. This is an animated series by Toei adapting Go Nagai's manga of the same title (1972–1974).
12. MBS, 98 episodes from April 3, 1971 to February 10, 1973.
13. TV Asahi, 84 episodes, from April 5, 1975 to March 26, 1977.
14. TV Asahi, 35 episodes, from April 9, 1977 to December 24, 1977.
15. "Marvel's Man in Japan," n.p.
16. Ibid.
17. Curiously, the first episode of the original *Kamen Rider* show is titled "The Mysterious Spider-Man."
18. Jason Hofius and George Khoury, *Age of TV Heroes* (Raleigh: TwoMorrows, 2010), 104. It is interesting to remark that this was not the only similarity—most probably, all of them were purely coincidental—between Supaidaman and several American superheroes. Some of them were especially evident in its genesis: forced to take shelter in a cave because of an extraterrestrial invasion, just like Dr. Donald Blake right before finding Thor's hammer (*Journey into Mystery* #83, Marvel, August 1962); being chosen to succeed an ailing hero with superhuman abilities, either an alien in the case of the Silver Age Green Lantern (*Showcase* #22, DC, October 1959) or an ancient wizard in the case of the Golden Age Captain Marvel (*Whiz Comics* #1, Fawcett, February 1940).
19. The debut of this character situates the film before the eleventh episode, where he appears in the series for the first time.
20. A former publisher of Marvel Comics remarked the fact that the influence of the *Supaidaman* formula was not limited to the field of live action: "the series had a major impact on Japanese anime by popularizing the trend of using *mecha* (or giant robots) to defeat other giants controlled by humans." Shirrel Rhoades, *Comic Books: How the Industry Works* (New York: Peter Lang, 2008), 284.
21. TV Asahi, 52 episodes from February 3, 1979, to January 26, 1980.
22. Gene Pelc, "Gene Pelc," *Comics Interview*, no. 3 (May 1983): 4.
23. Ibid.
24. TV Asahi, 51 episodes from February 3, 1980, to January 31, 1981. Like *Supaidaman*, this series generated a film for theatrical exhibition in the Toei Manga Matsuri film festival; it premiered on July 12, 1980. Also, both plot and length were similar to those of the television episodes.
25. TV Asahi, 50 episodes from February 7, 1981 to January 30, 1982.
26. "Gene Pelc," 4.
27. Fox Kids, 145 episodes from August 28, 1993, to November 27, 1995.
28. Jerry Beck, ed., *Animation Art* (London: Flame Tree, 2004), 175.
29. A possible exponent of how important these productions were for Toei is the fact that the company mascot is the cat Pero, the main character of *Puss in Boots* (*Nagagutsu o haitaneko*), directed by KimioYabuki (1969).
30. Amy Kiste Nyberg, *Seal of Approval: The History of the Comics Code* (Jackson: University Press of Mississippi, 1998), 172.
31. Pierre Comtois, *Marvel Comics in the 1970s: An Issue by Issue Field Guide to a Pop Culture Phenomenon* (Raleigh: TwoMorrows, 2011), 153.
32. This is the title of the 1983 American release by *anime*-specialized distributor Harmony Gold. The original title is *Yami no Teio: Kyuuketsuki Dracula*, which translates more literally as "Dracula: Vampire Emperor of Darkness." It was directed by Akinori Nagaoka and Minoru Okazaki, and it first aired on Asahi TV in 1980 as a television special.
33. "Dracula: Sovereign of the Dead," *Anime Bargain Bin Reviews*, last modified October 26, 2007, http://www.anime-games.co.uk/VHS/anime/dracula.php. For example, see also Chris Sims, "The Hilariously Terrible 'Tomb of Dracula' Anime Is 1.5 Hours of Insanity," *Comics Alliance*, last modified October 30, 2011, http://comicsalliance.com/comicsalliance-vs-the-hilariously-terrible-tomb-of-dracula-an/?trackback=tsmclip.
34. Stevie Susan, *The Anime Paradox: Patterns and Practices Through the Lens of Traditional Japanese Theater* (Leiden: Brill, 2013), 10.
35. Probably, the most ridiculous scene introduced in the transposition is the fight between a sword-wielding Quincy—his wheel-chair pushed by Rachel—and Frank, whose impossible jumps elevate him several meters, in typical *anime* action.

36. Peter Sanderson, "The Dead Yet Move: Toei's Animated TOMB OF DRACULA Movie," *Comics Feature*, no. 12–13 (September–October 1981): 58.

37. "Japanese Producer Animates Wolfman/Colan Dracula Series," *The Comics Journal*, no. 63 (Spring 1981): 20.

38. Jonathan Clements and Helen McCarthy, *The Anime Encyclopedia: A Guide to Japanese Animation Since 1917* (Berkeley: Stone Bridge Press, 2006), 286.

39. Particularly, the 1985 film *Vampire Hunter D* (*Banpaia Hanta Di*), directed by Toyoo Ashida, whose eponymous hero is the hybrid son of Dracula and a mortal woman, like Janus in *Dracula: Sovereign of the Dead*. See Natalie Bartlett and Bradley D. Bellows, "The Supernatural Ronin: Vampires in Japanese Anime," in *Bram Stoker's Dracula: Sucking Through the Century*, edited by Carol Margaret Davidson (Toronto: Dundurn Press), 284. Also Wayne Stein and John Edgar Browning, "The Western Eastern: Decoding Hybridity and CyberZen Goth(ic) in *Vampire Hunter D* (1985)," in *Draculas, Vampires, and Other Undead Forms: Essays on Gender, Race, and Culture*, edited by John Edgar Browning and Caroline Joan (Kay) Picart (Lanham, MD: Scarecrow Press, 2009), 279–293.

40. *The Monster of Frankenstein* #1–5 (January 1973–September 1973) continued as *The Frankenstein Monster* #6–18 (October 1973–September 1975).

41. Michael Browning, "Flashback: The Monster of Frankenstein," *Back Issue*, no. 36 (October 2009): 12.

42. Under this title, Harmony Gold distributed in America in 1984 the film *Kyōfu densetsu kaibutsu: Furankeshutain* (literally "Mystery! Frankenstein Legend of Terror"), directed by Yugo Serikawa.

43. *Frankenstein* (1931) and *Bride of Frankenstein* (1935).

44. *G.I Joe: The Movie*, directed by Don Juwich (1987). *Transformers: The Movie*, directed by Nelson Shin (1986). *My Little Pony: The Movie*, directed by Michael Joens (1986).

45. Stew Shearer, "Japanese Spider-Man Could See Marvel Comics Revival," *The Escapist*, last modified January 13, 2015, http://www.escapistmagazine.com/news/view/139441-Marvel-Editor-Open-to-Supaidaman-Comic-Book-Revival.

Japanese Characters and Culture in Marvel's American Films

Stephen Miller

Japan, and the Japanese, began prominently featuring in film adaptations of Marvel comic books starting in the 1980s. However, the country and its people play prominent roles in much earlier film adaptations of comic books from other publishers, with some appearances dating back, almost, to the beginning of the genre itself. The 1941 Republic Pictures serial *Adventures of Captain Marvel*, the first film adaptation of a comic book (as opposed to a comic strip), makes no reference to the island nation.[1] But by the end of 1941, the U.S. would be at war with Japan, and Japanese characters would be introduced in animated shorts and live-action serial episodes based on famous DC properties such as Superman and Batman as early as 1942 and 1943, respectively.

Predictably, these wartime depictions of the Japanese in early comic book movies are uniformly villainous, reflecting the sudden shift in representations of the Japanese in other media toward a dehumanizing, propaganda-inspired formula including ruthlessness, cruelty, cunning, and fanatical loyalty to the Japanese state.[2] For example, although Paramount's *Superman* (1941–1942) cartoon under Fleischer Studios, the first episodes of which were released in 1941, makes no mention of Japan, the series quickly changes tone after the animation duties move to Famous Studios in 1942. The very first episode produced by the new studio, entitled *Japoteurs*, pits Superman against Japanese saboteurs attempting to commandeer a new military aircraft during its test run. These Japanese villains are bucktoothed caricatures, nameless and without dialogue; when faced with defeat and capture, they, cowardly, attempt suicide. A few episodes later, Clark Kent uses his captivity in Yokohama, Japan as an opportunity for Superman to wreak havoc behind enemy lines. Here, Superman's famous regard for life is apparently absent, with countless Japanese deaths implied onscreen as he sinks and destroys numerous manned naval craft.[3]

This historical dehumanization of the Japanese in comic book films is important to keep in mind when considering how the portrayal of Japanese characters evolves over time in Marvel comic–based films. Marvel would continue this association of Japan with cruel villains and violent organizations in its own post-war film output, dropping the obsolete military as a source for inspiration in favor of shadier choices: Japanese organized crime syndicates, known popularly as "yakuza"; and modern-era holdovers of feudal clans of spies and assassins, known popularly as "ninja."

In the beginning, portrayals of the Japanese in Marvel films differ little from the wartime stereotypes established by previous comic book movies, but over a progression of several live-action films that include *The Punisher* (1989), *Blade* (1998), *Elektra* (2005), *G.I. Joe: Rise of Cobra* (2009), *G.I. Joe: Retaliation* (2013) and *The Wolverine* (2013), representations of Japan become deeper, more sophisticated, and more humanized. Marvel finally breaks away completely from the yakuza and ninja villain stereotypes, showing multiple Japanese characters unequivocally as heroes in its most recent film adaptation to feature them, *Big Hero 6*.

The Punisher

The first Marvel film to feature Japanese characters was Mark Goldblatt's *The Punisher*, which was released in West Germany in October 1989. Earlier the same year, Warner Bros. had released Tim Burton's first installment of his dark re-imagining of *Batman* (1989) on the big screen. Superficial comparisons are easily made between the Punisher and Batman: lacking superpowers, both are vigilantes that use their brains, equipment, discipline and determination to bring the criminals that killed their families to justice. Although Burton's *Batman* itself lacks Japanese characters, the first Punisher movie takes full advantage of the coinciding release of that Batman film to refer instead to the original, Columbia's 1943 serial of the same name—particularly through the shared use of the Japanese as main villains.

Both Batman and the Punisher battle organized crime units led by ruthless Japanese in their respective initial cinematic outings: in Lambert Hillyer's 1943 serial, Batman battles a cabal under the leadership of the evil spy, Dr. Daka, a humble servant of His Majesty Hirohito; while in Goldblatt's *The Punisher*, Frank Castle fights against the incursion of the Japanese yakuza under their ruthless leader, Lady Tanaka. The names of the two villains are hardly the only thing they have in common. They are both modeled along "Yellow Peril" stereotypes, employing inhuman tactics and exhibiting unflagging loyalty to their cause.[4]

The strategies of both villains involve forcing local mafia members to join them, and they have no mercy for those who either refuse, or prove to be of no further use. Prince Daka kidnaps and brainwashes various victims who refuse to submit willingly, feeds a would-be deserter to his alligators, poisons a henchman captured by the police so he cannot talk, and considers a Japanese soldier fortunate to have been able to die in the service of the Empire just to deliver some secret information. Likewise, Lady Tanaka kidnaps the children of the local mob bosses to sell them into slavery, poisoning those that refuse to join her; it is also revealed that she has trained her adopted daughter to be a deadly assassin, and that she killed her own twin brother in a display of loyalty in order to become the head of the yakuza.

These kinds of behaviors on the part of the Japanese villains garner the disgust of the American characters, including other villains. Wartime pejoratives such as "Nipponese," "Nips," and "Japs" used throughout both films reflect this. For example, echoing the Italian mob boss that balks at working for "some bunch of Nips," Mr. Foster explains before being fed to Dr. Daka's alligators that he is sick of the "Jap New Order." And although the moral standards of Batman and the Punisher may be miles apart, even when it comes to the hero killing the bad guys Frank Castle seems to have more in common

Lewis Wilson's Batman than Michael Keaton's; whereas the former values human life to the extent that his being forced to take the Joker's forms the climax of the 1989 film, the latter was responsible for the deaths of several villains, driving a trio of them off of a cliff in one episode, while in other episodes indirectly causing another three to be eaten by Daka's alligators, including Daka himself. Although not approaching Frank Castle's "work in progress"—one hundred and twenty-five murders in five years—in terms of the level of violence, the 1943 Batman is actually closer than the 1989 one to the first depiction of Batman in comics, in which he kills a villain by punching him into a vat of acid.[5]

One element added to the Batman canon with the 1943 film was the Bat Cave. This affords Batman a secret hideout to go with his secret identity, just as the city sewers serve as the Punisher's escape. But the heroes aren't the only ones with hideouts—both Daka and the yakuza have their own secret bases. Daka's is accessible with numbered keys through a secret door in a funhouse in Little Tokyo called the Cave of Horrors, and Tanaka's is hidden at the top of a 41-story building, accessible from the elevator only with a special key.

Both hideouts are decorated inside with Japanese works of art, including a giant statue of Buddha and various wall paintings in Dr. Daka's; and a statue of Raijin, a torii, Noh masks, erotic feudal-era wall hangings, and garish samurai helmets, masks, swords, spears, and other martial implements in Lady Tanaka's. In addition to Tanaka's penthouse complex, complete with traditional paper walls, sliding doors, and a kendo dojo, her yakuza also use a funhouse called "Coney Island Funnyland" as a front similar to Daka's. Just as Daka, using Linda Page as bait, succeeds in capturing Batman with his zombies when the hero discovers the true nature of the Cave of Horrors, Lady Tanaka is able to lure the Punisher to the abandoned theme park by dangling the kidnapped children of the mob bosses as bait; there, her ninja-like followers overpower him.

When Castle awakes, he is chained to a torture rack. Lady Tanaka proceeds to ask him a series of questions, among which: *"Who sent you?"* His humorous response—*"Batman"*—simultaneously underscores and explains the other numerous references and parallels to the 1943 serial found in *The Punisher*. After failing to get any information from him, Lady Tanaka and her bodyguards leave Castle in the hands of a Mr. Ito, who, despite lacking the doctor epithet, appears in a white lab coat with a stethoscope around his neck—perhaps one last reference to "Dr." Daka? The influence of the original Batman film is wide indeed—after all, even the 1989 *Batman* could not help but lift the sinister theme music from the old serial.[6]

The Punisher hereby explicitly integrates preexisting comic book movie archetypes of Japanese characters into Marvel films, along with their associations to underground, criminal societies. Along with formalizing Japanese organized crime with the term "yakuza," *The Punisher* also introduces the image of the Japanese as degenerate and perverted, particularly in the night club scene—characterizations which do not appear in previous cinematic adaptations of comic books, but which do go on to feature in future Marvel films.

Blade

Directed by Stephen Norrington, New Line Cinema's *Blade* (1998) was the first theatrical Marvel film to really succeed at the box office, grossing over $131 million worldwide and spawning two sequels. The first film particularly makes numerous references to Japan, featuring a number of Japanese supporting characters. Indeed, the unholy mural featured in *The Punisher* nightclub scene depicting a vampires making love to a black panther on a flaming red cross appears to have been a prescient allusion, because this time around the Japanese characters are not just figuratively inhuman, they are literally so—vampires, in fact!

As if in a follow-up to the nightclub scene from *The Punisher*, the Japanese are introduced in *Blade* when the titular hero visits a Japanese nightclub with neon signs on the outside. One of signs is the sacred Hindu mantra "Om" (or Aum), written in Bengali script (ওঁ). This mantra represents the beginning, middle, and end of everything.[7] The specific placement of this symbol outside of the Japanese nightclub is possibly a reference to the 1995 Tokyo subway sarin gas attacks perpetrated by the Japanese doomsday cult known then as "Aum Shinrikyo," which takes its name from the same mantra.[8]

Just as Deacon Frost and his vampire followers in *Blade* search through the "vampire bible" for clues about how to bring back the blood god La Magra to usher in an age of vampire rule without humans, Shoko Asahara—the leader of Aum Shinrikyo—and his followers syncretized doomsday traditions from various world religions into a belief that the world was coming to an end, with only members of the cult destined to survive the destruction of humanity.[9] And just as the vampires force new members into their ranks by converting them, Aum Shinrikyo assured continued membership with elaborate psychedelic rituals and the threat of death should a member attempt to leave—both of which mirror the ruthless tactics used by Daka and Tanaka to keep their own subordinates from defecting.[10]

The other neon sign outside of the club is a combination of a stylized version of the Chinese character for "four" above Hexagram 18 from the Yi Jing (or I Ching).[11] The Sino-Japanese reading of the character for four (四, "shi") is homophonous with the word for death (死, "shi"), and thus the number is often superstitiously associated in Japan with that concept.[12] Hexagram 18 ("gu3," 蠱, or ☶ followed by ☴) means "work on what has decayed."[13] Taken together, these are clearly a reference to the vampires that run the club, whom Blade easily identifies through smell.

One of them, the doorman, billed as "Japanese" in the credits and played by the Polynesian Sidney Liufau, attempts to stop Blade from entering in halting Japanese. Blade forces his way in, where a pair of Lolita-esque Japanese dancers in revealing school uniforms are performing a lascivious rap on stage before an audience of middle-aged and older Japanese businessmen wearing sunglasses. This performance echoes those of the strippers, the male ballerina, and the female bodybuilder in the yakuza-run nightclub in *The Punisher*. After pushing past Kenji the bartender, played by Jeff Imada, Blade finds a secret entrance—reminiscent of the secret entrance to Daka's hideout—behind a freezer door in the kitchen. From there a secret elevator, as in *The Punisher*, leads to the bad guys' inner sanctum.

There are a number of other scattered references to East Asia and Japan made throughout *Blade*: Blade's fighting style seems to take cues from Eastern martial arts; Gerald Okamura plays the leader of an Asian house of vampires; an Asian-looking fighter attempts to stop Blade when he reaches Deacon Frost's penthouse, itself decorated with statues of the Four Heavenly Kings; and Blade is shown meditating before an ikebana display in a small tokonoma-like shrine with burning incense. The film ends with "Ni Ten Ichi Ryuu," a composition titled in Japanese.

In Guillermo del Toro's *Blade II* (2002), ninja-like vampire emissaries appear to carry Japanese wakizashi on their backs, and the action relies heavily on CGI, evoking a feeling of Japanese animation.[14] A supporting character even explicitly references Batman as he jokingly calls Blade "the Dark Knight."

On the note of Japanese animation, it is worth mentioning that the Blade film series does not represent the first major overlap between Marvel characters, Japan, and vampires in film. By including Dracula, David Goyer's *Blade: Trinity* (2004), the third film in the series, forms an indirect connection with an earlier Japanese animation based on *The Tomb of Dracula* series, the same Marvel property from which Blade originated.[15] This animation was the first of two produced by the animation division of Japanese studio Toei after reaching a deal with Marvel to obtain the rights to adapt their comic properties. Produced and first released in Japan in 1980 under the title *Yami no Teiou: Kyuuketsuki Dorakyura* (or, *Emperor of Darkness: Vampire Dracula*), the TV movie features Dracula but not Blade nor any Japanese characters or settings.[16] The final depiction of Dracula in *Blade: Trinity* completes the circle, providing some association with the older TV animation. Blade would also ultimately end up getting another Japanese-animated TV treatment in 2011 in the final installment of Madhouse's Marvel Anime series.[17]

Elektra

The next Marvel character with Japanese influences to appear in film is "Elektra," marking the proper beginning of the tradition of depicting ninja as such in Marvel film. In her cinematic debut in Mark Steven Johnson's *Daredevil* (2003), Elektra is shown to have some mastery of martial arts, including the use of sai, but her training as a "kunoichi"—a female ninja—is not specifically explored until the sequel named for her character.

Rob Bowman's *Elektra* (2005) centers on the conflict between two ninja factions, the evil Hand and the good Chaste, and features a number of Japanese characters, including Master Roshi, the leader of the Hand, played by Cary-Hiroyuki Tagawa; his son Kirigi, played by Will Yun Lee; and Meizumi, Master Roshi's right-hand man. Still, the film does little to advance the depiction of Japan beyond the stereotypes established up until that point; far from nuanced, the named Japanese characters are still exclusively and unwaveringly evil. Continuing the absolute and extreme characterizations of Japanese loyalty from previous films, Meizumi is forced by Kirigi to commit ritual suicide with a Japanese knife to atone for his ninja's failed attempts against Elektra. With a modern building for headquarters and a business-like atmosphere, the Hand mixes elements of the yakuza found in *The Punisher* with its own take on ninja to make for doubly despicable villains.

Although there are good ninja, the only prominent members of the Chaste—Elektra herself, the prodigy Abby, and their leader Stick—are all Westerners. Even the Japanese writing featured in the movie has negative connotations: Elektra, during her time outside the Chaste as a hired assassin, has 死, the Chinese character for "death," on her sai; while Kirigi has the word 対抗, "resistance," tattooed on his neck, and 空, meaning "emptiness" or "void," written on the back of his clothing.[18]

The film does feature at least one neutral Japanese-inspired concept, and that is the ancient art called Kimagure, which allows the user to "control time, the future, even life and death." The Japanese word *kimagure* literally means "whim" or "caprice."[19] The ambivalent nature of this concept, although not heavily expounded upon in the movie, would be a sign of the next set of developments in the world of Marvel film with the live-action G.I. Joe films.

G.I. Joe

The Tomb of Dracula was not to remain the only Marvel property to be animated by the Japanese and feature Japanese characters in film adaptations. Marvel would continue to work with Toei's animation division in Japan, co-producing with the U.S.–based Sunbow Studios a number of animated TV shows between 1983 and 1987. Among these, three series with ties to Hasbro toy lines were selected for presentation on the big screen: Michael Joens' *My Little Pony: The Movie* (1986) managed to beat out Willard Huyck's *Howard the Duck* (1986) by little more than a month for the distinction of being Marvel's first domestic theatrical feature film. Nelson Shin's *The Transformers: The Movie* followed later in August of 1986, and Don Jurwich's *G.I. Joe: The Movie* was ultimately relegated to a direct-to-video release in 1987 after the box-office failure of the preceding two features. None of these movies, however, prominently feature Japanese characters.

Although G.I. Joe and the Transformers were not original Marvel properties, Marvel did publish comics for them—the former starting in June of 1982, more than a year before the animated series started. This is significant because, although G.I. Joe comics had been published by various studios, including DC (*Showcase #53*) and the United States Military (*Yank #1*) since the 1940s, Marvel rebranded the series with the subtitle "A Real American Hero," employing Japanese-American Vietnam veteran Larry Hama as a writer to introduce new characters with elaborate back-stories.[20]

Among these original additions by Marvel were several Japanese characters, including Thomas Arashikage (aka "Storm Shadow"), the ninja clan to which he belonged, and his father and head of the clan, the Hard Master.[21] Snake Eyes, an American who joins the ninja clan, further reflects Hama's interest in Japanese martial arts, which included judo, kyudo, and iaijutsu.[22] This unique prospective that Hama brought to the franchise would remain with it long after Marvel ceased to be officially involved with Hasbro, with depictions of Snake Eyes, Storm Shadow, the Arashikage clan and its Hard Master making their way into the live-action Paramount G.I. Joe films, Stephen Sommers' *G.I. Joe: Rise of Cobra* (2009) and John M. Chu's *G.I. Joe: Retaliation* (2013).

Finally, with the Hard Master—played by Gerald Okamura from *Blade*—there is a Japanese character in the Marvel film world that is not evil. He kindly takes in the film's version of Snake Eyes when the latter is just a starving boy. The Hard Master's role in the films, however, takes a back seat to Storm Shadow, who is depicted as an unrepentant villain in the first installment. It is not until the second film that we see Storm Shadow join forces with the Joes, after discovering that it was Zartan's treachery and deceit that led the ninja to mistakenly join Cobra in the first place. If *Rise of Cobra* gave us our first Japanese hero, *Retaliation* tells the first story of redemption for a Japanese villain.

The Wolverine

Fox followed New Line Cinema's *Blade* almost two years later with Bryan Singer's *X-Men* (2000), which was an even bigger success. Just as in the *Blade* film series, Japan would be touched on in the *X-Men* series in more than one instalment, with the references primarily focused in one film—in this case, James Mangold's *The Wolverine* (2013).

Not only does the film feature a record number of Japanese characters and actors for Marvel, but is actually set and shot mostly in Japan—a first for a Marvel film, outside of the 1970s Japanese *Spider-man*, which bears little resemblance with the original Marvel character outside of their common name.[23] (Although it is left unclear if parts of *Elektra* take place in Japan, the action in the film implies that the bases of the Hand and the Chaste lay in or close to North America.)

The Wolverine begins by revisiting the idea of the Japanese as a wartime enemy by placing Wolverine in hiding in a well in a military base outside of Nagasaki in 1945, just before the atomic bomb codenamed "Fat Man" is about to drop. There he dissuades Yashida, a young and sympathetic Japanese soldier, from performing ritual suicide with the latter's superiors, and saves him from the blast of the bomb by protecting him at the bottom of the well. Yashida, played by Ken Yamamura, witnesses Wolverine's healing power, and survives to tell his children the tale of the fierce and wonderful *kuzuri*, or "wolverine," that saved his life.[24]

As Yashida, now a grandfather and the head of his own Japanese technology conglomerate played by Haruhiko Yamanouchi, nears his death, he remembers the magnificent healing powers of the man that saved his life, and sends his adopted granddaughter—a mutant, Yukio, played by Rila Fukushima—to fetch Wolverine and bring him back, so that he can convince Wolverine to freely hand over his healing power and his immortality. Yashida attempts to frame Logan's powers as a curse, appealing with the Buddhist notion that life is suffering, and dangling before Logan the samurai notion of an honorable death. Logan, predictably, refuses.

But that is only the beginning. After Yashida fakes his own death, Logan prevents the mogul's granddaughter, Mariko (played by Tao Okamoto), from committing suicide, and soon falls in love with her. In his efforts to protect her, he is caught up in a political struggle to gain control of the Yashida business empire. Will Yun Lee makes his second appearance in a Marvel film, this time as Harada, the childhood sweetheart of Mariko and leader of a gang of ninja. He sides with her crazed grandfather, who has built a nearly unstoppable suit of armor designed to render Logan harmless and drain his powers; meanwhile, Mariko's father, Shingen (played by Hiroyuki Sanada), himself a skilled swordsman, plots with her arranged fiancé, Noburo (Brian Tee), to have her killed so that the business will be left to himself, instead of to her as his father had willed.

These story elements give the movie rich opportunity to superficially explore various aspects of Japanese culture. For example, in one scene, Mariko corrects Logan on how to set his chopsticks down when eating rice. As Mariko explains, placing them upright in rice is considered bad manners, because it resembles incense at a funeral—a ceremony we actually get to see earlier in the movie—and thus may be construed as an omen of death.[25] Logan is not a quick learner and commits the same mistake soon after being corrected. Of course, along with Yukio's prophecy that Logan will soon die, the audience is led to believe this foreshadows Wolverine's death, but by the end of the movie it could be interpreted to have instead spelled doom for Shingen, Harada, Yashida, and his mutant doctor, the Viper.

The Wolverine draws a line between yakuza and ninja, including them both as distinct yet related factions. Despite some of the tired stereotypical, unrealistic images—mafia members are spotted, as in *The Punisher*, by their body tattoos; and are depicted, for example, openly holding automatic weapons in public, when such a thing would be unthinkable in a country like Japan where almost all guns are illegal.[26] However, the movie makes real strides in depicting scenes of everyday life in Japan. From the comical attendant at the love hotel who insists in Japanese to Wolverine that she doesn't speak English, to the idyllic apple merchant and wood-chopping scenes in the Nagasaki countryside, *The Wolverine* captures the spirit of Japan like no other Marvel film. Still, with characters like Yashida, Shingen, and Noburo, the movie does not necessarily deviate far from established comic book movie traditions, depicting the Japanese at the very least as ruthless and inscrutable. Still, Yukio and Mariko constitute perhaps the first Japanese main characters in a Marvel film to be portrayed as unambiguously good.

As with the Blade series, minor references to Japan and East Asian can be found throughout the other X-Men films. Fox would present the first Japanese character in the X-Men cinematic universe in the second film of that franchise, Bryan Singer's *X2* (2003); although this character is introduced as Yuriko, Stryker's personal assistant, it is later revealed that she serves him only because she is under the effects of his mind control serum, harkening back to the mind control tactics of Dr. Daka. Played by Kelly Hu, the character is billed as "Yuriko Oyama/Deathstrike" in the credits, but her back story is never explored in the movie: she is just another successful subject of the adamantium bonding process, like Wolverine. Psylocke, a minor character in Brett Ratner's *X-Men: The Last Stand* (2006), is played by an actress of partial Japanese descent, but the character is given no firm connection to Japan. Lastly, Agent Zero, played by Daniel Henney in Gavin Hood's *X-Men Origins: Wolverine* (2009), is portrayed as Asian, but his back story is not discussed either.

Big Hero 6

Don Hall and Chris Williams' *Big Hero 6* (2014) is the first Marvel animated film to feature Japanese characters. From the very opening shots, it is different from its live-action predecessors in its depiction of Japan. Japanese architecture, toponyms, writing, food, artistic designs and more are integrated into an American backdrop. In the first shot, the Golden Gate Bridge is pictured with torii-shaped towers. In the second shot, the new name for San Francisco—"San Fransokyo," a hybridization of the old name with Tokyo—is literally spelled out in Roman characters on an illuminated sign, repeated again on the side of a skyscraper in Japanese in the third shot. The fourth shot shows a cluster of tethered wind turbines modeled after Japanese "koinobori" (carp-shaped wind socks) floating above the city. The fifth and sixth shots feature signs exclusively in Japanese advertising everything from an indoor golf practice areas and ramen, to businesses with names that translate to "Kamii Real Estate, "Manga Café," and an "Eel House Matsune."

As soon as the action begins, we see robots modeled after samurai armor, Japanese writing on shirts and as graffiti on walls, chopsticks in hair, Japanese umbrellas—in short, a constant stream of references to Japan. Within five minutes, the main character, Hiro Hamada, introduces himself, making his Japanese descent clear from the very start of the movie. His brother, Tadashi Hamada, appears shortly after, played by a returning Daniel Henney; Go Go (Jamie Chung) rounds out the list of explicitly Japanese protagonists. Instead of an interest in martial arts or a membership in an underground society, the three share a more modern stereotype typically associated with Japan—a love of robotics and mechanical engineering.

With a villain called Yokai (the Japanese word for "spirit" or "fairy") that wears what one character describes as a "Kabuki mask," and with Hiro almost succumbing to a violent impulse for revenge, the movie appears at one point to be falling back onto well-worn stereotypes about Japan.[27] However, in contrasting twist to that of *The Wolverine*, these arcs resolve to reveal that the villain is not even Japanese at all, and that Hiro is able to avenge his brother's senseless death without killing anyone. Oddly enough, the first Marvel animated film to depict Japanese characters does so with more depth and realism than any of the live-action ones before it: *Big Hero 6* is almost entirely free of the anachronistic references to violent archetypes from early and pre-modern Japanese history, such as yakuza, ninja, and samurai, which abound in Marvel's other comic book-to-film adaptations.

With the doing-away of Japan's offensive military at the conclusion of World War II and Japan's becoming a close ally of the United States thereafter, perhaps popular culture was left with nothing but notions of Japan's long-past history as viable subjects to romanticize and sensationalize. Starting with Japanese organized crime in *The Punisher* in 1989, Marvel would begin its treatment of Japan in film with an emphasis on stereotypically violent archetypes from Japan's past. This pattern would continue through a series of live action films, until a change of direction with 2014's animated *Big Hero 6*.

Understandably, all of the Japanese characters portrayed in *The Punisher* are cartoon villains, just like in the earlier wartime film adaptations of Batman and Superman. *Blade* continues the standard of the Japanese as the bad guys, with the brief appearance of a Japanese vampire night club. *Elektra* takes it another step and introduces an evil society of ninja called "the Hand." The G.I. Joe films continue the tradition of ninja and Japanese villains, tempering previous black-and-white scenarios with the possibility of redemption. Only with *The Wolverine* do we begin to have uncompromised Japanese protagonists, alongside the usual villains. *Big Hero 6* takes us full circle to the point where several heroes, including the lead, are Japanese, while the main villain is not.

And full circle has come to the depiction of Japanese in Marvel films. Where they started out as two-dimensional and very reminiscent of the caricatures of Japanese villains seen during World War II, by the time of *The Wolverine* Japanese characters—like Mariko, Yukio, and Harada—had at least attained the status of being written as heroes just as often as villains. With *Big Hero 6*, we have in Hiro and Tadashi Hamada perhaps the first unambiguous Marvel heroes of Japanese descent ever to grace the big screen—and this time without all the stereotypical trappings of samurai, ninja, and yakuza. Although it is difficult to predict what Marvel has in store next for cinematic audiences, the influence of Japan is sure to continue, and with it a more nuanced and well-rounded view of the island nation where comic books are—after all—perhaps even more popular than here in the U.S.[28]

NOTES

1. Raymond William Stedman, "Shazam and Good-by," in *The Serials: Suspense and Drama by Installment* (Norman: University of Oklahoma Press, 1971), 125.
2. John W. Dower, *War without Mercy: Race and Power in the Pacific War* (New York: Pantheon, 1986), 20.
3. *Superman*, directed by Seymour Kneitel, Paramount Pictures, 1942.
4. Dower, *War without Mercy: Race*, 20.

5. Bill Finger and Bob Kane, *Detective Comics #27* (n.p.: Detective Comics Inc., 1939).
6. Mark S. Reinhart, *The Batman Filmography*, 2d ed. (Jefferson, NC: McFarland, 2013), 117.
7. Annette Wilke and Oliver Moebus, *Sound and Communication: An Aesthetic Cultural History of Sanskrit Hinduism* (Berlin: De Gruyter, 2011), 435–456.
8. Kyle B. Olson, "Aum Shinrikyo: Once and Future Threat?," *Emerging Infectious Diseases* 5, no. 4 (August 1999): 513–516, doi:10.3201/eid0504.990409.
9. Ian Reader, *Religious Violence in Contemporary Japan: The Case of Aum Shinrikyo* (Honolulu: University of Hawai'i Press, 2000).
10. Robert Jay Lifton, *Destroying the World to Save It: Aum Shinrikyo, Apocalyptic Violence, and the New Global Terrorism* (New York: Henry Holt, 1999).
11. James Legge, Ch'u Chai, and Winberg Chai, *I Ching: Book of Changes* (New Hyde Park, N.Y.: University Books, 1964).
12. Mark McBennet, "Japanese Superstitions: Death and the Number 4," Japan Zone, http://www.japan-zone.com/omnibus/superstition.shtml.
13. Elizabeth Moran and Joseph Yu, *The Complete Idiot's Guide to the I Ching* (Indianapolis: Alpha, 2002).
14. Keith McDonald and Roger Clark, *Guillermo Del Toro: Film as Alchemic Art* (New York: Bloomsbury Academic, 2014), 163.
15. Marv Wolfman and Gene Colan, *The Tomb of Dracula #10* (New York: Marvel Comics, 1973).
16. *Yami no teiô kyuketsuki dorakyura*, directed by Akinori Nagaoka and Minoru Okazaki, Toei Animation, 1980.
17. *Blade*, directed by Mitsuyuki Masuhara, Sony Pictures Entertainment, 2011.
18. Izuru Shinmura, *Kojien*, 6th ed. (Tokyo: Iwanami Shoten, 2008).
19. Ibid.
20. Larry Hama, *G.I. Joe: A Real American Hero #1*, illus. Herb Trimpe (New York: Marvel Comics, 1982).
21. Larry Hama, *G.I. Joe: A Real American Hero #21*, illus. Larry Hama, ed. Danny O'Neil and Linda Grant (New York: Marvel Comics, 1984).
22. Larry Hama, "Larry Hama (conducted by Rod Hannah of Zartan's Domain in July 1998)," interview by Rod Hannah, Joe Guide, last modified July 1998, http://joeguide.com/interviews/larrryhama_rh.shtml.
23. *Supaida-man*, directed by Koichi Takamoto, Toei, 1978.
24. Shinmura, *Kojien*.
25. McBennet, "Japanese Superstitions: Death and the Number," Japan Zone.
26. *Law Controlling Possession, Etc. of Fire-Arms and Swords* (Tokyo: EHS Law Bulletin Series, 1978), PDF.
27. Shinmura, *Kojien*.
28. Saira Syed, "Comic Giants Battle for Readers," BBC Business, last modified August 18, 2011, http://www.bbc.com/news/business-14526451.

PART 4

Setting Up the Marvel Cinematic Universe

Sowing the Seeds
How 1990s Marvel Animation Facilitated Today's Cinematic Universe

Liam Burke

"The Golden Age of Comic Book Filmmaking" is how *Batman* (1989) executive producer Michael E. Uslan described the unprecedented number of comic book film adaptations produced since the dawn of the new millennium.[1] This trend began in 2000 when Bryan Singer's *X-Men* grossed $300 million on a modest $75 million budget, and gathered pace when *Spider-Man* broke box-office records two years later. With the Marvel Cinematic Universe the comic book film adaptation reached its commercial peak. However, despite the popularity of *Spider-Man* and *The Avengers* (2012), superheroes did not make the leap from comics to screen in a single bound; rather it was a series of incremental steps.

Drawing on the transtextual relations Gérard Genette puts forward in *Palimpsests*, film scholar Robert Stam suggests that film adaptations are "hypertexts derived from preexisting hypotexts that have been transformed by operations of selection, amplification, concretization, and actualization."[2] He expands this point by suggesting, "diverse prior adaptations can form a larger, cumulative hypotext that is available to the filmmaker who comes relatively 'late' in the series."[3] For instance, when asked on the *X-Men* DVD commentary whether the 1992 animated series *X-Men* (1992–1997) had influenced his live action adaptation, director Bryan Singer replied, "Tremendously. The animated series [... featured] the characters that had risen through the comic franchise and had become part of a more public lexicon, I wanted to take advantage of that." Thus, the popular films of today owe much to earlier adaptations. This essay will consider one of the most important yet overlooked steps in the comic book character's journey from niche interest to mainstream success: animated series. In particular, it will focus on the animated *X-Men* series to which Bryan Singer was so greatly indebted, and its sister show *Spider-Man* (1994–1998).

Marvel Gets Animated

Before the success of the 1990s, Marvel struggled to realize its characters in other media. The publisher's first foray into animation was the much-maligned *The Marvel*

Super Heroes developed by Grantray-Lawrence, a company more accustomed to producing cartoons for advertising than television shows. *The Marvel Super Heroes* first aired in 1966 as daily six-minute installments, with each day dedicated to a different hero: Captain America, Hulk, Iron Man, Thor, and Sub-Mariner. Each of the segments was produced on a modest budget of $6,000,[4] with the creators reducing costs by Xeroxing the original comics and adding movement through camera pans or limited animation (primarily moving mouths and flailing hands). In *Spider-Man: Confidential,* Edward Gross suggests, "the word *animated* overstates the situation. A better description might be filmed comic-book panels with lips that occasionally moved. It was abysmal."[5] The publisher and fans were more than aware of the show's limitations with a 1966 story in *The Merry Marvel Messenger* acknowledging the series' shortcoming: "A lot of you have spotted a few fumblin' flaws in the show, and you should see how many we found, ourselves! Just like many of you, your brain-bustin' Bullpen realizes that the animation isn't up to Walt Disney."[6]

The publisher's top-tier heroes were spared the ignominy of *The Marvel Super Heroes*. *Fantastic Four* received a comparatively luxurious adaptation by Hanna-Barbera Productions that began airing on ABC in 1967. That same year, Spider-Man also swung into Saturday mornings on ABC for the hero's eponymous animated series, which again was produced by Grantray-Lawrence. Although the animation was a step above the company's cut-and-paste approach on *The Marvel Super Heroes*, rote villains, predictable plots, and simplistic character design dogged the production. Nonetheless, *Spider-Man* and the other Marvel series were effective in raising the profile of these characters, with future Marvel creators crediting these shows with introducing them to comics. For instance, former X-Men editor Bob Harras recalled how he "saw those Marvel animated shows, and I remember the shock of going to the local newsstand and seeing a *Sub-Marnier* comic. I had never made the connection between the cartoons and the comic books."[7]

In a pattern that would be repeated years later, the success of these early cartoons prompted Marvel to turn its attention to live action. However, beyond the popularity of the fugitive-inspired series *The Incredible Hulk* (1978–1982), none of Marvel's characters succeeded in television. *Doctor Strange* (1978) and *Captain America* (1979) each anchored TV movies that failed to develop into series. A 1977 Spider-Man TV movie did garner the ratings necessary to prompt the production of an ongoing CBS show starring Nicholas Hammond in the dual role of Spider-Man and Peter Parker. However, *The Amazing Spider-Man* lacked any comic book villains, with the hero tackling everyday thugs in a series that Gross described as "bland, maintaining none of the character or edge that had distinguished Spidey as a hero in the first place."[8] Unsurprisingly, the live action show was cancelled after 13 episodes.

Marvel heroes faced similar difficulties in animation during the 1970s with fans being treated to two ill-advised shows based on the Fantastic Four. In 1978 DePatie-Freleng Enterprises produced *The New Fantastic Four* animated series, which swapped out the Human Torch for a new character Herbie the Robot. Even more egregious was *Fred and Barney Meet the Thing,* which was produced by Hanna-Barbera one year later. The show packaged a revival of *The Flintstones* with a series that re-imagined Fantastic Four curmudgeon The Thing as a teenage boy, Benjy Grimm, who would become the rock encrusted hero when he joined magic rings and said the incantation, "Thing ring, do your thing!" Just like *The Amazing Spider-Man*, these shows only lasted 13 episodes.

After the disappointments of the 1970s, fans finally began to see adaptations of their heroes that more closely resembled what they enjoyed in the comics. In 1981, Marvel owners Cadence Industries bought DePatie-Freleng Enterprises (DFE), the studio responsible for the animated titles for *The Pink Panther* movies as well as the Human Torch-less Fantastic Four series. This company was soon dissolved forming the basis of animation studio Marvel Productions. David Perlmutter, in *America Toons In,* describes how Marvel's "involvement in animation had been engineered by its creative driving force, Stan Lee, who saw it as a logical step toward expanding Marvel's corporate bottom line beyond the low-profit comics industry and into areas where it could reach more diverse audiences."[9] However, the company's credits extended far beyond adaptations of its publishing arm, with an emphasis placed on creating shows for other licenses such as *Muppet Babies* (The Jim Henson Company), *Dungeons & Dragons* (TSR), *Transformers* (Hasbro), and the Avengers-like *Defenders of the Earth,* which saw King Features comic strip characters Flash Gordon, The Phantom, and Mandrake the Magician teaming up to stop Ming the Merciless.

Among these high-profile collaborations, Marvel Productions also found time for characters from its own library with two Spider-Man series developed in 1981 to launch the studio. The first to air was *Spider-Man and his Amazing Friends* (1981–1983); a Saturday morning NBC animated series that found Peter Parker rooming with fellow Empire State University students (and superheroes) Bobby Drake (Iceman) and Angelica Jones (Firestar). A number of commentators have suggested that the series was Marvel's response to the success of the DC comics–based *Super Friends,* with the show featuring regular guest appearances from heroes such as Captain America, Hulk, and Iron Man.[10] While the series failed to match the longevity of *Super Friends,* as Derek Johnson points out, *Spider-Man and his Amazing Friends* successfully "leveraged interactions among different characters in a shared Marvel Universe to multiply audience appeals."[11] This strategy would prove central to Marvel's eventual domination of Hollywood a few decades later.

The team dynamic of *Spider-Man and his Amazing Friends* was arguably at odds with the feared and hated vigilante of the comics. Former head of Marvel Productions and Fox Kids, Margaret Loesch, described the show's development in an interview with website *Blast from the Past* as follows:

> I was meeting with the head of kid's programs at NBC and I said to her: "Listen, I just have a question. Why did you want to add his 'amazing friends' to Spider-Man? And she said: "How can we have a loner star in a TV show?" I told her that the whole point is that Peter Parker is a loner, that's his plight in life.… She told me it wouldn't work for TV.[12]

Those looking for a more faithful web-slinger found some relief in *Amazing Friends'* sister show *Spider-Man* (1981–1982), which David and Greenberger describe as skewing "a bit older" and sticking "more closely to the continuity of the comics."[13] The series shared designs and music with the better-remembered *Amazing Friends,* but focused on Peter Parker's struggles with his popular villains and dual identity. While Gross contends "the series was pretty formulaic,"[14] it did reaffirm Spider-Man's place as a transmedia icon, a status not shared by the X-Men.

A Sub-Mariner segment of the 1966 "animated" series *The Marvel Super Heroes* marked the first appearance of the X-Men outside of comics, but the guest role would have done little to broaden the mutant team's recognition. With the rights for Fantastic Four still held by Hanna-Barbera, Grantray-Lawrence opted to substitute the X-Men for Marvel's first family in "Dr. Doom's Day," an episode based on *Fantastic Four* #6 and *Fantastic Four Annual* #3. However, rather than use the mutant team's comic book name, the

X-Men were referred to as the "Allies for Peace" in the episode as they carried out the heroics clearly intended for the Fantastic Four.

Following this ignominious debut the X-Men continued to be underrepresented as Marvel adapted other heroes for live action and animated shows. The mutant team's fortunes were equally bleak on the comic book page, with the comic struggling for sales during its early years. However, a 1975 revival saw the popularity of the characters steadily increase to the point that *The Uncanny X-Men* was Marvel's top-selling title in the mid–1980s. This success went unnoticed, however, by the wider world, prompting Mallory to describe the characters as "pop culture's best kept secret"[15]—a secret Marvel Productions was eager to share.

This ambition goes some way towards explaining why, on *Spider-Man and his Amazing Friends,* the hero was flanked by long-time X-Man Iceman and newly created mutant Firestar. Firestar's origin as an X-Man was revealed in the second-season episode "A Fire-Star Is Born." The episode finds Iceman and Firestar ditching Spider-Man to attend an X-Men reunion replete with Storm and Wolverine in their first adaptation. While the X-Men would make further guest appearances in *Spider-Man and his Amazing Friends,* the best-selling comic book characters had yet to enjoy their own show. Marvel Productions sought to rectify this disparity in 1989 with "Pryde of the X-Men," a pilot episode for a planned syndicated series.

Although "Pryde of the X-Men" was not developed into a series, the pilot provided producers and fans with a glimpse of how the X-Men might function in their own audiovisual adaptation. In the episode, new mutant Kitty Pryde is recruited by Professor Xavier to join his peacekeeping force, the X-Men. After a brief introduction to each of the heroes, "terrorist mutant" Magneto attacks the team before stealing a "mutant power circuit," which necessitates an outer space showdown in which Kitty proves herself to be a hero.

Although Sidney Iwanter, who would oversee the 1990s series, described the pilot as a "template for what not ever, ever to do with the Fox X-Men series,"[16] the show did anticipate later adaptations. For instance, the trope of using a young female recruit as the audience's surrogate in this strange new world not only reappeared in the 1992 Fox series, where Jubilee filled the role, but also in the first feature length adaptation of the characters, *X-Men,* with the audience following Rogue's journey into the world of mutants.

The show, which Mallory describes as "briskly paced and terrifically designed,"[17] also became the basis of a Konami produced *X-Men* arcade game, which had an innovative dual screen that allowed six players to play alongside each other at once. Thus, even as a "failed" pilot, "Pryde of the X-Men" demonstrated the capacity of adaptations to develop merchandise. This tactic would become one of the underlying motivations for the 1990s Fox shows. In addition to the arcade game, "Pryde of the X-Men" is perhaps best remembered for the decision to outfit Canadian X-Man Wolverine with an Australian accent. Producer Will Meugniot later explained that Marvel Entertainment Group mandated the Australian accent as the publisher's parent company, New World Entertainment, "was trying to develop an Australia-based *Wolverine* movie" to capitalize on the interest in Outback heroes like *Mad Max* and *Crocodile Dundee*.[18] While this Wolverine presaged the casting of Australian actor Hugh Jackman as the popular X-Man, it was also an early example of Marvel using animation to prime ideas for big screen production—a process that would become commonplace moving in to the 1990s.

Ultimately, the inability of "Pryde of the X-Men" to develop into a series was attributed to the show's complexity; Meugniot recalled a studio representative asking, "It looks nice, but why is that Wolverine guys [sic] so mean?"[19] Marvel Productions would not survive long enough to mount another X-Men series, with the studio "resigning itself to corporate hackwork" by the late 1980s.[20] A chief factor in the decline of the Marvel Productions was the loss of CEO Margaret Loesch to the fledgling Fox Kids Network in 1990. During her time at Marvel Productions Loesch had fought to get comic book adaptations picked up by the networks. She would later reflect that her "single biggest disappointment was that we could not get an *X-Men* series off the ground, no one was interested."[21] Loesch attributed this impasse to narrow-minded network executives who could not see the value in the material. Loesch told *Blast From the Past* that when she became to President of Fox Kids, she "called up Stan [Lee] and said: 'Ok, I couldn't sell it, but now I want to buy it.'"[22]

By the time *X-Men* aired in 1992 the landscape had changed for television animation and superheroes. Jason Mittell identifies a number of factors that "helped restore the legitimacy and broad appeal of animation" during this time,[23] including the wider availability of Japanese animated films like Katsuhiro Otomo's *Akira* (1988), the success of primetime cartoon *The Simpsons* (1989—), and the Disney Renaissance, which reached its critical peak with the 1992 Academy Award Best Picture nomination for *Beauty and the Beast*. Furthermore, the success of the Tim Burton's *Batman* in 1989 allowed for more adult approaches to superheroes, as typified by the series that found a darker knight finally descend into animation, *Batman: The Animated Series* (1992–1994). Back in their native form, superheroes were also generating wider interest, with the first issue of a new X-Men title selling a reported 8.1 million copies in 1991—sales figures even the mainstream media could not ignore.[24] The X-Men also made successful inroads into the toy market, with Mallory crediting a 1991 line of action figures produced by Toy Biz for introducing "the characters to a whole new audience of youngsters."[25]

It was during this fertile period that Margaret Loesch and Fox premiered *X-Men* as part of the Saturday morning "Fox Kids" line-up on October 31, 1992. For the series, Loesch recruited many Marvel Productions alumni, including the team behind "Pryde of the X-Men" Rick Hoberg, Larry Houston, and Will Meugniot, who served as storyboard artist, line producer, and supervising producer respectively on the new show. The responsibility of writing the series bible and serving as showrunner fell to Eric Lewald, who was suggested to Loesch by Fox Kids Vice President Sidney Iwanter following the writer's work editing scripts for the *Beetlejuice* animated series. Despite this experienced team, in a retrospective interview with *Blast from the Past*, Lewald described how "given the previous weak track record of Marvel animated adaptations, there was great fear that X-Men would fail."[26]

Drawing heavily on the comic books, *X-Men* broke with animated superhero traditions by maintaining a continuing storyline, touching upon complex themes of prejudice, and featuring a band of mutants who did not always get along. For instance, the opening two-part episode "Night of the Sentinels" centered on a disastrous mission in which one X-Man, Morph, dies and another, Beast, is taken prisoner by the authorities, prompting Wolverine to sucker punch fellow hero Cyclops for his inept leadership. These X-Men might have been superheroes but they were far from Amazing Friends. What did amaze broadcasters was the show's ratings, with Fox Kids President Loesch noting, "we went from number three to number one because of one event: the premiere of *X-Men*."[27] With X-Men, and the stratospheric success of the live-action series *Mighty Morphin Power*

Rangers (1993–1995), Fox Kids dominated Saturday morning programming in the early 1990s. Inevitably Loesch would turn her attention to developing other Marvel properties, and, in a move that would be echoed by the film adaptations a decade later, Marvel's most recognizable character, Spider-Man, followed the success of X-Men.

Premiering on Fox Kids on November 19, 1994, *Spider-Man: The Animated Series* adopted a similar approach to *X-Men* by emphasizing continuing storylines, comic book fidelity, and greater character depth. Also like the earlier series, artists who had previously worked at Marvel Productions populated the show's creative team. While *Batman: The Animated Series* writer Martin Pasko initially developed the series, showrunning responsibilities ultimately fell to writer John Semper, who had worked on *Defenders of the Earth* for Marvel Productions. In addition to Semper, Supervising Producer Bob Richardson and Art Director Dennis Venizelos also came from the ranks of Marvel Productions. However, the biggest influence on this new series was arguably Toy Biz executive and future head of Marvel Studios, Avi Arad.

The manufacturer Toy Biz established its reputation by producing the action figures for Tim Burton's 1989 *Batman* film and securing an exclusive license with Marvel. When Marvel attempted to renegotiate that deal, Toy Biz heads Avi Arad and Isaac Perlmutter managed to work out a compromise whereby Toy Biz would maintain exclusivity while Marvel would acquire 46% of the toy manufacturer. Recognizing that the financial viability of both Toy Biz and Marvel was dependent on licenses, Arad and Perlmutter "were committed to putting their characters on the screen."[28] As a Toy Biz executive, Arad had been "a vocal producer of the *X-Men* animated series."[29] The success of that show saw Arad ultimately eclipse Stan Lee as Marvel's liaison with Hollywood. Arad was even more involved with *Spider-Man: The Animated Series*, with showrunner Semper describing how "Avi has wild ideas—mostly for individual scenes—and my job was to put them into some kind of shape."[30] In 1996 Marvel Entertainment Group (MEG) filed for Chapter 11 bankruptcy protection. After two years of uncertainty and infighting, MEG was merged with Toy Biz. This deal cemented Avi Arad's control of Marvel and enabled him to develop a slate of feature length films that would eventually blossom into the Marvel Cinematic Universe. However, much of the groundwork for this film empire was established through the development of the 1990s *X-Men* and *Spider-Man* animated series.

While there were other attempts during the 1990s to replicate the success of these flagship shows, they were all short-lived and ultimately unsuccessful. For instance, *The Incredible Hulk* animated series developed for UPN in 1996 was considered too dark by network executives, prompting a change in tone and title for the second (and final) season, *The Incredible Hulk and She-Hulk*.[31] *The Marvel Action Hour*, which began in 1994, split its running time between Iron Man and Fantastic Four and included introductions by Stan Lee, but it also only lasted two seasons, while *The Avengers: United They Stand* suffered from the lack of A-list Avengers: Captain America, Iron Man, and Thor. Fox Kids also developed a *Silver Surfer* animated series that deftly blended cell (celluloid) and computer animation, but it was cancelled after one season. By the time *X-Men* and *Spider-Man* ceased production in 1997 and 1998, respectively, they had become the longest running shows based on Marvel characters.

Creators on both series contend that the influence of these shows extends far beyond their initial runs. For instance, Loesch, who spearheaded these adaptations, recently recounted, "I think Fox Kids definitely was the impetus for the whole comic book revolution, since we dramatically raised the whole awareness of the Marvel characters."[32] Yet, how much does the Golden Age of Comic Book Filmmaking owe to these 1990s animated series?

Digests and Prototypes

French film scholar André Bazin argued that adaptation was a process of "digest" as the literature is "made more accessible through cinematic adaptation."[33] However, where a film adaptation of a novel might need to compress a couple of hundred pages of a book into a two hour running time, an adaptation of a serialized comic will often need to distil years, if not decades, of stories. Loesch acknowledged this difficulty, noting, "Our challenge with *X-Men* was that it had been in the books for thirty years and had gone through so many evolutions, we had to figure out where we picked it up ... so we created sort of an amalgam."[34] Indeed, the series was successful at combining heroes such as Cyclops and Jean Grey who appeared in the first issue of the comic (September 1963) with more recent additions like Jubilee and Gambit, who were introduced in 1989 and 1990 respectively.

Similarly, John Semper notes of *Spider-Man: The Animated Series*, "Spider-Man had never properly been brought to life on screen prior to my show, so we did a lot of things for the first time.... We didn't have multi-million dollar feature length films to reference."[35] Thus, these animated series did not have the benefit of successful audiovisual versions of the heroes to guide the adaptations. By comparison, when the feature length films went into production, the complicated publication histories of these characters had already been reconciled by the Fox Kids series. For instance, while the feature length *X-Men* film could have made use of any of the dozens of heroes who populated the books, the film tapped into the larger hypotext by only using mutants that had been popularized by the animated series. Similarly, much like the animated series, *Spider-Man* elected to drop Peter Parker's ill-fated college sweetheart Gwen Stacy in favor of later love interest Mary Jane Watson, who was more familiar to audiences from the animated series as well as recent comics.

One of the greatest obstacles for comic-book movies has been the realization of the hand drawn heroes in live action. Pascal Lefèvre discusses this issue in his essay "Incompatible Visual Ontologies: The Problematic Adaptation of Drawn Images," where he describes how the "characteristic differences of the two media" give rise to "adaptation problems" that include the difficulty of "translating drawings to photography."[36] Cartoonist and commentator Robert C. Harvey also picks up on the medium-specific differences between the forms, suggesting that "animated cartoons have a foot in both camps: they use the mechanical methods of film to present images drawn by hand. Consequently, animated cartoons are a third medium."[37] This third medium serves as the ontological bond between comics and cinema, with the 1990s series establishing a model for how these characters might function when they went from static to motion pictures.

The creators on the animated series actively sought to narrow the semiotic gap between the forms. The end-credits for the *X-Men* animated series featured computer generated models of the hand-drawn heroes that allowed audiences to imagine what the characters might look like as live action heroes (and even action figures). *Spider-Man* went one step further, featuring some of the earliest uses of computer-generated imagery

(CGI) in an animated series. As Supervising Producer Bob Richardson noted, "we attempted to add CGI backgrounds to the show at a time when it was unheard of for a children's television show [… this gave] the show a live-action film quality to further enhance the 'realism' that we were looking for and treat each episode almost like a mini-movie."[38] When Spider-Man was finally adapted to "live action," the film heavily relied on CG characters to carry out the high-flying heroics. Lev Manovich contends, "digital cinema is a particular case of animation that uses live action footage as one of its many elements."[39] While offering a convincing illusion of reality, the digital images of today's feature films are as constructed as their comic book and animated counterparts. Thus, shows like *Spider-Man* anticipated the "live action" adventures of cinema's superheroes.

It is frequently suggested that, with publishers, broadcasters, and film studios all falling under mammoth media conglomerates, comics have become the research and development stage for wider transmedia endeavors.[40] If comics are the research and development branch of entertainment companies, then animation might be considered the prototype phase, as companies regularly refined Intellectual Property as animated series ahead of wider diffusion. For instance, while the lure of mass merchandising incentivized Avi Arad to develop comic book characters for big screen success, Marvel first developed these heroes on the lower risk platform of animation. These prototypes exceeded expectations with X-Men "spun off into apparel, trading cards, video games, and fourteen million action figures and Pizza Hut meal deals."[41] Thus, the successful animated series would have helped allay the concerns of 20th Century–Fox and Sony Pictures, thereby facilitating the big budget film adaptations.

Audiences and Fans

Even in the heyday of the comic book speculator boom, when issues of Spider-Man and X-Men were selling millions of copies, comics were becoming a rarefied pastime dependent on a collector market to sustain the industry. Although the earlier animated series ensured that Spider-Man enjoyed wider recognition, it was not of the same magnitude as big-screen stars Superman and Batman, while the X-Men were little known outside of the comic book community.

However, the ratings success and lengthy runs of the 1990s Fox Kids series brought these characters to the attention of many who would never read a comic. By the time the feature films were released, these Saturday morning Kids TV watchers were at the height of their spending power as teenagers and young professionals. The films actively courted this audience by playing upon nostalgia for these earlier shows. For instance, the trailer for the X-Men film mirrored the opening titles of the animated series, with the individual heroes introduced by title cards before a quick display of their unique power. The film also included a cameo from actor George Buza, who voiced Beast in the *X-Men* animated series. Similarly, the 2002 Spider-Man film evoked earlier adaptations with a busking musician providing a rendition of the mantra-like theme song from the 1960s Spider-Man cartoon ("Spider-Man, Spider-Man! Does whatever a spider can!").

Furthermore, Wilson Koh suggests that the spider bite sequence in the live action film evokes the opening credits of the Fox Kids series, adding, "the result is a text which provides its audiences with a comforting and celebratory confirmation of their existing extra-textual knowledge regarding the Spider-Man character."[42]

Spider-Man: The Animated Series was not only successful at raising the profile of its titular hero but also the show's frequent guest stars. In 1998, comic book film adaptation *Blade*, based on the little known *Tomb of Dracula* character, surprised box office commentators when it grossed $131 million on a $40 million budget. However, *Blade* had recently gained wider attention when the vampire hunter was included as a supporting character in the season long *Spider-Man* story arc, "Neogenic Nightmare." Showrunner Semper explains, "There was NO Blade film in the works at all … I believe that it was my use of the character that inspired Avi [Arad] to pursue it as a movie."[43]

Beyond developing greater recognition of the characters, these series also furthered the belief that they could be taken seriously. While *Spider-Man* showrunner Semper complained about the limitations of Saturday morning censorship, the shows did manage to bring a hitherto unseen level of maturity to animated adaptations.[44] For instance, *X-Men* set out its stall as a more adult series by having one the heroes die in the opening two episodes, and adhering to the comic's central theme of prejudice. The *Spider-Man* creative team sought to emphasize Peter Parker's love life as a way to distinguish the show from previous animated efforts and also attract a more mature audience. Both strategies were successful, with the shows garnering older audiences than traditional Saturday morning fare.[45] Thus, by the time *X-Men* and *Spider-Man* shuffled into cinemas, they were better positioned to target a broader demographic.

Beyond the mass audience, one group likely to tune into the new shows were comic book fans, and these adaptations did much to gain their approval. David and Greenberger note that despite its many flaws, the Xeroxed production of *The Marvel Super Heroes* ensured that the episodes "were, of necessity, extremely faithful to the source material."[46] However, since that first effort, adaptations of Marvel comics had had a very loose commitment to such fidelity.

Under the stewardship of Loesch, the Fox Kids series displayed greater faithfulness to the comics than any adaptations in animation or live action. Many of the story arcs from the X- Men comics were adapted directly to the animated series, including "The Phoenix Saga" and "Days of Future Past," while the heroes' distinctive designs were based on popular comic artist Jim Lee's recent reinterpretation of the characters. Although the Spider-Man series included less direct adaptations, showrunner Semper noted, "I didn't want people to feel that we were really deviating from the essence of what had happened with Spider-Man in the sixties."[47] Indeed, as Perlmutter observed, the Spider-Man series "was far more faithful to the spirit and intent of the original comic books than the previous TV animated versions."[48]

Engendering the goodwill of comic book fans and other pop culture enthusiasts became increasingly important to producers moving into the late 1990s, as the web emboldened this vocal minority and gave them wider reach. As Henry Jenkins observed of this participatory era, "none of this is new. What has shifted is the visibility of fan culture."[49] As I discuss in detail in *The Comic Book Film Adaptation: Exploring Modern Hollywood's Leading Genre*, producers in this Golden Age of Comic Book Filmmaking displayed previously unseen levels of fidelity in their film adaptations, such as adapting fan-favorite storylines like *X-Men: Days of Future Past* (2014) or mirroring iconic comic book moments.[50] However, it was the Fox Kids series that developed this model of appeasing long-time fans through faithful adaptations, while developing a wider audience open to the idea that comic book characters could be more than children's entertainment.

Storytelling and Shared Universe

Many commentators have noted that comic book storytelling relies on continuing narratives in which any form of definitive conclusion is endlessly deferred.[51] This serialization was eschewed by early television adaptations, which tended to conclude each plot within a single episode. However the Fox Kids shows, taking their cue from the comics, adopted ongoing storylines that Semper compared to a "soap opera."[52] This approach not only allowed for more complicated storylines, but also facilitated greater audience investment, as viewers could not afford to miss a single episode. For instance, the second episode of *Spider-Man*, "The Spider Slayer," introduced inventor Spencer Smythe and his son Alistair, who build a robot to hunt Spider-Man for the criminal Kingpin. The episode concludes with Alistair vowing retribution against Spider-Man following Spencer's accidental death, a plotline that was continued in the appropriately titled episode "Return of the Spider Slayer." Although earlier adaptations maintained little continuity between installments, the franchise-minded filmmakers of the Golden Age of Comic Book Filmmaking have adopted the comic book–style storytelling that served these Fox Kids' shows so well (see Cogan and Massey, this volume). For instance, much like the animated series' Spider Slayer arc, the climax of feature film *Spider-Man* finds the hero blamed for the death of Norman Osborn by Osborn's son (and Peter's friend) Harry. Harry, like Alistair Smythe in the series, promises, "I'll get Spider-Man for this, if it's the last thing I do," a storyline that was gradually developed across the film's two sequels.

In Marvel Comics, this continuity allowed for the building of a shared universe collectively inhabited by the publisher's heroes. *Spider-Man and His Amazing Friends* tapped into that mythology giving audiences a taste of a larger Marvel Universe. Fox Kids' *Spider-Man* went one step further weaving in guest appearances from popular characters such as the X-Men and Fantastic Four, alongside lesser-known heroes like Blade, Punisher, and Daredevil, all of whom would be the subject of feature length adaptations over the next decade. Semper believed that his *Spider-Man* show would be exceptional in its use of a larger continuity,[53] but he could not have anticipated that Marvel Studios would develop a shared universe of films that turned comic book continuity into bustling box office. Nonetheless, Semper and his collaborators on *Spider-Man* and *X-Men* can take the credit for developing the first comic book adaptations to embrace the continuing storylines and larger universe that up until then had been confined to comics.

Conclusion

In the post–*X-Men* boom of comic-book movies a number of animated series were produced including *X-Men: Evolution* (2000–2003), *Spider-Man: The New Animated Series* (2003), *The Spectacular Spider-Man* (2008–2009), and *Wolverine and the X-Men* (2009). Yet none of these shows achieved the success or longevity of the 1990s Fox Kids series. *X-Men* and *Spider-Man* accomplished what no animated show based on a Marvel comic has before or since: the adaptations compressed characters with decades of publication history into a format that could be easily digested by fans and non-fans alike, providing a template for later big screen adaptations; they brought a wider audience and greater credibility to characters often dismissed as kids' stuff ahead of their feature length debuts; and they turned comic book continuity into some of the most complex and engaging narratives ever developed in an adaptation until the Marvel Cinematic Universe. More recent MCU animated shows such as *Ultimate Spider-Man* (2012–) and *Avengers Assemble* (2013–) have eclipsed the runs of these Fox Kids' series. Nonetheless, that these 1990s shows achieved these aims in an era of speculator market crashes, bankruptcy declarations, merchandising concerns, and stifling censorship is worthy of celebration. Thus, animation is not so much the missing link, but rather the forgotten bridge between the comics that are respected as the source text and the excitement that greets each new blockbuster movie.

Notes

1. Liam Burke, *The Comic Book Film Adaptation* (Jackson: University of Mississippi Press, 2015), 23.
2. Robert Stam, "Beyond Fidelity: The Dialogics of Adaptation," in *Film Adaptation*, edited by James Naremore (New Brunswick: Rutgers University Press, 2000), 66.
3. Ibid.
4. David Perlmutter, *America Toons In: A History of Television Animation* (Jefferson, NC: McFarland, 2014), 106.
5. Edward Gross, *Spider-Man Confidential: From Comic Icon to Hollywood Hero* (New York: Hyperion, 2002), 108.
6. Roy Thomas and Peter Sanderson, *The Marvel Vault* (Philadelphia: Running, 2007), 97.
7. Tom DeFalco, *Comics Creators on X-Men* (London: Titan, 2006), 171.
8. Gross, 125.
9. Perlmutter, 216.
10. Mallory, 154; Gross, 141.
11. Derek Johnson, "Cinematic Destiny: Marvel Studios and the Trade Stories of Industrial Convergence," *Cinema Journal* 52, no. 1 (2012): 7.
12. Scott, "Interview with Margaret Loesch, President of Fox Kids (1990–1997)," *Blast from the Past*, last modified August 22, 2014,
13. Peter David and Robert Greenberger, *The Spider-Man Vault* (Philadelphia: Running, 2010), 170.
14. Gross, 141.
15. Michael Mallory, *X-Men: The Characters and Their Universe* (New York: Universe, 2008), 133.
16. Scott, "Interview with Sidney Iwanter, VP of Fox Kids (1990–1998)," *Blast from the Past*, last modified August 22, 2014, http://www.blastfromthepasttv.com/siwanterinterview.html.
17. Mallory, 159.
18. Ibid., 162.
19. Ibid., 163.
20. Perlmutter, 300.
21. Mallory, 163.
22. Scott, "Interview with Margaret Loesch."
23. Jason Mittell, *Genre and Television: From Cop Shows to Cartoons in American Culture* (New York: Routledge, 2004), 80.
24. Ben Morse, "SDCC 2010: Marvel Breaks World Record," Marvel.com, last modified April 30, 2010, http://marvel.com/news/comics/13598/sdcc_2010_marvel_breaks_world_record.
25. Mallory, 134–136.
26. Scott, "Interview with Eric Lewald, Executive Story Editor of X-Men," *Blast from the Past*, last modified August 22, 2014, http://www.blastfromthepasttv.com/elewaldinterview.html.
27. Mallory, 167.
28. Thomas and Sanderson, 182.
29. Sean Howe, *Marvel Comics: The Untold Story* (New York: Harper, 2012), 355.
30. Gross, 158–159.
31. Stu Harvey and James Harvey, "The Incredible Hulk Interviews—Dick Sebast," *Marvel Animation Age*, last modified November 7, 2014, http://marvel.toonzone.net/hulk/interviews/sebast/.
32. Scott, "Interview with Margaret Loesch."
33. André Bazin, "Adaptation, or the Cinema as Digest," in *Film Adaptation*, ed. James Naremore (New Brunswick: Rutgers University Press, 2000), 26.

34. Mallory, 164.

35. Shany Golan, "Semper, John, Jr. Interview," *AnimDesk*, last modified January 31, 2014, https://www.animdesk.com/john-semper-jr.

36. Pascal Lefèvre, "Incompatible Visual Ontologies: The Problematic Adaptation of Drawn Images," in *Film and Comic Books*, edited by Ian Gordon, Mark Jancovich, and Matthew P. McAllister (Jackson: University of Mississippi Press, 2007), 3.

37. Robert C Harvey, *The Art of the Comic Book: An Aesthetic History* (Jackson: University of Mississippi Press, 1996), 175.

38. Stu Harvey and James Harvey, "Bob Richardson Talks Spider-Man: The Animated Series," *Marvel Animation Age*, last modified October 21, 2012, http://marvel.toonzone.net/spideytas/interviews/richardson/.

39. Lev Manovich, *Language of New Media* (Cambridge: MIT Press, 2002), 302.

40. Burke, 77.

41. Howe, 355.

42. Wilson Koh, "Everything Old Is Good Again: Myth and Nostalgia in Spider-Man," *Continuum* 23, no. 5 (2009): 740.

43. Stu Harvey and James Harvey, "John Semper Discusses the 10th Anniversary of Spider-Man: The Animated Series," *Marvel Animation Age*, last modified October 22, 2012, http://marvel.toonzone.net/spideytas/interviews/semper10/.

44. Ibid.

45. Howe, 355.

46. David and Greenberger, 162.

47. Gross, 154.

48. Perlmutter, 300.

49. Henry Jenkins, *Convergence Culture: Where Old and New Media Collide* (New York: New York University Press, 2006), 135.

50. The oft-cited panel from *The Amazing Spider-Man #50* in which the hero dumps his costume in a trashcan was recreated for the feature film *Spider-Man 2*.

51. Danny Fingeroth, *Superman on the Couch: What Superheroes Really Tell Us about Ourselves and Our Society* (New York: Continuum, 2005), 34; Randy Duncan and Matthew J. Smith, *The Power of Comics: History, Form and Culture* (New York: Continuum International, 2009), 120; Umberto Eco, "The Myth of Superman," *Diacritics* 2, no.1 (1972): 17.

52. Gross, 156.

53. Stu Harvey and James Harvey, "John Semper Talks Spider-Man: The Animated Series," *Marvel Animation Age*, last modified October 21, 2012, http://marvel.toonzone.net/spideytas/interviews/semper2/.

The Death of the First Marvel Television Universe

Arnold T. Blumberg

From 1978 to 1982 on the television series *The Incredible Hulk*, David Bruce Banner wandered the country a fugitive, searching for a cure for his rage-induced transformation into a green-skinned brute. When the show was cancelled, Marvel's longest-running live-action adaptation of one of its comic book characters came to an end. Six years later, Banner and his bewigged, white-eyed alter ego returned in three TV movies that not only continued his tragic adventures, but also attempted something unprecedented up to that point. In 1988's *The Incredible Hulk Returns* and 1989's *The Trial of the Incredible Hulk,* Banner met a Norse thunder god named Thor and a blind lawyer-turned-crime fighter called Daredevil. Featuring live-action Marvel heroes meeting one another and building the beginnings of a cohesive continuity for the first time—and even featuring a Stan Lee cameo years before that became a de facto requirement—these TV movies/backdoor pilots failed to draw an audience willing to follow the guest heroes into shows of their own and lacked support from the production companies. And so a Marvel Television Universe ("MTU") never materialized. When the Hulk himself perished in the final TV movie in 1990, unambiguously titled *The Death of the Incredible Hulk,* all hope of making a Marvel small screen saga died with him. But where did it go wrong, this ambitious, but ultimately unsuccessful, attempt to create a Marvel Television Universe decades before the MCU would establish itself and find its way back to the small screen via *Agents of S.H.I.E.L.D., Agent Carter,* and the many Netflix series ... including *Daredevil* himself? Was there anything they did *right*? And what would a Marvel Television Universe of the 1990s have looked like if history went a different way?

Marvel Media Hit and Miss

We truly live in the Marvel Age of Media. At the time of this writing, the latest installment in the sprawling and hugely successful Marvel Cinematic Universe, *Avengers: Age of Ultron,* is doing predictably big business at the box office around the world. With many more feature films planned, television shows on ABC and Netflix, and a plethora of merchandising tie-ins as well as the occasional comic book, Marvel, in association with parent company Disney, has triumphed over all competitors to establish a live-action universe of heroes and villains the likes of which has never before been seen in media history.

But it wasn't always like this. Rival publisher DC had shepherded flagship characters like Superman, Batman, and Wonder Woman to popular live-action film and television projects through the decades, but Marvel had managed just one *Captain America* movie serial in 1944. Not a single Marvel character appeared in American movie theaters again for forty years and when it did, it was *Howard the Duck.* After years of trying to arrange deals to see more of their characters adapted into live-action productions, Marvel found some success in that area when several of their heroes made it into people's homes via a handful of TV movie pilots in the mid- to late 1970s. While only two of them made it to series (and theaters overseas via releases of pilot and compilation films)—Spider-Man and the Hulk—it was the Green Goliath that would prove to be the runaway rampaging TV triumph that could have served as the foundation for something even grander. Decades before Robert Downey, Jr., introduced moviegoers to a Marvel Cinematic Universe, Bill Bixby might have done the same with a Marvel Television Universe on CBS and NBC.

The Incredible Hulk *Storms the Small Screen*

By 1977, the Hulk had already appeared in cartoons, and Marvel had made a deal to sell the character's movie rights, but when Universal head Frank Price acquired the rights to develop Marvel's Jade Giant into a television star along with eleven other Marvel characters in an unbelievable package deal that cost him just $12,500, he went straight to CBS. Using cardboard effigies of the characters to sell the network on live-action television shows built around the likes of Captain America, Ms. Marvel, and more, Price succeeded in convincing CBS to move ahead with pilots for two of them: Spider-Man and the Hulk.[1]

For fans watching these shows at the time, one of the most disappointing aspects of finally seeing their heroes brought to life was that their adventures were so ... ordinary. With such a rich tapestry of threats both local and cosmic, and a long litany of characters to employ in endless stories of heroic escapades, the *Spider-Man* and *Hulk* television shows disregarded the Marvel Universe in its entirety, borrowing only a few distinctive elements from both main characters and then placing them in an otherwise realistic world populated entirely by gangsters and assorted adversaries culled from police procedurals found all around the TV dial. Only on rare occasions did either series incorporate fantasy elements beyond the limited abilities of the title characters. The creative claustrophobia certainly helped to spell an early end for Spidey after two short seasons totaling just thirteen episodes aired between 1977 and 1979, although the Green Goliath proved more resilient thanks to a slightly more reasoned strategy for grounding the character in reality.

To turn the Hulk's comic book exploits into a viable television series, CBS turned to producer Kenneth Johnson, who had already impressed genre audiences as a writer and producer on *The Six Million Dollar Man* and *The Bionic Woman*. In developing the series, it was decided to test the waters by producing a two-hour pilot film that could also be released theatrically overseas. In the event, two such films were produced, both airing in November 1977. CBS was pleased by the performance of the two *Hulk* pilot films and scheduled its first run of hour-long episodes to begin mid-season in 1978. The journey of David Banner, alias the Incredible Hulk, had begun in earnest.

Johnson's decision to develop *The Incredible Hulk* around a very realistic framework, reducing the title creature's powers and size to that of a still very impressive former Mr. America (Lou Ferrigno in less-than-convincing green body paint and a fright wig), and relying heavily on the likability and tragic nuance of star Bill Bixby's portrayal of Dr. David Banner (not Bruce as in the original comic books due to a network executive declaring that name "too gay"), ultimately proved to be a sound approach. Unlike the short-lived *Spider-Man* series, which seemed to languish without exploring more fanciful scenarios, *The Incredible Hulk* captured an audience with its take on the internal dynamics of the Jekyll-and-Hyde character as he was thrust into weekly adventures that required him to aid new friends and then move on once more *à la* the show's thematic template, *The Fugitive*. As with that classic TV series, Johnson had taken inspiration from Victor Hugo's *Les Misérables,* and the result was a solid premise for a realistic Hulk saga.[2]

In every episode, Banner—on the run from reporter Jack McGee (Jack Colvin) and accused of a murder he did not commit—would adopt an alias (always maintaining his initials in a peculiar lack of concern for the potential of pattern recognition), get involved in some local trouble due to his unswerving devotion to justice and compulsion to help the underdog, suffer a beating or two thus facilitating his anger-triggered transformation into his muscled alter ego, and then by episode's end bid farewell to those he helped and sling a bag over his shoulder to wander down the road to the plaintive sound of the show's unforgettable piano-based theme tune, "The Lonely Man" by Joe Harnell.

The success of the show, due in no small part to Bixby's utter conviction in the role, left a lasting mark on pop culture and even influenced the 2008 MCU film *The Incredible Hulk* (only the second installment in that universe and a swift attempt to undo the damage caused by director Ang Lee's poorly received 2003 *Hulk*) to incorporate recognizable iconography from the TV show's origin sequence in the opening montage. By the early 1980s, no other Marvel Comics character had greater success in other media. Although the Hulk's television incarnation—or at least the world around him—was quite different that that of his comic book progenitor, it was this version of the character that made its way into millions of homes occupied by fans and non-fans alike, solidifying the Hulk's place in the upper echelons of mainstream pop culture and even boosting sales of his comics.[3]

At this point, it may be surprising to many reading today that with a long-running television series performing well in the ratings, Marvel and the production team did *not* take advantage of the opportunity to mine Marvel's back catalog for characters and stories. Imagine the impact in the early '80s if *The Incredible Hulk* had aired multi-part episodes with appearances by Nicholas Hammond's Spider-Man or Reb Brown's Captain America (whose two 1979 TV movies packed with motorcycle hijinks typical of the era were received less than favorably) or perhaps Peter Hooten's Doctor Strange (whose sole TV movie appearance during the CBS Marvel era was doomed to fail when programmed opposite *Roots*). To be fair, there were "special" episodes of the Hulk series that fans still remember fondly precisely because they pushed the boundaries in terms of fantasy, from Banner's encounter with a meteorite that temporarily altered the nature of his transformation into the Hulk to a meeting with the first man to become a green-skinned brute long before Banner tested his fateful theory. But apart from those, the chances of a CBS/Universal Marvel Television Universe, while tantalizing and at least theoretically possible, never materialized, and an Avengers or Defenders team comprised of the television versions of Spider-Man, the Hulk, Captain America, and Doctor Strange was not to be.

The Incredible Hulk was still performing well in the ratings when it was unceremoniously cancelled in 1982 with only seven episodes completed in its fifth and final season. In an attempt to dissuade CBS head of programming Harvey Shephard from going through with the cancellation, Johnson offered a season premiere event that would feature Banner transfusing blood with his sister, turning her into a "She-Hulk" (more on that later); Shephard turned him down, and Banner's television travels came to an end after 82 regular episodes in May 1982.[4]

The Marvel Television Universe: A Second Chance?

Although the possibility of something larger growing out of the *Incredible Hulk* TV series at CBS ended with its cancellation, that very same incarnation of the character would provide a second, perhaps greater opportunity to establish an MTU when he returned to the small screen after an absence of six years. The notion of bringing back the most successful live-action adaptation of a Marvel hero for a series of TV movie reunions was surely not a leap worthy of the Green Goliath himself—the viewers would be there, and Bixby's conviction would drive the new adventures as well as he did in the weekly series. But what *was* surprising was the idea that this would *not* be a return to the realistically grounded escapades seen in the original show but rather something far more fantastic in its aspirations.

Spurred by new Marvel owners New World Pictures, who were eager to expand the development of the comic book heroes into multiple live-action properties, the return of the television Hulk was spearheaded by none other than Bixby himself, only this time with the NBC network serving as the Jade Giant's home rather than CBS. Bixby never contacted Johnson to serve in any production capacity, but perhaps the huge shift in tone from realism to fantasy made Bixby realize that Johnson would never have agreed to return.[5]

Most significantly, the resurrection of the Bixby/Ferrigno Hulk was intended less to bring that character back for an extended run and more to use the Hulk's TV popularity to introduce audiences to other Marvel characters that could then go on to star in series of their own. Banner was brought back to wander that long and lonely road once again, but instead of encountering a succession of ordinary people wrestling with real-world problems, he would now meet up with fellow Marvel heroes in surprising guises. First up, a certain thunder god with a bit of an identity problem…

The Incredible Hulk Returns

Airing on May 22, 1988, only two days shy of the sixth anniversary of the show's final original first-run episode, *The Incredible Hulk Returns* saw Bixby take control as producer. He brought in former *Incredible Hulk* creative contributor Nicholas Corea (a supervising producer and producer from 1978 to 1981 as well as director, story editor and writer on multiple episodes) to serve as writer and director for this first "reunion" film, although crewmembers later revealed that Bixby also handled some of the directorial responsibilities.[6]

Beginning with basically the same title sequence and theme from the original series, *The Incredible Hulk Returns* found Banner, now using the name "Banion," living in relative peace after having avoided a transformation into the Hulk for the last two years. Banner had even found love with biogenetics expert Margaret Shaw (Lee Purcell), whose work at the Joshua Lambert Institute gave Banner the opportunity to secretly build a gamma transponder that could rid him of the Hulk forever. Unfortunately, a chance encounter with a fellow named Donald Blake (Steve Levitt) and a plot to steal the transponder interrupted Banner's plans and not only brought back his green alter ego but forced him to team up with a bizarre being from another realm known as Thor (Eric Allan Kramer).[7]

Sadly, the film's production values do not stand the test of time. Shabby settings (including an appearance by an infamous sequentially lit prop that turned up in countless productions throughout the late '80s and early '90s), stilted shooting, extremely variable Hulk makeup (to say nothing of the horrible new wig, designed to hide Ferrigno's new model hearing aid), flat lighting, amateurish synthesized music, and cheap special effects leave *The Incredible Hulk Returns* looking and sounding like a curio from a bygone era perhaps best forgotten.

More importantly, as a first attempt to introduce another Marvel hero through the Hulk, *The Incredible Hulk Returns* fell short. One of the most obvious weaknesses here was the irreconcilable clash between the realistic world that Bixby's Banner inhabited and the overtly cartoonish, mystical origin story shared by Levitt's Blake concerning his possession of Thor's hammer and control over the Thunder God's appearances. The two worlds simply did not mesh; Bixby looked incredulous during the origin storytelling and every subsequent time he had to share a scene with Kramer, which was nothing compared to the faces of many people at home.

One of the greatest strengths of the nascent MCU was the way it managed to take people to Asgard and blend Thor's tale into the growing reality of the Marvel movie series by shifting it from a story with mystical or spiritual underpinnings to a foundation in alien technology and scientific concepts. Chris Hemsworth's MCU Thor is a powerful alien being misunderstood as a god by ancient humans; in the *Returns* version, Thor was definitely a magical being, an exiled ancient Viking warrior (no Asgard here) forced to serve penance and tethered to the owner of his hammer, Donald Blake.

There are so many other missteps in the portrayal of Thor in this film, dooming any chance at building an MTU with his incarnation. Making Blake a separate individual that "channeled" the thunder god by screaming "Odin" (every *single* time) instead of an alternate identity was an unnecessary complication that undercut the potential for exploring Thor's character by seeing him in a human guise, as well as the possibility of paralleling him with Banner and the Hulk—two beings with a Jekyll and Hyde personality.

As for personality itself, Hemsworth's Thor conveys a brashness born of privilege but still possessing a deep and abiding nobility and moral center. Kramer's Thor was a beer-guzzling buffoon, a muscle-bound moron keen to punch things with little provocation and then find wine and women to cap off the evening. The resulting underpowered, carousing, and annoying Thor more closely resembled Marvel's comic book take on Hercules.[8] Both versions of Thor learn lessons of humility through variations of exile and both have a clarity of purpose when it comes to crusading for an honorable cause, but they are otherwise drastically different characters.

A fleeting image or two of the Hulk and Thor standing side by side in combat, echoing the same kind of easy pairing that would later lead to the two characters assuming a similar stance in *The Avengers*, provided too little of the sort of team-up thrills promised by the promotional material associated with *The Incredible Hulk Returns*. Even the costume and prop design failed to impress. Kramer's fur ensemble made him look less like a hero and more like a flamboyant biker wielding a mallet, while Hemsworth's far more faithful armored outfit and hefty hammer enables audiences to accept the alien Thunder "God" as a hero by appearance alone.

Although *The Incredible Hulk Returns* did so well in the ratings that a follow-up TV movie was a certainty, the many failings in the realization of Thor's character prevented any further appearances by this incarnation of the thunder god. Any remaining prospects for a Thor spinoff series died with the writers' strike that consumed Hollywood at the time and transformed the power structure at the networks. Had they conjured a Thor television show, however, Kramer foresaw exploring more of the thunder god's experiences in the real world as a man from a "much different time,"[9] perhaps echoing some of the character work now being seen via Hemsworth's Thor.

The Trial of the Incredible Hulk

Less than a year later on May 7, 1989, the Hulk was back … but without the god of thunder. Directed by Bixby with a script by Gerald Di Pego, *The Trial of the Incredible Hulk* continued the plan to establish an MTU despite a certain Viking-sized misstep. The results this time would prove far more promising, but turn out to be just as disappointing.

Now, David "Belson" Banner had relocated to a strangely generic metropolis suffering under the malevolent machinations of a master criminal named Wilson Fisk (John Rhys-Davies). A black-clad vigilante known as Daredevil had been trying to protect the city from Fisk, and when Banner ran afoul of the law and drew the attention of kindly attorney Matt Murdock (Rex Smith), he learned that Daredevil and Murdock were one and the same. The two unlikely allies then teamed up to stop Fisk and save an innocent woman named Ellie (Marta DuBois) that was caught up in the ruthless businessman's world.[10]

The music didn't get any better in this installment, but in retrospect *Trial of the Incredible Hulk* had far more right than many fans thought when it first aired. Tellingly, much of the Daredevil part of the movie—which, to be fair, was most of it—was astonishingly close in the creative choices made to those that shaped the production of the 2015 Netflix *Daredevil* series, from the dynamics of the struggle between Murdock and the master manipulator Fisk (in both adaptations, his familiar comic book name "The Kingpin" was never uttered) to the design of Murdock's superhero guise.

The all-black ensemble with mask that completely covered his eyes was met with derision in 1989—what hero would lose his strategic advantage and reveal to his opponents that he's blind by wearing something that clearly obscures his vision? Three years later, Frank Miller's 1993–1994 five-issue miniseries, *Daredevil: The Man Without Fear*, retroactively added details to the beginning of Murdock's quest for justice, revealing that he wore very similar clothes before adopting his distinctive red garb. By the time the Netflix series took inspiration from Miller's work and utilized a nearly identical black outfit to the *Trial* movie, including the eye-covering bandana, no one was outraged, especially since the thirteen-episode run concluded with the revelation of a version of Daredevil's traditional red costume. For all we know, a *Daredevil* series born of the *Trial* movie might one day have done the same.

Daredevil's origin was also handled almost as faithfully in *Trial* as in the 2015 series, although off camera. *Trial* made note of his boxer father, as well as the incident with the old man in the street and the toxic waste truck that led to Murdock's blindness and enhanced senses. The one major addition was the relationship with police Captain Tendelli, whose Commissioner Gordon–like role and "Daredevilphone" put this version of the character more in line with DC's Batman. *Trial* also inexplicably omitted Murdock's friends Foggy Nelson and Karen Page, replacing them with cyphers Christa Klein and Al Pettiman, while the firm Nelson & Murdock unnecessarily became Murdock & Klein.

If Rhys-Davies' Fisk was nowhere near as nuanced a portrayal as that of Vincent D'Onofrio in the 2015 *Daredevil*, neither was he as sympathetic a villain as the latter incarnation. He was, however, effective enough to have warranted a return should the Smith Daredevil have continued into a weekly series. Rhys-Davies even had a commitment to the role that went above and beyond the call of duty; while he appeared with hair and a beard, he had offered to shave himself bald in keeping with the character's comic book look. In the end, the production team proceeded with a hirsute Fisk. Hair or no hair, Fisk was fine as a foe, and even had a satisfyingly realistic goal: he wasn't out for world domination, he just wanted to unite all organized crime into a national syndicate under his control. He did inhabit a base that seemed far more elaborate and Bondian than would be warranted by his operations, but we'll let him have his ostentatious display of chrome and glass villainy. It is baffling, though, where all of the references to video and performance were heading; was Fisk supposed to be a frustrated television producer?

This is not to say that *Trial* didn't fall short of what it could have been. One of the missteps was certainly in the choice of setting. Rather than establish Matt Murdock and his crime-fighting alter ego in the environs of Hell's Kitchen, as much a character in Daredevil's saga as any actual individual inhabitant of that beleaguered neighborhood, the adventure played out in the aforementioned generic metropolis (shot in Vancouver) that offered none of the gritty distinction that should accompany a corrupt city desperately in need of Daredevil's heroic presence. The town was bright and clean, not swathed in shadow and soot, and Murdock didn't even live down in the streets with the people he wanted to save, removing himself instead to a sprawling, well-appointed penthouse rather than the cavernous, cathedral-like den of his 2015 counterpart.

Perhaps the biggest flaw in the story of *Trial* was that the Hulk wound up as a supporting player in his own film, and not much of one. He was a reactive rather than proactive (or even active) character, his escape from prison—a prime opportunity for some green-skinned action—took place entirely off screen, and he was absent for the entire final act of the film, remaining on the sidelines while Daredevil took care of business. Perhaps Banner's only significant contributions were to provide a crucial pep talk to Murdock when he began to lose heart in his battle against Fisk, and his admittedly moving reference to Murdock as a "brother in the world."

Still, Daredevil meshed much more organically with Bixby's Hulk saga than Thor and provided a far more viable option for a 1990s MTU. Sadly, however, the future for Smith's Daredevil was the same as Kramer's Thor, even though Smith was temporarily on track to have his own series with Bixby serving as producer and director of multiple episodes. Development of the project switched from NBC to ABC, where it was doomed to languish and die.[11] ABC did preside over the completion of at least one draft of a *Daredevil* pilot script before ending development; the writer was Stirling Silliphant, an Academy Award winner whose work included feature films *In the Heat of the Night*, *The Towering Inferno*, and *The Poseidon Adventure*, as well as television series like *Perry Mason*, *Alfred Hitchcock Presents*, and *Naked City*, a particularly grimy look at crime in the city that was perfectly in keeping with the street-based adventures of a horned Hell's Kitchen hero like Daredevil. But even Silliphant's credentials didn't protect the Man Without Fear from the executives with the axe at ABC.[12]

While ABC's decision to acquire and bury the show was the primary reason *Daredevil* didn't happen at the time despite the movie's success in the ratings, there were larger issues that might have prematurely ended any expansion of a Marvel Television Universe, which can best be summed up as a case of unfortunate timing. About a month after *Trial* aired, Tim Burton's *Batman* arrived in theaters and forever transformed the way mainstream audiences perceived the superhero genre. The bar had most definitely been raised, and when compared to the big budget treatment of the Dark Knight, Daredevil's *Trial* debut—with its garish cinematography, synth score, and stilted dialogue—couldn't hope to compete. Where *Batman* embraced some of the most comic-like aspects of its main character and took moviegoers to school, training them to appreciate everything that comic book heroes had to offer, *Trial* was still of an era where superheroes were watered down to near unrecognizability in order to appeal to an audience unfamiliar with their exploits.

The Death of the Incredible Hulk ... *and Beyond*

The night of February 18, 1990, brought the debut of what was to be the television Hulk's final adventure, but *The Death of the Incredible Hulk* also generated disappointment through the fan viewing community on several levels. Once again directed by Bixby and written by Di Pego, the movie had a title that seemed to signal the end of the revival that had begun with *The Incredible Hulk Returns* (although comic book fans certainly knew that death was hardly if ever to be taken seriously when their heroes were concerned). Advance word on the plot of the movie, meanwhile, made another thing clear: there would be no appearance by another Marvel character as with the previous two installments. Although Russian espionage agent Jasmin (Elizabeth Gracen) might have shared some traits with the Black Widow, now played by Scarlett Johannson in the MCU, there was no overt attempt to draw any parallels with any comic book counterpart or any indication that this connection was ever intentional.[13]

In later years, various interviews with key players behind the scenes revealed that there could have been a number of additional Hulk "team-up" adventures, including one featuring the return of the *Spider-Man* cast led by Nicholas Hammond as well as an installment introducing Iron Man. A fourth TV movie, tentatively titled *Revenge of the Incredible Hulk* or *Rebirth of the Incredible Hulk*, was also planned, and Bixby was actively shopping it to the networks. Despite stories that claim Bixby's declining health due to prostate cancer (the condition that ultimately led to his death in 1993) put an end to development of future TV movies, some colleagues including Di Pego asserted that NBC had already called a halt to any plans due to the massive ratings drop suffered by *Death*.[14]

There were also extensive plans for a pilot that would launch a series based on *She-Hulk,* with Bill Bixby's Banner returning to set the title character on the road to superheroism. *Incredible Hulk* producer and writer Jill Sherman Donner was brought in by New World in 1990 at the behest of Bixby to spearhead the development of the pilot, which would have revealed that Banner had faked his death in *Death* (that helicopter fall looked pretty convincing) and retreated to the Caribbean, where he would wind up helping assistant district attorney Jennifer Walters after a near-fatal shooting by giving her a blood transfusion. Gabrielle Reece was already cast for the role of She-Hulk, one that would mirror Ferrigno's Hulk by being similarly mute and animalistic, with Mitzi Kapture as alter ego Walters. Oddly enough, Donner decided that Reece's She-Hulk would have been colored gold rather than green; her eyes would have been emerald-hued however, framed by shockingly red hair.[15] Although production apparently began, the powers that be were unhappy with Kapture and the project was cancelled before much material had been shot (including none of Reece as She-Hulk).[16]

A character whose comic book series was originally created at the behest of Stan Lee expressly for the purpose of heading off any attempts by Universal to create a similar character and own the rights to her independently of Marvel,[17] She-Hulk could have offered another path toward creating an extended television universe for live-action Marvel adaptations. But the troubled pilot development eventually led nowhere. As we can see, there's an unfortunate pattern to the fate of all these productions that guaranteed a 1990s MTU was fated never to exist.

The MTU That Never Was

As we've seen, there are a number of reasons why a CBS/Universal or NBC/New World Marvel Television Universe never happened. As far as the CBS era is concerned, with only *The Incredible Hulk* succeeding out of the multiple projects attempted, there wasn't much upon which to build. The failures of *Spider-Man, Doctor Strange,* and *Captain America* would have required introducing still more Marvel characters in the hopes of expanding the universe beyond the Hulk's lonely journey, and that wasn't going to happen as long as there was no actual desire to try. By the time CBS was rolling out its few Marvel offerings, the executive that had brought the heroes to the network was gone. In his place was someone that feared CBS becoming a "cartoon network."[18]

A bigger issue for either network was the lack of a central creative guiding hand like Marvel Studios' current guru, Kevin Feige, whose every decision shapes the ever-growing MCU and keeps all the various production components consistent with one another and in service to the power of the building brand. In the latter days of the Hulk TV movie revival, the only figure that might have come close to that role was Bixby. The potential for Bixby to take a leading position in shaping the MTU was considerable, not least because of his positive relationship with virtually everyone involved in the production process. *Trial*'s Daredevil himself, Rex Smith, commented that everyone making the movie "had a personal friendship, on top of a working relationship" with the star. Smith's observation that Bixby possessed a powerful combination of "confidence and style" might suggest that should plans have moved forward, it was David Banner himself that might have shepherded an interconnected MTU in existence at NBC.[19] Sadly, his death in 1993 would have precluded any progress on that front.

As for the ubiquitous face of Marvel, Stan Lee, his role has always been as that of a visible figurehead and embodiment of the creative enterprise, putting in his requisite appearances in each MCU film (a gimmick that actually began with his appearance as jury foreperson in the dream sequence of *Trial*!) and their related promotional campaigns with all of his trademark enthusiasm. But "The Man" himself probably derailed whatever might have developed back at CBS when he publicly groused about the shortcomings of the *Spider-Man* television show. Despite his praise for Johnson's realistic take on the Hulk, the negative comments could not have been received well.

Speaking of Johnson, could *he* have become the Kevin Feige of his time? It seems unlikely. He was already long gone when the New World/NBC projects came about, and indeed, he was a bit perplexed by Bixby's lack of communication about them. And when he was helming the CBS television series, his interest was with that show only; even that was a hard sell for the network without offering him an additional incentive in the form of an adaptation of *Ivanhoe* that was then never made.[20] Ultimately, we're left with no known figure that could have assumed the role of an MTU guru.

Conclusion

Today it's hard to believe that the potential of a vast universe of Marvel movies and TV shows eluded so many executives for so long. And although today we live in a renaissance of live-action superhero adaptations, including a Marvel Cinematic Universe that has grown into multiple television series as well, there was however briefly the possibility that a Marvel Television Universe might have grown and even flourished on CBS in the 1980s or NBC in the 1990s. In that alternate reality—dubbed Earth-400005 by the online Marvel Database[21]—Lou Ferrigno's Incredible Hulk stood shoulder to shoulder with Eric Allan Kramer's Thor, Rex Smith's Daredevil, Nicholas Hammond's Spider-Man, Peter Hooten's Doctor Strange, Reb Brown's Captain America, Gabrielle Reece's She-Hulk, and who knows how many others in a television team of Marvel heroes dedicated to defending the Earth and avenging every wrong perpetrated on the innocent.

Notes

1. Sean Howe, *Marvel Comics: The Untold Story* (New York: Harper Perennial, 2012), 195–196.
2. Glenn Greenberg, "The Televised Hulk," *Back Issue!* 70 (2014): 21.
3. Howe, *Marvel Comics*, 205.
4. Greenberg, "The Televised Hulk," 24.
5. Ibid.
6. Ibid.
7. *The Incredible Hulk Returns*, directed by Nicholas Corea (1988; Image Entertainment, 2011), DVD.
8. Eric Goldman, "Thor's TV History," *IGN*, last modified November 6, 2013, http://www.ign.com/articles/2013/11/06/the-avengers-thors-tv-history.
9. John Bierly, "Interview: Eric Allan Kramer," *Impact*, last modified June 15, 2013, http://www.johnbierly.com/118.
10. *The Trial of the Incredible Hulk*, directed by Bill Bixby (1989; Image Entertainment, 2011), DVD.
11. Bierly, "Interview: Eric Allan Kramer," *Impact*.
12. Howe, *Marvel Comics*, 261.
13. *The Death of the Incredible Hulk*, directed by Bill Bixby (1990; 20th Century–Fox Home Entertainment, 2003), DVD.

14. Greenberg, "The Televised Hulk," 26.
15. Brian Cronin, "Comic Book Legends Revealed #499," *Comic Book Resources,* last modified November 27, 2014, http://goodcomics.comicbookresources.com/2014/11/27/comic-book-legends-revealed-499/2/.
16. Brian Cronin, "TV Legends Revealed: Did Bill Bixby Star in a She-Hulk Pilot," *Comic Book Resources,* last modified November 26, 2014, http://spinoff.comicbookresources.com/2014/11/26/tv-legends-revealed-did-bill-bixby-star-in-a-she-hulk-pilot/.
17. Howe, *Marvel Comics,* 220–221.
18. Ibid., 215.
19. Bierly, "Interview: Eric Allan Kramer," *Impact.*
20. Brian Hiatt, "How 'The Incredible Hulk' Conquered Seventies TV," *Rolling Stone,* last modified May 1, 2015, http://www.rollingstone.com/tv/features/how-the-incredible-hulk-conquered-seventies-tv-20150501.
21. "Earth-400005," *Marvel Database,* http://marvel.wikia.com/Earth-400005.

Frozen in Ice
Captain America's Arduous Journey to the Silver Screen

David Ray Carter

Marvel's Captain America was ranked as the sixth "greatest superhero of all time" by online magazine *IGN*, and the character's inclusion near the top of that list could be seen as surprising.[1] While Captain America has for some time been one of the most recognizable figures in comics, he was at the time the highest ranked character not to have had a commercially successful film or television series; only one of two such heroes in the list's top ten. By way of comparison, the five superheroes ranked ahead of Captain America had been involved in no fewer than twenty five live-action adaptations, all of which were massive commercial hits and had been made after Captain America's creation in 1941. Even characters considered significantly less important, like the 90th-ranked Ghost Rider, had been made into moderately successful feature films, further highlighting the conspicuous lack of a successful Captain America adaptation.

Captain America finally joined the ranks of successful, modern superhero adaptations with 2011's *Captain America: The First Avenger* from Marvel Studios and Paramount Pictures, a film that eventually grossed more than double its substantial budget. *First Avenger*'s timing and subtitle demonstrate its importance to the Marvel Cinematic Universe (MCU). *Captain America* was the final chapter in the build up to Marvel's *coup de grace*, 2012's *Marvel's The Avengers*, currently the fifth highest-grossing film of all time and, as such, the most successful superhero film of all time by a considerable margin.[2] As with his showing on the *IGN* list, Captain America's placement in such an esteemed position was something of an enigma. Of his fellow Avengers comprising the MCU's "first wave," Captain America was the only one to have had *bona fide* critical and commercial failures in the past. Captain America was alone in this distinction on the IGN list as well, being the only hero to have a checkered past with regard to cinematic or television adaptations, with the notable exception of the much lower-ranked Supergirl.

Captain America's lack of a successful live-action adaptation was not due to a lack of effort. To fully appreciate the magnitude of Marvel's success with *First Avenger* and its sequel, *Captain America: The Winter Soldier*, it is necessary to more closely examine the previous, failed attempts to adapt the character. Captain America had been the subject of a 1944 serial, two 1979 television movies, and a 1990 film. None of these efforts, however, can be viewed as being successful from a critical or commercial standpoint, and they have also not been held in any esteem by comic book fans. Although these works share the same source material as the more recent successful versions, each was made in a different time for a different audience. In these earlier works we find distinct versions of the character that are at times familiar but often wildly divergent from the Captain America of the comics. Through an analysis of the unique reasons why each version was unsuccessful, we will more clearly see which elements of the MCU's version of the character contributed to its eventual triumph with fans.

Soldier Without a War: The Republic Serial

Adaptations of comic book superheroes in other media began in earnest in 1940, when DC Comics' Superman joined his pulp and newspaper strip counterparts in making the leap into his own syndicated radio show.[3] The following year saw comic book adaptations taking the logical next step into movie serials with the release of Republic Pictures' *The Adventures of Captain Marvel*, starring the Fawcett Comics character.[4] Fawcett's Captain Marvel became property of DC Comics in the 1970s, as did the star of the second Republic/Fawcett adaptation, *Spy Smasher*, featuring the character of the same name. Columbia Pictures entered the comic adaptation market with 1943's *Batman* and Republic looked again to comics in 1944 for the inspiration of a new, fifteen-chapter serial: *Captain America*.[5] Captain America's big screen debut therefore predates that of the more popular Superman by several years, a curious fact and one that played a large role in how *Captain America* came to be.

As the fourth comic book superhero to star in a movie serial, Captain America occupies a prestigious place in superhero cinema history. However, the serial also has the distinction of being the first such adaptation to break significantly from its source material. The aforementioned *Adventures of Captain Marvel*, *Spy Smasher*, and especially *Batman* made changes to their subjects based on budgetary limitations or what producers believed would appeal more to audiences. Yet the hero depicted in *Captain America* is not simply a modified version of the one seen in *Captain America Comics*; he is literally a different person. *Captain America* contains almost none of the character's most readily identifiable traits, something that is most likely Republic's intention.

The hero of *Captain America* is District Attorney Grant Gardner, not wimp-turned-*übermensch* Steve Rogers.[6] Gardner has no superhuman abilities, just a keen mind and above-average fighting skills. In lieu of the Captain's trademark shield, Gardner's Captain carries a pistol, which he uses liberally against several of his enemies. Captain America is not supported by his sidekick Bucky Barnes, but by Gail Richards, Gardner's attractive but formidable assistant. The largest break from the source material was in Captain America's *raison d'être*, however. Despite the fact that America was still involved in both the European and Pacific theatres at the time, no mention at all is made of World War II, the Nazis, or the Axis Powers. *Captain America* sees the hero face off with the Scarab, a villain with no designs on world domination.

In the serial's first chapter, *The Purple Death*, we learn the secret identities of both Captain America and the Scarab. The Scarab is in fact Dr. Cyrus Maldor (Lionel Atwell), a museum curator who uses the hypnotic drug "the purple death" to compel his former partners into committing suicide. The police fail to stop the murders, so the mayor enlists the help of District Attorney Gardner, who is known for using his friendship with the mysterious Captain America to solve tough cases. Gardner/America deduces the Scarab's next victim, but arrives too late to save him; his involvement, however, alerts the villain to his existence and the Scarab shifts his focus to stopping Captain America.

Subsequent chapters follow the standard cliffhanger formula as the Scarab uses experimental technology taken from his scientist victims to menace Captain America. Although *Captain America* was Republic's most expensive serial to date, most of these devices are not actually used, as Captain America always thwarts the Scarab at the final moment and, thus, his plans did not have to be realized (expensively) on screen. In contrast to most serial heroes of the day, *Captain America* spends little time on dialogue and devotes the majority of its fifteen chapters to start-to-finish action. Compared with Columbia's talkative *Batman*, *Captain America* is the more exciting of the two despite its deviations from the comic source. Captain America is actually killed via explosion in chapter nine's conclusion in one of the better-realized cliffhanger moments from superhero serials. Chapter ten is renamed *The Return of Captain America: The Avenging Corpse*, but subsequent chapters do not feature the new title.

Captain America is an entertaining and well-made serial, rivaling *The Adventures of Captain Marvel* as the pinnacle of comic book serials.[7] *Captain America* has aged better than the four DC Comics costumed hero serials—*Batman*, *Superman*, *Batman and Robin*, and *Atom Man vs. Superman*—which, despite financial success, were considered subpar serials at the time. The significant changes to the character are problematic, however, when analyzing it as a true representation of the character. The aforementioned DC Comics properties have their faults, but each was in some ways additive to the mythos of those characters, with key aspects such as the Batcave and Kryptonite appearing the serials prior to their comic book debuts. *Captain America* bore such little resemblance to the Simon and Kirby character that no such cross-media influence took place, and the serial had little to no effect on its comic counterpart.

There is evidence to support the idea that *Captain America* was a name-only adaptation, ironically stemming from a rights issue when attempting to adapt Superman for the silver screen. Paramount Pictures had a claim to Superman through their cartoon series, which forced Republic to rework a planned 1940 adaptation into *The Mysterious Dr. Satan*, starring a Batman-esque hero, Copperhead. The similarities between Copperhead and the Grant Gardner Captain America are such that Harmon and Glut posit that *Captain America* was originally conceived as a sequel to *The Mysterious Dr. Satan* and thus linked Captain America to the aborted Superman project.[8] The authors also note that Timely balked at Republic's changes to the character, but that Republic stood firm on depicting their version. Harmon and Glut's theory is speculation, and with the wide array of similarities between comic book characters, pulp heroes, and serial heroes in the 1940s, it is difficult to accurately determine the true inspiration for *Captain America*. Adding another complication is the fact that Columbia's 1943 *Batman* changed the character to essentially be Captain America: a government agent fighting a Japanese mad scientist. Furthermore, the Captain America of the comic books was not dissimilar to Fawcett's Spy Smasher, the subject of a Republic serial in 1942; a more likely reason for *Captain America*'s break from the comics, then, is Republic's desire for a unique product.

Captain America has little relation to the modern conception of the character, but is less removed from the version depicted in *Captain America Comics* of the period than has been previously observed. Though the costumed Captain America eschewed firearms in favor of his fists, both Steve Rogers and Bucky Barnes are shown using machine guns in their Army garb in issues #2 and #4, respectively.[9,10] The bulk of *Captain America Comics*' stories from 1941 to the time of the serial's production in 1944 dealt with World War II–themed villains, but as early as *Captain America Comics* #6, the Captain and Bucky were squaring off against the Camera Fiend, Fang, and the Hangman, all of whom have more in common with *Captain America*'s Scarab than with the Red Skull.[11] By 1943, Captain America's involvement in the war was often limited to the covers only, such as April 1943's #25, which features the Captain and a machine gun wielding Bucky fighting the Japanese on a snowy mountainside, but internally has the duo tackling demons and interdimensional giants.[12] Some issues feature Betty (later Betsy) Ross as a companion to Captain America serving the same purpose as *Captain America*'s Gail Richards: a damsel-in-distress or, alternatively, a capable assistant, depending on the story. A multi-issue storyline in 1978 saw Captain America revealing that he played himself in the movie serial and made the changes to protect his identity.[13]

Post–World War II, *Captain America Comics* morphed into a strictly crime-fighting title with rare political overtones, more related to the changing political landscape than to the influence of the serial. Though briefly revived as "Captain America.... Commie Smasher!" for three issues in 1954, *Captain America Comics* stopped production and the character would not be seen again until Marvel's *The Avengers* #4, which saw Jack Kirby and Stan Lee revive the character both had worked on during his original 1941 to 1954 run.[14] Captain America's Golden Age compatriots the Sub-Mariner and the Human Torch had both previously been revived by Marvel in changed incarnations, but Captain America was reintroduced as the same character as seen in the Timely comics, with the Avengers acknowledging his status as a legendary crime-fighter.

Despite the popularity of the revived Captain America, it would be quite some time before he reappeared in other media. Spurred on by the success of the *Batman* television series, Marvel released *The Marvel Super Heroes* in 1966, an animated series consisting of vignettes starring Captain America, Iron Man, Thor, Sub-Mariner, and the Hulk. Though poorly animated by 1966 standards, the shorts were extremely faithful to the source material and were often verbatim remakes of specific comic issues.

Captain America in the Seventies: Turkey and Television

A live-action Captain America would not be seen again until 1973 in one of the most bizarre films in the annals of superhero cinema, the Turkish film *3 Dev Adam*. Literally translated as "three giant men" or "three mighty men," the film is also known by the more descriptive title *Captain America and Santo vs. Spider-Man*. The plot of the film is exactly that. Criminal mastermind Spider-Man's counterfeiting scheme is challenged by the national heroes of the United States and Mexico, Captain America and *luchador* El Santo, respectively. The trio of heroes resembles their more well-known counterparts in name and costume only, with such notable deviations as El Santo removing his mask and Spider-Man's depiction as a sadistic killer. *3 Dev Adam* has become a cult classic for its outlandish depictions of known characters despite the fact that an English-subtitled version was not available until 2008 in a limited-run DVD edition. As strange as it may seem to western audiences, *3 Dev Adam* was by no means anomalous for Turkish action cinema in the early seventies. Exploitation cinema regularly ignored copyrights to produce cheaply made versions of popular films, and this was especially true in Turkey, where properties were more closely tied to their source materials. Captain America and Spider-Man were not the only comic book characters to appear in Turkish cinema; Pete Tombs and Giovanni Scognamillo observed that the primary influence in Turkish cinema of the period was American serials of the 1940s.[15] It should then come as no surprise that while *3 Dev Adam*'s Captain America has little to do with his comic counterpart, he is almost an exact copy of the Grant Gardner version seen in Republic's *Captain America*. *Captain America*'s acrobatic fighting style and lack of a shield are both clues, but perhaps most telling is the lack of wings on the hero's head; an obscure, minor detail shared by both.

It would be the late seventies before Captain America would be seen again in an official live-action adaptation. Marvel had missed out on the "Batmania" of the midsixties, but partnered with CBS to bring several properties to life in the seventies, including the short-lived *The Amazing Spider-Man* and the more successful *The Incredible Hulk*. Both series began their lives as made-for-TV movies, so Marvel used the same approach in bringing Dr. Strange and Captain America to television in 1978 and 1979. *Dr. Strange* had the misfortune of airing opposite *Roots* and was not optioned for a series, but *Captain America* was successful enough to be followed by a sequel later the same year.

Captain America, 1979, is more faithful to its source material than the 1944 serial, but still makes drastic changes to the character.[16] After serving in the Marines, Steve Rogers decides to spend his life as an artist, travelling the California coast in a customized van. Stopping in at a friend's residence, he finds that an old friend, Hayden, and the mysterious Dr. Simon Mills have been attempting to contact him. Rogers is attacked by unknown saboteurs en route to see Dr. Mills, but he is even more shocked by what he learns upon his arrival. Mills was the partner of Rogers' father, a brilliant scientist who invented FLAG—Full Latent Ability Gain—a "super steroid" that can unlock anyone's physical and mental potential. Mills has been unsuccessful in testing FLAG, and believes that the younger Rogers' shared genetic traits with his father make him a prime candidate for the serum. Steve declines Mills' offer, preferring the life of a travelling artist to potential death as a test subject.

Steve arrives at his friend Hayden's home only to find the man dying, attacked by another unknown assailant. Mills arrives soon after and informs Steve that Hayden had been working on the hydrogen bomb and was suspected of selling classified secrets. Steve refuses to believe this and works to find Hayden's killers on his own, but he is nearly killed when he confronts a gang claiming to be responsible. Rather than letting him die, Mills injects Steve with FLAG against his previous wishes, saving his life and giving him the superhuman abilities Mills and the elder Rogers hoped it would. Rogers still refuses to work for Mills, denying even a (off-screen) request from the President, but eventually acquiesces after Mills proposes he take on the "Captain America" moniker given to his father, complete with a costumed identity. As Captain America, Steve foils a plot to detonate a hydrogen bomb in Phoenix and later agrees to continue to help the government when his special abilities are needed.

The Captain America of the comics had evolved beyond his World War II origins by 1979, but *Captain America* ignores all comic plotlines of the sixties and seventies for an interpretation of the character more akin to television's *The Incredible Hulk*. The updated origin story of the film borrows elements from the original but likely seemed a more plausible alternative to the unfrozen Nazi-fighter of the comics. CBS' version presented an updated version of the Captain's costume that more closely resembled that of Evel Knievel, a change that was likely intentional given the large amount of time the film devotes to motorcycle stunts. Furthering the importance of motorcycles to the plot, the Captain wears a motorcycle helmet instead of his cowl, and his shield doubles as his motorcycle's windshield. In the movie's climactic scene, Steve is shown wearing the comic book version of his costume.

This final scene unites the comic and television versions of the character, but also serves to highlight the biggest flaws with CBS' *Captain America*. Donning the familiar costume, Rogers announces that he's going to serve the government dressed as his father did— the first and only time the film mentions the elder Rogers being a costumed hero. Similar continuity issues and poor acting performances throughout hamper the film far more than the changes to the Captain America mythos. As noted above, depicting Captain America as a wandering, reluctant hero was most likely done to add similarity to the popular *Incredible Hulk* series, although *Captain America*'s reluctant hero is more likely viewed as cowardly rather than simply hesitant.[17] Steve Rogers' initial refusal to help Mills appears to be a selfish act and is the most jarring difference between the televised and comic versions.

In November of 1979, Captain America returned to CBS in *Captain America II: Death Too Soon*, broadcast over two nights.[18] The more-straightforward plot pits Captain America against Christopher Lee's General Miguel, who douses Portland with a rapid-aging chemical and offers to sell the U.S. government the antidote for a massive ransom. More accomplished than its predecessor in several regards, *Captain America II* more closely resembles the comic version of the character and, indeed, has a more fantastical, stereotypical "comic book" plot than other superhero media of the period. Continuity issues are improved significantly, and the film is helped immensely by the presence of Christopher Lee, despite it not being his best work.

Though neither film is a direct adaptation of the comics, both *Captain America* and *Captain America II: Death Too Soon* are not far removed from the stories told in *Captain America/Captain America and the Falcon* during the mid- to late seventies. It was not uncommon for the Captain to battle mad scientists and would-be world conquerors in between skirmishes with costumed villains, aliens, and monsters. They share some consistencies, but regular readers of *Captain America* would have not viewed CBS' version as the same character. The televised Captain spends the majority of time out of costume, while Captain America was rarely seen as Steve Rogers in his own title or in *The Avengers*. While a limited inclusion of the title hero worked well in *The Incredible Hulk*, the large focus on Steve Rogers over Captain America is ultimately the films' biggest flaw.

Neither *Captain America* nor *Captain America II* was particularly impactful with audiences. The popularity of superhero television series was on the wane, with CBS ending production on *The Amazing Spider-Man* and *Wonder Woman* before the end of 1979. This, coupled with a desire by the network to no longer be viewed as "the superhero channel," likely had as much to do with the failure of *Captain America* to make the leap into a series as the shortcomings of the films themselves. Both were released theatrically in European markets, a common practice at the time and the same route taken by the first and final episodes of *The Amazing Spider-Man*.

Off Broadway and Direct-to-Video: The 1980s and 1990s

It would be over a decade before Captain America was seen in a live-action format again. Again, this was not due to a lack of effort on the part of Marvel and others in the entertainment industry. Producer Shari Upbin spent three years in the mid-eighties unsuccessfully trying to get a Captain America musical off the ground, first on Broadway and later off Broadway.[19] Completed, but never performed, little is known about the project other than *Blazing Saddles* star Cleavon Little was at one point attached as a villain.

A proposed Captain America film did not fare any better. Producers Menahem Golan and Yorum Globus of the Cannon Group purchased the rights to both Captain America and Spider-Man in 1984, placing ads in *Variety* in both that year and the following announcing the production.[20] Cannon primarily released low-budget horror and exploitation films and would occasionally purchase the rights to existing properties in order to make sequels, as was the case with *Superman IV: The Quest for Peace*. Erroneously calling Captain America "Stan Lee's Marvel comic strip character," trade ads listed James R. Silk, a screenwriter for several low-budget Cannon projects, as being attached.[21] *Death Wish* series director Michael Winner would later be attached as director of the film, but by the decade's end both he and Silke would be replaced, and the film would be stalled by financial troubles at Cannon.[22]

Captain America was eventually made after Golan left Cannon for 21st Century Film Corporation and, more importantly, after the massive critical and commercial success of Tim Burton's 1989 *Batman*. Completed and scheduled for release in 1990, it was only briefly released theatrically in the United Kingdom and did not arrive in the United States until being released direct-to-video in 1992. Directed by Albert Pyun, *Captain America*'s production troubles had taken their toll, resulting in a film that underwhelmed despite being the most faithful adaptation of the character then to date.

Captain America opens with the origin story not of Captain America, but rather of the Red Skull.[23] A young Italian boy is taken from his family by the Fascists and given an experimental serum created by fascist scientist Dr. Vaselli that will enhance his mental and physical abilities but horribly disfigure him. Dr. Vaselli objects to seeing her work used in such a manner and flees to America, refining her formula for use in the U.S. government's super-soldier program. Steve Rogers, a disabled young man, is chosen for the project—codename: Captain America—but is the only successful test subject; Dr. Vaselli is murdered immediately after Rogers is transformed. Given a red, white, and blue costume and indestructible shield of Vaselli's design, Rogers as Captain America is dropped into a Nazi stronghold to prevent the launch of a rocket capable of reaching the White House. Captain America is handily defeated by the better-trained Red Skull and strapped to the rocket, getting a small measure of revenge by forcing the Red Skull to cut off his own hand before being launched. Captain America manages to divert the rocket from its course, but is photographed by a young boy in the process, and ultimately crashes in Alaska, where he is buried in ice.

Fifty years later, Captain America is accidentally discovered by a team of researchers and emerges alive from the block of ice. In the intervening years, the Red Skull has hidden his identity through plastic surgery and leads a cabal of wealthy and powerful men responsible for the assassinations of JFK, RFK, and Martin Luther King, Jr. Their next target is President Thomas Kimball, coincidentally the young boy who saw Captain America save the White House. Recognizing the Captain in a news article, Kimball dispatches his friend and reporter Sam Kolawetz to find him, but Captain America refuses to believe that it is really fifty years in the future and escapes upon seeing that Kolawetz carries a Japanese tape recorder. Lost in a world he doesn't understand, Steve Rogers makes his way to the home of his former girlfriend, now an elderly woman.

The Red Skull has President Kimball kidnapped during an environmental summit in Rome. Fearing that assassination would turn Kimball into a martyr, the Red Skull's cabal instead plans to place a mind control device in him, effectively turning the Presidency over to the Red Skull. This spurs Rogers to don the Captain America uniform once again, and he travels to Italy with Sharon, the daughter of his 1940s girlfriend, in tow. An encounter with Skull's daughter Valentina leads them to the cabal's hideout and a second confrontation between Captain America and the Red Skull with the life of the president and the fate of southern Europe hanging in the balance.

Captain America is more faithful to the comics than its predecessors but shares with them low production values and an inadequate cast. Made for less than a fifth of the budget afforded to Tim Burton's *Batman*, the 1990 *Captain America* barely improves on the visual aesthetics seen in its 1979 predecessor. Budget appears to have dictated both the narrative and the structure of the film. The Red Skull's plastic surgery allows for him to be seen in his traditional depiction only once, Rogers spends very little time in costume, and the action moves to Europe (with its lower shooting costs) at the first opportunity. In another cost-saving move, Matt Salinger was tapped to play the Captain despite having never had a previous starring role. Salinger did bring a small amount of name recognition to the role, however; he's the son of reclusive author J.D. Salinger. Pyun's direction is capable here and superior to many of his other outings, and many of the film's problems originate rather more with the script by crime novelist Lawrence J. Block and television scriptwriter Stephen Tolkin. *Captain America* features a well-realized villain with clear motivations in the form of the Red Skull, and relegates Captain America to a two-dimensional foil with little purpose.

The 1990 *Captain America* was, however, the first adaptation of the character to include an accurate version of his comic costume and the version of his origin seen in *Captain America Comics* #1 and revised in *The Avengers* #4. It also distinguishes itself by being the first to pit the Captain against his nemesis the Red Skull, and furthermore the first to even mention the Nazis or World War II. However the fact that it gets these elements correct makes the reasoning behind the changes the film does make all the more confusing. The Red Skull is changed from being German to Italian, with no reason for the modification being obvious (with the possible exception of allowing the film to take place in Europe, as *Captain America* was filmed prior to German reunification). Steve Rogers' boyhood home is moved from New York to California; again most likely a change dictated more for budgetary than artistic reasons.

Except for a comic adaptation of the film, Pyun's *Captain America* had little influence over the *Captain America* comic book of the early nineties, but surprisingly *Captain America: The First Avenger* incorporated several ideas that were first seen in the 1990 film. The 1990 *Captain America*'s plot point of the Red Skull being an earlier, imperfect version of the super-soldier was incorporated into *The First Avenger* with few changes. Additionally, the manner in which Captain America became encased in ice was ascribed to a plot by Baron Zemo in *Captain America* #112. *Captain America* 1990 assigns this responsibility to the Red Skull, with the culprit and method being the same as seen in *The First Avenger*: a long-range weapon capable of reaching the United States.

Captain America: The First Avenger and its sequel *The Winter Soldier* set box office records and are among the most popular entries in the Marvel Cinematic Universe, a remarkable feat regardless of the circumstances, but one made all the more impressive by the fact that four official attempts to bring Captain America to life prior to that were unsuccessful. *The First Avenger* had the largest budget of any Captain America project to date, but ultimately it was the fact that it avoided the pitfalls of its predecessors that made it resonate with audiences. *The First Avenger* avoided making the unnecessary changes to the Captain America mythos that diminished the 1944 and 1979 attempts. More important, however, is the fact that it accurately portrayed the Captain America from the comic books that has drawn in readers for over 75 years. *Captain America: The First Avenger* finally gave audiences Marvel's true icon, a hero that was brave, honest, and impeccably moral and good. As proven by the previous attempts to bring him to life, anything else isn't the real Captain America.

NOTES

1. IGN, "IGN'S Top 100 Comic Book Heroes," *IGN*, last modified May 6, 2011, http://www.ign.com/top/comic-book-heroes.
2. Box Office Mojo, "All Time Box Office: Domestic Grosses," *Box Office Mojo*, last modified February 27, 2015, http://boxofficemojo.com/alltime/domestic.htm.
3. Thomas V. Powers, "Superman … in the media," *Metropolitan Washington Old Time Radio Club*, last modified February 2005, http://www.mwotrc.com/rr2005_02/superman.htm.
4. Jim Harmon and Donald F. Glut, *The Great Movie Serials: Their Sound and Fury* (New York: Routledge, 1973), np.
5. Ibid., np.
6. *Captain America*, directed by Elmer Clifton and John English (1944; Hollywood, CA: PR Studios, 2009), DVD.
7. Jim Harmon and Donald F. Glut, *The Great Movie Serials: Their Sound and Fury* (New York: Routledge, 1973), np.
8. Ibid.np.
9. Joe Simon, and Jack Kirby, *Captain America Comics* #2, April 1941 (Meridian, CT: Timely Comics, Inc.), 7.
10. Joe Simon, and Jack Kirby, *Captain America Comics* #4, June 1941 (Meridian, CT: Timely Comics, Inc.), 8.
11. Joe Simon, and Jack Kirby, *Captain America Comics* #6, August 1941 (Meridian, CT: Timely Comics, Inc.), np.
12. Uncredited, *Captain America Comics* #25, April 1943 (Meridian, CT: Timely Comics, Inc.), np.
13. Don Glut, and Sal Buscema, *Captain America and the Falcon* #219–220, March 1978–April 1978, (New York: Marvel Comics).
14. Stan Lee, and Jack Kirby, *The Avengers* #4, March 1964 (New York: Marvel Comics), np.
15. Pete Tombs, *Mondo Macabro: Weird & Wonderful Cinema Around the World* (New York: St. Martin's Press, 1997), 103–107.
16. *Captain America* & *Captain America II: Death Too Soon*, directed by Rod Holcomb and Ian Nagy (1979; California: Shout Factory, 2011), DVD.
17. See Burnham, elsewhere in this volume, for further discussion of the turn toward the hesitant superhero in the 1970s.
18. *Captain America* & *Captain America II: Death Too Soon*, directed by Rod Holcomb and Ian Nagy (1979; California: Shout Factory, 2011), DVD.
19. Geoff Gehman, "How 'Captain America' Plans Unraveled," *The Morning Call*, April 3, 1988.
20. William S. Wilson, and Thomas T. Sueyres, "The 'Never Got Made' Files #66: Cannon's *Captain America* (1984–87)," *Video Junkie*, last modified July 22, 2011, http://originalvidjunkie.blogspot.com/2011/07/never-got-made-files-66-cannons-captain.html.
21. Ibid.
22. Ibid.
23. *Captain America*, directed by Albert Pyun (1990; Los Angeles, CA: Shout Factory, 2013), Blu Ray.

The Primetime Heroics of Small Screen Avengers
Finding Sociopolitical Value in Marvel TV Movies

JEF BURNHAM

In their introduction to *The 21st Century Superhero*, Richard J. Gray II and Betty Kaklimanidou defend the study of superhero narratives appearing in film and television by arguing that, in general, "popular culture [...] produces multilayered narratives that contain and spread ideological and political messages to a wide audience."[1] By focusing specifically on the relevance of contemporary texts to our global society in the 21st century, the authors reveal that the particular sociopolitical issues broached by any superhero narrative are intrinsically timely in nature. Thus, these superhero narratives serve as cultural artifacts that "negotiate, respond to and/or defuse some of the most significant socio-political [sic] issues" of the eras in which they are produced.[2]

In the revelation of this broad social relevance lies what Gray and Kaklamanidou as well as Matthew Pustz identify as the educational value of superhero narratives.[3] Specifically, superhero narratives can provide audiences with a greater understanding of historical events as well as the mechanisms whereby our cultural memories of those events are formed.[4] However, Gray and Kaklamanidou refer predominantly to the value of superhero narratives in film, and Pustz to those in comic books. Except in my own related research[5] and perhaps in Patrick A. Jankiewicz's *You Wouldn't Like Me When I'm Angry*, nowhere has the value of a made-for-TV movie adaptation of Marvel Comic been advocated as cultural property. Jankiewicz's exploration of CBS's *The Incredible Hulk* (1977) TV movie focuses only on its significance in relation to the popularity of the Hulk it bolstered and its position as but one of many Marvel TV movies, without ever examining its broader, sociopolitical ramifications.[6]

This absence of a dedicated analysis of Marvel TV movies' social value is made all the more conspicuous given that no fewer than thirteen live action, feature-length, made-for-TV movies were adapted from Marvel comic books prior to their success with the Marvel Cinematic Universe.[7] The bulk of the Marvel TV movies aired on CBS between 1977 and 1979, during which time the network premiered seven TV movies featuring four of Marvel's most recognizable heroes. These titles include *The Amazing Spider-Man* (1977), *The Incredible Hulk* (1977), *The Incredible Hulk: Death in the Family* (a.k.a. *Return of the Incredible Hulk*, 1977), *Dr. Strange* (1978), *The Incredible Hulk: Married* (1978), *Captain America* (1979), and *Captain America II: Death Too Soon* (1979). The remaining six Marvel TV movies include *The Incredible Hulk Returns* (NBC, 1988), *The Trial of the Incredible Hulk* (NBC, 1989), *The Death of the Incredible Hulk* (NBC, 1990), *Generation X* (Fox, 1996), *Nick Fury: Agent of S.H.I.E.L.D.* (Fox, 1998), and finally, *Blade: House of Chthon* (Spike, 2006).

In light of the absence of such a study of these works, I seek herein to reveal the educational value of viewing Marvel TV movies as cultural artifacts. I draw specific inspiration in this regard from Douglas Gomery's framing of *Brian's Song* (1971) within the sociopolitical climate of the early 1970s,[8] as well as Elayne Rapping's attempts to codify the TV movie as a genre according to the form's social relevance.[9] To that end, this analysis begins with an exploration of the 1979 *Captain America* TV movie as a reflection of American's malaise in the late 1970s before turning to a case study of *Nick Fury: Agent of S.H.I.E.L.D.* and *Generation X* as embodiments of what Robert Jewett and John Shelton Lawrence dubbed the "American monomyth."[10] In doing so, I will reveal that not only do Marvel TV movies reflect the concerns of the sociopolitical climate in which they were produced, but that they also perpetuate our specifically American understanding of the hero's social function.

Reflections of the American Sociopolitical Climate

In Pustz's essay on "America's Malaise as Demonstrated in Comic Books of the 1970s," he positions comic books of the 1970s as cultural artifacts that embody and provide insight into the "mood of pessimism" that plagued the United States during that era.[11] Throughout the decade, the American people became palpably pessimistic about the nation's future. President Jimmy Carter referred to this in his prime-time, television/radio address to the nation on July 15, 1979, as a "crisis of confidence," one that Pustz asserts resulted from numerous factors including "the military defeat in Vietnam, 'stagflation,' the Arab oil embargo, Watergate, and even the kidnapping of Patty Hearst."[12]

According to Pustz, comic books of the 1970s came to illustrate Americans' despair or "malaise" during that era through their depictions of similarly malaise-stricken superheroes. Thus, the five major symptoms of this crisis of confidence identified by President Carter[13] ultimately translated into comic books in four primary ways:

> First, superheroes of this period frequently suffered from their own "crisis of confidence" and often ended up abandoning their costumed secret identities. Second, it was common to find superheroes suffering from a lack of direction—much like Americans who were uncertain about the future. Third, superheroes in the 1970s were frequently faced with overwhelming power, problems and threats that seemed impossible to overcome. The final demonstration of malaise is personified by superheroes who lost their powers...[14]

Pustz identifies manifestations of these trends in titles of the 1970s as varied as *Superman*, *Inhumans*, *The Incredible Hulk* and *Captain America*. What's more, he pinpoints specific *historical* events for which many of the *fictional* events portrayed in these titles served as metaphors or otherwise referenced. For example, the assassination of a Nobel Peace Prize winner in a 1970 issue of *Teen Titans* draws on the real-life assassinations of Martin Luther King, Jr., and Robert Kennedy, while the 1973–1974 Secret Empire storyline in *Captain America* clearly evokes the Watergate scandal.[15] In much the same way as the comic books of the era do, the 1979 Marvel TV movie, *Captain America*, also reflects the crisis of confidence facing the American people in the 1970s through its malaise-stricken hero and metaphorical address of Americans' distrust of the oil industry.

Captain America *(1979) and the Powerless Superhero*

Pustz also states that America's malaise in the 1970s was defined primarily by "a feeling of being powerless in the face of change while also not really understanding the forces that were transforming the world."[16] This feeling of powerlessness underscores the journey of *Captain America*'s Steve Rogers throughout the movie's narrative, as it finds him grappling emotionally with his distrust of the American government and later physically with the vilified oil industry. Steve thus grapples with despair, just as the era's comic book heroes do as stated in Pustz's analysis. Moreover, when Pustz's argument about manifestations of America's malaise in 1970s comic books is applied, *Captain America* employs not one, but three of the four tropes identified by the author.

In capturing the mood of the 1970s, the TV movie's depiction of Captain America's origin deviates significantly from the comic book source material. After all, *Captain America* #1, published by Timely Comics in 1941, explicitly addresses the sociopolitical concerns of people in that era as the cover famously depicts Captain America punching Hitler in the face. That the *Captain America* TV movie does not retain this focus on the conflicts of the 1940s reinforces Gray and Kaklamanidou's claim that an adaptation of a comic book, when "produced and released with a delay of several years and/or decades, [...] is used as a comment on the contemporary sociocultural circumstances and does not respond to the time period in which the source was written and/or published."[17]

To that end, the TV movie's Steve Rogers is plagued not by the Nazi menace but by an overwhelming malaise that finds him on "the path that leads to fragmentation and self-interest," against which President Carter warned the American people six months after *Captain America* debuted on January 19, 1979.[18] In the opening of the movie a friend inquires where Steve has been since his release from the Marines two weeks earlier. Steve here confesses that his absence owes to the self-interested, fragmentary lifestyle he has adopted ("I've been comin' down the coast slow and easy. You know, kickin' back"), then voices plans to spend the coming years living on the road in his van. He thereby exhibits the "lack of direction" that defines Pustz's second manifestation of malaise in superhero narratives.[19] Like the Hulk of Marvel Comics in the 1970s[20] and David Banner of CBS's *The Incredible Hulk*, Steve would live as a nomad adrift. Only, he *chooses* this lifestyle of his own volition, motivated by malaise rather than necessity.

Steve's is a crisis of confidence reminiscent of Pustz's first manifestation of malaise whereby superheroes abandon their responsibilities in favor of a policy of noninterference. As such, when Dr. Simon Mills offers to administer the FLAG (Full Latent Ability Gain) serum to Steve and make him a super-powered crime fighter for the government, Steve declines, expressing disillusionment with national service. Even after Simon uses FLAG to save Steve's life following a motorcycle accident, Steve remains adamantly self-interested, again declines a position working for the government, and refuses to express any gratitude. In these scenes, the movie additionally hails a principal marker of malaise as identified by President Carter. Although once a devoted Marine, Steve has seemingly lost faith in his "ability to have a positive impact on the government" and feels "powerless to initiate change or stop the country's downward spiral" no matter how powerful FLAG might make him.[21]

Stephen Strange, in the 1979 Marvel TV movie *Dr. Strange*, similarly refuses to battle evil alongside the sorcerer Lindmer in spite of his own virtually unmatched, innate magical abilities. While *Dr. Strange* may not specifically refer to governmental service, in it and *Captain America* both, the protagonist's refusal of responsibility stunts narrative progression and this results in both movies failing to meet Gomery's requirement that a TV movie's protagonist serve as the narrative's primary causal agent.[22] When viewed specifically as cultural artifacts of the 1970s, the characters' apathy toward the "greater good" and their refusals to participate in their narratives' central conflicts are clear manifestations of America's malaise. This positions these TV movies as *successful* reflections of the era in which they were produced rather than mere narrative *failures*.[23]

Additionally, Steve's apathy toward the needs of the American government in *Captain America* is complicated by the intervention of an "overwhelming power," one that seems impossible to overcome, in keeping with Pustz's third manifestation of malaise in superhero narratives.[24] Although an adamant non-interventionist, Steve's wanderings are put on hold when he becomes ensnared in a plot by oil tycoon Lou Brackett to destroy Phoenix, Arizona with a neutron bomb and abscond with $1.4 billion in gold bullion from the International Gold Repository. The sheer complexity of Brackett's plan coupled with the incredible number of resources and murderous henchmen at his disposal place Steve at a seemingly insurmountable disadvantage, even with his super powers. So overwhelming is Brackett's power, in fact, that neither Steve nor any government employee, including his handler Simon Mills, has the faintest inclination about Brackett's plot until well over an hour into the movie. Moreover, when confronting Brackett during the climax, Steve proves grossly ineffectual and accidentally triggers the neutron bomb himself, thereby requiring Simon to step in and undo his error.

Pustz explains that such depictions of superheroes as powerless against their enemies were common in superhero narratives of the 1970s.[25] This central narrative and thematic concern with powerlessness in fact pervaded most Marvel TV movies of the era, not just *Captain America*. In *The Incredible Hulk*, David cannot control the Hulk or save the women he loves, Stephen cannot stop the evil Morgan le Fay and save his pseudo-love interest Clea without the direct intervention of Lindmer in *Dr. Strange*, and Peter Parker nearly commits suicide in *The Amazing Spider-Man* while rendered powerless by a cult leader's mind control. Powerlessness functions as a central narrative conceit in the follow-up Captain America and Hulk movies as well. In the conclusion of *Captain America II*, General Miguel holds Portland, Oregon hostage, having doused the city in a cellular aging compound to which he holds the only antidote.[26] Captain America ultimately triumphs over Miguel not through his own narrative agency, but as a result of the General's miscalculation when throwing a vial of said aging compound. Furthermore, in *The Incredible Hulk: Death in the Family*, David is powerless to prevent Julie, a young, disabled girl, from being murdered by her family without first transforming into the Hulk and losing conscious control of his body. And in *The Incredible Hulk: Married*, David is once again incapable of saving the life of a woman he loves, even when transformed into the Hulk.

Fear of the Oil Industry in Captain America

Pustz notes that comic books of the 1970s more often focused on heroes who had lost their way or suffered from a crisis of confidence than on broad problems facing American society,[27] hence the previous section's focus on the *character* of Steve Rogers. Yet, *Captain America* also addresses issues plaguing America as a whole during the 1970s. Namely, through its incorporation of an oil tycoon as antagonist, *Captain America* speaks to the nation's ongoing energy crisis in the 1970s and ultimately offers a solution to the crisis paralleling the one proposed by President Carter later that year.

The United States faced a severe energy crisis moving into 1979, the second of its kind that decade. In 1978, four months of revolution by oil workers had forced Iran to "cut its export production from 5.5 million barrels a day to zero."[28] The effects such an oil shortage could have on the world economy in 1979 were well-documented following the Arab oil embargo of 1973–1974, which sent the price of oil skyrocketing. As *Time* reported in March 1979, "the danger is that rocketing fuel prices will aggravate inflation, force governments to fight back by clamping down on domestic growth, and for the second time in a decade plunge the world economy into an oil-greased slide."[29] Americans had no way to accurately predict the actions OPEC would take in the face of the Iranian shortage coupled with the declining value of the dollar.[30] Moreover, they were met with reports emphasizing worst-case-scenarios, such as the *Time* piece quoted above, and with "crisis propaganda manufactured by the Department of Energy."[31] As a result, Americans panicked, began stockpiling oil and gasoline, and thereby *created* the energy crisis they had so feared in 1979.[32]

The same fear of the oil industry that led Americans to waste 150,000 gallons of gasoline in 1979 as their cars idled in lines at gas stations around the country also informs the central conflict of *Captain America*, which features oil tycoon Lou Brackett as the primary antagonist.[33] It follows then that Brackett, synecdochally representing the entire oil industry as perceived by Americans, proves wholly irrational and unpredictable in his plot to nuke a major American city as part of a robbery. Brackett's plan represents an exploitation of the American people for financial gain not unlike the price-gouging strategies of OPEC. Meanwhile, the unprovoked attempt to kill pre–Captain America Steve Rogers using a staged oil spill and an "oil-greased slide" off a mountain road embodies perceptions of the industry's flagrant disregard for Americans on a personal level.

"The American ideal": It's a Little Tough to Find These Days, Isn't It?

Elayne Rapping asserts that the importance of TV movies arises from their ability to offer narratives in which issues of political importance are not merely presented, but negotiated.[34] Steve Rogers' transformation into Captain America in the TV movie, for example, offers a productive solution to the concerns of a malaise-stricken people when faced with a severe oil shortage. It does so, however, without addressing the issue explicitly, as Rapping asserts TV movies must.[35] Yet this study has already shown that social issues can be poignantly explored in a TV movie subtextually, as *Captain America* does America's malaise in the 1970s. The Marvel TV movie therefore has the potential to shape public perception of political issues without ever having explicitly evoked them.

To that end, Steve eventually realizes that he can actually make a difference as Captain America and joins Simon Mills to serve the government as Captain America on a permanent basis. This narrative turn prefigured President Carter's solution to the oil crisis as voiced in his "Address to the Nation on Energy and National Goals" in July 1979 by nearly six months. In that address, President Carter called on the American people, from the collective members of Congress to the individual citizen, to join in an effort to conserve energy wherever possible.[36] Only through such collective actions did President Carter envision America overcoming this malaise and finding a solution to the energy crisis at hand.

As Steve joins forces with government representative Simon Mills, *Captain America* depicts precisely such a unification of citizen and government in an effort to prevent the oil industry from corrupting the "American ideal"—a task that neither an individual nor the government could perform independently. This is why Steve's refusal to cooperate with Simon throughout most of the movie not only stunts the forward progression of the narrative, but also the government's efforts to stop Lou Brackett. Only when Steve (the individual American citizen) unites with Simon (the government) can they actually make headway in thwarting Brackett's plan (a crisis brought on by the oil industry). In this, as in President Carter's address, the movie asserts the necessity of abandoning isolationism and self-indulgence to cooperate with the government. To this end, the climactic failure of Captain America to confront Brackett and disable the neutron bomb without Simon's assistance reflects the need for the people and the government to unite against the energy crisis if they're to ever restore "American values."[37]

Thus, the *Captain America* TV movie prefigured the energy crisis of 1979 in its reflection of the American people's fears of the oil industry, as well as President Carter's proposed response to the crisis in July of 1979. Of course, *Captain America* still fails to *superficially* address broadly relevant social issues as required by Rapping's definition of the TV movie. However, abandoning that rigid model of the TV movie in favor of analyzing the text as a cultural artifact exposes productive social messages at a more subtextual, thematic level instead.

This approach in fact proves useful when applied to Marvel TV movies produced during other eras as well. *Blade: The House of Chthon* opens with the return of Krista Starr from Iraq and scarred by memories of war, indicating the potential for a productive analysis of the movie within the context of post–9/11 America. Also, *The Incredible Hulk Returns* might be analyzed according to its reflection of the contradictory populist and elitist ideologies of Reaganomics, given that the altruism characterizing David Banner's actions in the 1978–1982 series is here replaced by flagrant self-interest.[38] That said, the social relevance of Marvel TV movies extends beyond the ways in which they reflect historical events and prevailing cultural attitudes. They also perpetuate a unifying national fantasy about the role of the hero in democratic society as illustrated by the following case studies of *Nick Fury: Agent of S.H.I.E.L.D.* and *Generation X* in relation to the American monomyth.

The American Monomyth

Rapping declares that the conservative medium of television is "an important public sphere within which social meanings and myths are constructed and circulated."[39] While

Marvel TV movies may not meet her requirements of the TV movie form, they indeed serve as sites wherein both social meaning and myths are constructed and disseminated. Specifically, the myths they construct perpetuate conservative ideologies relating to the role of powerful individuals in the perpetuation of American society.[40]

Responding to psychoanalyst Rollo May's claim that there exists no mythic system in the culture of the United States,[41] Lawrence and Jewett identify a widely accepted myth rooted in "motifs of superheroic redemptive violence" underpinning a myriad of popular culture artifacts and news media responses to political events.[42] While variations on the model exist, the basic structure of the American monomyth takes the following form:

> A community in a harmonious paradise is threatened by evil; normal institutions fail to contend with this threat; a selfless superhero emerges to renounce temptations and carry out the redemptive task; aided by fate, his decisive victory restores the community to its paradisiacal condition; the superhero then fades into obscurity.[43]

According to Lawrence and Jewett, the American monomyth informs the narratives of such varied popular culture texts as *The Matrix* (1999), *The Lion King* (1994), the *Death Wish* films, and the *Star Trek* franchise. The inclusion of *Star Trek* here points to the monomyth's applicability to groups of heroes in certain instances, not just individuals. To that end, George H. Lewis explores how *Teenage Mutant Ninja Turtles* (1990), and the *Turtles* franchise in general, in part revolutionized the American monomyth by allowing an isolated but "smoothly functioning team" or gang to embark on the monomythic quest otherwise attributed to individuals.[44]

The American monomyth is ultimately the product of an ever-increasingly less religious society and reflects a secularization of "Judeo-Christian dramas of community redemption [by] combining elements of the selfless servant who impassively gives his life for others and the zealous crusader who destroys evil."[45] In this, the monomyth fulfills Americans' latent spiritual needs by replacing religious icons with superheroes.[46] While the monomyth thus fulfills an obvious social function, at its core it espouses an undermining of the foundational principles of American democracy.

Although depicted in monomythic narratives as the saviors of the American people and their way of life, monomythic superheroes "are never elected to public office, never submit to the restraints of law or constitution, and never contribute to the discussion that is the very stuff of democracy."[47] For Lawrence and Jewett, then, the American superhero is intrinsically fascist,[48] while Lewis similarly situates Americans' appreciation for the Ninja Turtles in a collective faith in bureaucratic control.[49] Gray and Kaklimanidou describe this sort of ideological emphasis on "might makes right" in superhero narratives as supporting the "cult of the individual."[50] For them, the cult of the individual spreads a positive message about the capacity of the individual to effect change in society and the "necessity of a government with limited authority."[51] Lawrence and Jewett, by contrast, cast the monomyth in a negative light given its fascist bent and the tendency of public discourse to advocate "total, violent solutions" to crises as a result of people's faith in its "might makes right" message.[52]

Nick Fury: Agent of S.H.I.E.L.D. *(1998) and* Generation X *(1996)*

Whether or not the American monomyth's effects on society prove to be negative, it clearly informs the narratives of Marvel TV movies, as exemplified by *Nick Fury* and

Generation X. Both Nick Fury and the mutant teenagers who would be collectively known as Generation X[53] act in the interest of the United States of America despite their outsider statuses.[54] When Nick Fury first appears, he is a former agent of the Supreme Headquarters International Espionage Law Enforcement Division (S.H.I.E.L.D.) and has since isolated himself from society by retiring to a remote location in the Yukon. In the America of *Generation X*, genetic mutations resulting in super powers have been declared illegal by the U.S. government, even though the genetic "X Factor" causing these mutations manifests naturally and randomly during puberty. As such, the mutants of Xavier's School for Gifted Youngsters reside there in order to isolate themselves from society and avoid compulsory imprisonment in the government's mutant internment camps.

Nick Fury and Generation X ultimately prove to be the only people capable of redeeming their respective societies from the evils that threaten them. Yet, in part due to their outsider statuses, they do so without democratic approval. In the opening of *Nick Fury*, S.H.I.E.L.D calls Fury out of retirement to take on the newly revitalized terrorist organization known as HYDRA. Yet, in order to prevent HYDRA from releasing the untreatable Death's Head virus on Manhattan, Fury must ultimately defy S.H.I.E.L.D. directives as well as the express orders of his incompetent superiors. In doing so, his actions reflect the very anti-democratic, fascist behavior that defines the monomythic hero.[55] Similarly, as unregistered mutants, Generation X defies U.S. law by virtue of their very existence and, without the permission or knowledge of the American people, the mutants use their powers to fight on the nation's behalf. Their mission: stop the megalomaniacal Russell Tresh from taking over the "dream dimension" from whence he can control people's minds. Thus, both Nick Fury and Generation X act outside the parameters of democracy and take fascistic control over the future of society.

This begs the question: if they violate the principles of the very system they seek to redeem, how do they qualify as heroes at all? Monomythic heroes can transcend the democratic process in these narratives by virtue of their selflessness and their ability to resist temptation as they carry out their redemptive quests. This selflessness arises in *Nick Fury* when the fatally-poisoned Fury decides to personally infiltrate HYDRA's base though physical activity which accelerates the poison's effects. Generation X display an even nobler selflessness as they fight to protect a society that has unjustly vilified and institutionally discriminated against their kind.

Additionally, Fury exhibits the monomyth's prescribed "sexlessness" by resisting the advances of a beautiful INTERPOL agent and then permanently staying a kiss with his former lover. He resists temptation in both instances in favor of discussing the conflict at hand (his redemptive task). In *Generation X*, Banshee, Skin and Refrax all resist significant temptation. Banshee makes no advances toward Emma Frost in spite of their banter's sexual undertones; Skin pursues a romance with a non-mutant "townie" in the dream dimension, where anything is possible, but he chooses only to dance with her; and Refrax calls off a make-out session with Buff when his X-ray vision unexpectedly flares up, so as not to look through her clothes. In these ways, the Marvel TV movie's "monomythic heroes suppress their needs in order to achieve a selfless perfection."[56] This "selfless perfection," defined by their resistance of temptation, serves as proof that the hero's cause is pure, confirms his/her moral infallibility, and thereby justifies the hero's violation of democratic processes.[57]

Such cultural myths, no matter how contrary to the foundational principles of that culture, ultimately persist thanks to constant recycling in mass media, which in turn reinforce and perpetuate those myths' core values.[58] To that end, the American monomyth's values find significant reinforcement in the Marvel TV movie since such selfless, isolated and sexually unfulfilled monomythic heroes define Marvel TV movies as a whole (not just *Nick Fury* and *Generation X*). All Marvel TV movie heroes risk their lives to save those who have not requested assistance or even democratically approved of the hero's existence. Even Steve Rogers undertakes his journey as governmental crime fighter Captain America without democratic approval. His identity is known only to Simon, scientist Dr. Wendy Day, and the president, *not* the American people or even Congress.

Turning to isolation and sexlessness, *House of Chthon*'s Blade, as a half-human/half-vampire, belongs to neither society and only forms allegiances that aid him in his quest to rid the world of vampires. Peter Parker never expresses interest in a woman in *The Amazing Spider-Man*, nor does he appear to have any friends whatsoever. Stephen Strange's charge as Lindmer's apprentice in *Dr. Strange* explicitly compels him to renounce pleasures afforded mortal men, especially the love of women. And although *Captain America*'s Steve Rogers kisses Wendy once, their relationship stalls when Steve becomes engrossed in defeating Lou Brackett.

Furthermore, David Banner can wander the back roads of America righting the wrongs he encounters only after the women he loves die in *The Incredible Hulk*, and once again hits the road at the conclusion of *The Incredible Hulk: Married* following the death of his second wife. The final *Hulk* TV movies additionally find David involved with two women, but even those relationships fail to produce blissful unions as he abandons them to fulfill the narratives' redemptive quests.

Conclusion

That Marvel TV movies fail to explore social issues superficially, or even through the lens of dominant family ideology as Rapping asserts TV movies should,[59] by no means signifies that they are inherently without sociopolitical value. After all, Rapping herself asserts that, for all its shortcomings, television as a medium "succeeds more than other forums [...] in embodying a version of public debate on matters of common concern that has credibility and authority."[60] In this regard, Marvel TV movies have the potential to connect with a wide audience by appealing to their common concerns. As in *Captain America*'s address of the 1970s energy crisis, such texts can offer practical solutions to pressing social issues and, when viewed retrospectively, afford modern viewers a glimpse into the processes whereby society's political ideals were negotiated in bygone eras. Marvel TV movies achieve additional social relevance in that all thirteen of those listed at the outset of this chapter reflect the American monomyth, perpetuating a unifying, if fallacious, national fantasy about the redemptive power of applied fascism within a democratic society. Thus, Marvel TV movies can help us tap into our collective, national subconscious to better understand the ways in which we promote the myths of American exceptionalism and self-determinism, even as they allow the cultural climates of the eras in which they are produced to inform and even stifle the forward progression of their narratives.

Notes

1. Richard J. Gray II and Betty Kaklamanidou, "Introduction," in *The 21st Century Superhero: Essays on Gender, Genre and Globalization in Film*, edited by Richard J. Gray II and Betty Kaklamanidou (Jefferson, NC: McFarland, 2011), 5.

2. Ibid. This quote specifically refers to superhero narratives produced during the 21st century, which they claim are more sociopolitically charged than those produced in other eras. However, it is my intention to show that even the dissection of a Marvel TV movie pilot that failed to spawn a series or achieve basic narrative coherence for that matter reveals inherent, timely social relevance therein. This approach is supported by Gray and Kaklimanidou's own methodological framing of 21st century superhero narratives as specific reflections of 21st century issues, *not* those of the era in which the source material was produced ("Introduction," 2–3).

3. Gray and Kaklamanidou, "Introduction," 3; Matthew Pustz, "Comic Books as History Teachers," in *Comic Books: An American Cultural History*, edited by Matthew Pustz (New York: Continuum, 2012), 2–4.

4. Pustz, "Comic Books as History Teachers," 4; Christine Muller, "Power, Choice, and September 11 in *The Dark Knight*," in *The 21st Century Superhero: Essays on Gender, Genre and Globalization in Film*, edited by Richard J. Gray II and Betty Kaklamanidou (Jefferson, NC: McFarland, 2011), 46–59.

5. Jef Burnham, "From Panels to Primetime: Made-for-TV Movies Adapted from Marvel Comics Properties," *DePaul University: College of Communication M.A. Theses*, last modified August 2013, http://via.library.depaul.edu/cmnt/22.

6. Patrick A. Jankiewicz, *You Wouldn't Like Me When I'm Angry! A Hulk Companion* (Duncan: BearManor Media, 2011), 89–90.

7. This number increases when considering two-episode storylines from Marvel television series that were subsequently edited into a feature-length movie for theatrical or video release, including *Spider-Man Strikes Back* (1978) and *Spider-Man: The Dragon's Challenge* (1979). This essay explores only Marvel TV movies that originally aired as TV movies.

8. Douglas Gomery, "*Brian's Song*: Television, Hollywood, and the Evolution of the Movie Made for TV," in *Why Docudrama?*, edited by Alan Rosenthal (Carbondale: Southern Illinois University Press, 1999), 91–92.

9. Elayne Rapping, *The Movie of the Week* (Minneapolis: University of Minnesota Press, 1992), 32–37.

10. John Shelton Lawrence and Robert Jewett, *The Myth of the American Superhero* (Grand Rapids: William B. Eerdmans, 2002).

11. Matthew Pustz, "'Paralysis and Stagnation and Drift': America's Malaise as Demonstrated in Comic Books of the 1970s," in *Comic Books: An American Cultural History*, edited by Matthew Pustz (New York: Continuum, 2012), 136.

12. Ibid., 136–137.

13. The five symptoms of America's crisis of confidence, according to Pustz, include Americans' loss of "faith in their ability to have a positive impact on the government," as well as their "diminished expectations for the future," materialism, and "distrust of all manner of institutions" ("'Paralysis and Stagnation and Drift,'" 137).

14. Pustz, "'Paralysis and Stagnation and Drift,'" 138.

15. Ibid., 139.

16. Ibid., 145–146.

17. Gray and Kaklamanidou, "Introduction," 2–3. Working from Brian McFarlane's conclusions about sociocultural circumstances in adaptation from *Novel to Film*, Gray and Kaklamanidou substitute the medium of the novel with the comic book, highlighting the universality of this principle of adaptation theory. In the same way, although Gray and Kaklamanidou specifically discuss the adaptation of comics to film, the principle holds true to the transition of material from comics to television, as my subsequent analysis of *Captain America* confirms.

18. Jimmy Carter, "Address to the Nation on Energy and National Goals: 'The Malaise Speech,'" *The American Presidency Project*, accessed February 22, 2015, http://www.presidency.ucsb.edu/ws/?pid=32596.

19. Pustz, "'Paralysis and Stagnation and Drift,'" 138.

20. Ibid., 141–142.

21. Ibid., 137.

22. Gomery, "*Brian's Song*," 88.

23. This is not to say that *Captain America* or *Dr. Strange* succeed at a narrative level. Most structuralist approaches would find them intrinsically narratively flawed. To emphasize a movie's failures, however, results in an appraisal of negative value (i.e., it then serves primarily as an example

of what *not* to do) and such analyses often preclude the possibility of any positive value. This is especially true when the positive value of a text lies in alternative readings of the same elements that give it negative value, as with *Captain America*.

24. Pustz, "'Paralysis and Stagnation and Drift,'" 138.

25. Ibid., 141–144. Pustz points to the powerlessness experienced by Marvel Comics' Hulk, Deathlok, and the humans of Jack Kirby's *Eternals* among others.

26. Here, the people of Portland also embody the powerlessness experienced by Americans in the 1970s, as their rapid aging prevents them from participating in the plot to save them.

27. Pustz, "'Paralysis and Stagnation and Drift,'" 141.

28. "The Oil Squeeze of '79," *Time* 113, no. 11 (March 12, 1979): 44.

29. Ibid.

30. Ibid.

31. Peter Deutsch, "The Phony Oil Crisis," *The Nation* 228, no. 15 (April 21, 1979): 423.

32. Jeremy Leggett, *Half Gone: Oil, Gas, Hot Air and the Global Energy Crisis* (London: Portobello Books, 2005), 150.

33. Ibid.

34. Rapping, *The Movie of the Week*, xxxii–xxxiii.

35. Ibid.

36. Carter, "Address to the Nation on Energy and National Goals," n.p.

37. Ibid.

38. Jane Feuer, *Seeing Through the Eighties: Television and Reaganism* (Durham: Duke University Press, 1995), 12. The central focus of Jane Feuer's book is this very tension between the populist and elitist components of Reaganist ideology as manifested in 1980s television.

39. Rapping, *The Movie of the Week*, xvii.

40. Quoting William G. Doty, Lawrence and Jewett assert that all "myths establish conservative benchmarks" (*The Myth of the American Superhero*, 9).

41. Lawrence and Jewett, *The Myth of the American Superhero*, 6.

42. Ibid., 5.

43. Ibid., 6.

44. George H. Lewis, "From Common Dullness to Fleeting Wonder: The Manipulation of Cultural Meaning in the Teenage Mutant Ninja Turtles Saga," *Journal of Popular Culture* 25, no. 2 (Fall 1991): 36.

45. Lawrence and Jewett, *The Myth of the American Superhero*, 6.

46. Ibid.

47. Ibid., 351.

48. Ibid.

49. Lewis, "From Common Dullness to Fleeting Wonder," 36.

50. Gray and Kaklimanidou, "Introduction," 4.

51. Ibid., 5.

52. Lawrence and Jewett, *The Myth of the American Superhero*, 338–340.

53. Though the TV movie never refers to this group of mutants as Generation X, as they are known in the comics, I refer to them here collectively as Generation X for brevity's sake.

54. Lawrence and Jewett, *The Myth of the American Superhero*, 47.

55. Ibid., 351.

56. Ibid., 357.

57. Ibid., 47.

58. Robert Westerfelhaus and Robert Alan Brookey, "At the Unlikely Confluence of Conservative Religion and Popular Culture: *Fight Club* as Heteronormative Ritual," *Text & Performance Quarterly* 24, no. 3/4 (July 2004): 307.

59. Rapping, *The Movie of the Week*, xl.

60. Ibid. xxxi.

PART 5
The Attempt of Progressivism in the Marvel Universe

Damsels in Transgress
The Empowerment of the Damsel in the Marvel Cinematic Universe

Joseph Walderzak

The 21st century movie consumer has been bombarded with a surfeit of films adapted from comic book source material. The development of this subgenre has inspired a wealth of academic work that has both legitimized the study of such films and brought incisive analysis to issues of gender, race, and sexual identity, among numerous others. Despite the breadth of scholarship concerned with the comic-based action genre, work dedicated to the "damsel character," whose existence is as historical as the filmic superhero or action hero himself, has been problematically absent. This omission is all the more troubling due to the fact the damsel character has been revised from a helpless, listless, object of basic desire in need of heroic rescuing to a strong-willed, intelligent woman who is just as capable of saving the hero as he is of her. The Marvel Cinematic Universe (MCU) includes some of the most significant and notable damsels: Jane Foster, Betty Ross, and Pepper Potts. These characters provide an intriguing sample of a subgenre which is a paragon of female empowerment. The nature of this empowerment, the damsel serving a heroic role, challenges the critics of post-feminism. This interpretation of empowerment highlights a more nuanced understanding of an ongoing and heterogeneous post-feminist paradigm. In some regard, the MCU damsel is perfectly symbolic of the problematically, paradoxical post-feminist figure; her professional success and individual agency are compromised because the damsel's very nature demands succumbing—if only temporarily—to the worst features of traditional femininity. In these moments, whether they are hysterical rescue scenes or romantic devotion to the hero, the damsel's representation is seemingly marred, with feminism treated as unnecessary and female joy reverting to being tied to men. However, when these scenes are understood with more subtlety, and contextualized within the damsel's own heroism, they demonstrate the pitfalls of interpreting any relapse into traditional femininity as fundamentally problematic and highlight the potential strength of traditional femininity in the era of post-feminism.

The Damsel and the Post-Feminist Paradigm

Certainly, there exists a popular conception of the damsel. Images ranging from Disney princesses to classic Hollywood noir, to hysterical victims in horror and disaster films, to comic book and film icon Lois Lane, pervade popular culture. Christina Amadou describes the damsel's function as aiding the plot and developing the main characters, noting they are often offered as prizes to the heroes for their bravery and skill, while Jeff Brown defines the damsel as a "hysterical figure who needs to be rescued."[1] These definitions fail to identify the totality of the damsel's role and rather describe particular moments of damsel representation, which happen to also highlight historical trends. Unfortunately, these conceptions of the damsel have become so pervasive that the term itself is imbued with negativity; this creates a dilemma of how to discuss the expanded and empowered role of the MCU damsel. Simply discarding the term "damsel" because its negative connotations are inapplicable to the MCU female characters is an enticing but ultimately problematic solution. First, the characters are still commonly referred to as "damsels" by scholars, critics, and fans alike. The argument expressed here regarding damsel representation is overtly oppositional to what is commonly conveyed in popular and scholarly criticism, and exemplified by the excerpts from Amadou, Brown, and various other works that are referenced within this writing. While this opposition could best be expressed by jettisoning the terminology of damsel altogether, doing so would obscure the dialectic taking place. An instructive example of a similar dilemma is how Amanda Lotz criticizes the popular label "antihero," but in so doing perpetuates the "imprecise" language—because not doing so would fail to contextualize her argument.[2] To resist perpetuating popular, yet problematic, terminology is to resist rehabilitating the misconceptions associated with those terms. Therefore, the language of damsel is retained in order to maintain a historical lineage which properly contextualizes the character's transformation.

There has been a momentous revision of the damsel in the 21st century, notably within the MCU, but these alterations have not been so dramatic as to render the character unrecognizable. Ultimately, damsel is defined here as a female character who is central to the plot, important to the film's hero, involved in a rescue scene, and *whose heroics are unexpected*. Notably this definition rejects Amadou and Brown's conception of the damsel, particularly notions of the character as intrinsically hysterical or a reward for the hero. Rather, the parameters are free from thematic assumptions which allow for the character to be culturally contextualized without prejudice of past iterations. This understanding of the damsel strips it of pejorative associations, or rather historically locates those associations to particular eras of damsel representation. The only notable female character omitted by this definition is Jane's trusted friend Darcy Lewis, whose role is far more comic relief than central to the plot.[3] Natasha Romanoff's early scenes in *Iron Man 2* (2010) suggest a damsel role, however after her secret identity is revealed her heroism becomes expected by the audience.[4] The difficulty of defining Peggy's role in *Captain America: The First Avenger* (2011) will be explored in detail below. Enough exceptions exist so that damsel and female character cannot be treated as synonymous; the damsel role, and how it has been transformed, are both markedly specific.

The MCU damsels' empowerment manifests itself through two recurrent tropes. First, the "hero-partner" trope is introduced to identify the damsel's role as a proper partner to the film's hero. The expectation of a helpless, hysterical figure has become archaic; the MCU damsel is equipped with agency that enables her meaningful partnership with the hero. Second, the "reciprocal-rescue" trope challenges the damsel's most hackneyed role—that of bait for the hero to rescue, often as part of the villain's plan. While this plot contrivance still appears, the hero's rescue of the damsel is often reciprocated or precipitated by the damsel's rescuing of the hero. For instance, Pepper is only in need of rescue during the climax of *Iron Man* (2008) because of her own heroic acts. In fact, Stark's rescue of Pepper is enabled and precipitated by her rescue of him. On other occasions, the damsel's need for rescue is only derived because of her coming to another's rescue, such as when Jane moves pedestrians to safety in the climax of *Thor* (2011). Beyond these tropes, the MCU damsel has shifted from offering the hero an unfounded and unconditional love, to a conditional love with ethical expectations. Finally, the damsel's professional ambitions and success have been emancipated from that of the hero. These tendencies are illustrative of a transgressive MCU damsel who is revising her history and producing a challenge to the critics of the post-feminist paradigm.

The MCU damsel positions herself as a response to both post-feminism and its astute critics. Some of the most interesting and important works on gender and popular culture in recent years are exemplified by the post-feminist criticism of Brown, Susan Bordo, Susan Douglas, Angela McRobbie, and Sherrie Inness, among others. While there still exist some challenges and debate in regard to concretely defining post-feminism, there is plenty of agreement that post-feminism describes the attitude where any exercise of female agency is positively empowering.[5] This perspective, which its critics contend has led to the reclaiming of sexist images of femininity and overt sexualization, has reduced empowerment to a superficial level.[6] McRobbie problematizes the language of empowerment itself claiming institutions, predominantly the media, have incorporated "empowerment" and "choice."[7] This incorporation by media institutions allows for regressive behaviors and vacuous choices to be framed as empowering. She describes the post-feminist attitude as a "double entanglement" in which an expansion of choice is mitigated by an increase in social punishment for breaking with normative conventions.[8] Elsewhere, Bordo critiques a culturally-situated false sense of empowerment, based on choice, which enables a post-feminist paradigm that willfully underplays culture's normalization of individuals and reinforces patriarchy.[9] Douglas critiques the incorporation of empowerment in her analysis of what she calls "embedded feminism," in which female achievements are part of the landscape, and "enlightened feminism," referring to the proliferation of sexist stereotypes whose disparaging qualities are deemed harmless in the age of gender equality.[10] For Douglas, empowerment has come to be defined, via the power of marketing, through consumption and the pursuit of beauty in an age where women are told they have gained everything else. The language of empowerment is part of the creation of a false assumption that all has been won, an assumption constantly reproduced through media and ultimately supportive of patriarchy.[11]

These cogent criticisms of post-feminism suggest that any claims of media representations of empowered females must be properly contextualized and justified. The MCU damsel is exceptional as a surprising genre development, but more important it is the type of character that would draw the ire of post-feminist critics. To borrow Douglas's language, MCU damsels embody "embedded feminism." Their professional achievements are presented as part of the landscape and as a result, feminism is implicitly suggested to be redundant as equality is evidently achieved. According to these critics of post-feminism, this grants immunity to the female characters when they digress into traditional representations of femininity, such as merely existing as a romantic fixture for the male or, conversely, being fixated on pursuing romance. Superficially, the MCU damsel would exemplify post-feminist concerns since the characters are successful, oblivious to feminism and, ostensibly, have limitless life choices; these embedded features often are ancillary to the damsel's romantic role. Even Peggy's mid-century professional success and individualism is presented as unexceptional. Likewise, the professional success of Pepper and Jane is foregrounded, but is not as relevant to the narrative as their romantic relationships with their respective superheroes. These types of perfunctory observations fail in acknowledging the nuance of damsel representation; post-feminist criticism mistakenly interprets any vestige of traditional femininity as deleterious. The MCU damsel demonstrates how genuine acts of heroism and empowerment can subsist in a post-feminist media paradigm.

An eagerness to criticize in the name of post-feminist backlash is rampant in superhero scholarship. One illustrative example is Betty Kaklamanidou's exploration of the X-Men films. Kaklamanidou claims the "damsels" of the X-Men cinematic universe are presented as weak, in search of love and support, yet fails to offer convincing substantiation.[12] Interestingly, Kaklamanidou's consideration of damsels includes the heroes Storm, Jean Grey, and Rogue, as well as tragic-villain Mystique. Kaklamanidou wields the term "damsel" to disparage any female representation no matter whether the characters serve in that role or not; this implementation differs from the way damsel is deployed here in which the character archetype is defined by its narrative function and not its negative connotations. Kaklamanidou criticizes Storm's eventual stewardship of Xavier's School for Gifted Children at the end of *X-Men: The Last Stand* (2006) as by default. In fact, all the character's traditionally feminine characteristics are reduced to being weaknesses, despite their ostentatiously transgressive implementation. Not unlike the X-Men superheroines, aspects of the MCU damsel could attract post-feminist critics inclined to interpret any digression into traditional femininity as problematic. Yet, the MCU damsel, while flawed, demonstrates how post-feminist constructions can be empowering. The MCU damsel's role as a romantic figure or plot contrivance distorts the entirety of the characterization and how even these (so-called) regressions are far more complicated than their traditional features suggest. Approaching the MCU damsel as a heroic figure illuminates an interpretive strategy to texts featuring a form of female representation which is not overtly sexualized, which features choices that are not vacuous affirmations of patriarchy, and where equality is foregrounded rather than assumed. The MCU damsel's equality and the consequences of their agency are most overwhelmingly apparent in the hero-partner and reciprocal-rescue scenes to be discussed in more depth below.

The Early 21st Century Marvel Damsel and Nostalgia

How the damsel of the MCU has evolved must be understood through a brief consideration of the portrayal of similar characters in previous superhero films featuring Marvel characters—specifically, Sam Raimi's Spider-Man trilogy. This is to say that the female characters in the MCU films stand as strikingly empowered figures when compared to Mary Jane Watson of the Spider-Man trilogy, who frequently embodied the hysterical and helpless norms which defined the 20th century damsel figure. While one cannot disregard the troubling aspects of female presentation in Raimi's Spider-Man trilogy, many of the limitations may be attributable to stylistic choices. Wilson Koh convincingly posits that Raimi imbued Spider-Man with nostalgia in order to enact timelessness, citing the notable absence of technology among other features and imagery.[13] Koh does not directly comment on how this nostalgic style contributed to the presentation of Mary

Jane, although one can easily extend his argument to understand her character. Her working as a waitress in the "big city," being harassed by a sexist boss, and trying to make it as an actress all add to the nostalgic style and harken to female representations from a bygone era. Thus, it is appropriate to read Mary Jane's characterization as heavily influenced by nostalgia. In spite of this, however, each subsequent film began to progressively empower Mary Jane. This empowerment established an important precedent within the superhero subgenre. Subsequent genre films could either continue this transgressive trajectory or regress to the damsel's most problematic features, to which Raimi's *Spider-Man* (2002) almost perfectly adheres.

In *Spider-Man*, the romance between Peter and Mary Jane is the central plot device, as noted by Robert Weiner.[14] Mary Jane is depicted as sweet (she defends Peter Parker on the bus and throughout his school travails as a victim of hyperbolic bullying) as often as she is frantically helpless, most frustratingly when clinging to a breaking terrace rather than trying to make her way to safety during Green Goblin's raid on the parade. Spider-Man is required to save Mary Jane repeatedly throughout the film and one wonders, *is there is anything she could do to avoid her state of helplessness*. Her ambition and independence are significantly counter-balanced by her superficiality and fragility, love-struck over Spider-Man and ending the first film on a lachrymose note as she somberly handles Peter's rejection. These maudlin moments are hard to imagine in *Thor*, *Captain America: The First Avenger*, or *The Incredible Hulk* (2008), when the damsels are faced with similar romantic challenges. While it becomes less true in subsequent Raimi Spider-Man films, one cannot easily refute Adamou's claim that Mary Jane's importance is as a structuring element and reassurance of the hero's heterosexuality.[15]

Spider-Man 2 (2004) places Peter as the surrogate for Mary Jane's inability to act or, at times, even think. While Peter reconciles his responsibility as Spider-Man and his desire to be free from the power, he is also making decisions for her, bluntly stating, "I can't let you take that risk" when she meekly, yet movingly, suggests they be together. Capitulating to the hero's demands is treated as natural in the film but will prove itself untenable to the MCU damsel if the hero's request interferes with her own heroism. Peter's policing of Mary Jane solidifies his "highly ethical stance," according to Adamou.[16] Yet, while the second film's existential crisis concerning the divide between Peter Parker/Spider-Man is given its due critical praise, Mary Jane undergoes an equally admirable transformation. By the end of the film, no longer willing to endure being without agency, she pleads, "I know you think we can't be together, but can't you respect me enough to let me make my own decision? I know there'll be risks but I want to face them with you. It's wrong that we should be only half alive ... half of ourselves.... Isn't it about time somebody saved your life?" The language of "halfness" lends itself to a psychoanalytic exegesis outside of the scope of this analysis; Adamou suggests Mulvey's concept of objectification is maintained by cinematic damsels such as Mary Jane.[17] Robert Peaslee, offers a Freudian analysis, arguing that Mary Jane "consents to ménage-a-trois, of sorts, accepting both 'Spider-Man' and Peter."[18] Convincingly assessing the myriad of Oedipal triangles within *Spider-Man* and *Spider-Man 2*, Peaslee's positioning of Mary Jane as her own oedipal agent is the most significant to the interpretation of her burgeoning transformation. Mary Jane attempts to reconcile her "halfness," transgressing Peter's boundaries, through demanding respect and asserting her right to take risks and to be the one doing the "life-saving." Her development may not be as conspicuously philosophical or psychological as Peter's, but it is just as revelatory.[19] By some measure, the MCU addresses

Mary Jane's crisis by producing brave damsels able to take risks and embrace a romance with the hero.

In the finale of *Spider-Man 2*, she joins the fight against Dr. Otto Octavius. Her inability to save Spider-Man (she is brushed aside easily by one of Octavius's metallic tentacles) does not matter as much as her move to action and rejection of helplessness. Her change may be the result of her becoming conditioned to the ritual of being kidnapped, held as bait, and predictably saved. Nevertheless, what amounts to quotidian rescue routines still emboldens a shift in Mary Jane from passive helplessness to active aggression. This transformation is exhibited by her behavior in the climax of both *Spider-Man 2* and *Spider-Man 3* (2007), in which the acquiescence towards villains and crooks is replaced with combativeness, even if the results prove unremarkable in the world of super-humans. This is developed further in *Spider-Man 3* when, after being kidnapped and used as bait for Spider-Man, she drops cinder blocks on Venom, resulting in enough distraction to free Spider-Man from his grasp. Unfortunately, Mary Jane's character development has been overlooked by scholars such as Justin Schumaker, whose praise of "Hit-Girl" in *Kick-Ass* (2010) comes by way of a dubious comparison to Mary Jane.[20] While the Mary Jane of *Spider-Man 3* remains marred by a need for constant reassurance and petty jealousy, Schumaker disregards Mary Jane's active role in her rescues and uses her as a distressed damsel to contrast against the masculinity of Hit-Girl. Not only does Schumaker conflate the roles these women play, he avoids how the women are similar despite their contrasting roles. While positing Mary Jane as requiring rescuing at some point and Hit-Girl as the "savior of captured men," he fails to articulate Mary Jane's attempts—albeit futile—to participate in her own rescue and Hit-Girl's need for rescue by "Kick-Ass" in the film's climax.[21] Even the nostalgic spectacle of the Spider-Man trilogy sees Mary Jane progress to a more active damsel. Although barely comparable to the gender politics of the MCU, the progression of Mary Jane throughout the Raimi trilogy signaled an impending development of the damsel. Female characters in other 21st century films featuring Marvel characters, such as Roxanne Simpson in *Ghost Rider* (2007), proved that the damsel empowerment of the Spider-Man trilogy was not an anomaly. Roxanne is professionally successful, exorcises the hero from Johnny Blaze's doomed soul, and fires a shotgun at Blackheart in the film's climax to save Johnny. The nascent forms of empowerment in films featuring Marvel characters would become solidified within the MCU as the damsel emerged as a legitimate hero.

The Heroic MCU Damsel

The "hero-partner" and "reciprocal-rescue" tropes expose how moments of perceived weakness are almost always the result of the damsel's own heroism (not the very lack of those characteristics, as in past damsel incarnations) and how these moments fail to undermine the embedded empowerment of the characters by transgressively deploying traditional femininity. The hero-partner trope is the story element wherein the damsels' actions are akin to the superhero; likewise, the reciprocal-rescue describes scenes where female character's endangerment is the result of their rescue of someone (often the superhero himself). Pepper, appearing in four films thus far, is the central damsel figure of the MCU. Pepper's professional success is demonstrated by her tenacious and indefatigable running of Tony Stark's affairs in *Iron Man* and her leadership of Stark Industries in *Iron*

Man 2, *Iron Man 3* (2013) and *The Avengers* (2012). Pepper has a stern approach to Tony's petulant behavior, perhaps best exemplified in her dismissal of Tony's boorish and fatuous testimony to the Senate Armed Forces committee in *Iron Man 2*. Nearly every scene concerning Tony and Pepper involves a battle of her professionalism and his immaturity or arrogance. While Tony's genius is the reason for the company's success, and therefore Pepper's success is terminally contingent on Tony, the film equally suggests it is Pepper's shrewd business skills which render the brazen Tony to be just as dependent on her. This dependency is alluded to in a scene in *Iron Man* when Pepper quips to Tony, "I don't think you could tie your shoes without me." This level of superiority is elucidated by Pepper's cognizant efforts to demarcate herself from the women in Tony's life, particularly by making subtle disparaging comments about his one-night stand in *Iron Man*. Her self-consciousness reflects a preoccupation with not being viewed as "chasing him" and retaining her professionalism, as she explains to Tony when dancing with him in *Iron Man*—the lone scene of that film in which Pepper is remotely sexualized.

Pepper fulfills the hero-partner trope in *Iron Man*'s climatic sequence, which commences when Pepper is sent by Tony to steal computer files and, in the film's lone true moment of suspense, is confronted by the villain Obadiah Stane. After retrieving the files, which reveal Obadiah's involvement in Tony's kidnapping, she leads a team of S.H.I.E.L.D. agents to the ominous "Section 16," opportunistically declaring she knows a short-cut. When James Rhodes appears on site, she directs him to go check on Tony, who she anticipates is in trouble. When Rhodes arrives, he finds Tony left nearly incapacitated by Obadiah and is able to revive him. In this sequence, Pepper proves Obadiah's guilt, uncovers his plans, and indirectly saves Tony, demonstrating the role of hero-partner and fulfilling the reciprocal rescue. It is this behavior which situates her in need of rescuing from Obadiah, equipped with a weaponized iron suit, in the film's resolution. In this moment, Pepper stands defenseless and strangely clueless in front of him and temporarily reverts to a regressive damsel performance in her moment of rescue. However, Pepper follows this behavior by again proffering a heroic rescue: she destroys the arc reactor, saving a compromised Tony from Obadiah's assault. While Pepper's tentativeness and trepidation in destroying the reactor must be noted, it is important to view this as merely a distraction; the fact that Pepper is in the heroic position, regardless of precise circumstances, is exemplary.

These tropes continue in *Iron Man 2* when Pepper accompanies Happy, Tony's driver, to provide Tony with his suit after Ivan Vanko attacks him on the racetrack. This initial rescue is quickly reciprocated when Pepper reverts to a screaming damsel performance as Ivan methodically attacks her. Again, her need for rescue should not be isolated from its context, as Ivan's threat to Tony was just as dire before Pepper came to his rescue. Her involvement in *Iron Man 2*'s resolution is not as integral as it was in *Iron Man*, but she is still markedly involved as she harangues Justin Hammer, Ivan's financier and Tony's rival, and essentially quarterbacks the daunting rescue efforts. While Pepper's importance as hero-partner, and the nature of her reciprocal rescue, are not as significant in *Iron Man 2*, she remains an empowered partner to Tony.

Given Pepper's role in the film, it is hard to reconcile Susanne Kord and Elisabeth Krimmer's interpretation of Pepper as a romantic fantasy for Tony.[22] Kord and Krimmer, like so many scholars, are focused on topics apart from damsel performance and offer their criticisms as part of a casual aside; the topic is evidently not important or interesting enough to devote substantial or appropriate time to, but too enticing to neglect completely. If Pepper is representative of any type of fantasy to Tony, it would be one of understanding, thwarting his alienation. Pepper is distinguished, repeatedly, from the type of women Tony views romantically and it is this very fact (Pepper's strength), which makes her so important (and attractive) to him. Kord and Krimmer comment that she is fully devoted to Tony but do not explain how this is expressed or, at the least, why this differs from Tony's devotion to her or how it intrinsically makes her weak. Tragically, these gender critiques accept patriarchal categories of strength and weakness. In fairness, Pepper's devotion to Tony has limits, as is often expressed in her reactions to his infringement on her ability to run the company and in their ethical debates. Further, Kord and Krimmer berate Pepper for not having any agency of her own, stating that all of her actions are the result of following Tony's orders. However, neither her decision to send James to save Tony in *Iron Man* nor her racetrack rescue in *Iron Man 2* were done on Tony's orders; rather, Tony's life was threatened and Pepper's exercising of her agency is what allowed for him to be saved. Even if one generously and mistakenly accepts an interpretation of Pepper as only following Tony's orders, the tasks Pepper does for Tony consist of successfully running a billion dollar company and executing the previously detailed heroics. It is difficult to convincingly malign one's agency when their actions are so starkly impressive. Critics seem to find any vestige of traditional femininity, be it devotion, tenderness, or love—never mind damsel hysterics when facing imminent danger—compromising of any empowerment, no matter the nature of the femininity.

Pepper is most prominent in *Iron Man 3*, a film which both exemplifies the heroic agency of the damsel but, more significantly, complicates and problematizes the nature of this empowerment. Early scenes affirm her success running Stark Industries, signing numerous papers while walking through the lobby of Stark Industries and being badgered by Happy. During Aldrich Killian's presentation, a distracted Pepper self-deprecatingly claims she does not understand a pithy, but certainly permeable, quote offered by Aldrich. Concerns over Pepper's ability to maintain her composure around a handsome intelligent man are quickly allayed when she rejects Aldrich's research proposal; her personal and professional maturity are also foregrounded when she rebuffs Tony's slightest showing of jealousy, finds his grand romantic gestures ostentatious, and is somewhat unsympathetic about Tony's mercurial behavior even after he reluctantly confides in her about his anxiety over "New York" (the traumatic events of *The Avengers*). Pepper's heroism first emerges during the attack on Tony's Malibu house. Tony sends the iron man suit to protect her from the explosion and debris and she, despite the unfamiliarity of the suit, immediately reciprocates by rescuing Tony from falling debris and then, following Tony's orders, saves the visiting scientist Maya Hansen. Following that rescue, Tony steals the suit from Pepper in order to rescue himself. Painfully for the audience who has witnessed myriad acts of heroism from Pepper, Tony lacks faith in Pepper's ability to rescue him. Tony's misogynistic tendencies manifest again later in the film when Maya explains to Pepper that "what I actually am is a biological coder running a team of forty out of a privately funded think tank, but, sure, you can call me a botanist," after taking offense to the notion of Tony telling Pepper she was simply a "botanist." Pepper's agency takes on an even more heroic context when she can commiserate with Maya over being overshadowed and reduced by Tony's misogyny. This rare female comradery proves short-lived when Maya's malevolent partnership with Aldrich is revealed. Notably, when Aldrich arrives to kidnap Pepper her first reaction is to yell for Maya to run before considering her own safety.

From the scene of the kidnapping through the end of the film, Pepper's representation and empowerment prove aberrant from the two installments which lends hope that the problematic features will prove evanescent. Pepper is held as bait for Tony, a subgenre trope which the MCU had previously jettisoned as hackneyed and which perpetuates regressive gender scripts. In this sequence Pepper is sexualized: chained up, eyes darkened with eyeliner, her shirt removed—rather inexplicably—leaving her in a sports bra. Tony is held under identical circumstances later in the film but the similarities prove superficial as Tony, remaining fully clothed, is able to free himself from the restraints and successfully accost his captors. While this scene thus invites criticism, it is notable that what is most visible is the impressive musculature of Pepper's (or that of Gwyneth Paltrow) abdomen rather than the typically fetishized areas of the female body. So while she is forced into a traditional damsel role, her body contradicts the weakness of the archetype by conforming to the female action heroine, the "rambolina" to borrow the language of Yvonne Tasker.[23] It is this heroine figure which garners the most acclaim, with critics heaping praise on the muscularly chiseled and aloof Charlize Theron in *Mad Max: Fury Road* (2015) or heralding Emily Blunt's *Edge of Tomorrow* (2014) as "the most feminist summer action flick in years."[24] Combined with her more understated heroics earlier in the film and franchise, Pepper's empowerment can be viewed as universally appeasing, alienating particular views of ideal empowerment while alternatively embracing them elsewhere in the films.

The climax of the film fully embraces Pepper as a sexualized, lean yet muscular, superheroine. As the final battle commences, Tony is unable to rescue a trapped Pepper and she plummets to her presumed death, saved only by Aldrich's serum experimentation. As the fight escalates, Tony is left without a suit, or any more to call upon, and awaits an all-but-certain execution from Aldrich. Pepper emerges from the wreckage and saves Tony. This sequence transcends the typical reciprocal-rescue trope as Pepper's rescue of Tony was unreciprocated; Tony was unable to prevent her deadly plummet. Before completing the heroic act of killing Aldrich (the second villain of the series she has eliminated, compared to Tony's joint effort with Iron Patriot [War Machine] in defeating Ivan), Pepper impressively evades and adroitly destroys an iron man suit targeting all individuals with infected heat signals. The visual of Pepper destroying an iron man suit is particularly empowering and satisfying—even if Pepper is supernaturally transformed—and can be read in such a way Pepper is a threat to iron man beyond her abnormal heat signal. Peaslee's analysis of the Oedipal triangle of Peter Parker, Spider-Man, and Mary Jane lends itself to application here with Pepper able to kill—albeit only symbolically—the patriarchal figure of Iron Man.

Clearly, damsel empowerment reaches a new level in *Iron Man 3* as Pepper both inhabits an iron man suit and also gains super-strength and near-indestructibility. Yet, this empowerment comes at a cost of overt sexualization, a trend Brown and Tasker have skillfully analyzed as problematically intrinsic to superheroine representation. Worse yet, Tony seems to take pleasure in her sexualization, asking why she does not dress like that at home and thus immediately diminishing Pepper's empowerment (and perhaps showing Tony, not Iron Man, to be the true patriarchal figure of their oedipal triad). Moreover, the entire sequence possibly proves Kord and Krimmer's initially forced "romantic fantasy" argument to be an inevitability of the genre.

Pepper's empowerment becomes more strikingly patent and perhaps neutralizes its exploitative nature but still takes a more vacuous and less transgressive form than the subtly balanced heroics of *Iron Man* and *Iron Man 2*. Further, the proliferation of odd and inexplicable rescues does somewhat diminish Pepper's heroism. For instance, a young boy saves Tony, the POTUS uses the Iron Patriot suit to save Colonel James Rhodes, and even the conflicted Maya attempts—unsuccessfully—to save Tony from Aldrich by threatening to take her own life. Rescues become so abundant in a film, in which Tony is frequently powerless, that it allows for Pepper's heroics to be obscured or perhaps reduced to suggestions of mere tokenism. Yet, any such claims prove fallacious when considered in context of Pepper's consistent heroism, success, and centrality to the plot. Her donning of the iron man suit and temporary physical empowerment are not fleeting enactments of tokenism but, rather, conspicuously symbolic forms of the exact type of power she has wielded throughout her appearances in the MCU.

In *The Incredible Hulk*, Dr. Betty Ross further complicates damsel empowerment by deploying traditional femininity as the only means of compromising the Hulk. Like Pepper, Betty's professional success as a doctor of cellular biology is part of the accepted landscape. Importantly, only a few years after Bruce Banner's transformation, Betty's professional efforts are directed to research outside of the scope of "curing" Bruce. Additionally, Betty has romantically moved on from Bruce; the film's narrative reveals that while her feelings for Bruce have not diminished, her singular devotion to him has. Her role as a hero, a partner to Bruce, is far more subtle than Pepper's, but equally meaningful. In Bruce's quest to counteract the radiation poisoning responsible for his Hulk mutation, Betty provides important data that she concealed from military requisition and had been saving. Betty also attempts to rescue the Hulk from being attacked; while unsuccessful, this effort demonstrates her bravery to come to the aid of a being whose strength renders any rescue superfluous. This rescue attempt defies Bruce's directive to "go as far away from me as you can." Additionally, she elbows a soldier and stands fearlessly in front of a tank, contesting military power, and by extension, patriarchal authority as her father, General Ross, leads the attack. In the film's climax, she is rescued by the Hulk from a fire he inadvertently started, but her endangerment is caused by her trying to placate the Hulk, much like she successfully does in an earlier scene when secluded in a cave. Ultimately, Betty is relegated to a tasteful, albeit problematic, fantasy form when the Hulk is effectively exiled. Her primary power is her pacification of the Hulk in the film's finale and, although it requires bravery, it is accomplished through nurturing and affection. This type of nurturing power is established in *Hulk* (2003) when Betty ends their romantic relationship because she feels Bruce is not honest with himself, a push to inspire a self-discovery in him. Betty possesses a rare power over both Bruce and the Hulk, but this strength is construed as definitively traditional, though it defies the affirmation of patriarchy. Betty threatens to disown her father in order to coerce a more benevolent approach to capturing Bruce and demonstrates an ability to live happily without Bruce. Betty's traditional femininity resists criticism because she deploys her empathy, nurturing, and compassion as a way to control the Hulk and soothe the untransformed Bruce (which ultimately addresses the central problem of the whole film). These characteristics do not serve patriarchal duties nor are they linked to a fixation on finding love. As a damsel, Betty challenges gender scholars who interpret any retreat into patriarchal values as undermining feminism; the MCU damsel reveals the transgressive potency of traditional traits, particularly when coupled with agency and independence.

Jane Foster (*Thor* and *Thor: The Dark World* [2013]) is an amalgamation of Betty's ambitious scientist and the strained romantic fulfillment and climatic heroics of Pepper.

Jane is introduced in *Thor* as a young and accomplished astrophysicist who is extremely serious about her career and treated as an equal by her mentor Erik Selvig. Her scientific ingenuity is foregrounded when S.H.I.E.L.D. confiscates her research gear; she pleads, "I made this equipment myself" during her ardent resistance to the seizure. Jane's cognizance of her lack of femininity is displayed when she is embarrassed by her disorderly confines and, flustered, confesses to Thor to never entertaining company. While her attraction to Thor is initially entirely scientific—she colludes with Erik to secure Thor's release from S.H.I.E.L.D. in a deal for him to retrieve her research journals—her interest in him predictably turns romantic. Nevertheless, when under attack in the film's climax, Jane disregards Thor's orders to hide, announcing, "if you're staying than so am I." This suggests that they are equals despite Thor's deity status. In this scene, Jane escorts pedestrians to safety, demonstrating heroism in the face of danger, her bravery being reciprocated by Thor's (and fellow Asgardian warriors') protection. Despite initially lacking the prominence of other MCU damsels, Jane is introduced as similarly intelligent, professionally successful, and able to perform myriad heroic acts.

Much like the conflicted representation of Pepper in *Iron Man 3*, Jane is far more central to the narrative in *The Dark World*, but the nature of that centrality is potentially worrisome. Her early scenes in the film are focused on her fixation and pining over Thor (who is unable to visit Earth due to the events at the conclusion of *Thor*). During an awkward date, her friend and unpaid intern, Darcy Lewis, shows up with urgent news and comments that she expected Jane to be at home in her pajamas, "eating ice cream, and obsessing about Thor." Unable to suppress her problematic romantic feelings and find companionship elsewhere like Betty, Jane is left to futile attempts at dating as a mere form of distraction (or even a reason to get off the couch, if Darcy's comments are to be believed). When Thor arrives on Earth, Jane plays the part of the insecure petulant girlfriend confessing to crying and waiting for Thor to show up as promised. Thor's role as galactic protector only serves as assuring when they are face to face, but fails to assuage her emotions in his absence. Her reaction is a severe departure from the precedent of romantic behavior established by Pepper and Betty. Unfortunately, Jane is unable to balance these neurotic moments with displays of strength, as she spends the vast majority of her scenes in various states of unconsciousness after being infected by the Aether. These scenes range from her in a complete state of stillness, simply serving as a beautiful thing to look at, to when she needs aid while walking during their journey back to Earth. In this scene, she requires rescuing from Loki, which proves to be the singular instance of an unreciprocated damsel rescue in the MCU. Once Thor and a recovered Jane make it to Earth, and are joined by Erik and Darcy, it is Erik who understands and provides an explanation to the audience of the gravitational convergence, despite Jane's focus on the subject.

In the climax, Jane finally achieves a heroic position when she is able to use her gravitational device to protect pedestrians and aid Thor. Jane appears far more courageous than Erik when he cowers in fear when Jane first utilizes her device. The scene plays as comic relief and perhaps his fear reflects his lack of faith in Jane's scientific ingenuity, but it still positions Jane's bravery above Erik (who, unlike Jane, had a central and ultimately heroic role in *The Avengers*) while yet failing to draw a parallel with the film's hero as had become a norm in the MCU. Once the danger escalates, both Erik and Jane predominantly run for cover while attempting to get her contraption to work properly, often operating as a comedic and visually arresting diversion to the true action. Jane does aid Thor in the finale, but it is from a safe distance by way of her device. Most frustratingly, when a ship begins to slowly descend towards Thor, falling from battle, she comes to his rescue by laying herself across him. Clearly, given the situation, Jane's act would fail to protect Thor and rather than attempting to truly rescue him (drag him from harm's way, for instance) she instead concedes her own life. Her heroism is reduced to an irrational lovelorn, self-sacrifice. Compounding this situation is the fact that Erik is able to pragmatically save both Thor and Jane by use of Jane's gravitational device, a logical solution given its pervasive use throughout the duration of the climatic sequence. In the film's final scene, Jane is again left in a dejected state, thought to be abandoned by Thor once again, which is a bittersweet conclusion for those who hope the damsel figure would resist retreating to being a romantic vessel of heterosexual confirmation. As the most recent damsel performance of the MCU, Jane's characterization in *The Dark World* is concerning as the MCU goes forward. While Pepper in *Iron Man 3* was often problematic, these features were offset by both a complex characterization and immense signs of strength. These most recent damsel performances illuminate how the precedent of damsel empowerment established by the MCU is far from stable and how quickly transgressive representation can revert back to its regressive archetype. One hopes the heroism of the damsel becomes truly inured and must acknowledge that the fulfillment of romantic narrative demands and their nurturing of the heroes does not mitigate their strength but, rather, has the potential to fortify their own heroism.

Conclusion

Despite the mid–20th century setting and her romance with Steve Rogers, Peggy Carter's role is both too minor and too powerful to be convincingly considered a damsel. In her first introduction, she barks orders to the soldiers competing for the super soldier program, maligns them by calling them "ladies," and swiftly punches a soldier when insulted by him. The only scene in which Peggy appears to require rescuing is preceded by her chasing an assailant, acting unmoved when a car explodes behind her, firing a number of shots and killing the driver, and again remaining unfazed when the car comes speeding towards her. When Steve dives atop of her to save her from getting hit by the car, she frustratedly exclaims, "I had him." Peggy willfully puts herself in the line of danger, and Steve's rescue can be read clearly as an overzealous exercise of his stereotypical heroism rather than a result of Peggy's desperation. Like the other MCU damsels, Peggy operates as a partner to the film's hero. When Steve aims to rescue the 107th, it is Peggy who procures a plane and pilot in Howard Stark. After Bucky's (presumed) death, it is Peggy who rejuvenates Steve's spirits and convinces him to continue his mission. Despite these scenes, which bare similarities to others featuring the MCU damsels, Peggy has far more in common with the MCU superheroine, Black Widow. The fact that a show on network television (*Agent Carter*, ABC 2015–) is centered on the character would seem to support the fact that her heroism is expected by the audience. Importantly, this show is a significant feminist text, as her heroism is exceptional in both its centrality to the narrative and how it is contextualized within the sexism and animosity of a 1950s workplace; however this text is outside of the scope of this study, which is solely interested in female characters who provide unexpected acts of courage and heroism. Peggy may be every part the mid-century dame, but she is no damsel—and perhaps this is the most significant gender revision of the MCU.

The MCU damsel is not immune to post-feminist criticism. The characters do ignore inequality and perpetuate an ersatz feminist victory, but the appearance of traditional femininity does not serve to exacerbate these faults. Rather, the characters transgressively revise traditional femininity and deploy it as heroism, exposing the sophistic link between traditional femininity and happiness exclusively through men. In other words, MCU damsel representation does not sacrifice the gains of feminism even if it does not acknowledge the urgency of that movement's continued existence. Problematic representations merit criticism, but refreshing images of intelligent women in powerful roles who are acting heroically without the aid of super powers, despite their flaws, also demand acknowledgement. If they also happen to be romantically linked to these heroes—and due to this, become entangled in dangerous situations, which highlight their (physical) weakness—it must be contextualized within their heroism and accomplishments. MCU damsels do not struggle with the post-feminist and film cliché of "having it all"; they simply succeed at having it all. Jane does not have to choose between her science and her relationship with Thor and she willfully accepts the fact that he leaves with only a promise to return. Pepper and Tony have a supportive and loving relationship despite the fact she is tasked with running Stark Industries. Betty's ability to repress her feeling for Bruce does not hinder her from being a highly respected and successful scientist. Damsel or not, Peggy's military career is not threatened when her feelings for Steve develop. The MCU damsel, being undeniably attractive but not hypersexualized, is a glossy comic book ideal of femininity. Importantly, past genre iterations failed to embrace a feminine power capable of comprising various forms, particularly the blend of traditional masculinity (capable fighting, courageous, scientific, military association) and traditional femininity present in the MCU.

The MCU damsels' partnership with the hero in rescuing civilians or their rescue of the hero himself, particularly in the most climatic and dangerous moments, demonstrates their agency; this strength should not be treated as circumspect because they may lack masculine exteriors or retain romantic and nurturing relationships with the protagonist. The trend of feminism via masculine enactment runs rampant throughout Hollywood, typified by emulating physical masculinity and fetishizing the exposed female figure in the action genre specifically. The post-feminist paradigm interprets this as progress whereas others question at what point these advances become dangerously assumed and the disparaging images sabotage the empowered framework that allowed for their creation. Both approaches assume a relationship between empowerment and masculinity that is central to the paradox the MCU damsel exposes. The MCU damsel is very much heroic in a genre that typically requires super powers or massive strength by instead enacting altruistic qualities, such as intelligence, bravery, and selflessness, and in the process rendering strong qualities as gender neutral and potentially broadening how viewers come to identity empowerment.

The MCU damsel emboldens traditional female characteristics and challenges the monopolization of strength and power by traditional masculine representation, either by redefining power or through appropriating masculinity while avoiding tactless emulation. Moreover, the damsel character poses a challenge to contemporary understandings of power and how we have conflated it with gender—it rightly asks why costumed or exaggerated muscularity is a more authentic form of power than vision, compassion, or collaboration. The MCU does not have exclusive claims to damsel empowerment: films such as *The Girl with the Dragon Tattoo* (2011) and the television series *Sherlock*

(2010–) deploy clever role reversals to challenge traditional gender scripts. Moreover, films based on DC comic characters are even more exceptional in this regard than the MCU. Rachel Dawes (*Batman Begins* [2005] and *The Dark Knight* [2008]) and Carol Ferris (*Green Lantern* [2011]) provide the most striking embodiment of the damsel as hero and partner to the superhero, as well as delivering the most courageous reciprocal rescues. Like the MCU damsel, the context of the DC damsel's heroism is obscured by their fleeting retread into traditional damsel behavior, requiring rescue or serving as the hero's love interest. Even DC's iconic damsel, Lois Lane, has undergone a notable revision, rescuing Superman from drowning in the climax of *Superman Returns* (2006). Inhabiting the world's most commercially successful films, these performances represent a nuanced and transgressive representation of gender that challenges post-feminism and its critics simultaneously by heterogeneously complicating and neutralizing the concept of power. It is in these characters, not in those with capes, suits, or skin-tight leather, that the discussion of empowerment should be debated in a dubious post-feminist world.

Notes

1. Christina Adamou, "Evolving Portrayals of Masculinity in Superhero Films: *Hancock*," in *The 21st Century Superhero*, edited by Richard Gray II and Betty Kaklamanidou (Jefferson, NC: McFarland, 2011): 103. Jeffery A. Brown, *Dangerous Curves: Action Heroines, Gender, Fetishism and Popular Culture* (Jackson: University of Mississippi Press, 2011), 26.

2. Amanda Lotz, *Cable Guys: Television and Masculinities in the 21st Century* (New York: New York University Press, 2014), 63.

3. Reporter Christine Everhart's (*Iron Man* and *Iron Man 2*) role is far too insignificant for inclusion. Maya Hansen (*Iron Man 3*), while integral to the plot and—at times—fulfilling the damsel role, is excluded due to her malevolent motivations.

4. The expectation of heroism, like that of a sidekick, applies to the majority of female characters of the MCU including S.H.I.E.L.D. agent Maria Hill (*The Avengers, Captain America: The Winter Solider, Avengers: Age of Ultron*), empowered Wanda Maximoff (*Avengers: Age of Ultron*), warrior Sif (*Thor, Thor: The Dark World*), deity Frigga (*Thor, Thor: The Dark World*), S.H.I.E.L.D. agent Kate/Agent 13 (*Captain America: The Winter Soldier*), and conflicted assassins Gamora and Nebula (*Guardians of the Galaxy*).

5. Brown, 148.

6. Susan J. Douglas, *The Rise of Enlightened Sexism: How Pop Culture Took Us from Girl Power to Girls Gone Wild* (New York: St. Martin's Griffin, 2010), 6.

7. Angela McRobbie, *The Aftermath of Feminism: Gender, Culture and Social Change* (London: Sage, 2009), 1.

8. McRobbie, 6.

9. Susan Bordo, *Unbearable Weight: Feminism, Western Culture and the Body* (Berkeley: University of California Press, 1993).

10. Douglas, 8–9.

11. Ibid., 10.

12. Betty Kaklamanidou, "The Mythos of Patriarchy in the X-Men Films," in *The 21st Century Superhero*, edited by Richard Gray II and Betty Kaklamanidou (Jefferson, NC: McFarland, 2011), 61–74.

13. Wilson Koh, "Everything Old Is Good Again: Myth and Nostalgia in Spider-Man," *Continuum: Journal of Media & Cultural Studies* 23, no. 5 (2009): 735–747.

14. Robert G. Weiner, "Three Stories, Three Movies and the Romances of Mary Jane and Spider-Man," in *Web-Spinning Heroics: Critical Essays on the History and Meaning of Spider-Man*, edited by Robert Moses Peaslee and Robert G. Weiner (Jefferson, NC: McFarland, 2012), 170.

15. Adamou, 103.

16. Ibid.

17. Ibid.

18. Robert Moses Peaslee, "Spidey Meets Freud: Central Psychoanalytic Motifs in *Spider-Man* and *Spider-Man 2*," in *Web-Spinning Heroics: Critical Essays on the History and Meaning of Spider-Man*, edited by Robert Moses Peaslee and Robert G. Weiner (Jefferson, NC: McFarland, 2012), 182.

164   Part 5: The Attempt of Progressivism

19. Peaslee's Freudian interpretation of the Peter Parker/Spider-man crisis situates Spider-Man as the repressive patriarch. Peters "kills" Spider-Man, signified by his abandonment of the Spider-Man costume in a trash can, to escape repression, impotence.

20. Justin Schumaker, "Super-Intertextuality and 21st Century Individualized Social Advocacy in Spider-Man and Kick Ass," in *The 21st Century Superhero,* edited by Richard Gray II and Betty Kaklamanidou (Jefferson, NC: McFarland, 2011), 129–142.

21. Ibid., 142. Schumaker's discussion of Hit-Girl as a savior does draw an interesting comparison to the "savior" motif detected by Peaslee regarding *Spider-Man* in Spider-Man and *Spider-Man 2.*

22. Susanne Kord and Elisabeth Krimmer, *Contemporary Hollywood Masculinities: Gender, Genre and Politics* (New York: Palgrave Macmillian), 2011.

23. Yvonne Tasker, *Spectacular Bodies: Gender, Genre and Action Cinema* (New York: Routledge, 1993).

24. Chris Nashawaty, "Edge of Tomorrow," *Entertainment Weekly,* 13 June 2014, 62.

Elektra
Critical Reception, Postfeminism and the Marvel Superheroine on Screen

Miriam Kent

A spin-off of *Daredevil* (Mark Steven Johnson, 2003), *Elektra* (Rob Bowman, 2005) stars Jennifer Garner as the ruthless assassin anti-heroine based on the popular character created by Frank Miller.[1] Bowman's film received an overwhelmingly negative response from critics, but it remains significant for its contribution to representations of female superheroism and as one of the foundational texts from the earlier period of Marvel's filmic superhero boom. Thus far, it is the only film based on a Marvel property to be led by a titular female character. It is therefore noteworthy that there have been no attempts to put other Marvel superheroines in their own films since, although, as of this writing, there have been announcements for a *Captain Marvel* film.

This chapter offers an interrogation of *Elektra*'s critical reception, alongside articles promoting the film prior to its release, to illuminate the question: *what is at stake in films presenting powerful superheroines?* While the film itself negotiates issues related to femininity and power, concentrating on *Elektra*'s promotional texts can offer a broader idea of dominant discourses present in Western culture at the time. This can shed light upon anxieties that arise when considering the female superhero, which potentially affect generic and industrial factors shaping the production of such films.

Let's first outline the cultural context of *Elektra*, referring to academic debates about the representation of physically tough women as well as post-feminist culture. These ideas are then related to how the film was promoted in articles before its release. As Jonathan Gray argues, "Hollywood invests considerable effort and money into 'hyping its products' before they are released."[2] This "hype" contributes to meanings generated by the texts. Then, let's examine the critical reception of the film, considering reviews from newspapers and online news sites in North America and the UK. The value of critical reception as a measure of the dominant discourses surrounding a film has been established by theorists such as Janet Staiger[3] and Barbara Klinger.[4] Thus, we'll see how the discourses present in the reviews and the dominant cultural contexts are relatable. Doubtless, issues concerning female empowerment, objectification and postfeminist rhetoric are rife within these reviews. Demystifying these discourses proves valuable in discerning the state of gender representation at the time.

Ideally, *Elektra* might have been the forerunner of many Marvel films featuring titular superheroines. However, it took until late 2014 for Marvel to even announce another solo superheroine film.[5] Despite being academically neglected, *Elektra* remains significant, suggesting that Hollywood still has a strained relationship with the notion of the superheroine on screen. The purpose of this chapter is to shed light on that relationship and question how it has been maintained over time.

Postfeminism and Superhero(ine)ism

The female action heroine has received considerable attention since, at least, the 1980s and 1990s, when a slew of tough action women began to appear. Physically resilient, muscular characters such as Ellen Ripley and Sarah Connor have been rich points of discussion. Significantly, Yvonne Tasker suggests that such characters embody "musculinity," a mode of presentation whereby female action characters adopt muscles, a traditionally masculine signifier, in a "transgressive" way.[6] Such portrayals later died out in favor of slender-bodied action women. A consideration of these heroines against those discussed by Tasker reveals the complexities present in the representation of female heroism.

These issues have also been addressed by theorists who interrogate the role of postfeminist culture in representations of superheroines. Postfeminist culture flourished in the 1990s and has been discussed by numerous writers. Angela McRobbie, for example, argues that postfeminist culture involves "an active process by which feminist gains of the 1970s and 1980s come to be undermined."[7] Postfeminist rhetoric therefore enacts modes of representation that portray feminism as redundant, whilst also incorporating the notions of female empowerment for which feminism has fought. The notion that women *can* be strong and heroic is often taken for granted, rendering attention to feminist issues unnecessary. Meanwhile, as Diane Negra claims, "postfeminism fetishizes female power and desire while consistently placing these within firm limits."[8]

Postfeminist sentiments are recognizable in the emphasis on sex appeal in portrayals of superheroines. Here, women's sexualization is empowering, a tendency that is apparent in the costuming of superheroines in Marvel films, for example. This sexualization has been examined by a number of authors, many of whom draw on Laura Mulvey's seminal theories regarding the cinematic binary opposition between active/male and passive/female, a phenomenon driven by the male gaze and the pleasure of looking (scopophlia).[9] Richard Gray, for instance, argues that, for action heroines such as those in *X-Men* (Bryan Singer, 2000), power is directly correlated to their levels of "hotness." The more control these characters wield over their powers, Gray maintains, the "hotter" and more sexually appealing they become.[10] Likewise, Marc O'Day refers to "action babes," who "can be seen to function simultaneously as the action subject of narrative and the erotic object of visual spectacle"[11] rather than remaining a passive object of the male gaze. Both writers draw attention to the emphasis contemporary action films place on heroines' appearance and sex appeal. Importantly, such portrayals incorporate feminist discourses of women's empowerment whilst largely privileging specific configurations of that empowerment (namely slim, white, heterosexual, feminine beauty).

Neither O'Day nor Grey refers to the cultural implications of these postfeminist representations. On the other hand, Lisa Purse questions the need for such postfeminist portrayals of female superheroism, concluding that they have resulted in an unbalanced presentation of women encompassing "the 'acceptable face' of female empowerment."[12]

Hence, the prevalence of slender, delicately feminine, white superheroines speaks to a need for media portrayals to provide images of empowered, tough women, while remaining well within the confines of conventional, easily recognizable categories of gender. Cristina Stasia similarly argues that the postfeminist superheroine "not only manifests anxieties about changing gender roles, but indicates a lack of anxiety as popular culture fulfils the prophecy of the term postfeminism: convincing women they live in a post-patriarchy."[13]

As a film based on a Marvel property, *Elektra* carries many of the burdens present in comic book representations of heroines, as well as those of mainstream Hollywood. Both comic books and blockbuster films have traditionally been aimed at (heterosexual) men.[14] Mike Madrid discusses the often problematic representations of superheroines throughout the decades, from superheroines who have been frequently portrayed as feeble or incapable[15] to others who became crazed murderers due to their inability to control their powers,[16] which can be seen as a result of these representational pressures. While these trends have undergone considerable development in recent years, their presence in comic history is still significant. Similarly, *Elektra* faced the problem of having to make a violent, ruthless female assassin accessible to a PG-13 audience (since the majority of Marvel adaptations fall under this rating in order to gain as wide an audience as possible).[17] The film thus had to appeal to large audiences (in line with dominant Hollywood trends shaped by young male viewers) and also speak to male comic book fans, while finally also presenting a sanitized picture of a violent and potentially transgressive character.

It is thus possible to position *Elektra* within these postfeminist discourses. Cinematic Elektra is a young, physically fit, white woman with disposable income (due to her job as an assassin-for-hire). Having died in *Daredevil*, she is resurrected and trained in an ancient form of martial arts. She is then assigned a job to assassinate a single-father named "Mark" and his daughter "Abby." Feeling a bond between herself and her targets, she spares their lives, only to discover that Abby is "The Treasure," a child prodigy with extraordinary fighting abilities who is sought by the predatory ninja outfit, "The Hand." Elektra must then protect Abby from numerous villains. Postfeminist sentiments shine through during the film, for instance through the many close-ups of Garner's immaculate face and slender body. In terms of physicality, Garner possesses the typical athletic fitness often presented in such films, an issue discussed more in the next section. However, there are also contradictions within the text. For instance, while frequently focusing on fragments of Elektra's body in an indulgent display of sexual allure, the film is cautious to also feature her fighting skills (for example, the opening fight takes place almost entirely in the dark). Similarly, the film exploits maternal themes as Elektra becomes a substitute mother to Abby, and the film must negotiate how to juggle the seemingly incompatible positions of assassin and mother. These tensions are perhaps most indicative of the postfeminist rhetoric of the surrounding culture of the time, which, as Tasker and Negra note, is "inherently contradictory."[18]

Elektra and the Promotion of "having it all"

The themes that surfaced within promotional press articles surrounding *Elektra* are inextricably linked to an overarching postfeminist rhetoric concerned with issues of contemporary femininity. This modern vision of strong femininity incorporates a number of dominant features that reach back to the feminist discourses of women's empowerment whilst simultaneously including seemingly paradoxical sentiments (for example, an emphasis on sex appeal). Promotional articles centered on Garner as the film's star, but the recurring themes focused almost solely on her good looks and attractive body. Subsequently, these discourses tie in to the postfeminist notion of "having it all." Since these were the traits through which the film was promoted, an examination of these articles offers some indication of the pressures exerted on female superheroism.

Given the highly gendered nature of the contemporary celebrity,[19] these themes come as no surprise. Su Holmes and Diane Negra, for instance, argue that when considering female celebrities, there is an insistence in the media to focus on the body, sexuality, marriage and motherhood—discourses which are not applied to male celebrities.[20] It is thus possible to characterize the media discourses surrounding Garner during the promotion of *Elektra* as a symptom of these practices. However, the fact that they have been used in conjunction with discourses referring to female superheroes is noteworthy and requires further examination.

The articles promoting *Elektra* were primarily invested in sexualizing Garner. Thus, statements referring to the actress' attractive looks were foregrounded through the use of adjectives such as "dazzling,"[21] "gorgeous"[22] and "stunning."[23] However, most of this sexualization was derived from the costume Garner wore as Elektra (which comprised a red satin bustier and matching leather pants) as well as her physically fit body. Regarding the costume, writers of these articles consistently referred to statements made by Garner, in which she reveals that the costume was so tight that she was unable to wear any undergarments. Hence Ian Burchell's headline, "Elektra's Warrior: Sexy Jen's All Swords ... and No Knickers,"[24] and Adam Stone's "Elektra Flies Solo ... and Goes Commando."[25] These writers highlighted the sexual appeal for the heterosexual male audience at which the film was targeted, while the quotation from Garner outlined that the costume was specifically devised to appeal to male fans, after they expressed disappointment with the costume she wore in *Daredevil*.

> Most of the time [fans] were upset about the suit I wore. They said it was too black and not sexy enough. This time it's red and very, very sexy, so I think a lot of Elektra fans will be happy.... The only thing I did discover about this costume is there's no room for panties—not even a G-string. So now everyone will know Elektra goes commando.[26]

These statements are clearly intended to provide a titillating point of interest for potential cinemagoers. Indeed, Stone noted. "with her perfect figure squeezed into an impossibly tight and revealing red jumpsuit, Jennifer is aware that the story will be the last thing on the mind of many in the audience."[27] They are likewise framed as light-hearted, with Garner showing no qualms about expressing this personal information. As such, Garner is portrayed as being completely at ease with her sexuality, a point I return to later.

Also linked to this subject were more general comments about Garner's attractiveness. To complicate matters, though, these statements were combined with "girl power" rhetoric. According to Stéphanie Genz and Benjamin Brabon, girl power takes the form of "a popular feminist stance ... that combines female independence and individualism with a confident display of femininity/sexuality."[28] Proliferated in the 1990s, girl power rhetoric is inextricably linked to postfeminist culture such that it is interested in empowering (young) women and co-opting feminist sensibilities while stressing the redundancy of second-wave feminism. Thus, girl power discourses offer a celebration of femininity, but their link to capitalism and commodified versions of feminism often result in the sloganization of feminist rhetoric.[29] Hence, promotional articles on *Elektra* referred to the character's physical strength as shaped by "girl power." Barry Koltnow, for instance, remarked that "Jennifer Garner is that rare Hollywood combination: Sex symbol and tough chick."[30]

Further, much of Garner's girl power is derived from her slender but physically fit body. Jackie Guendouzi outlines the importance of the slender body in promoted images of empowered women in the media.[31] Surpassing the previously dominant ideal of the thin woman, the toned woman is seen as more desirable, although this sort of body type is harder to achieve due to requiring a punishing fitness regime.[32] Thus, as Rosalind Gill argues, postfeminist culture promotes this body type as part of its investment in the "monitoring, surveillance, discipline and re-modelling"[33] of the female body. Gill similarly argues that such body ideals are by nature limiting and exclusive, as "postfeminist sensibility re-centres both heterosexuality and whiteness, as well as fetishizing a young, able-bodied, 'fit' ... female body."[34] Therefore, these articles celebrated Garner's sexual appeal in terms of her fitness. Stone, for example, highlights that Garner stays in "tip-top shape,"[35] while Koltnow focuses on the physically taxing nature of Garner's workouts, referring to the "lumps and bruises" she endured while training for the role.[36]

Another focus in promotional articles was the film's inclusion of a kiss between Garner and actress Natassia Malthe, who played Elektra's foe, the toxic woman "Typhoid" (based loosely on Typhoid Mary from the comics). Here, Burchell drew attention to "a steamy lesbian snog with her deadly enemy Typhoid Mary."[37] The articles capitalized on a heterosexualized vision of lesbian sexuality that served a (heterosexual) male gaze, while promoting a liberated sexuality for Garner. As Tricia Jenkins notes, such images presenting "luscious lesbians" had been on the increase throughout the late 1990s and early 2000s.[38] But the comments quoted from Garner, again, present a woman who is entirely at ease with her sexuality, for instance when she comments that "when the time came, it was just a kiss."[39] As noted earlier, a celebration of female sexuality is often present in postfeminist culture, and Garner hereby indicates her status as a sexually liberated woman. However, it must also be noted that the articles[40] likewise drew attention to Garner's relationship with former co-star Ben Affleck, again reasserting heterosexuality.

The culmination of these discourses results in an image of Garner "having it all," an ideal promoted through postfeminist culture which posits that women do not have to choose between falsely dichotomized notions of having feminist ideals and indulging in femininity.[41] As Hannah Sanders notes, it is "the assumption that feminism's goals have been achieved and all that modern women have to do is choose a lifestyle from the endless range of options available to them."[42] The articles present Garner as having reached the ultimate combination of feminine achievements—confidence, beauty, a fit body, professional fulfillment, being at ease with her sexuality, and, of course, a man. Garner is assigned the position of the ideal postfeminist subject who is sexy but strong, physically fit but still slender, comfortable with her sexuality but not straying too far from heterosexual ideals. These factors are shown to be enriching to Garner's subjectivity (for example, she notes that the physical training she undertook gave her confidence).[43] Similarly, Garner's professional achievements are taken for granted, making way for discussions of her physical beauty. In one interview, Garner directly refers to these discourses, stating, "I know that when *Elektra* comes out, there's going to be a whole wave of articles which are going to emphasize my look or whatever. I can cope with it because I think that my work will still be the thing upon which I'm ultimately going to be judged."[44] Here, Garner accepts that the media may focus on her appearance, but claims that this does not matter, as she takes for granted that her acting abilities will be recognized. She subsequently comments, "I've known for a long time that your looks will only take you so far.... But I wouldn't mind if I was known for being a good actress who's also kind of nice to look at."[45] The overarching discourses of these statements is that Garner can afford to be scrutinized for her looks because it has already been established that she is a skilled actress, allowing the media to indulge in her beauty. The feminist goal of having a good career and being a respected professional has been achieved; it is now possible to turn the focus back to points which might once have even been deemed frivolous by second wave feminists, who are presumed to stand in opposition to traditional models of femininity fostered by patriarchal structures of womanhood.

In this sense, Garner is able to "have it all," and yet, as Genz notes, the very notion of having it all is fraught with inconsistencies.[46] Thus, an examination of these articles illustrates the complexities present in contemporary feminine subjectivity, which become yet more complicated when combined with notions of female superheroism. These complexities are also present in the critical reception of the film, although with slightly different results.

Critical Reception of the Postfeminist Superheroine

As discussed, postfeminist women must negotiate the task of "having it all." In the case of Garner, promotional articles maintained an almost unanimous image of the actress as a contemporary woman who has succeeded in this task. However, this ideal can at times rebound, as can be seen in the critical reception of *Elektra*, which was overwhelmingly negative. Critics were quick to condemn various traits of the film, many of which were undeniably gendered. As such, the postfeminist ideals were projected onto the film, resulting in contradictory and convoluted reasons as to why the film was received poorly. These reviews thus shed light on the multifaceted expectations critics had regarding a female superhero whilst also illuminating the cultural pressures which are placed upon such characters.

Critics, like the promotional articles, focused on matters of Garner's physical appearance. In fact, her beauty was a vehicle through which gender-based discourses regarding superheroic representation were expressed, and this was greatly localized onto Garner's body. The *Washington Times*' reviewer wrote that, in the film, Garner "struts like an athlete, has abs of titanium and boasts lips that make Angelina Jolie's look masculine by comparison,"[47] while Bob Townsend of the *Atlanta Journal-Constitution* referred to her "pneumatically chiselled build and solemnly sensuous face."[48] As noted earlier, postfeminist culture is invested in the promotion of a particular, toned brand of fit femininity. However, what makes these statements noteworthy is their incorporation of both fitness and beauty discourses. Hence, critics often combined their praise for Garner's fit body with reference to the Elektra costume. For example, Christy Lemire maintained that the role is "a perfect fit for the perfectly fit actress.... She saunters across the room in a red lace-up bustier and low-slung red leather pants."[49] In typically contradictory postfeminist fashion, these reviews acknowledged Garner's striking physicality, but the discussion focused on her sexy outfit. Likewise, it should be noted that even critics who gave a negative review of the film regarded Garner's sex appeal positively, characterizing it as an asset of the film. Furthermore, critics also invoked sloganized girl power phrases to refer to Garner: Jami Bernard titled her review "Martial Tart,"[50] while others utilized phrases such as "buxom badass,"[51] "blade-hurling babe"[52] and "Jennifer Garner kicks butt."[53]

The red leather costume effectively took center stage across the reviews, with some critics referring to it ironically as a source of ridicule. Benjamin Strong, for instance, wrote that "whether or not you'll appreciate [*Elektra*'s] modest charms depends entirely on whether you too have been anticipating Garner's new outfit,"[54] while others drew parallels between the costume and Victoria's Secret underwear.[55] Indeed, the complexities of the postfeminist embrace of sexual exhibitionism become more apparent in certain reviews which implied rigid prerequisites for acceptable sexual femininity. Nick Schager argued that "Garner looks delicious in a rose-red bustier and matching hot pants, and the girls-gone-violent film fleetingly taps into its potential for sensuality during Elektra's soulful mouth-to-mouth moment with Typhoid."[56] He appreciated the heterosexualized display of the girl-on-girl kiss, but concluded that "unfortunately, this fetching killer's tiresome hang-ups—ill-matched with slow-motion shots of her strutting like a second-rate fashionista auditioning for *America's Next Top Model* … cause all traces of eroticism, intrigue, and gravity to evaporate."[57] Here, Schager argues that specific levels of sensuality are enjoyable, but through drawing parallels with a reality series that offers young women the chance to become models, he effectively makes distinctions between acceptable and unacceptable visions of feminine sexuality. As such, he found *Elektra*'s sensuality enjoyable until it became, in his eyes, trashy. Similar sentiments came from Townsend, who referred to Elektra's attire as a "scanty bright-red costume that could also be very useful to a highly paid call girl,"[58] a response that is reminiscent of director Rob Bowman's argument that the filmmakers could not make an exact copy of Elektra's comic book costume for fear that "she would look like a hooker."[59] As Gill notes, postfeminist culture promotes a particular kind of sexual freedom, but also stresses the need for discipline and self-monitoring of the female body.[60] Certainly, such inconsistent sensibilities are well and truly established within these reviews.

The complexity of these discourses of acceptable (superheroic) femininity become more exaggerated when critics directly refer to issues of women's empowerment in action cinema. Mick LaSalle wrote:

> It's Garner going around in a tight red outfit, killing people. She is without emotion, as close as a human being can get to being a machine. More to the point, she is as close as a woman can get to being a man. This is film feminism in the 21st century: Take a cruel, bloodthirsty, homicidal character, but instead of making the character a man, make it a woman. Then pretend you've created an exemplar of female strength. I liked this fake feminism better when it was called misogyny.[61]

LaSalle's statement raises a number of points that have been present in debates about action heroines for decades. When muscular heroines such as Ellen Ripley and Sarah Connor gained popularity in the 1980s and 1990s, viewers became concerned with the notion that such action heroines were overly masculinized women, or "men in drag."[62] Regardless of whether or not this is the case, the fact that these debates have persisted indicate the contentious nature of the action heroine and the tensions she faces. LaSalle focuses on the aspects of the character he perceives as masculinized—violence, cruelty, etc.—arguing that such representations are "fake feminism" since these female characters are stripped of their femininity (incidentally, LaSalle makes no references to the feminized aspects of the character, such as the maternal subplot). His reference to Elektra's "tight red outfit" also suggests that it is this sexualized brand of violence that he sees as particularly problematic. Though LaSalle's intentions are not quite clear, his review does illustrate the complexities of representing action heroines in the age of postfeminism.

However, LaSalle's arguments become more fascinating when compared to other critics who invoked similar themes. Bernard, for instance, chose to focus on the feminized aspects of the character: "the movie bows to convention, perhaps fearing that audiences won't accept a woman with a hide this thick. Elektra is stripped of the unrepentant ferocity that made her a crossover hit in the first place. Here, she quickly succumbs to her gooey, maternal side."[63] Comparing the character to her representation in the comics, Bernard argues that Elektra is not represented as "tough enough." But it is this "unrepentant ferocity" which LaSalle disliked because it made her what Elizabeth Hills refers to as a "figurative male."[64]

Further, Manohla Dargis dedicated much of her review to issues of female representation in superhero films.[65] Dargis recognizes the tensions present in these representations, claiming, "culturally there's always something disturbing, even disrupting about a woman who walks (or flies) alone."[66] She ultimately concludes that the superheroines of Hollywood pale in comparison to those presented in Hong Kong cinema, "where for decades alpha gals have been soaring through the air and kicking up their high heels to battle villainy."[67] Indeed, many critics made negative comparisons between *Elektra* and the action films of Hong Kong,[68] but Dargis effectively articulates what these other reviewers do not: the heroines in these films are not viewed as exceptional within their culture. Through these discourses, Dargis was one of few critics to actively acknowledge that there even *are* issues that arise when considering the representation of action heroines.

Still, comparisons to other films were made in *Elektra*'s reception, most notably Garner's previous film *13 Going on 30* (Gary Winick, 2004), a fantasy comedy in which a teenage girl wishes she was "thirty, flirty and thriving" and wakes up in the body of a grown woman (Garner). *13 Going on 30* has likewise received attention for its engagement with postfeminist sensibilities, for example its promotion of eternal girlhood and "girl-women."[69] However, *Elektra*'s critics largely expressed disappointment that Garner's performance did not match that of her previous film. Claudia Puig, for instance, maintained: "Jennifer Garner, adept as she is at physical stunts and action moves, is far more appealing when she's playing charming and adorable, as she did so winningly in *13 Going on 30*"[70] and Bernard suggested that Garner was "far more enjoyable in the light comedy *13 Going on 30*."[71] Likewise, Strong wrote: "director Rob Bowman squanders the impressive comic facility Garner demonstrated in *13 Going on 30*."[72] These statements are interesting, considering the enormous difference between the two respective characters played by Garner. The dichotomy between the characters becomes amplified by the fact that Elektra in the comics is stoic, violent and edgy, leaving little room for the type of cute humor desired by these critics. Rather than praising her diverse selection of roles (let alone, whether she plays them well), critics instead were disappointed that Garner did not demonstrate her comic acting ability in *Elektra*. This is to say that they preferred Garner when she was playing a charming, cute, light-hearted character that is essentially a child in a woman's body. Such sentiments indicate an anxiety in the portrayal of superheroines. It could, for instance, be said that these critics found it challenging to accept Elektra's harsh characteristics in light of Garner's previous performance. To sum up Purse: Elektra did not match the "acceptable face" of female heroism linked to the actress's screen image, which they held as an ideal.

Thus, the film's reception illustrates the tensions present in representations of female superheroes. Within these reviews, notions of feminine power are constantly negotiated and re-negotiated. The reviews are complex and multifaceted, engaging and compromising with dominant postfeminist sentiments. Overall, I would argue that it was impossible for *Elektra* to demonstrably "have it all" in these reviews. For instance, Garner was praised for her sex appeal but simultaneously ridiculed for it. Meanwhile, Elektra was at times perceived as too tough, and yet also not tough enough. Finally, critics expressed disappointment that Garner was not able to play the character as light-hearted and comic. Judging by the film's reviews, it is clear that postfeminist pressures place conflicting demands on the notion of the superheroine: she must be sexy, but not too sexy; tough, but not too tough; she must be cute, witty and funny, but still be commanding. She must, in other words: have it all. This indicates the limiting, frustrating nature of postfeminist culture, demonstrating the highly complex nature of such representations. As such, it is perhaps no surprise that it has taken Marvel this long to consider releasing another female-led superhero film.

Conclusion

As my discussion of promotional texts surrounding *Elektra* suggests, there is a strained relationship between the notion of the superheroine and Hollywood's representations of them. Whilst the promotional articles capitalized on Garner's status as a postfeminist woman succeeding in having it all, *Elektra*'s negative critical reception was related to its inability to juggle the varying demands which having it all entails. Within these texts, feminist notions of women's empowerment became intertwined with discourses that potentially disavow feminism. Likewise, the issues concerning the representation of action heroines are revealed when examining the discourses surrounding a film that features such a heroine. This indicates the proliferation of such issues throughout Western society, which is thus not limited to academia but also penetrates the popular sphere, whether or not critics were consciously aware of it as such.

It is hence possible to consider Marvel executives' hesitation in announcing another female-led superhero film as a symptom of anxieties surrounding the representation of heroines. Recent comments from Kevin Feige, Marvel Studio's President of Production, for instance, expressed a reluctance to "pluck" a female character, in this case Black Widow, super spy in *The Avengers* (Joss Whedon, 2012), from an established franchise.[73] The danger, states Feige, is that by putting an established superheroine in her own film, Marvel would not get "credit" for making a successful movie.[74] Be that as it may, Feige's bizarre explanation shows how superheroines are regarded as requiring special handling from filmmakers. If anything, these statements support my findings and showcase the complexities of the postfeminist superheroine in Hollywood film.

With this in mind it is notable that a *Captain Marvel* film is in the works. Meanwhile on the small screen, *Marvel's Agent Carter* (ABC, 2015–)[75] has gained considerable traction, having been renewed for a second season, while Netflix is offering *Marvel's Jessica Jones*.[76] Given that television has been considered to have offered the female superheroine an arena in which to experiment and flourish in the past,[77] these developments are perhaps not surprising, although the added dimension of the internet and online streaming services should also be noted. Also of interest is the positioning of these new female superheroic texts within an era marked by shifting discourses of a post-recession media landscape and the gendered implications thereof.[78] *Elektra* was a product of a series of cultural discourses that by the time of its release had firmly taken hold. It is hard to say what form, if any, these discourses will take when a solo Marvel superheroine film sees the light of day, although it is almost certain that the figure of the superheroine on screen will remain a complex cultural phenomenon.

Notes

1. Frank Miller and Klaus Janson, "Elektra," *Daredevil* #168, January 1982, Marvel Comics.
2. Jonathan Gray, *Show Sold Separately: Promos, Spoilers, and Other Media Paratexts* (New York: New York University Press, 2010), 47.
3. Janet Staiger, *Interpreting Films: Studies in the Historical Reception of American Cinema* (Princeton: Princeton University Press, 1992).
4. Barbara Klinger, *Melodrama and Meaning: History, Culture and the Films of Douglas Sirk* (Bloomington: Indiana University Press, 1994).
5. Lucas Siegel, "Marvel Announces BLACK PANTHER, CAPTAIN MARVEL, INHUMANS, AVENGERS: INFINITY WAR Films, CAP & THOR 3 Subtitles," *Newsarama*, October 28, 2014, http://www.newsarama.com/22573-marvel-announces-black-panther-captain-marvel-inhumans-avengers-infinity-war-films-cap-thor-3-subtitles.html.
6. Yvonne Tasker, *Spectacular Bodies: Gender, Genre and the Action Cinema* (London: Routledge, 1993), 149.
7. Angela McRobbie, "Post-Feminism and Popular Culture," in *Interrogating Postfeminism: Gender and the Politics of Popular Culture*, ed. Yvonne Tasker and Diane Negra (Durham: Duke University Press, 2007), 27.
8. Diane Negra, *What a Girl Wants? Fantasizing the Reclamation of Self in Postfeminism* (Oxon: Routledge, 2009), 4.
9. Laura Mulvey, "Visual Pleasure and Narrative Cinema," in *Film Theory and Criticism: Introductory Readings*, ed. Leo Braudy and Marshall Cohen, 6th ed. (New York: Oxford University Press, 1975), 841.
10. Richard J. Gray, "Vivacious Vixens and Scintillating Super Hotties: Deconstructing the Superheroine," in *The 21st Century Superhero: Essays on Gender, Genre and Globalization in Film*, ed. Richard J. Gray and Betty Kaklamanidou (Jefferson, NC: McFarland, 2011), 75–93.
11. Marc O'Day, "Beauty in Motion: Gender, Spectacle and Action Babe Cinema," in *Action and Adventure Cinema*, ed. Yvonne Tasker (Oxon: Routledge, 2004), 203.
12. Lisa Purse, *Contemporary Action Cinema* (Edinburgh: Edinburgh University Press, 2011), 85.
13. Christina Lucia Stasia, "'My Guns Are in the Fendi!' The Postfeminist Female Action Hero," in *Third Wave Feminism: A Critical Exloration, 2d ed.*, ed. Stacy Gillis, Gillian Howie, and Rebecca Munford (Basingstoke: Palgrave Macmillan, 2007), 238.
14. Jeffrey A. Brown, *Dangerous Curves: Heroines, Gender, Fetishism, and Popular Culture* (Jackson: University Press of Mississippi, 2011), 53; Peter Krämer, "A Powerful Cinema-Going Force? Hollywood and Female Audiences since the 1960s," in *Identifying Hollywood's Audiences: Cultural Identity and the Movies*, ed. Melvyn Stokes and Richard Maltby (London: BFI, 1999), 93.
15. Mike Madrid, *The Supergirls: Fashion, Feminism, Fantasy, and the History of Comic Book Heroines* (Ashland, OR: Exterminating Angel Press, 2009), 109.
16. Ibid., 173.
17. Thomas Schatz, "New Hollywood, New Millennium," in *Film Theory and Contemporary Hollywood Movies*, ed. Warren Buckland (Oxon: Routledge, 2009), 33.
18. Yvonne Tasker and Diane Negra, "Introduction: Feminist Politics and Postfeminist Culture," in *Interrogating Postfeminism: Gender and the Politics of Popular Culture*, ed. Yvonne Tasker and Diane Negra (Durham: Duke University Press, 2007), 8.
19. Su Holmes and Diane Negra, "Introduction," in *In the Limelight and Under the Microscope: Forms and Functions of Female Celebrity*, ed. Su Holmes and Diane Negra (New York: Continuum, 2011).
20. Holmes and Negra, "Introduction."

21. Iain Burchell, "Elektra's Warrior; Sexy Jen's All Swords ... and No Knickers," *Daily Star*, January 7, 2005.
22. Ibid.
23. Adam Stone, "Elektra Flies Solo ... and Goes Commando," *Daily Record* (Scotland), January 3, 2005.
24. Burchell, "Elektra's Warrior."
25. Stone, "Elektra Flies Solo."
26. Jennifer Garner in Alun Palmer, "Elektra-Fying; Jennifer Garner on Her Hot New Film," *The Mirror*, January 07, 2005.
27. Stone, "Elektra Flies Solo."
28. Stéphanie Genz and Benjamin A. Brabon, *Postfeminism: Cultural Texts and Theories* (Edinburgh: Edinburgh University Press, 2009), 77.
29. Sarah Banet-Weiser, "Girls Rule! Gender, Feminism, and Nickelodeon," *Critical Studies in Media Communication* 21, no. 2 (2004): 119–39.
30. Barry Koltnow, "Getting a Charge from Elektra," *Hamilton Spectator* (Ontario), January 11, 2005.
31. Jackie Guendouzi, "'She's Very Slim': Talking about Body-Size in All-Female Interactions," *Journal of Pragmatics* 36 (2004): 1636.
32. Ibid., 1649.
33. R. Gill, "Postfeminist Media Culture: Elements of a Sensibility," *European Journal of Cultural Studies* 10, no. 2 (2007): 149
34. Ibid., 163.
35. Stone, "Elektra Flies Solo."
36. Koltnow, "Getting a Charge from Elektra."
37. Burchell, "Elektra's Warrior."
38. Tricia Jenkins, "'Potential Lesbians at Two O'Clock': The Heterosexualization of Lesbianism in the Recent Teen Film," *Journal of Popular Culture* 38, no. 3 (2005): 491–504.
39. Stone, "Elektra Flies Solo."
40. Palmer, "Elektra-Fying"; Stone, "Elektra Flies Solo."
41. Stéphanie Genz, "Singled Out: Postfeminism's 'New Woman' and the Dilemma of Having It All," *The Journal of Popular Culture* 43, no. 1 (2010): 98.
42. Hannah E. Sanders, "Living a Charmed Life: The Magic of Postfeminist Sisterhood," in *Interrogating Postfeminism: Gender and the Politics of Popular Culture*, ed. Yvonne Tasker and Diane Negra (Durham: Duke University Press, 2007), 74.
43. Koltnow, "Getting a Charge from Elektra."
44. Garner in Palmer, "Elektra-Fying."
45. Garner in Ibid.
46. Genz, "Singled Out."
47. Garner Tries Out New Alias," *Washington Times*, January 13, 2005, http://www.washingtontimes.com/news/2005/jan/13/20050113-113646-3425r/print/.
48. Bob Townsend, "'Elektra' Pretty Complex for a Comic Book Heroine," *Atlanta Journal-Constitution*, January 14, 2005.
49. Christy Lemire, "Garner Perfect for 'Elektra,'" *York* (PA) *Dispatch*, January 13, 2005.
50. Jami Bernard, "Martial Tart: Alive and Kickin'," *Daily News* (New York), January 14, 2005.
51. Nick Schager, "Elektra," *Slant*, January 12, 2005, http://www.slantmagazine.com/film/review/elektra.
52. Bob Strauss, "Elektra Back from the Dead—But Why?" *Daily News of Los Angeles*, January 14, 2005.
53. Townsend, "'Elektra.'"
54. Benjamin Strong, "Mediocre Marvel Probes Elektra's Complexes, Costumes," *Village Voice*, January 11, 2005, http://www.villagevoice.com/content/printVersion/188704/.
55. Dann Gire, "Mourning Becomes the Brain-Dead 'Elektra,'" *Chicago Daily Herald*, January 14, 2005; Manohla Dargis, "Moral Conflict Plus a Hot Bod: What More Does a Girl Need?" *The New York Times*, January 14, 2005, http://www.nytimes.com/2005/01/14/movies/14elek.html?_r=0.
56. Schager, "Elektra."
57. Ibid.
58. Townsend, "'Elektra' Pretty Complex."

59. Rob Bowman in Barry Ronge, "Fly or Flop?," *Sunday Times* (South Africa), January 9, 2005.
60. Gill, "Postfeminist Media Culture," 149.
61. Mick LaSalle, "Lady in Red Adds Zero Zing to Soulless, Violence-Prone 'Elektra,'" *SFGate*, January 14, 2005, http://www.sfgate.com/movies/article/Lady-in-red-adds-zero-zing-to-soulless-2738825.php.
62. Harvey R. Greenberg, "FEMBO: 'Aliens' Intentions," *Journal of Popular Film and Television* 15, no. 4 (1988): 164–71; Elizabeth Hills, "From 'Figurative Males' to Action Heroines: Further Thoughts on Active Women in the Cinema," *Screen* 40, no. 1 (1999): 38–50.
63. Bernard, "Martial Tart."
64. Hills, "From 'Figurative Males' to Action Heroines."
65. Dargis, "Moral Conflict Plus a Hot Bod."
66. Ibid.
67. Ibid.
68. Lemire, "Garner Perfect for 'Elektra'"; Matt Soergel, "'Elektra' Not Fully Charged," *Florida Times-Union*, January 14, 2005.
69. Alison Winch, *Girlfriends and Postfeminist Sisterhood* (Basingstoke: Palgrave MacMillan, 2013), 28.
70. Claudia Puig, "'Elektra' Is a Fight to the Finish," *USA Today*, January 13, 2005, http://usatoday30.usatoday.com/life/movies/reviews/2005-01-13-elektra-review_x.htm.
71. Bernard, "Martial Tart."
72. Strong, "Mediocre Marvel."
73. Kevin Feige in David Faraci, "Kevin Feige on Marvel's Responsibility to Be Diverse and a Possible Captain Marvel Movie," *Badass Digest*, March 14, 2014, badassdigest.com/2014/03/14/kevin-feige-on-marvels-responsibility-to-be-diverse-and-a-possible-captain/.
74. Feige in Ibid.
75. Merrill Barr, "'Agent Carter' Season 2 Confirmed at ABC," *Forbes*, May 8, 2015, http://www.forbes.com/sites/merrillbarr/2015/05/07/agent-carter-season-2-renewed-cancelled/.
76. Robin Parrish, "Netflix's Next Marvel Series: Who Is Jessica Jones?" *Tech Times*, May 16, 2015, http://www.techtimes.com/articles/53354/20150516/netflixs-next-marvel-series-who-jessica-jones.htm.
77. Sherrie A. Inness, "Introduction—'Boxing Gloves and Bustiers': New Images of Tough Women," in *Action Chicks: New Images of Tough Women in Popular Culture* (New York: Palgrave Macmillan, 2014), 10.
78. Diane Negra and Yvonne Tasker, "Introduction," in *Gendering the Recession: Media and Culture in the Age of Austerity* (Durham: Duke University Press, 2014).

Gods and Freaks, Soldiers and Men
Gender, Technologies *and* Marvel's The Avengers

JEREMIAH FAVARA

In May of 2012, Marvel Films released *Marvel's The Avengers*, which recorded the second largest opening weekend gross in history en route to taking in over $1.5 billion worldwide and becoming the fifth-highest grossing film of all time.[1] Part of what makes *The Avengers* such an interesting site of study is the way the film takes a variety of different superheroes—Black Widow, Iron Man, Thor, and Captain America, to name a few—and mashes them together, muddling the different histories, technologies, and mythologies of each superhero. Focusing on the 2012 film, while drawing on other films in the Marvel Cinematic Universe, this chapter explores the ways that cinematic superbodies acquire meaning through gendered discourses conflated with technology.[2] More specifically, the Marvel Cinematic Universe is used as a site for exploring the ways that ideas about masculinity, technology, and bodies inform various myths of super-masculinities.

The Avengers film is one of the latest iterations of a team of superheroes who first appeared in comic books in 1963. Creating a shared universe of superheroes is a distinct feature of the world of comics and of the Marvel Cinematic Universe, of which *The Avengers* is a part, and is reminiscent of narrative models from comics in the 1960s.[3] Since 2008, eleven films in the Marvel Cinematic Universe have grossed more than $8 billion worldwide. The increased prevalence and success of superhero films reflects a unique situation in which comic books are read by only a small segment of Americans, but their characters and images are a highly popular cultural presence.[4]

As the culmination of the first phase of the Marvel Cinematic Universe, *The Avengers* brought together established characters—and the stars that play them—from the first five Marvel films, including Black Widow, Nick Fury, Iron Man, Thor, and Captain America. Iron Man, played by Robert Downey, Jr., is the longest standing member of the Marvel Cinematic Universe, prominently featured in *Avengers: Age of Ultron* (2015), *Iron Man 3* (2013), *Marvel's The Avengers* (2012), *Iron Man 2* (2010), and *Iron Man* (2008). Both Thor, played by Chris Hemsworth, and Captain America, played by Chris Evans, featured in solo films; *Thor* (2011) and *Captain America: The First Avenger* (2011), leading up to *The Avengers*. Black Widow, played by Scarlett Johansson, and Nick Fury, played by Samuel

L. Jackson, have featured prominently in the Marvel Cinematic Universe, each appearing in multiple films across both phases of the Universe. In the 2012 film, the Avengers are composed of six superheroes brought together by Nick Fury and S.H.I.E.L.D.: Iron Man, Captain America, Thor, the Hulk, Hawkeye, and Black Widow. Though Hawkeye and the Hulk are prominently featured in *The Avengers*, their presence in the overall Marvel Cinematic Universe is of a lesser degree than Black Widow, Nick Fury, Iron Man, Captain America, and Thor. By focusing on these five characters, while also attending to the character of Falcon, played by Anthony Mackie in *Captain America: The Winter Soldier* (2014), this chapter explores the organization of gender, race, and the role of technology in constructions of cinematic superbodies.

In order to look at the gendered production of cinematic super-bodies one needs to look beyond the representational aspects of superhero narratives to the embodied production of superheroes. Superhero narratives in the Marvel Cinematic Universe contain ideals of gender that are articulated across both fictional and non-fictional contexts. On-screen superheroes are realized through convergences of the real life bodies of the actors that portray them and fictional narratives situated in fantastical settings bolstered by computer-generated imagery. Attending to the media coverage surrounding celebrities and their bodies, particularly in the case of actors that portray superheroes, and the work of crafting bodies that can realistically portray heroes with superpowers, allows one to see how Marvel's films rely on an embodied production of superheroes.

Drawing on paratextual discussions of the gendered bodies of the actors who portray superheroes, I explore the construction of cinematic superbodies as sites where ideals of gender, race, and technology converge. In order to explore representations of superbodies within the fictional spaces of film, while accounting for the flesh-and-blood bodies that provide the foundation for the construction of cinematic superbodies, I draw on the concept of gender capital. When discussing gender capital, I borrow from Bridges' definition of gender capital as the value afforded to contextually and historically relevant presentations of gendered selves.[5] The value afforded through gendered presentations result from the management of both physical and discursive meanings of gender, bodily, and cultural capital across a variety of settings.[6] The use of gender capital as an analytic for exploring the production and representation of gendered superbodies allows a focus on the processes through which gendered ideals emerge, are reinforced, and challenged across the contexts that converge in the production of superhero narratives. The process of constructing a cinematic superbody is not limited to representations on the screen. Rather, cinematic superbodies are crafted in the gym routines of actors, the media coverage of the ways actors prepared their bodies to realistically portray superheroes, and the representations of the superheroes that actors embody in films. As such, this paper takes seriously the ways that discourses about celebrities represent cultural values of gender and race and inform how celebrities act as material embodiments of fictional superheroes in film.[7]

The Embodied Production of Cinematic Superbodies

In the lead up to the release of *The Avengers* several news stories about Scarlett Johansson's preparation for her role as Black Widow were released. The website popsugar.com, which describe themselves as a global women's lifestyle brand where women's passion points—including celebrity, entertainment, and fashion—connect, featured a story detailing how Scarlett Johansson got into superhero shape for *The Avengers*. Focusing on specifics of Johansson's fitness routine, such as her diet, exercise program, and combat training, the story tells us that "Scarlett Johansson kicks major butt as Black Widow in *The Avengers* ... all while wearing a black catsuit.... To prep for the physically demanding role, Scarlett worked for almost two months."[8] Similar stories from *Shape* and *Self* magazines discuss Johansson's physical preparation for the role, while focusing on her body: "Reprising her role as the butt-kicking Black Widow in *The Avengers* ... the sexy superhero makes wearing a body-hugging, skin-tight leather costume look easy."[9] Both stories emphasize the intense work and training that goes into playing a superhero while framing Johansson as "sexy" and "gorgeous." These stories demonstrate the ways that Johansson's body, as the embodiment of a cinematic superhero, is inscribed with ideas about gender, sexuality, and desire. Balsamo demonstrates how women's use of bodybuilding technology to sculpt their bodies is inscribed with ideas about gender and sexual objectification.[10] Balsamo sees athletic female bodies as being somewhat transgressive, although cultural processes keep such bodies in place through the persistence of gender hierarchies.[11] Johansson's preparation to portray a superhero is framed with an emphasis on her body as both physically capable and sexually desirable, situating her cinematic superbody firmly within gendered narratives where bodies of women are sexualized and objectified. References to Johansson's body as one that is desirable, both as an object of sexual desire and bodily aspiration, maintain a gender order in which the bodies of women are objectified and seen as being in need of correction in the form of a superhero-worthy workout routine.

We first see Black Widow in *The Avengers* bound to a chair, wearing a dress, surrounded by three men. In a seemingly straightforward interrogation scene, a frightened looking Black Widow is struck and threatened with torture. A phone call for Black Widow, on one of the interrogator's phones, changes the dynamics of the interrogation and flips Black Widow's apparent position as the victim to that of one in charge of the situation. A male voice on the phone tells us that Black Widow needs to come in, to which she responds that she is in the middle of an interrogation and is getting valuable information. Placing the caller on hold, Black Widow proceeds to fight, and easily defeat, the three men before picking up the phone, grabbing a pair of black heels, and walking out of the room.

Black Widow's introductory scene speaks to a tension at work in *The Avengers* and the Marvel Cinematic Universe more broadly. It is Black Widow's representation within a stereotypical version of femininity—as victim in lipstick and a tight dress—that allows her to gain valuable information from her interrogators while also serving as a bait-and-switch for viewers. The initial representation of Black Widow as a victim in peril quickly changes to a representation of a female superhero that is more than capable of defending herself. Black Widow exercises power on her own terms, yet still within a male-dominated world. Black Widow is one of seven women in *The Avengers* with speaking roles. At times, Black Widow is shown to be more than capable of defending herself; she knocks out Hawkeye in a fight and is the only Avenger that is able to harness alien technologies in the final fight scene. Yet at other times, Black Widow is shown to be vulnerable and in need of protection; when encountering the Hulk, for example, Black Widow is helpless, only to be saved at the last minute by Thor. These instances point to the ways that Black Widow demonstrates a tension at work where, as the only female superhero in the first phase of the Marvel Cinematic Universe, she is in some ways transgressive while remaining in place within the gendered order of a male-dominated world. Black Widow is an ass-kicking superhero and a prominent member of Marvel Cinematic Universe. She is capable of handily defeating men, aliens, and other superheroes in combat—while clad in a form-fitting suit—and doesn't yet have a standalone film. The three Avengers who have been featured in multiple standalone films—Thor, Captain America, and Iron Man—demonstrate how the world of *The Avengers* and the Marvel Cinematic Universe more broadly is constructed through the convergence of material bodies of celebrities and representations of fiction and fantasy in ways that reinscribe superhero narratives as being the domain of men and masculinities.

Masculinities and the Production of Cinematic Superbodies

Scholars have demonstrated the ways that superhero stories preserve normative discourses of gender and sexuality while relying on gendered narratives emphasizing superheroes as physically strong men acting as vanguards of white, heterosexual masculinity.[12] Early stories of patriotically clad superheroes in the late 1930s and early 1940s, such as Captain America, promoted gendered images of what America was and what about America was worth fighting for.[13] This is not to say that superheroes have always functioned in ways that promote and preserve normative ideals of gendered bodies. As Taylor contends, the bodies of superheroes represent a site of possible departure for ways of thinking about gendered bodies that provide glimpses of androgynous corporeal possibilities.[14] Although superbodies in comic books may represent sites for the construction of transgressive bodies, mainstream film versions of superhero stories often rely on the safest visions of their characters. The reliance on flesh-and-blood actors contributes to the ways that cinematic superbodies are representative of gendered ideals. Cinematic superbodies emerge through, and rely upon, real bodies that are inscribed with ideas about gender, race, and sexuality before they reach the screen.

In the lead up to the release of *The Avengers*, as well as their respective standalone films, a series of stories circulated across the mediascape focused on the superhero workout routines of Chris Hemsworth, Robert Downey, Jr., and Chris Evans. Articles about the superhero workout routines of the actors that play Thor, Iron Man, and Captain America focus on the work of crafting the body of a superhero. An article from *Men's Fitness* details how Downey, Jr., needed a heroic build to portray Tony Stark and the diet and exercise routine necessary to "build Downey into a character capable of going toe-to-toe with fighter jets and terrorists."[15] The articles often discuss the look of a superhero physique and the work of crafting a realistic superbody. Downey Jr.'s preparation is discussed as being about the importance of forging "a physique truly worthy of Iron Man."[16] Coverage of Downey Jr.'s preparation to portray Iron Man is particularly interesting, given that his status as a superhero is primarily due to Iron Man's suit, rather than the strength or physique of Tony Stark's body. Downey Jr.'s bodily transformation is less about his characterization and more about media and audience expectations of the type of physique expected of actors portraying superheroes. Another article from *Men's Fitness* focuses on Evans' diet and workout routine in preparation to portray Captain America, saying, "Unfortunately for Evans, Super-Soldier Serum isn't a real thing, so he had to get his massive, chiseled physique the old-fashioned way."[17] Hemsworth's preparation to portray Thor is discussed in terms of how "the leap from page to screen would require someone whose physique was more fitting of [a] deity than a mortal."[18] In an article from *Men's Health*, Hemsworth's preparation is discussed as a transformation whose goal was to "look super-realistic in the context of a mythological blockbuster."[19] The presence of articles emphasizing the bodily transformation undertaken by actors required to craft their cinematic superbodies underlines the embodied foundations upon which representations of superheroes rest.

The emphasis on transformation is framed in the articles with a focus on each actor's ability to realistically portray a superhero. A convincing portrayal of a superhero is situated with a focus on the body, particularly the way a superbody ought to look. Focusing on how he can stand out among the other Avengers, Evans is quoted as saying, "the preparation for Captain America was really about me bulking up looks wise."[20] Other articles mention "Chris Evans' hot body" and Hemsworth's "ripped-looking body."[21] The discussion of superbodies isn't limited to descriptions of stars' superbodies but also contains a prescriptive element detailing how other men can similarly craft their bodies. A number of articles contain character-specific workout plans—"The Iron Man Plan,"[22] "The Captain America Workout,"[23] and "Thor's Upper Body 'Grinder' Workout"[24]—for readers to follow. These articles are not the first time characters from the Marvel universe have been featured in workout plans. In the 1976 *Stan Lee Presents: The Mighty Marvel Strength and Fitness Book,* mostly male superheroes, including Thor, Hulk, Captain America, and Falcon, were shown in detailed exercise routines with instructions for readers.[25] The routines emphasize strength, muscle, and body building similar to contemporary workout routines focusing on looks and the body. An article discussing Hemsworth's preparation to play Thor contends, "This workout may not give you the strength to wield the greatest weapon in the Marvel universe, but it can help you look like a Norse god,"[26] while another article provides "a workout schedule that can help you get the superhero physique you so badly want."[27]

The focus on the bodies of superheroes, both as a transformative process that Evans, Downey Jr., and Hemsworth undertook and a process hailing the participation of other men, contributes to the gendered production of masculine bodies. As Balsamo contends, bodies are gendered as products of technological transformation as well as products of discursive inscription.[28] Bodybuilding as a technology sculpts the physical bodies that become superbodies while marking them as embodiments of masculine ideals. Bridges found bodybuilding to be an important site for the masculine display and performance of gender.[29] As Kimmel contends, work on the body is viewed as an important aspect of physical expressions of masculinity.[30] Bodybuilding acts as a form of monitoring gender bodily capital that, when taken up in mainstream superhero narratives, demonstrates how such practices are aligned with dominant ideals of masculinity.[31]

There is a further gendered distinction when comparing articles that discuss Johansson's preparation with those of the other Avengers. The majority of articles about Johansson's preparation for *The Avengers* mention her stunt double, while articles about the male Avengers only mention stunts to reiterate that these men do their own. An article from *Men's Fitness* mentions that "Robert does all his own stuff when it comes to fights. When the camera's on him, it's really him doing it."[32] In a discussion of his portrayal of Thor, an article states, "Hemsworth tries to do as many stunts as he can with his own body."[33] The emphasis on physique is framed as extending into the abilities of male superbodies to use their bodies in masculine ways. The ability to use the body in a masculine way—in the case of superbodies, this refers to stunts and fighting—is an important characteristic of hegemonic masculinity.[34] Though the construction of superbodies is framed as being about looks and physique, looks become synonymous with performance for male bodies in a way that is not extended to Johansson. This distinction points to the ways that cinematic superbodies are constructed through technologies of bodybuilding, but in ways that reinforce notions of gendered bodies and the value afforded to those bodies.

The superbodies of actors that portray superheroes, as crafted through bodybuilding, act as technologies for gendered bodies that provide cues about cultural inscriptions of gender as well as of race. All the actors discussed, and the characters they portray, are white. Each of the six superheroes in the first phase of the Marvel Cinematic Universe, all of whom are featured in *The Avengers*, are white. Though people of color are present throughout *The Avengers*, often as soldiers, scientists, or bystanders, only a few people of color fill roles with speaking lines. Though *The Avengers* and the Marvel Cinematic Universe are overwhelmingly white, the presence of bodies of color points to the ways that cinematic superbodies are crafted through cultural hierarchies of race, particularly in the characters of Sam Wilson/Falcon and Nick Fury. It is not until the ninth film in the Marvel Cinematic Universe—*Captain America: The Winter Soldier*—that a cinematic superbody of color is introduced in the character of Falcon.[35] Given Falcon's status as the first African-American superhero in mainstream comics, his inclusion in the Marvel Cinematic Universe illuminates the relationships between race and cinematic superbodies.[36] Similar to his white counterparts, during the lead up to the release of *Captain America: The Winter Soldier*, Anthony Mackie's preparation to portray Falcon was the focus of articles on superhero workout routines.

In an article discussing various actors preparation for *The Winter Soldier*, including Evans, Johansson, and Mackie, Mackie's preparation is discussed through an emphasis on his training regime, particularly the 1,000 push-ups Mackie did daily.[37] The work involved in crafting Mackie's body as a realistic superbody is seen as part of involvement in the Marvel Cinematic Universe. "Mackie also says that, 'if you're a part of the Marvel Universe, you have to be pretty consistently in shape.'"[38] Similarly to coverage of other actors, there is an emphasis on the way Mackie's body looks, with nods towards Evans' body and the role of costume in displaying their superbodies. Mackie is quoted as saying, "I was in the gym like a monster working out for that movie, and I said, 'If Chris gets to wear tight shirts, I want tight shirts!'"[39] The work of constructing Mackie's superbody is part of Mackie's inclusion within an already existing universe, both in terms of the Marvel Cinematic Universe as well as the bodily expectations put forth by other actors' preparations. Mackie is quoted as saying, "[W]hen I see him [Evans] built like a Greek statue.... My whole goal was to get as buff as he was."[40] The comparative and competitive aspect of Mackie's and Evans' bodily preparations coincide with representations of the characters they portray. The opening scenes of *Captain America: The Winter Soldier* show Sam Wilson/Falcon running and being repeatedly passed by a much faster Steve Rogers/Captain America. In the lead up to the final battle scene in the film, Falcon claims, "I do what he does, just slower" in reference to Captain America.[41] This statement serves to situate Falcon in the role of a sidekick—loyal to Captain America but somehow lesser than. Falcon's position as a superhero sidekick coincides with racialized narratives of superheroes that privilege white masculinity. Falcon's presence serves to reinforce gendered and racialized hierarchies in superhero narratives.

Another article that discusses Mackie's workout plan and the importance of physique in portraying Falcon contends that Mackie will be the first African American superhero in a Marvel movie because Samuel L. Jackson's portrayal of Nick Fury "doesn't really count because he doesn't have 'super' powers."[42] Though Fury fights alongside the other Avengers and uses high-tech weaponry, the above quote demonstrates how readers are led to believe that Fury specifically, as a person of color in the Marvel Cinematic Universe, is different than Falcon because of his lack of powers. As such, Fury's body is not crafted as a cinematic superbody in the same ways as Falcon, Captain America, Black Widow, Thor and Iron Man. Samuel L. Jackson plays Nick Fury in *The Avengers* as well as in two other films in the Marvel Cinematic Universe. Fury is the only character of color in *The Avengers* that has more than a few speaking lines and appears consistently across multiple scenes. Fury is undoubtedly a central character of the Marvel Cinematic Universe, yet the construction of Fury as a cinematic body is markedly different than that of the characters and actors discussed. Of the characters discussed thus far, Fury is the only character not considered as a superhero in paratextual discussions of the film. Danny Fingeroth, who has close to 20 years experience working for Marvel Comics, defines superheroes as being distinct from other heroes by having fantastic magical, science, or technologically based powers.[43] Though Fury has access to power in the form of technology, the technologies he utilizes are not wedded to his identity in the same way as Black Widow's Bite or Iron Man's suit. Fury's status as a non-superhero results in his being differently positioned within a world of white cinematic superbodies. Fury's representation does not require Jackson to invest in bodybuilding technology to craft his body as super. Fury's lack of superpowers act to limit his involvement in *The Avengers* in particular ways.

Fury is in charge of the Avengers initiative, meant to bring the various superheroes together to combat threats, yet such a position comes with the thankless task of managing and herding an unruly group of superheroes. Fury is largely absent from the main action sequences, playing a supporting role, particularly in the last third of the film. Though Fury acts as the catalyst for the various superheroes assembling and working together in the climactic final battle scene of the film, he undoubtedly takes a back seat to the Avengers. As the Avengers fight off an alien invasion, Fury watches the action unfold on a series of screens. Though Fury's position of power enables him access to technology and a seemingly infinite cache of weapons—of which the individual Avengers are a part—his lack of a superbody prevents him being an active participant in many of the film's pivotal sequences. Fury's position points to the ways that it is specific superbodies that gain capital in conjunction with off-screen uses of bodybuilding as a technology inscribed with ideals of gender and race.

Masculinity and Cinematic Superbodies

Superbodies in films are constructed through a combination of real actors—with accompanying embodiments of celebrities—and computer-generated imagery that is both beholden to, and apart from, everyday reality. Bodies act as foundations for fantastic representations taking place in a universe of aliens, lightning-wielding demi-gods, and weaponized cyborgs while anchoring such a world in distinctly gendered ways. Though we can picture Captain America as a scientifically enhanced super-soldier, we can only do so through the body of Chris Evans. The same holds true for Iron Man and Thor and the actors that portray them. The limits of how we can imagine the bodies of cinematic superheroes manifest in the embodiment of superheroes. The bodily capital demonstrated in the production of Captain America, Iron Man, and Thor as superbodies, enabled by investments in bodybuilding as a gendered technology, anchor these fictional characters to ideals of masculinity. The technological practices of building superbodies place technology at the center of an exploration of cinematic superbodies. The superbodies of Captain America, Iron Man, and Thor are technologically embodied inscriptions of gendered ideals that carry into the representational spaces of film.

From the opening scenes, *The Avengers* is about technology—about struggles between alien technologies, human military technology, and the technology and weaponry of the various superheroes. Throughout *The Avengers*, superbodies are constructed according to different historical and technological sources of gender capital. A large aspect of the plot of *The Avengers* is about conflict and tensions between different embodiments of superheroes, from the entrepreneurial technology of Iron Man to the traditional soldiering of Captain America. Steve Rogers—Captain America—is introduced during a scene in a gym. Rogers is shown punching a bag repeatedly as flashbacks take us back to his experiences fighting in World War II. Rogers is referred to as the "world's first superhero" and the patriotic uniform of Captain America—"stars and stripes"—is described as "old fashioned."[44] Captain America is consistently situated as a man out of time. His clothes, ideals, and knowledge are all called out in the film to remind us that Captain America is stuck 70 years in the past, in a bygone era. Rogers' physical strength, as an embodiment of masculinity, and patriotic, team-playing ideals are linked to the 1940s. The gendered ideals of the era define Captain America and place him in opposition to other ideals of masculinity embodied by other superheroes. Rogers' superbody is represented as a product of science and his status as a superhero is intimately linked to historically contingent ideals of patriotism and masculinity. In an argument, Tony Stark/Iron Man tells him, "You're a laboratory experiment, Rogers. Everything about you came out of a bottle."[45]

Just before Stark's comment, Rogers tells Stark, "Big man in a suit of armor; take that off, what are you?"—to which Stark replies, "Genius, billionaire, playboy, philanthropist."[46] Stark is situated as being from an entirely different era defined by different ideals of masculinity. Stark embodies a form of masculinity in which technological and scientific knowledge are highly valued. Stark's superbody is cybernetic, a conflation of human and machine, made possible not only by Stark's knowledge of science and engineering but also by his extravagant wealth. Stark is represented as selfish, as not playing well with others, as the antithesis to the team-playing ideals embodied by Captain America. Stark's powers—and his cybernetic superbody—are situated in a different historical conceptualization of masculinity associated with entrepreneurialism, wealth, science, and technology. In his conflicts with other superheroes, Stark often makes references to their bodily strength and power. After witnessing Captain America fight for the first time in the film, Stark quips, "You are pretty spry for an older fellow. What's your thing, pilates?"[47] After a fight with Thor, Stark taps him on his bare bicep saying, "No hard feelings, Point Break. You've got a mean swing."[48] These references to the embodied physical strength of Thor and Captain America situate the ideals of masculinity represented by Stark in opposition to older ideals of masculinity that privilege physical strength and bodily power over wealth and scientific and technological knowledge.

These examples point to the ways that the identities of Iron Man, Thor, and Captain America emerge through forms of masculinity imbued with notions of technology and the body. Each of their bodies are made super through technological practices. Thor's bodily power stems from his status as a god from another world while Captain America's stems from scientific intervention in the form of a special serum. While their characters' bodies are shaped through magical and scientific interventions, the embodied cinematic versions of Thor and Captain America display the technological investments made by Hemsworth and Evans. It is the bodily gender capital gained by Hemsworth and Evans and their investment in bodybuilding that allows for a cinematic representation of their character's bodies as super. References within the film further demonstrate how gendered narratives of superheroes revolve around, and ultimately must land upon, the body. Iron Man's bodily power stems from Stark's status as a cyborg, as both reliant on the suit for survival and as technologically and mechanically enhanced. References to Iron Man's suit as his status of power demonstrate how his superbody is constructed through the conjunction of technology, both the fictional technology of his suit and the special effects technology that allows audiences to see such a fiction. The ways in which the film represents ideas about superbodies is generally through competition and conflict. The following exchange, occurs in the midst of a fight between Iron Man and Thor:

> THOR: "You have no idea what you're dealing with."
> IRON MAN: "Uh, Shakespeare in the park? Doth mother know you wear-eth her drapes?"
> THOR: "This is beyond you, metal man."
> IRON MAN: "Tourist."[49]

The above exchange demonstrates how much of *The Avengers* is based around competition and conflict between ideals of masculinity that are not in sync with one another. Iron Man attempts to diminish Thor's masculinity by comparing him to a cross-dressing and childish figure while also pointing to Thor's status as an outsider. Thor's masculine embodiment—as expressed through physical strength and supernatural powers—is situated as beyond time. Thor is referred to as a "demi-god" that is both more advanced and less modern than the contemporary human world in which he finds himself. Exchanges between Thor, Captain America, and Iron Man, particularly in the first half of the film, call out ideas about their superbodies as aspects of what makes them super. The competing myths of masculinity at work in *The Avengers* revolve around the technological sources of the power that make the heroes super, the different technologies of their weapons—Thor's hammer, Captain America's shield, Iron Man's suit—and their bodies as products of technology. Recurring themes of competition and conflict emerging from ideas about bodies and technology frame *The Avengers* as being largely about a series of masculinity challenges.

Borrowing from Bridges and Messerschmidt, masculinity challenges refer to confrontations between competing masculinities stemming from insults and unachieved expectations of masculinity within certain contexts.[50] The body is central to masculinity challenges, particularly ideas about size and the ability to use your body in masculine ways.[51]

Many of the interactions between Iron Man, Thor, and Captain America are framed as a series of challenges and insults—often revolving around the source of their powers, their scientific or technologically enhanced bodies, and their enactments of masculinity that reference the body. In the context of *The Avengers* the bodies that are contested and challenged as embodiments of masculinity are necessarily imbued with technological enhancement. Taking seriously the notion that superheroes represent the values of the society in which they are produced, *The Avengers* illuminates a cultural moment in which meanings of masculinity are articulated through relationships between bodies and technology, both materially and discursively. Superhero narratives point to the ways that we imagine gendered and raced meanings of material and imagined technologies. Technologies are an integral aspect of the distribution of bodily gender capital at work in the production, and representation, of cinematic superbodies.

Conclusion

In order to grasp the ways that superhero narratives convey ideals of gender, race, and bodies in a contemporary moment where most audiences encounter superheroes in films, one must account for the way that cinematic superbodies are crafted both on- and off-screen. Cinematic superbodies are produced through the convergence of material embodiment and discursive representation. Technology is central—both as a bodily investment imbued with inscriptions of gender and race, and as an integral aspect of superhero narratives—to *The Avengers* and the Marvel Cinematic Universe. Exploring the gendered bodies of superheroes as sites of meaning before they reach the screen requires a framework that accounts for physical and discursive meanings of gender. The framework of gender bodily capital enriches how we think of the production of gender, particularly ideals of masculinity, within the contemporary moment. *The Avengers*' reliance on material bodies provides an example of the limits of fictional and fantastic spaces of film. We can imagine and see superheroes on an unprecedented scale in films, but we can only do so through characters embodied in traditionally gendered ways. To capture the transgressive potential of fiction and fantasy as a site for rethinking gendered and raced bodies, perhaps we need to re-imagine how such bodies are constructed and represented before they reach the screen.

Notes

1. Marvel's The Avengers," *Box Office Mojo*, accessed July 7, 2015. http://boxofficemojo.com/movies/?id=avengers11.htm.
2. In discussing technology, I refer to technology as a set of processes involving material objects, discursive practices, and techniques.
3. Bart Beaty, "Introduction," *Cinema Journal* 50, no. 3 (2011): 106.
4. Greg M. Smith, "Surveying the World of Contemporary Comics Scholarship: A Conversation," *Cinema Journal* 50, no. 3 (2011): 135.
5. Tristan S. Bridges, "Gender Capital and Male Bodybuilders," *Body & Society* 15, no. 1 (2009): 83–107.
6. Ibid.
7. Richard Dyer, *Heavenly Bodies: Film Stars and Society* (London: Routledge, 2004) and David Marshall, *Celebrity and Power: Fame in Contemporary Culture* (Minneapolis: University of Minnesota Press, 1997).
8. Michele Foley, "How Scarlett Johansson Got in Superhero Shape for the Avengers," *Popular Fitness*, accessed February 3, 2015, http://www.fitsugar.com/Scarlett-Johansson-Diet-Fitness-Routine-Avengers-22993592.
9. "How Scarlett Johansson Got in Superhero Shape," *Shape Magazine*, accessed February 3, 2015, http://www.shape.com/celebrities/interviews/how-scarlett-johansson-got-superhero-shape.
10. Anne Balsamo, *Technologies of the Gendered Body: Reading Cyborg Women* (Durham: Duke University Press, 1995).
11. Ibid.
12. Cord Scott, "Written in Red, White, and Blue: A Comparison of Comic Book Propaganda

from World War II and September 11," *The Journal of Popular Culture* 40, no. 2 (2007): 325 and Neil Shyminsky, "'Gay' Sidekicks: Queer Anxiety and the Narrative Straightening of the Superhero," *Men and Masculinities* 14 (2011): 288 and Helen Shugart, "Supermarginal," *Communication and Critical/Cultural Studies* 6, no. 1 (2009): 98.

13. Cord Scott, "Written in Red, White, and Blue."

14. Aaron Taylor, "'He's Gotta Be Strong, and He's Gotta Be Fast, and He's Gotta Be Larger Than Life': Investigating the Engendered Superhero Body," *The Journal of Popular Culture* 40, no. 2 (2007): 344–60.

15. Sam Dehority, "Robert Downey Jr.: 'He Was Skinny,'" *Men's Fitness*, accessed February 3, 2015, http://www.mensfitness.com/life/entertainment/robert-downey-jr-he-was-skinny.

16. "Robert Downey Jr.'s Iron Man Workout," *Men's Fitness*, accessed February 3, 2015, http://www.mensfitness.com/training/build-muscle/robert-downey-jrs-iron-man-workout.

17. John Mitchell, "How to Get Jacked Like a Superhero," *Men's Fitness*, accessed February 3, 2015, http://www.mensfitness.com/training/build-muscle/how-to-get-jacked-like-a-superhero/slide/1.

18. "Chris Hemsworth Thor Workout," *Men's Fitness UK*, accessed February 3, 2015, http://www.mensfitness.co.uk/exercises/celebrity-workouts/1919/chris-hemsworth-thor-workout.

19. The Thor Star's Intense Training Turned Hemsworth into a Superhero. You Want to Get a Godlike Physique? Train like an Immortal," *Men's Health*, accessed February 3, 2015, http://www.menshealth.co.uk/living/men/chris-hemsworth-interview.

20. Matthew Power and Aundre Jacobs, TRAIN Magazine, last updated May 2, 2014. "Bodybuilding.com—Captain America's Training Plan," accessed February 3, 2015, http://www.bodybuilding.com/fun/chris-evans-captain-america-training-plan.html.

21. "How the Stars of 'Captain America: The Winter Soldier' Get Into Superhero Shape," *Yahoo Celebrity*, accessed February 3, 2015, https://celebrity.yahoo.com/blogs/celeb-news/how-the-stars-of—captain-america—the-winter-soldier—get-into-superhero-shape-191913283.html and "Chris Hemsworth: Building a Superhero's Body," accessed February 3, 2015, http://man.bodyandsoul.com.au/mens+fitness/male+workouts/chris+hemsworth+building+a+superheros+body,21083.

22. "Robert Downey Jr.'s Iron Man Workout." *Men's Fitness*.

23. Matthew Power and Aundre Jacobs, TRAIN Magazine, last updated May 2, 2014. "Bodybuilding.com—Captain America's Training Plan," accessed February 3, 2015, http://www.bodybuilding.com/fun/chris-evans-captain-america-training-plan.html.

24. Matthew Power and Aundre Jacobs, TRAIN Magazine, last updated Jan. 7, 2014. "Bodybuilding.com—Race God to Norse God: Chris Hemsworth Thor Two Workout," accessed February 3, 2015, http://www.bodybuilding.com/fun/race-god-to-norse-god-chris-hemsworth-thor-two-workout.html.

25. Agile Ann Picardo, *Stan Lee Presents: The Mighty Marvel Comics Strength and Fitness Book* (New York: Simon & Schuster, 1976).

26. Power and Jacobs. "Race God to Norse God"

27. Power and Jacobs, "Captain America's Training Plan."

28. Balsamo, *Technologies of the Gendered Body*.

29. Bridges, "Gender Capital."

30. Michael Kimmel, *Manhood in America: A Cultural History*, 3d ed. (New York: Oxford University Press, 2011).

31. Bridges, "Gender Capital."

32. Dehority, "Robert Downey Jr."

33. Power and Jacobs, "Race God to Norse God."

34. James W. Messerschmidt, "Becoming 'Real Men' Adolescent Masculinity Challenges and Sexual Violence," *Men and Masculinities* 2, no. 3 (January 1, 2000): 286–307. doi:10.1177/1097184X00002003003.

35. Although the character of James Rhodes/War Machine is the first superhero of color in the Marvel Cinematic Universe, fighting alongside Iron Man in *Iron Man 2* (2010), his body is not crafted as a cinematic superbody. Neither of the actors who portray Rhodes—Terrence Howard and Don Cheadle—were featured in workout routines or articles discussing their physical preparation for the role.

36. Adilifu Nama, *Super Black: American Pop Culture and Black Superheroes* (Austin: University of Texas Press, 2011).

37. "How the Stars of 'Captain America: The Winter Soldier' Get into Superhero Shape," *Yahoo*

188 Part 5: The Attempt of Progressivism

Celebrity, accessed February 3, 2015, https://celebrity.yahoo.com/blogs/celeb-news/how-the-stars-of—captain-america—the-winter-soldier—get-into-superhero-shape-191913283.html.

38. "Anthony Mackie on Captain America, Spandex, and Crashing the Avengers Sequel," *Vulture*, accessed February 3, 2015, http://www.vulture.com/2014/04/anthony-mackie-on-avengers.html.

39. Ibid.

40. Ibid.

41. Anthony Russo and Joe Russo, *Captain America: The Winter Soldier*, Action, Adventure, Sci-Fi, 2014.

42. "Anthony Mackie on His Superhero Workout for Captain America 2!" accessed February 3, 2015, http://perezhilton.com/fitperez/2012–09-18-anthony-mackie-opens-up-about-superhero-workout-for-captain-america-two.

43. Danny Fingeroth, *Superman on the Couch: What Superheroes Really Tell Us About Ourselves and Our Society* (New York: Bloomsbury Academic, 2004).

44. Joss Whedon, *The Avengers*, Action, Adventure, Sci-Fi, 2012.

45. Ibid.

46. Ibid.

47. Ibid.

48. Ibid.

49. Ibid.

50. Bridges, "Gender Capital" and Messerschmidt, "Becoming 'Real Men.'"

51. Messerschmidt, "Becoming 'Real Men.'"

An Archetype or a Token?
The Challenge of the Black Panther

JULIAN C. CHAMBLISS

In August 2006, Lions Gate Entertainment advertised a new animated feature based on the Avengers. Part of agreement forged between Marvel Enterprises and Lions Gate Entertainment in 2004 "to develop, produce and distribute original animated DVD features based on certain characters within the Marvel Universe" the animated film produced by Lion Gate foreshadowed Marvel Studios' live action offerings.[1] Drawing on myriad stories from Marvel Comic publishing, their effort began in 2006 with two Avengers films and featured the Black Panther's origin in its second release.[2] The decision highlighted the centrality of the Black Panther to comic fans and hinted at the challenge posed by adapting the character in contemporary media.

This essay examines the Black Panther's centrality as a figure of engagement with race and identity in the African Diaspora. As such, the article suggests the minimal inclusion of the Black Panther in the Marvel Cinematic Universe (MCU) is a reflection of a persistent white privilege linked to the alignment between power and identity in the superhero genre. By creating an African superhero from a country untouched by European imperialism, Stan Lee and Jack Kirby began a dialogue about the implication of black agency throughout the Africa Diaspora. The Black Panther reflects broader debates about the impact of black social power within the United States and the postcolonial experience in Africa.[3] Therefore, anxiety linked to domestic racism and desire linked to the African diaspora places the Black Panther in a contested space where questions about freedom, legitimacy, and equity are put on display.

The adaptation of the Black Panther in *Ultimate Avengers 2: Rise of the Panther* (2006) produced by Ron Hohauser, Avi Arad, and Craig Kyle is a prime example of this challenge.[4] The animated film utilized the Ultimate Marvel Comic Imprint version of the Avengers as its central inspiration. The Ultimate Universe began in 2000 and updated Marvel's 1960s characters to reflect contemporary geopolitical concerns.[5] This animated re-telling of the Black Panther origin story borrows from the 1966 version by having the Black Panther seek assistance from American heroes to resist invaders. However, the invaders in question are aliens who allied themselves with Nazi Germany during World War II and have sought to conquer the Earth ever since. The film employs an anti-imperialist message and assigns the Black Panther the role of oppositional hero. Yet, because the program is aimed at a youth audience, it lacks the overt political symbolism that historically links the Black Panther to his postcolonial identity. In this way, the animated film crystalizes the challenge posed by adapting Black Panther. As a black character, the Black Panther's inclusion triggers a consideration of inequality linked to the African Diaspora.

Just Like Us

Concerns about black superheroes and their meaning have increased in recent years. Scholars such as Adilifu Nama have suggested that these characters offer positive symbols despite the limited numbers.[6] Indeed, Bradford Wright's seminal cultural history of comics makes it clear the appearance of black heroes was a potent indication of changing societal standards in the United States.[7] The presence of the Black superheroes affirmed white integrationist assumptions in the 1960s, but rapidly began to evolve in the 1970s. The introduction of black characters reflects a cultural paradox. As Richard Reynolds explains in *Superheroes: A Modern Mythology*, themes of restraint and limitation are central parts of the genre. Yet, the introduction of racial minorities into superhero comic narratives arguably heightens the reader's understanding of societal dissonance as these characters act as markers of "real" debate linked to race and representation.[8] Trapped by this layered meaning, black characters struggle to find legitimacy among white readers.[9]

Uncertainty associated with bringing the Black Panther to MCU was captured by the comments of Louis D' Esposito in 2012. While Esposito saw *Guardians of the Galaxy* (at the time an unannounced forthcoming project) as a potential film from the studio, he thought Black Panther a more difficult proposition. He reasoned that creating Wakanda, a technologically advanced African nation, was an imaginative leap too far. He explained, "It always easier basing it here. For instance, 'Iron Man 3' is rooted right here in Los Angeles and New York. When you bring *in other worlds* [emphasis added], you're always faced with those difficulties."[10] Thus, it was easier for Esposito to believe a white audience could accept a talking raccoon and sentient tree fighting evil in another galaxy than the idea that Africans on earth are technologically superior to whites. Esposito's comments highlight a historical reality linked to minority characters.

Questions about the white audience's willingness to accept minority characters have shaped debates linked to incorporating representations of African Americans in popular culture. Steady advocacy from civil rights groups led to depictions of black people evolving from demeaning stereotypes in 1930s and 40s films to more diverse characters with identity and agency by the 1950s and 60s.[11] Rejecting subservient roles for African Americans in society, social activists have routinely demanded broader interpretations of minority life in American entertainment. However, critics have argued that new black protagonists remained mired in a racial subtext that required their actions conform to white expectations.[12] It is within this context that the Black Panther's legacy as a foundational character in popular culture must be understood.

By the mid–1960s the desire to acknowledge changing racial circumstances created by civil rights activism influenced character development in Marvel Comics' fictional universe. Marvel's emergence in 1961 ushered in an innovative storytelling style that challenged DC Comics' dominance. Led by editor and writer Stan Lee, Marvel Comics courted the comic-reading public, sending thank you notes to fanzines and creating letter pages in popular books such as the *Fantastic Four* and *Amazing Spider-Man*.[13] Marvel Comic heroes emphasized a "realistic" fantasy world with emotional entanglements that moved superhero confrontations away from simple good-versus-evil to embrace interpersonal and introspective conflicts.[14] Marvel's success ushered in a new era by expanding the audience for superhero comics to a rapidly changing youth culture. Initially, African-American heroes were limited to support roles in this revolution. This all changed with the Black Panther's 1966 introduction.[15]

T'Challa, the Black Panther, is an African king educated in the West and more concerned with protecting his homeland than battling crime. Indeed, his costume is not a costume; it is the traditional tribal dress for the leader of the state religion, the Cult of the Panther. Indeed, his moniker is also ceremonial; "Black Panther" is the title held by leader of the Panther cult. Created by Stan Lee and Jack Kirby, the Black Panther led a technologically advanced, xenophobic African nation that was never conquered by European powers.[16] Essentially the fusion of the military, religious, and political leadership, the Black Panther is far from the traditional hero. In part, this was the point. As an "exotic" African, T'Challa and the world he represented offered a counter-narrative to marginalizing depictions of Blackness common in the United States. Thus, everything about the character became a proxy for an imagined African experience free from the economic exploitation and cultural domination linked to European colonialism. In crafting this narrative, Lee and Kirby acknowledged the damage done by slavery to Africa (and Africans), and externalized the 1960s social and political consequences of correcting this injustice to an African continent *already* emerging from colonial rule. At the same time, Marvel presented a black character that acknowledged the changing racial dynamic, defining the African-American experience in the United States. As David Taft Terry has noted, Marvel essentially interpreted the broader advocacy questions of the 1960s to create a black character, but without black creative input. Thus, the presentation of the Black Panther reflected white aspirations more than black advocacy, and his otherness arguably sidestepped the complexity of achieving racial reconciliation in the United States.[17] Indeed, Lee and Kirby presented Wakanda as a melding of traditionalism and technology that was associated with "pseudoscience" common in the 1960s and posited alien visitation as a more plausible source of ancient Africa's cultural achievements than the Africans themselves.[18]

The struggle at the heart of the Black Panther debut further captured the interplay between white hopes linked to racial integration and black expectations in the United States. The Black Panther defeats and then asks for the Fantastic Four's assistance to repel a white invader, Ulysses Klaw. Klaw is a mercenary responsible for the death of T'Challa's father and attempts to steal Wakanda's unique natural resources, a rare mineral called Vibranium. Only found in Wakanda, Vibranium's unique properties make it highly valuable, and it serves as the foundation of the Wakandan economy and the source of the country's prosperity. Not surprisingly, the Black Panther and the Fantastic Four defeat Klaw. The significance of this story rested in its subtle acknowledgement of the negative effect of colonialism. The story aligned with broader beliefs within the United States about declining European power and the rise of self-governing efforts in Africa and Middle East, affirmed and supported through U.S. activism.[19] The sameness of the Black Panther's heroic action provided an affirmative message of integration by providing an example of a black hero that shared the same goals linked to mainstream white values. Marvel's actions were not revolutionary; instead they reflected the ongoing evolution of race in U.S. culture.

New Black View

By the mid 1960s popular entertainment offered numerous narratives that questioned the mainstream assumption of the rightness of U.S. policy and challenged Eurocentric notions of identity, power, and community. Clearly, anti-establishment messages became common as concerns over Vietnam and social critiques associated with race, class, and sexuality grabbed public attention. With a growing weariness linked to the struggle to achieve equality in society, a narrative of disillusionment in popular entertainment put "society" on trial in the United States.[20] Films and television questioned the validity of U.S. political and economic actions in both domestic and foreign settings.[21] This coincided with a growing polarization along ethnic and class lines in the United States that helped to splinter political consensus between suburban and urban groups. Los Angeles, the home of the American entertainment industry, served to highlight this shift. Inequality began to rise in the 1970s and according to Janet L. Abu-Lughod, despite healthy economic growth, the poverty rate rose and racial minorities in the city were trapped in a system of low wages, poverty, and racism.[22]

As ghettoization defined the inner city experience, these communities exploded in protest. By 1972, producers began to explore militancy linked to inner city African Americans in film, television, and print. Producers of these media exulted in the perceived violence to create a new genre called Blaxploitation. Often seen as reductionist and exploitive, Blaxploitation media also captured the complexity of this changing urban landscape. Films such as *Shaft*, released in 1971, provided a new image of black masculinity, and many films incorporated viewpoints that appealed to black audiences.[23] Indeed, the premise of *Blacula*, a horror film released in 1972, highlights this complexity. Dracula turns the title character into a vampire after he travels to Transylvania to ask for help stopping the slave trade. The entire film shifts the meaning of monstrosity and offers a counter narrative about the danger posed by race and sexual difference to U.S. society.[24] The box office success of these initial African-American themed films sparked entertainment producers to cater more to minority audiences.[25]

Marvel Comics moved to capitalize in July 1973 when the Black Panther became the featured character in an ongoing anthology series called *Jungle Action Featuring....* The first story arc, "Panther's Rage," was a multi-chapter adventure written by Don McGregor with art by Gil Kane and African-American artist Billy Graham among others.[26] In "Panther's Rage" T'Challa faces the consequences of an attempted coup. In crafting this story, McGregor expands on the initial premise introduced by Kirby and Lee and adds depth to the character, his country, and its people. The effort to deepen the cultural narrative was not accidental; instead McGregor hoped to push the boundaries and bring a *realistic* black hero to readers. As explained in *Jungle Action's* letter page "Jungle Re-Action," the Black Panther's story was "precedent-shattering" because of "who the hero happens to be. Not an abandoned child raised by apes or lions or armadillos or whatever. Not an accidental visitor to this jungle paradise—but its king; not one of the restless natives of B-movie fame, but a man who has a logical reason to be there ... because he was born there."[27]

The second and final arc of the *Jungle Action Featuring the Black Panther* was the *Panther vs. the Klan* story arc, which ran from January to November 1976. The subject matter, the Panther's confrontation with the Ku Klux Klan, was considered controversial in the Marvel editorial offices at the time.[28] The entire run of *Jungle Action Featuring The*

Black Panther garnered marginal popular appeal, yet the Black Panther did not disappear when the series was cancelled. Instead, Marvel launched a new solo title featuring the Black Panther written by comic legend Jack Kirby.

The return of Jack Kirby to Marvel in 1977 was a heralded event in the industry. After working for DC comics and creating characters such as the *New Gods*, Kirby returned to write and draw the *Black Panther*. However, while Black Panther's *Jungle Action* adventures strove to incorporate the changing African reality and diverse concerns expressed by African Americans, Kirby's take on the character failed to engage readers. As one letter explained, "After Panther's Rage and The Panther vs. The Klan there is only one word to describe King Solomon's Frog: obscene."[29] *Black Panther* was cancelled after fifteen issues. Relegated to guest appearances in various titles, the Black Panther was not the lead character in a comic book again until 1988.

Marvel's return to Black Panther joined a broader cultural dialogue linked to identity in U.S. culture. The end of the Cold War and the rise of globalization shifted domestic and international circumstances linked to race. Domestically, "culture wars" pitted liberal advocates for inclusion on race, gender, and sexuality issues against conservatives that lamented the loss of traditional values and cultural cohesion. This unease was captured in historian Arthur M. Schlesinger's *The Disuniting of America: Reflections on a Multicultural Society* (1992), which argued that the rise of multiculturalism overshadowed a traditional unifying American identity.[30] Schlesinger's critique was especially harsh on Afrocentric narratives that sought to refute Eurocentric perspectives and claimed Africa's centrality as a significant contribution to the world's cultural and scientific heritage.[31] In characterizing this post–Cold War cultural landscape, Nikhil Pal Singh suggested that the United States nurtured both "exclusionary and integrationist" ideas by simultaneously emphasizing a universalism based on a fusion of diverse practices from different people and detaching those traits from the complexity created by linking them to specific identities.[32] In this context the United States is a space of unity, and otherness and chaos are externalized to foreign locales and people. This period saw an emphasis on diversity that placed African Americans in leading roles in film, television, and music. Ultimately, just as Singh suggests, these media seemed to limit minority actions internally to either "exemplary" stereotypes or reaffirmed racist assumptions.[33] At the same time, popular narratives of Africa and Africans highlight instability and conflict.

This dynamic explains, in part, *Black Panther: Cry the Accursed Country,* a miniseries written by Peter Gillis and drawn by Denys Cowan that centered on T'Challa losing power after the Panther spirit leaves him for failing to act against the apartheid government of the neighboring country of Azania. Published in 1988, but written in 1983, the story was shelved by Marvel editors for fears that it would alienate readers.[34] The story's eventually publication, however, highlights how the Black Panther's symbolism once again paralleled a dualistic perception of blackness between domestic and international contexts. Beginning in the late 1970s, a coordinated activism championed by African American groups such as TransAfrica emerged to push the United States to limit involvement with South Africa.[35] The efforts resulted in massive protest on college campuses, corporate divestment and government sanctions.[36] As the public turn against apartheid grew, Marvel continued its focus on the Black Panther.

The Black Panther quickly reappeared in a story written by Don McGregor, the former of writer of *Jungle Action,* in *Marvel Comic Presents* #13. McGregor's "Panther's Quest" once again focused on South Africa as a setting for the Black Panther's adventures.[37]

McGregor was explicit in his desire to use the Panther to explore the African sociopolitical context for African American readers. He explained, "I had no idea how long the story would be. I was still researching apartheid, and trying to include as many facets of what was happening there at that time into the series. I spent a lot of time at the Shomberg Museum up in Harlem. The staffs were really helpful in getting me material, articles and photos."[38] Over 25 installments McGregor crafted a story that explored the human turmoil of apartheid. Perfectly timed, the story coincided with Nelson Mandela's release from prison in 1990. While heralded by the black community, Mandela's release opened the door to debate about possible turmoil in post-apartheid South Africa.[39] McGregor continued his focus on this uncertainty in *Panther's Prey* (1991), a four-issue miniseries that focused on T'Challa struggling against a new drug-dealing villain while trying to balance growing xenophobic sentiments within Wakanda. Continuing a pattern of cultural representation, the Black Panther's adventures in Africa resonated with the shifting dynamic associated with globalization immediately after the Cold War. By the end of the decade, Americans were less occupied with Africa, but the Black Panther's legacy as a racial symbol inspired new engagement.

A New Panther

In 1998 *Black Panther* #1, with writer Christopher Priest and artist Mark Texeira, began publication under the Marvel Knight Imprint.[40] At the time Marvel Comics, which had come out of bankruptcy, was under the editorial leadership of Joe Quesada. Quesada's own youthful experience as a minority seeking diversity in media influenced his views on Black Panther:

> I've always loved the character. As a kid who grew up on Marvel comics, I remember picking them up and I remember seeing the Black Panther for the first time, and what an incredible influence the character had upon me. I'm not black but I'm Hispanic, and I grew up in a neighborhood in Queens where I had friends that came from all walks of life and all different ethnicities. I had an opportunity to read comics from different companies, and seeing the Black Panther in *Fantastic Four*, to me, was so significant.[41]

Under his mandate, Christopher Priest was given the opportunity to recreate the Black Panther series. The writer remembers:

> Initially, I wasn't all that attracted.... I subsequently had a conference call with Joe (Quesada) and Jimmy (Palmiotti) and insisted Panther could no longer be this guy who got beat up, hit from behind—sometimes by little kids—or dragged behind motor vehicles. The Panther, as I understood him, was this incredibly wily strategist who beat the crap out of the Fantastic Four, largely on the strength of Ben Grimm's arrogance in assuming he'd be no threat to them.[42]

Priest's version of the Black Panther returned to the themes in *Jungle Action Featuring The Black Panther*, the *Fantastic Four* and *Avengers* to emphasize the Black Panther's actions and outlook, which offered a counterpoint to American heroes and their concerns.[43] Critics and fans alike recognize the innovative characterization and story, but lackluster sales led to repeated threats of cancellation.[44] Priest's *Black Panther* series set a new standard by embellishing the character's identity as an African and an outsider. Priest placed the Black Panther in a questioning role and rooted that oppositional perspective within his African identity. The result was a backlash from white fans. As Priest discussed on his website fans were

> outraged by our evolution of the character into an extremely capable and not always clearly heroic figure, a man of uncertainty and mystery who used all of the vast resources at his disposal to accomplish his goals.... Expletive-laden rants came in from people who know nothing about Panther, never really bought Panther on any regular basis, and who, frankly, think Panther is lame but who have bought into the severely errant illogic of the day—the de-evolution of a very clever and very unique character created by Stan Lee and Jack Kirby. Again and again I was asked, "How dare you change Panther!" to which I replied, "I didn't change Panther—other writers over the years changed Panther, losing sight of FF #52. *I* changed him back."[45]

Regardless of whether this series was a drastic change or a return to the original intent, Black Panther at the turn of the millennium reflected contemporary African-American skepticism about the intersection of race and power. In doing so, Priest unsettled the "integrationist" identity attached to the Black Panther in the 1960s. Moreover, by placing his adventures firmly within the United States and having the Black Panther act to affirm Wakanda's sovereignty, Priest's approach called western imperialism into question and put Black Panther in place to oppose it.

The Black Panther as a counterforce to western power would become the central premise of the next iteration of the Black Panther. Writer Reginald Hudlin and artist John Romita, Jr., teamed to produce a new *Black Panther* series in 2005. Pairing Hudlin, an established African American writer, director, and producer in Hollywood with the well-respected Romita, Jr., was intended to broaden the series' appeal. Heavily promoted, *Black Panther* catered to new readers more than the small established fan base. The opening six-issue story *Who Is the Black Panther?* made it clear that the Black Panther represented anti-imperialism and freedom by retelling the character's origin story as a generational narrative that emphasizes Wakanda's existence challenged white power and cultural presumption.[46] Reflecting black concerns about policies that marginalized Africans abroad and African Americans at home, Hudlin's *Black Panther* series addressed popular narrative within black contemporary culture such as imperialism linked to Bush Administration, inequality linked to New Orleans, and positioned Wakanda as superpower on par with the United States.[47]

The 2008 presidential campaign furthered embellished on the anti-imperialist debate in the United States. Stories crafted by African American writers dominated the character's presentation, and the Black Panther's original anti-imperial narrative was expanded upon to resonate with contemporary African American racial and political narratives in the United States. These views were skeptical of the "War of Terror" and aligned with domestic and foreign criticism and they influenced the development of the *Black Panther* animated mini-series produced by Reginald Hudlin, Haven Alexander, and David Busch for Black Entertainment Television (BET) network in cooperation with Marvel Knights Animation in 2010.[48] Conceived by Hudlin (the former head of BET Entertainment) and based on his 2005 comic book series, this depiction of the Black Panther presented the aggressively anti-imperialist message he offered in his comic book series. The *Black Panther* animated mini-series presented the European colonial aggression against Wakanda as a historic event overcome by the Black Panther's father in a series of flashbacks. Contemporary mercenaries then mount an invasion from the corrupt neighboring state of Niganda, backed by unspecified Western corporate interests. Featuring

Dondi Reese, a character derived from Bush administration Secretary of State Condoleezza Rice, the series presents the United States' offer to "assist" Wakanda as a pretense for invasion.[49] Thus the animated series makes the Black Panther a figure of resistance to both historic European colonialism and contemporary American imperialism in Africa.

The success of Marvel Studios has raised new questions about representation and sparked debate about representation linked to the Black Panther. Since 2008, fans and critics alike have questioned if and when the Black Panther would appear in live action films produced by Marvel Studios. Borrowing heavily from the same Ultimate Marvel Comic Imprint that informed the *Ultimate Avengers 2: Rise of the Panther*, the Marvel Cinematic Universe (MCU) has hinted at the possibility of the Black Panther through references to Wakanda in films such as *Iron Man 2* (2010) and most recently *Avengers: Age of Ultron* (2015). The announcement of a Black Panther film to be released in 2018 and the assurance that the Black Panther will play a "large role" in several films suggest producers will continue the pattern seen in animated films.[50] Indeed, the introduction of Ulysee Klaw in *Avengers: Age of Ultron* as a criminal arms dealer branded by Wakandians as a thief suggests that the Marvel Studio films will externalize turmoil linked to Africa to Wakanda.[51] In this way, the live action films continue the model of using the Black Panther as a symbol of anti-imperialist action outside the United States. However, *Avengers: Age of Ultron* goes further by making Klaw a convicted criminal. In doing so, the film depoliticizes the postcolonial resistance narrative within the Black Panther's origin. In making this shift, Marvel Studios producers replicate and enhance the process found in the comic books.

Conclusion

Just as Marvel Comics made its reputation on its ability to bridge the gap between its fantasy realm and the real world, the Marvel Cinematic Universe has deftly adapted myriad storylines. Key to this translation has been the manipulation of themes, motivations, and actions culled from stories written in the 1960s, 1970s, and 1980s, repurposed to address recent social and political circumstances. Aligning the Black Panther within these frameworks forces creators to acknowledge contemporary concerns about inequality in domestic and international circumstances. Speaking about the reality of this diversity question, Kevin Feige stated that he felt privileged to "get to make movies based on source material where people have been sensitive to that (diversity) for decades and decades."[52] Yet, the reality is that the announcements of the first Marvel Studios films featuring gender and racial minorities came after twelve films (*Iron Man, The Incredible Hulk, Iron Man 2, Thor, Captain America: The First Avenger, Marvel's The Avengers, Iron Man 3, Thor: The Dark World, Captain America: The Winter Soldier, Guardians of the Galaxy, Avengers: Age of Ultron* and *Ant-Man*) featuring white men. Thus, just as minority characters in comic books have appeared in carefully regulated spaces, Marvel Studios continues the same pattern by manipulating minority representation in manner that carefully reaffirms a wider societal message.[53] Thus, the Black Panther offers the same possibility and challenge for cinematic adaptations that he has served in print, to acknowledge the complexity of contemporary racial politics within a framework that will not offend white audiences, but affirms the reality of racial diversity.

Notes

1. "Marvel Enters Burgeoning Made-For-DVD Market Segment Through Landmark Deal with Lions Gate Entertainment," Marvel.com, May 25, 2004, http://marvel.com/news/movies/73/marvel_enters_burgeoning_made-for-dvd_market_segment_through_landmark_deal_with_lions_gate_entertainment.
2. Will Meugniot, Dick Sebast, and Bob Richardson, *Ultimate Avengers II*, Animation, Action, Adventure (2006).
3. Shona N. Jackson, "Risk, Blackness, and Postcolonial Studies: An Introduction," *Callaloo* 37, no. 1 (Winter 2014): 63–68,182.
4. Meugniot, Sebast, and Richardson, *Ultimate Avengers II*.
5. Jesse Schedeen, "The State of Marvel's Ultimate Universe," Www.ign.com, February 4, 2011, http://www.ign.com/articles/2011/02/05/the-state-of-marvels-ultimate-universe.
6. Adilifu Nama, *Super Black: American Pop Culture and Black Superheroes* (Austin: University of Texas Press, 2011).
7. Bradford W. Wright, *Comic Book Nation: The Transformation of Youth Culture in America* (Baltimore: Johns Hopkins University Press, 2003).
8. Richard Reynolds, *Super Heroes: A Modern Mythology* (Jackson: University Press of Mississippi, 1994), 15.
9. Jeffrey A. Brown, *Black Superheroes, Milestone Comics, and Their Fans* (Jackson: University Press of Mississippi, 2000).
10. Josh Wigler, "'Guardians of the Galaxy' Is 'a Great Concept,' Marvel Studios Co-President Says," *Splash Page*, July 14, 2012, http://splashpage.mtv.com/2012/07/14/guardians-of-the-galaxy-marvel-studios-co-president/.
11. Jennifer Thompson and Jessica Carew, "From Blackface to Blaxploitation: Representations of African Americans in Film," Duke University Library, accessed May 8, 2015, http://exhibits.library.duke.edu/exhibits/show/africanamericansinfilm/timeline/1950s.
12. Jeffery A. Brown, "Comic Book Masculinity and the New Black Superhero," *African American Review* 33 (Spring 1999): 25.
13. Matthew Putz, *Comic Book Culture: Fanboy and True Believer* (Jackson: University Press of Mississippi, 1999), 48.
14. Peter Sanderson, *Marvel Universe* (New York: Harry N. Abrams 1996), 18.
15. Ibid., 196–197.
16. Sanderson, *Marvel Universe*, 35–36.
17. David Taft Terry, "Imagining a Strange New World: Racial Integration and Social Justice Advocacy in Marvel Comics, 1966–1980," in *Soul Thieves: The Appropriation and Misrepresentation of African American Popular Culture*, ed. Tamara Lizette Brown and Baruti N. Kopano (New York: Palgrave Macmillan, 2014).
18. Sean Howe, *Marvel Comics: The Untold Story* (New York: Harper Perennial, 2013), 85.
19. "Reconsiderations: The Cold War Was the Truman Doctrine a Real Turning Point?" *Foreign Affairs*, accessed May 12, 2015, https://www.foreignaffairs.com/articles/russian-federation/1974-01-01/reconsiderations-cold-war-was-truman-doctrine-real-turning.
20. Leroy Ashby, *With Amusement for All: A History of American Popular Culture Since 1830* (Lexington: University Press of Kentucky, 2006), 395–396.
21. Ibid., 402–403.
22. Janet L. Abu-Lughod, "New Immigrants in a Changing Los Angeles," in *Major Problems in American Urban and Suburban History*, ed. Howard Chudacoff and Peter C. Baldwin (Boston: Houghton Mifflin, 2005), 483.
23. Gordon Parks, *Shaft*, Action, Crime, Thriller, (1971).
24. Brooks E. Hefner, "Rethinking Blacula: Ideological Critique at the Intersection of Genres," *Journal of Popular Film & Television* 40, no. 2 (June 2012): 65, doi:10.1080/01956051.2011.620038.
25. Ed Guerrero, *Framing Blackness: The African American Image in Film* (Philadelphia: Temple University Press, 2012), 69–70.
26. http://www.fanboyplanet.com/comics/js-panthersrage.php. Accessed 7/06/07.
27. Jungle Action featuring The Black Panther, Vol. 2, Issue 8 (New York: Marvel Comic Group, 1974) M. Thomas Inge Collection of Comic Art Reference at the Virginia Commonwealth University Library.

28. Howe, *Marvel Comics*, 180.
29. Black Panther, Vol. 1, Issue 3 (New York: Marvel Comic Group, 1977) M. Thomas Inge Collection of Comic Art Reference at the Virginia Commonwealth University Library
30. Arthur Meier Schlesinger, *The Disuniting of America: Reflections on a Multicultural Society* (New York: W. W. Norton, 1998), 16–17.
31. Heather MacDonald, "The Disuniting of America by Arthur M Schlesinger Jr," *Commentary Magazine*, June 1, 1992, https://www.commentarymagazine.com/article/the-disuniting-of-america-by-arthur-m-schlesinger-jr/.
32. Nikhil Pal Singh, "Culture/Wars: Recoding Empire in an Age of Democracy," *American Quarterly* 50, no. 3 (September 1, 1998): 509.
33. Jude Davies, "'Diversity. America. Leadership. Good over Evil': Hollywood Multiculturalism and American Imperialism in Independence Day and Three Kings," *Patterns of Prejudice* 39, no. 4 (December 2005): 397–415, doi:10.1080/00313220500347840; Jennifer Fuller, "Branding Blackness on US Cable Television," *Media, Culture & Society* 32, no. 2 (March 1, 2010): 285–305, doi:10.1177/0163443709355611; Denise Herd, "Changing Images of Violence in Rap Music Lyrics: 1979–1997," *Journal of Public Health Policy* 30, no. 4 (December 2009): 397–399, doi:10.1057/jphp.2009.36.
34. John J. Siuntres, "Word Balloon the Comic Book Interview Podcast: Double Feature John Romita Jr Part One—Denys Cowan Panel from Summit City Con," *Word Balloon the Comic Book Interview Podcast*, June 22, 2011, http://wordballoon.blogspot.com/2011/06/double-feature-john-romita-jr-part-one.html.
35. "What We Do," *TransAfrica*, accessed May 17, 2015, http://transafrica.org/what-we-do/.
36. Frederic I. Solop, "Public Protest and Public Policy: The Anti-Apartheid Movement and Political Innovation," *Policy Studies Review* 9, no. 2 (Winter 1989): 309–311.
37. Jim Beard, "Path of the Black Panther: A Retrospective Pt. 2," Marvel.com, June 4, 2014, http://marvel.com/news/comics/22621/path_of_the_black_panther_a_retrospective_pt_2.
38. Ibid.
39. Alex Duval Smith, "Why FW de Klerk Let Nelson Mandela out of Prison," *The Guardian*, January 30, 2010, http://www.theguardian.com/world/2010/jan/31/nelson-mandela-de-klerk-apartheid.
40. Jim Beard, "Path of the Black Panther: A Retrospective Pt. 3," Marvel.com, June 6, 2014, http://marvel.com/news/comics/22642/path_of_the_black_panther_a_retrospective_pt_3.
41. Ibid.
42. Ibid.
43. Christopher Priest, *Black Panther Vol. 1: The Client* (New York: Marvel Comics, 2001); Christopher Priest, *Black Panther: Enemy of the State TPB* (New York: Marvel Comics, 2002).
44. Beau Yarborough, "David v. Quesada: Squaring Off Over 'Captain Marvel' and 25," www.comicbookresources.com, March 18, 2002, http://www.comicbookresources.com/?page=article&id=962.
45. Christopher Priest, "The Death of the Black Panther: Quesada's Bitch Survives the Mean Season," DigitalPriest.com, 2008, http://digitalpriest.com/legacy/comics/panther/panther_death.html.
46. Reginald Hudlin, *Black Panther Vol. 1: Who Is The Black Panther* (New York: Marvel, 2006).
47. Adilifu Nama, "Brave Black Worlds: Black Superheroes as Science Fiction Ciphers," in *The Black Imagination: Science Fiction, Futurism and the Speculative*, ed. Julie E. Moody-Freeman and Sandra Jackson (New York: Peter Lang P, 2011), 40–41.
48. *Black Panther*, Animation, Action (2010).
49. Julian C. Chambliss, "Black Panther: Who Is the Black Panther," in *Critical Survey of Graphic Novels: Heroes and Superheroes, Vol. 1*, ed. Bart H. Beaty, Har/Psc edition (Ipswich, MA: Salem Press, 2012).
50. Marc Graser, "Marvel Announces New Wave of Superhero Movies," *Variety*, October 28, 2014, http://variety.com/2014/film/news/black-panther-inhumans-captain-marvel-marvel-announces-new-wave-of-superhero-movies-1201341076/.
51. Dan Van Winkle, "Andy Serkis Confirms the Character He'll Play in Avengers: Age of Ultron," www.themarysue.com, April 1, 2015, http://www.themarysue.com/andy-serkis-confirms-ultron-character/; Joss Whedon, *Avengers: Age of Ultron*, Action, Adventure, Sci-Fi (2015).
52. Gina McIntyre, "'Avengers: Age of Ultron': Kevin Feige Wires Marvel Movies for Conquest," *Hero Complex—Movies, Comics, Pop Culture—Los Angeles Times*, April 25, 2015, http://herocomplex.latimes.com/movies/avengers-age-of-ultron-kevin-feige-wires-marvel-movies-for-conquest/.
53. Nickie D. Phillips and Staci Strobl, *Comic Book Crime: Truth, Justice, and the American Way* (New York: New York University Press, 2013), 171–172.

PART 6

Genre Studies

The Daywalker
Reading Blade *as Genre Hybridity*

Naja Later

In *Blade* (1998), the titular vampire-human hybrid is taunted by Deacon Frost, his vampire nemesis: "You think the humans will ever accept a half-breed like you?"[1] The question articulates one of *Blade*'s fundamental conflicts, but more telling is Blade's confident indifference. When we struggle to situate *Blade* in the canon of Marvel cinema and superhero comics, it is because Blade's strength as a character and a story relies on his hybrid vigor. The Daywalker—a half-vampire immune to sunlight—thrives in liminal spaces. This liminality is textual, intertextual, and most significantly for this study, generic. To read Blade's marginality is to recognize the remarkable genre hybridity on display throughout the character's history. Focusing on the first *Blade* movie, I aim to illuminate the strengths of generic hybridity, as modeled by Jim Collins, that characterize the hero as a "border guardian," able to walk in multiple worlds by functioning as a hybrid being.[2] *Blade* borrows from the Western, martial arts, horror, Blaxploitation, the teen movie, and the newly evolving independence of the vampire genre—all to create a superhero film. The syntactic arrangement of semantics from these genres supports the narrative of a hero on the margins, protecting the boundaries around humans, and around the mainstream superhero. From the physical embodiment of the actor, to the cross-media intertextuality of comics and movies, Blade demonstrates the significance of hybridity and genre to Marvel storytelling. It can be suggested that this hybridity is what makes *Blade* an effective hero, and I seek to illustrate how his liminal position is key to his role among Marvel superheroes.

The first *Blade* film follows the titular hero, played by martial artist Wesley Snipes, in his campaign against vampire supremacy. Blade is born Eric Brooks to a woman who suffers a vampire bite while in labor and seemingly dies in childbirth. Granted select vampire powers and a minor bloodlust by this process, Blade hunts and destroys covens of vampires with the aid of Whistler, his companion and quartermaster. His prime enemy is Frost, a stylish and savvy vampire who plans to summon an ancient "blood god" to become the supreme vampire. To complete the summoning, Frost is working to eliminate a conservative vampire assembly who oppose him. Meanwhile, a hematologist named Karen is bitten by a vampire, rescued by Blade, and develops a cure for herself before turning. Blade is captured by Frost after escalating confrontations, and Frost reveals that Blade's mother survived to become a vampire. Frost takes advantage of Blade's shock at his mother's return to drain Blade's blood, which Frost uses to summon the blood god into himself. The draining leaves Blade severely weakened, and Karen volunteers her own blood to revive Blade for the final battle. He defeats Frost and the blood god using Karen's vampire cure, but afterward declines the cure himself so he may continue to fight evil as the Daywalker.

Blade is thus difficult to categorize by genre. Collins' model of genre hybridity accommodates the canon of blockbusters, which quote a range of genres too broad to be placed firmly within a classic generic category. In highlighting the hybrid's cultural value, Collins claims:

> The foregrounding of a highly eclectic range of intertexts in so many recent popular films needs to be investigated in greater detail, because the significance of these quotations [of popular generic tropes] cannot be adequately explained in terms of overheated intertextual relations or the diminished creativity of Hollywood screenwriters.[3]

In *Blade*, these quotations from an array of genres re-center the marginal hero as an essential archetype. Hybridity gives Blade power and makes his movies powerfully entertaining, while also obliging him to guard the borders of genre where necessary. This power can be read literally down to Blade's embodiment of the vampire-human hybrid. In *Blade*, *Blade II*, and *Blade: Trinity*, his Daywalker physiology unlocks a crucial plot device of the films' final acts.[4] Intertextually, this hybridity sustains and justifies Blade's mythology, championing a hero who slips between borders.

I will present a number of generic quotations and histories for consideration in the construction of *Blade* as a self-reflexive hybrid. The breadth of genres presented emphasize both his Daywalker heroism and his marginality in Marvel's superhero canon. For the purposes of this study, three generic categories are highlighted as constructing the liminal hero: the Western and its action descendants; horror, vampires, and the monstrous; and the comic book superhero.

To trace these quotations and the significance of their synergies, I will use Rick Altman's semiotic model of genre.[5] Altman breaks tropes into semantics, syntactics, and pragmatics; distinctions which reveal "patterns of generic change."[6] Altman's example of semantics include "common traits, attitudes, shots, locations, sets, and the like," while syntactics accommodate "certain constitutive relationships between undesignated and variable placeholders."[7] In other words: "The semantic approach thus stresses the genre's building blocks, while the syntactic view privileges the structures into which they are arranged."[8] Syntactically, *Blade* functions as a Western: a hero who stands between the forces of good and evil. He uses violence to defeat the ancient savagery and push forth order and reason. This syntactic is so significant to reading *Blade*, and is fundamental to so many Western-derivative genres, that it leads this investigation of generic influences. Semantically, *Blade* has the building blocks of a horror film: vampires, gore, grimy and isolated sets, a restrictive color palette, and so forth. Horror syntax furthers the narrative of borderlands, and the latent monstrosity of the Western's gunslinger hero. Finally, the pragmatic approach takes into account the inclusion of this chapter in the collection. Pragmatics extend beyond the film to its reception, to audiences' understanding that Blade is a Marvel hero as defined by Marvel's intellectual property, and their reading of the film in a wider context. A film that uses horror semantics and Western syntactics is placing itself on the edges of this genre, and contextualizing the comic hero movie pragmatically is essential to understanding the importance of hybridity and liminality on an intertextual level.

Blade *as a* Western

Like many contemporary action men, Blade owes much to the Western hero. He is Shane, Ethan Edwards, Hawkeye, Harry Callahan, Sanjuro, and Shaft. The frontier of the Old West—the line between civilization and savagery—is redrawn between humans and vampires. The Western hero, characteristically a gunslinger with a remarkable talent for killing, fights violence with violence on behalf of the civilized community. His own affinity for the forces of darkness, the source of his skill, continually pushes him to the margins of the civilization he champions. The Western hero is a troubling, ambivalent figure, but nonetheless a fundamental pillar of American mythology. Blade draws on generations of Westerns to foreground the hybrid nature of the gunslinger.

Read semantically, *Blade* may not initially appear to be a Western. Gone are the horses, the Monument Valley vistas, and the 19th-century setting. We may recognize the leather outfits, quick-draw gunfights, and pithy one-liners of the Western that were passed on to the action genre in the 1970s as Western semantics. Even the selectivity—the postmodern combination of these semantics with a katana-wielding, mixed martial artist, African American actor—indicates how the Western syntax of hybridity guides the semantics of *Blade*. Borrowing from other genres is how the gunslinger can exist at generic frontiers: he appropriates from chaos to support order, protecting the key narrative of the Western.

The syntax of the Western protagonist proves more enlightening in reading the genre's significance to *Blade*. Geoff King explains the syntax of the Western hero as follows:

> The dominant figure of the western hero is a frontiersman who combines a feeling for the wilderness with some of the qualities of civilization. Not the "superficial" niceties, maybe, but what is presented as the essence of civilization: a respect for the value of human life and liberty, perhaps. The frontiersman might have an understanding of the ways of Native American groups, an insight into some of their methods and customs, an ability to live on their terrain and to understand their languages. A clear distinction is usually made between this figure and the "Indian," however, the latter often viewed in racist terms as a "savage" entirely beyond the bounds of civilization. The frontier hero is often called upon to make a commitment to the "civilized" township or community.[9]

The syntax of *Blade* can, under King's model, be read as a Western. More specifically, the film's plot owes much to one archetypal Western: John Ford's *The Searchers*.[10] John Wayne's "Ethan Edwards" is a man with a mysterious and violent past, pursuing Comanche "savages" that have stolen his niece. Despite his ability to communicate with and predict the actions of the Comanches, he abhors them, believing that he must kill the girl if she has been turned to their ways. When she is rescued, Edwards turns his back on the community he has restored, walking once more into the wilderness. The semblance of this plot to the first *Blade* movie is obvious: the "savages" are translated as vampires, the innocent human Karen is bitten and then rescued by Blade—but, in a more feminist twist, cures herself. The third act elevates the civilization/savagery conflict to apocalyptic levels: as a hematologist who develops an antidote for vampirism, Karen represents the rational world of humanity, while the vampires attempt to raise a pagan "blood god" to subsume the world with monstrousness. As the Daywalker, Blade is granted the speed and skills to defeat the vampires, but like Ethan Edwards he is excluded from both worlds by his hybrid status. This similarity to *The Searchers* signposts the hero's relationship to the genre's core conflicts, and demonstrates the potential of *Blade*, as a character and a text, to hybridize key mythological tropes.

The syntax of the gunslinger myth has always carried elements of hybridity and liminality. Tad Gallagher notes that cynical Westerns with ambivalent heroes have been represented in cinema since 1902.[11] Richard Slotkin identifies the James Fenimore Cooper's 1827–1841 dime novels as a prototype for the hybridized hero archetype.[12] Slotkin writes of frontier heroes:

> Because the border between savagery and civilization runs through their moral center, the Indian wars are, for these heroes, a spiritual or psychological struggle which they win by learning to discipline or suppress the savage or "dark" side of their own human nature.[13]

With vampires replacing Indians, the border and center of Blade runs through his genetics. We may take the struggle between his dark side and human nature very literally. Slotkin's analysis of Fenimore Cooper's hero Hawkeye serves as a blueprint for reading both Ethan Edwards and Blade:

> As the "man who knows Indians," the frontier hero stands between the opposed worlds of savagery and civilization, acting sometimes as a mediator or interpreter between races and cultures but more often as civilization's most effective instrument against savagery–a man who knows how to think and fight like an Indian, to turn their own methods against them.[14]

This is a striking allegory for Blade's role in the movie. He is the instrument, wielding ostentatious weapons as part of his embodiment of this role: a "Blade." His knowledge of vampirism and the temptation of bloodlust are a source of great drama: he relies on synthetic blood to survive, and must drink from Karen to strengthen himself for the final battle. He stands against savagery only for the sake of "good" after losing his key motivation: avenging the death of his mother. When Blade continues to fight for humanity, it is reminiscent of his Western predecessors, working thanklessly for the benefit of society.

The replacing of "savages" with "monsters" was a common means to update the racist Western trope by the 1990s. As part of his analysis of genre hybridity, King frames *From Dusk Till Dawn*[15] as a Western that substitutes vampires for Indians: "Further beyond the boundaries of acceptability are the vampire hordes, the truly alien and savage others whose principal role is to be exterminated."[16] *From Dusk Till Dawn* uses vampires and humans as a frontier in a similar way to Blade, but splits the border through its temporal center—halfway through the movie—rather than through the physicality of the hero. The frontier is self-reflexive in these films: the boundary between humanity and vampires is also a boundary between traditional Western storytelling and chaotic, generic hybridity. This is how these films function as intertextual Westerns: the Western syntax of the frontier and its dissonant hero remains intact by drawing a generic frontier, with the hero straddling both civilization/savagery and Western/other genres.

The ironic dissonance of the hybrid hero is often played for pathos and seriality: as he establishes the frontier, he must leave the community behind to move to new borderlands. Although he may act on behalf of civilization, he possesses elements of savagery that keep him on the fringe. He harnesses these elements to act as a guardian, holding the wilderness at bay, knowing that this skill precludes him from assimilating into the community himself. After all, if Blade's quest succeeds, there will always be one vampire left. This is coded best in *Shane*, where the buckskin-clad hero arrives in the border town and saves them from the brutal outsiders—this time a gang of gunslingers.[17] In the discordant conclusion, he declines the invitation to join the community, declaring, "A man has to be what he is," and disappearing into the darkness. Shane is titular and mononymous, with a mysterious past and a near-supernatural skill for gun fighting. The community fears him as much as they value him, but the gunfighters recognize him as their own. *Blade* quotes this syntax by denying Karen's cure to his vampirism—a man who has to be what he is—acknowledging that the humans will never accept him. This tragic exclusion is brushed off in the diegesis, but a pragmatic reading reminds us that Blade's affinity for the borders also precludes him from being fully integrated into the Marvel canon.

The Western syntax continues to expand into new territories with the development of action genres in the 1970s. The limitations of Old West semantics meant the compelling syntax was adapted for new contexts: relevant comparisons for this study of *Blade* include the hardboiled cop movie, East-West fusion films, and Blaxploitation. In the forthcoming section I will briefly outline these genres to illustrate how they create a lineage of generic quotations from the Western to *Blade*, with a focus on the strength and tenacity of hybridity as a syntactic.

Beyond Western Borders

Blade is exemplary of the action genre's hybridization of Western narrative and characters imposed on the urban noir setting. Eric Lichtenfeld discusses this cross-generic quotation in his reading of *Dirty Harry* and the action genre:

> The most obvious marker of the genre's modernity would be the big-city backdrops that had longed served *noir*, detective, and gangster pictures and against which more classically Western conflicts would now be staged. Urban warfare was about to receive the Western gunfighter, who, to bring law to the lawless, would appropriate some of the dark terrain traditionally associated with other genres. This terrain would be physical in terms of geography (cities, their shabby police precincts, their sleazy motel rooms, etc.) and in terms of the body (the kinds of violence done to it, the weapons by which it is done.)[18]

Dirty Harry is exemplary in the one-cop-takes-a-stand action syntax from the 1970s onwards.[19] Moving the border into a city space creates a new dynamic between the civilized urban community of the day and the savage creatures of the night. The film follows another titular hero, a jaded cop abandoning his oaths as a lawman to chase "Scorpio," a rogue sniper. Harry Callahan is caught between an ineffectual police force and a shadowy, decadent killer threatening the city. Like the gunslinger, Harry discards his connection to the community: the cost of remaining its protector. The film is framed around his struggle against the law's restrictions and his ambivalent slippage into monstrosity to maintain his own ideology of order.

Dirty Harry can be called a "post–Western." Lichtenfeld foregrounds the pessimistic role of the hybrid action hero, adapted for audiences weary of the Western, as his own third faction between civilization and savagery. Lichtenfeld suggests that the gunslinger's ultimate denial of the community is as significant as his elimination of savagery in a triangulation of narrative forces:

> The triangle composed of Harry, the politicians, and Scorpio parallels the one of so many Westerns, a triangle composed of the hero, the civilized, and the savage (which can in turn include outlaws, Indians, and the wilderness itself). One point in the triangle is usually in contention

with the other two. This is especially true for the hero, who as "The Man Who Knows Indians" is constantly defined against the civilized and the savage. He must be; as his nature resonates with both, he is neither wholly, but rather, is stranded between them.[20]

This shifting of Harry's alignment indicates some of the more complex conflicts in the civilized and savage factions of *Blade*. The ambiguity of the hero pollutes the border, deepening his struggle to maintain external and internal order. Civilization does as much harm as good, at times: cops and humans hinder Blade at key strategic moments, while the old-world vampires opposing Frost threaten Blade very little. Frost and his coven are thoroughly modernized, donning gaudy street fashions and utilizing cyberpunk hacking technology to unlock the blood god. Action movies have ambiguous gunslingers meeting ambiguous villains: no-good hippie "Scorpio" is as much a product of civilization as its opposite.

Vampires appearing to be civilized—posing as humans, stealing them away, using their technology—makes them even more threatening to the community, and Blade's struggle to find and overwhelm them is more urgent than ever. These vampires are not appropriating to assimilate: the irreverent decadence of Frost's coven triggers a yearning for the ultimate wilderness of the "blood god." This struggle with bloodlust is what tenaciously positions Blade, like Harry, on the side of civilization: the hero only engages in violence to end violence.

Blade frames the dangers of savage excess in generic terms: while Blade is able to moderate his dependence on other genre tropes to strengthen himself, vampires indulge in chaotic genre quotations. This wilderness and moderation lead to my reading of the Eastern cinema influences on the film. References to Japanese and Hong Kong popular culture abound in *Blade*, but contextualizing their relevance still depends on the Western syntax: first for its influence on martial arts and Japanese period films, and second for its dichotomous organization of semantics.

I have mentioned that Blade recalls "Sanjuro," a Western hero so liminal he is neither a gunslinger nor a character from the Old West. The abstractly-named hero of Akira Kurosawa's film *Yojimbo* (1961), Sanjuro is a samurai who rescues a community by ending a schism between two violent groups overrunning their village.[21] J.L. Anderson notes that here "Kurosawa ... clearly acknowledges his interest in Westerns while maintaining perfect Japanese authenticity in his work."[22] Collins acknowledges that generic hybrids borrow in a "transnational" manner, and this is worth discussing in the context of Anderson's "authenticity."[23] *Yojimbo*'s story is richly transnational: Kurosawa's generous use of Western semiotics leads to an Italian remake *A Fistful of Dollars* set in North America.[24] Anderson's work suggests that this transnational quotation is not at the expense of "authenticity," but a demonstration of the flexibility of Western syntactics. To quote *Yojimbo* through the katana-wielding Blade is to quote the richness of the Western, while acknowledging that transnational quotations can still convey authenticity.

Blade's prime instrument against savagery is the iconic samurai weapon: the katana. It's used to resolve the vampire schism and restore order to the city, and is supported by an arsenal of guns, gadgets, throwing stars, and Snipes' formidable martial arts skills. This is another case of syntax meeting audience pragmatics: the knowledge of Snipes' multinational martial arts training and choreography outside the film's textual elements contributes to our understanding of his hybrid strength. The elevation of the Kung Fu choreographer as a star in 1990s American action cinema is documented by Leon Hunt, who claims that choreography and training are used to "authenticate" a film.[25] Blade's ability to draw on forces outside the Western give him strength and authenticity, but restrain the film from falling into trope-riddled chaos. Snipes' physicality is tightly controlled, markedly more so in *Blade* than his other works, and promotion of the star's black belt training in many disciplines intertextually reframes his moderated bloodlust—his knowledge of violence as an end to fight violence.

This is not to suggest that Eastern cinema is portrayed as "savage" in *Blade*. However, transnational quotation without the overtures of Snipes' and Blade's discipline suggests a risk of being lost in the inter-generic wilderness. This is where Frost's vampires stand for the "savage" side of transnational quotation. Their consumption of Eastern popular culture is rampant and vacuous in the film. Their semantic quotations from fashionable Eastern trends are coded with irreverence and excess in the context of vampires. This can be read in contrast to the syntactic and intertextual use of Eastern cinema for Blade's narrative: Blade once more working as an instrument of order against chaos. Blade exudes control in his stiff movement, his advanced fighting styles, and his repressed bloodlust. His fighting technique places him on the fringe of the traditional gunslinger, but it allows him to restore order through an extreme performance of discipline.

Discussing Snipes' star status and the intertextuality of *Blade* necessitates consideration of his context as a black action hero. Blade's comic book origin is directly influenced by the Blaxploitation cinema trend, and the film expresses some nostalgia for the genre. Blaxploitation emerged from the decline of the Western, borrowing many Western tropes and star actors. *Blade*, like its predecessors, is a monument to black masculinity, music, sexuality, heroism, and also struggle: unlike the traditional gunslinger, Blade's exclusion from the community for his violent prowess is coded with a powerful racial subtext. Along with the Western, William Crain's 1972 horror film *Blacula* is an exemplary Blaxploitation ancestor to *Blade*, featuring the first African American vampire star in cinema.[26] The influence of Blaxploitation on *Blade* serves to further his liminality as a hero, while once again using inter-generic quotation to create a powerful hybrid character.

Blade was created as a comic book character by Marv Wolfman and Gene Colon in 1973 in *Tomb of Dracula #10*, at the peak of the Blaxploitation cinema boom. Artist Gene Colan notes in an interview that he was visually based on Jim Brown, a Blaxploitation star of the period with a history of Western roles.[27] Without dwelling on the comic book incarnation of Blade, this is remarkable evidence of his cinematic intertextuality. Despite two decades passing between Blaxploitation and *Blade*, the former directly influences the character and his adaptability, and hopefully, the importance of a Blaxploitation context in reading *Blade* from Western to horror is briefly traced throughout this analysis.

Preceding examples mention the significance of the gunslinger's "mononymity." From *Shane* to *Shaft*, from Sanjuro (a name made up on the spot by the character) to "The Man with No Name," Western and Western-inspired heroes show a deep reticence about proper names.[28] It is never addressed in the movies why Eric Brooks uses the name Blade. Considering his role as a superhero, it is not uncommon to take on a title to fight evil. However, in the context of a black hero, this chosen title has complex connotations. Studying *Blacula*, in which African prince Mamuwalde is renamed Blacula when turned by a slaver vampire, Novotny Lawrence notes:

> This renaming [of Mamuwalde to Blacula] parallels that endured by African slaves at the hands of whites after they were unwillingly shipped to America, and it was vehemently preached against in rallies held by Malcolm X and the members of the Nation of Islam during the Civil Rights Movement.[29]

When it is revealed that Blade's mother—the origin of his name, Eric Brooks—is a willing vampire, the chosen title of Blade may signify the hero's independence and his iconic weapon. The revelation of his mother—the reminder that he is, in fact, Eric Brooks—is so shocking that vampires are able to capture and enslave Blade. He is forced into bondage, his blood drained to power the vampires' summoning ritual. The contentiousness of names, given or chosen, runs deep in Blaxploitation and *Blade*, complicating the obliquity of this Western trope. Again, Blade finds strength in the between: beyond the human name Eric Brooks and outside the vampire slur Daywalker, he is, with very little ado, Blade.

Quoting directly from a radical genre dealing with blackness demands that Blade's race be read into the hero's struggle. It remains true that the Western gunslinger is stranded between worlds, with a violence (and, shown in his animalistic drinking of Karen's blood, sexuality) too radical for civilization. When Frost taunts that "humans will [never] accept a half-breed," he addresses an actor who is African and American; who is trained in martial arts of many nations; and who plays a superhero-gunslinger role seldom offered to black actors by Hollywood. It is difficult to ignore that Blade is exploited by white villains, that he struggles to protect a community that characterizes him as a violent outsider, and that he is placed on the margins of Marvel's superhero canon. Ultimately, he is able to use these conflicts to his advantage, and like his Blaxploitation and Western predecessors, his hybridity creates heroism.

Horror, Vampires and Why There's an "Everything" in Between

In the video-store framework of generic categorization used by acclaimed horror theorist Carol Clover, *Blade* can be shelved in the horror section.[30] The vampires are the most obvious semantic guide for classifying *Blade* as horror, but even vampires have migrated to and settled in other genres. In the absence of horror's characteristic frights, *Blade*'s relationship to the horror genre requires further investigation. Horror in *Blade* is the horror of liminality—of ambiguity and its threat to space and bodies. Like the Western, horror is obsessed with the borderlands and the danger of the wilderness overpowering the safe world. Blade's core struggle is with monstrousness threatening to break forth and overwhelm its borders, whether in the guise of the "blood god" destroying mankind or his own bloodlust destroying his humanity. I suggest that the film itself is a "monster," threatening the borders between genres: it allows horror to creep into the Western, the martial arts film, the Blaxploitation piece, and the superhero story. As vampires infiltrate genres from the teen movie to the superhero comic, Blade's role is once more as a superhero-monster, patrolling the borderlands of these worlds and using their liminality to his advantage.

Tracing Blade's origins in comics helps to identify the importance of horror storytelling. Between the Golden and Silver Ages of comics in the 1940s and 1960s, superheroes fell out of favor, and Marvel published horror comics as its most popular genre.[31] The influence of these horror stories on the Silver Age heroes is evident, described by Gareth Schott and Andrew Burn: "At a cultural level 'the Hulk' was deliberately pieced together from fusing Frankenstein's misunderstood creature and the transformative personalities of Dr. Jekyll and Mr. Hyde."[32] *Tomb of Dracula* similarly borrows from the Gothic horror classics of the 1930s, and was among a small collection of Marvel horror titles launched in the 1970s.[33] Blade's popularity in comics was preceded by *Blacula*, another Dracula text with a black hero and one of the few popular Blaxploitation-horror hybrids. Lawrence claims that 1968's *Night of the Living Dead* "functions as an important prelude to Blaxploitation cinema because it is *the* singular example of a horror film that prominently features a three-dimensional black character as an integral part of the action."[34] Blade appears five years later, fighting back the undead as many of George A. Romero's later heroes continued to do. Colan acknowledges the timeliness of Blade as a black hero and his appearance in the comic medium: "Oh, I knew it was good, this character. Blacks were not portrayed in comics up to that time, not really. So I wanted to be one of the first to portray blacks in comics."[35] This period, in which horror was being introduced to new heroes, genres, audiences, and media, links *Blade* in his 1990s incarnation to horror storytelling stretching back over a century. While the film does not rely on many tropes of contemporaneous teen-star-slasher horror, a rich history of horror-hybridity informs the cultural landscape from which Blade first emerged.

The vampires of *Blade* cannot be said pay close homage to Bela Lugosi. As horror monsters, their key functions are deceptively effective. Unlike other undead brethren, vampires are easily able to infiltrate human society, maintaining their power and monstrosity in the shadows as "the assembly" do in *Blade*. Their ability to threaten the fringes, disguising their monstrosity until it is too late, makes them horrific while allowing them to infiltrate genres outside traditional horror. By the 1990s, and continuing now, a vampire movie is not one we would necessarily classify as a horror movie anymore. Deacon Frost's interpretation of vampirism is more *Near Dark* than *Nosferatu*—until he summons the ancient forces of evil.[36] Frost is played by then-teen heartthrob Stephen Dorff, and styled appropriately for haunting nightclubs in 1999. His coven dwell at the fringes of horror, shifting between action movie foes, ninjas, hackers, and style icons, all to bring back an archaic monster of true horror. *Blade* suggests to us that the chaos of ancient monstrosity has more in common with the genre-bending cyberpunk vampires than with our conventional, demarcated understanding of horror.

The syntax of the Western allows me to discuss the border's significance from a horror context. The Western hero embodies this struggle between good and evil: Blade battles with monsters, and risks becoming a monster. Monsters defy categorization: they may be half-man, half-beast—or a thing that lurks near the edges of the woods and maps, devouring those who stray too far. This is the Daywalker: a chimaera that prowls the boundaries of darkness. Marina Warner notes the hybrid power of ancient monsters:

> When people in the ancient world commissioned a curious gem with a strange hybrid creature or a metamorphosed beast-man cut into the stone, they were attaching to themselves the ambiguous powers of protection and fear generated by this source.[37]

Warner furthers this discussion of hybrid monsters to a colonial, cartographical context in her work on sea monsters:

> Many of these primordial monsters are hybrids defying nature. They belong to dark places, those underworlds under land and sea—volcanoes, ocean abysses—because they embody our lack of understanding, and mirror it in their savagery and disorderly, heterogenous asymmetries of shape.[38]

I highlight Warner's monsters because they are both horrifying and attractive. Their monstrosity is communicated through their hybrid, heterogenous body and the "darkness" of liminal worlds. Warner describes the "fear and awe" that "can't entirely be dispelled" around these monsters: these frontiers and their anthropomorphisms hold an important place at the limits of our imagination.[39] The colonialist conquest of "savagery"—which Slotkin notes included the conquest of African slaves—is not a satisfying victory in the cultural narrative.[40] Blade is a compelling hero because he represents liminality as a powerful, fascinating, and essential element of storytelling. It is an enjoyable film because it plays out on the border of rationality and irrationality, challenging the limits of genre. The gunslinger is as much a superhero as he is a monster, and he protects the important cultural space in which creativity, hybridity, and danger can flourish.

The "Marvel" Brand

I have discussed Blade's liminality to establish how and why his place in the Marvel canon is significant. Altman's pragmatics incorporate the "use factor" of semiotics: how different audiences might identify and categorize genres.[41] Audiences, particularly those since 1999, recognize "Marvel" as a brand, but one defined by complex factors of cross-media and legal intertextuality. Our recognition of *Blade* as a Marvel movie requires pragmatic knowledge outside the limits of film canon: we must know his comics history, his animated television series with other Marvel characters, and something of the studio deals on character licensing to understand why he should be included in the "Marvel" category.[42] As with other genres, his place in Marvel is liminal, but this is not a weakness: Blade's heroism is dependent on our enjoying the spaces between the margins of the comic page and the movie screen, just as it is between the worlds of superheroes and vampires.

Marvel comics have come to celebrate Blade as a member of their superhero lineup while maintaining his power as a fringe dweller. The most recent run of *The Mighty Avengers* featured an eclectic lineup of superheroes, including one that moonlit as Spider-Hero and Ronin in an ongoing tease around his identity. When he was revealed as Blade, our knowledge is rewarded: of course that hidden hero we don't immediately recognize would be the Daywalker.[43] We must know he comes from the comics between Marvel's horror and superhero genres, and remember that he holds off the occult side of Marvel's universe for the sake of mainstream superheroes. We know we forget that Blade is a Marvel hero, and the revelation depends on us enjoying his adventures on the borders of the Marvel universe, both pushing them and protecting them. This is because we are intertextual—able to follow Blade's mythos across media and between genres. Like the Daywalker, audiences thrive in marginal spaces. We explore the limits of what a superhero can be, and imagine spaces where monsters and horrors still exist. We are able to read this liminality in Blade's body, his story, his genre, and his medium, and enjoy it.

Blade champions hybridity for all the Marvel movies that follow, demonstrating the potential for generic quotation to enrich the superhero movie. Although it keeps him in the margins of Marvel, he champions those movies we might say dwell in the "day" of the superhero genre and those beginning to expand its boundaries. *Blade* makes space for the spy thriller of *Captain America: The Winter Soldier* and the comedy romp of *Guardians of the Galaxy*.[44] *Blade* precedes an era where our generic categories are impossibly specific and hybridized: Alexis C. Madrigal's investigation of Netflix's formula produces genres such as "Foreign Satanic Stories from the 1980s" and "Violent Thrillers About

Cats for Ages 8 to 10."[45] In hindsight, vampire Western "Blaxploitation martial arts superhero horror" is not an unusual genre. It suggests that hybrid vigor can avert the dreaded exhaustion of the superhero genre, and demonstrates how classic American mythology can experiment while retaining its cohesion. Although he didn't exist yet in what we call the Marvel Cinematic Universe, he creates a generically sound universe in which other Marvel heroes can flourish, enriched and empowered by hybridity. *Blade* foregrounds possibility of the superhero genre, pushing its boundaries outward. And rumors suggest he is soon to return.

Blade's Edge

Blade works as a Marvel hero because he isn't statically a Marvel hero. We have our Spider-Man and our Wolverine; but who keeps them safe from their comic book vampires? All spaces have borders, and those borders are rich with narrative opportunity. Blade is powerful because he is a Daywalker: we enjoy him because we, too, enjoy the shift between characters, media, universes, and genres. He personifies our fascination with liminal space and the creative, classic stories of heroism. Blade demonstrates from character physicality to cross-media histories the potential for hybridity in generic storytelling. At the cost of acceptance into the mainstream canon, Blade may save the Marvel universe.

Notes

1. *Blade*, directed by Stephen Norrington (1998; Los Angeles: New Line Cinema, 1998), DVD.
2. Jim Collins, *Architectures of Excess: Cultural Life in the Information Age* (New York: Routledge, 1995), 125.
3. Collins, *Architectures of Excess*, 126.
4. *Blade II*, directed by Guillermo Del Toro (2002; Los Angeles: New Line Cinema, 2002), DVD. Blade: Trinity, directed by David S. Goyer (2004, Los Angeles: New Line Cinema, 2005), DVD.
5. Rick Altman, *The American Film Musical* (London: BFI, 1989), 91.
6. Rick Altman, *Film/Genre* (London: BFI, 1999), 208.
7. Altman, *The American Film Musical*, 95.
8. Altman, *The American Film Musical*, 95.
9. Geoff King, *New Hollywood Cinema: An Introduction* (London: I.B. Tauris, 2002), 125–126.
10. *The Searchers*, directed by John Ford (1956; Los Angeles: Warner Bros., 2007), DVD.
11. Tad Gallagher, "Shoot-Out at the Genre Corral: Problems in the 'Evolution' of the Western," in *Film Genre Reader*, edited by Barry Grant (Austin: University of Texas Press, 1986), 204.
12. Richard Slotkin, *Gunfighter Nation: The Myth of the Frontier in Twentieth-Century America* (Norman: Oklahoma University Press, 1998), 14.
13. Slotkin, *Gunfighter Nation*, 14.
14. Slotkin, *Gunfighter Nation*, 16.
15. *From Dusk Till Dawn*, directed by Robert Rodriguez (1996; New York: Dimension Films, 2001), DVD.
16. King, *New Hollywood Cinema*, 126.
17. *Shane*, directed by George Stevens (1953; Hollywood: Paramount Pictures, 2000), DVD.
18. Eric Lichtenfeld, *Action Speaks Louder: Violence, Spectacle and The American Action Movie* (Middletown, CT: Wesleyan University Press, 2007) 23.
19. *Dirty Harry*, directed by Don Siegel (1971; Los Angeles: Warner Home Video, 2010), DVD.
20. Lichtenfeld, *Action Speaks Louder*, 29.
21. *Yojimbo*, directed by Akira Kurosawa (1961; New York: Criterion Films, 1998), DVD.
22. J. L. Anderson, "Japanese Swordfighters and American Gunfighters," *Cinema Journal* 2, no. 2 (Spring 1973): 9.

23. Collins, *Architectures of Excess*, 134.

24. *A Fistful of Dollars*, directed by Sergio Leone (1964; Los Angeles: Fox Searchlight, 1999), DVD.

25. Leon Hunt, "The Hong Kong/Hollywood Connection: Stardom and Spectacle in Transnational Action Cinema," in *Action and Adventure Cinema*, edited by Yvonne Tasker (London: Routledge, 2004), 227.

26. *Blacula*, directed by William Crain (1972; Beverly Hills: MGM, 2004), DVD.

27. Gene Colan, Tom Field, and Jon B. Knutson, "The Colan Mystique," *TwoMorrows Publishing*, last edited February 18, 2001, http://www.twomorrows.com/comicbookartist/articles/13colan.html.

28. *Shaft*, directed by Gordon Parks (1971, Los Angeles: Warner Home Video, 2006), DVD.

29. Novotny Lawrence, "Fear of a Blaxploitation Monster: Blackness as Generic Revision in AIP's *Blacula*," *Film International* 7, no. 3: 22.

30. Carol Clover, *Men, Women and Chain Saws: Gender in the Modern Horror Film* (Princeton: Princeton University Press, 1992), 5.

31. Sean Howe, *Marvel Comics: The Untold Story* (New York: HarperCollins, 2012), 30.

32. Gareth Schott and Andrew Burn, "RIPPED OFF! Cross-Media Convergence and 'The Hulk,'" in *Super/Heroes: From Hercules to Superman*, edited by Wendy Haslem, Angela Ndalianis, and Chris Mackie (Washington, D.C.: New Academia Publishing, 2007), 291.

33. Colan, "The Colan Mystique."

34. *Night of the Living Dead*, directed by George A. Romero (1968; Culver City: Sony Pictures Home Entertainment, 1999), DVD; Lawrence, "Fear of a Blaxploitation Monster," 16.

35. Colan, "The Colan Mystique."

36. *Near Dark*, directed by Kathryn Bigelow (1987; Santa Monica: Lionsgate, 2009), Blu-ray. *Nosferatu*, directed by F.W. Murnau (1922; New York: Kino Lorber films, 2013), Blu-ray.

37. Marina Warner, *Monsters of our own Making* (Lexington: University Press of Kentucky, 1998), 286.

38. Marina Warner, "Here Be Monsters," *New York Review of Books*, last edited December 19, 2013, http://www.nybooks.com/articles/archives/2013/dec/19/here-be-monsters/?pagination=false.

39. Warner, "Here Be Monsters."

40. Slotkin, *Gunfighter Nation*, 11.

41. Altman, *Film/Genre*, 210.

42. *Blade: The Series*, directed by Peter O'Fallon, Michael Robinson, John Fawcett, Felix Enriquez Alcala, Alex Chappie, David Straiton, Norberto Barba, Brad Turner, and Ken Giroti (2006; New York: Marvel Entertainment, 2006), DVD. *Marvel Anime*, directed by Mitsuyuki Masuhara (2011; Tokyo: Madhouse, 2012), DVD.

43. Al Ewing, Greg Land, Jay Leisten, Frank D'armata, and Edgar Delgado, *The Mighty Avengers* #9, April 2014 (New York: Marvel), 29.

44. *Captain America: The Winter Soldier*, directed by Joe and Anthony Russo (2014; Burbank: Disney, 2014), Blu-ray. *Guardians of the Galaxy*, directed by Ryan Gunn (2014; Burbank: Disney, 2014), Blu-ray.

45. Alexis C. Madrigal, "How Netflix Reverse Engineered Hollywood," *The Atlantic*, last edited January 2, 2014, http://www.theatlantic.com/technology/archive/2014/01/how-netflix-reverse-engineered-hollywood/282679/.

Body vs. Technology
Iron Man: The Rise of Technovore *and Cyberpunk Culture*

VANESSA GERHARDS

"The sky above the port was the color of television,
tuned to a dead channel."—William Gibson, *Neuromancer*

The aforementioned sentence is not only an introduction for Gibson's world, but it is also a description of the world as established in *Iron Man and the Rise of Technovore*[1] (dir. Hiroshi Hamasaki, 2013). In both cases, the audience perceives the characters as being surrounded by "white noise" (the dead channel) and trying to escape it at the same time. The world the reader steps into is "[d]ense, kaleidoscopic, fast-paced, full of punked-out, high-tech weirdos."[2] It is the world of Cyberpunk—in many cases, it is our world in the future, but with many alterations.

The objective of this essay is to show the interrelations of Cyberpunk and Cyber-culture and Marvel's animated film. The fusion of body and technology, which is one of the main themes of Cyberpunk, is omnipresent in the Marvel film and we can find many points of connection to "traditional" Cyberpunk fiction. This essay sets out to explore these connections with regard to the Cyberpunk heritage, showing that this genre is still a major force in literature and film.

After setting the scene, so to speak, with an attempt at defining Cyberpunk, the first part of the chapter is dedicated to the analysis of the focus of this investigation, *Rise of Technovore*. In the following parts, connections to three main pieces of work from Cyberpunk fiction are drawn: William Gibson's *Neuromancer* (1984) (Marvel Comics also released a graphic novel adaptation in 1989), Kathryn Bigelow's *Strange Days* (1995), and Alex Proyas' *Dark City* (1998). Each preceded *Rise of Technovore* by several years or even decades, and thus I argue that the Marvel film borrows its rich imagery from them and re-contextualizes them in the Marvel Universe. Apart from the imagery, there is also a strong link to the Gothic tradition. They are an expansion of the Gothic ideals and elements as established by classic novels such as Mary Shelley's *Frankenstein* or Bram Stoker's *Dracula*. The analysis will then focus on the dichotomies of body/technology and identity/memory.

The Rise of Technovore

The premise of *Rise of Technovore* is that Tony Stark's invention called "Howard" (a satellite system used to spot and hence apprehend crime) is about to be launched. The "Technovore" attacks the facility with the help of mercenaries and faces Iron Man in a short fight. Although Iron Man is able to survive the fight, the new enemy proves to be technically more advanced than him. It turns out that the Technovore wears an upgraded body armor, which is connected to its carrier: Ezekiel Stane (Stark later gains this intelligence with the help of The Punisher). As it is an Artificial Intelligence (AI), the Technovore betrays Ezekiel to follow its own aims of replacing humanity with AI beings, using the Howard satellite to hack into all the computers in the world. Naturally, Iron Man is able to defeat the Technovore and commit Ezekiel into S.H.I.E.L.D.'s custody.

In contrast to other Iron Man treatments, it is the antagonist who is technologically more advanced and, despite being defeated in the end, he represents the next step into the future of body modifications. Tony Stark still has to put on a separate suit to become Iron Man, but Ezekiel is physically linked to his armor. He is the host of the Technovore, which consists of "corrosive biological cells"; in return, they give him superhuman speed, strength and the ability to levitate. However, Ezekiel overestimates his control, so before launching its final attack, the Technovore turns him into a hideous monster, twisting his body and adding some eyes, showing the dangers of a physical fusion with A.I. or other cyber-technology. Hence, the film taps into the question situated at the core of Cyberpunk fiction: *How far can we go in changing the human body with the help of technology?*

The Cyberpunk World

Before beginning the analysis of the texts in question, it is important to take a brief look at the main features of Cyberpunk fiction. The actual term "Cyberpunk" has been in use since the early 1980s—it appeared first in Bruce Bethke's short story "Cyberpunk" in November 1983.[3] It is interesting to note that it was not a theoretical approach which initially used this term, but a literary piece of art. The Oxford Dictionary defines it as "a genre of fiction set in a lawless subculture of an oppressive society dominated by computer technology."[4] There are of course exceptions to this highly generalized description, but for this essay, it provides the common basis for *Rise of Technovore* and the other texts involved. *Neuromancer*, *Strange Days* and *Dark City* all share the premise of being set in oppressive societies, in which advanced technology has infiltrated every aspect of human life. In Bigelow's *Strange Days*, the characters stumble through their lawless world dominated by police brutality, crime and the "jacks" (data-discs containing the memories of others that users can experience themselves—including every emotion). Proyas' *Dark City* similarly reflects this definition, but the film also expands it by adding to the mix aliens with psychokinetic powers. By adding this last element, the film opens up more possibilities of interpretation, thus linking Cyberpunk more strongly to the genre of "science fiction." As shall be shown in the following close reading, these oeuvres all investigate the relationships between human nature and technology as well as between reality and the virtual world.[5]

The dichotomy of body/technology is at the core of the most famous and influential novel of the Cyberpunk genre: *Neuromancer* (1984). As the novel is generally regarded as the foundation of both the literary genre and the subculture, there has been substantial research on various themes central to the text, such as cyberspace, virtuality, identity and gender.[6] Therefore, this chapter will only focus on its connections with *Rise of Technovore*, which are mainly concerned with the issue of body and/vs. technology.

The novel is set in the future, but provides enough parallels to our contemporary society so the reader can identify with the characters. The premise of *Neuromancer* is that the technologies described—and used—have existed for some time, so that Case, the protagonist, cannot remember a time without them. He is described as a "cowboy," a "jockey in the matrix," who can hack into every system or computer he likes; basically, he is a thief. Most notably, the matrix can be accessed "directly"; one's consciousness is in the matrix, while the body remains connected to a deck. The experience of virtuality is thus immediate and physical, as the pains you feel in the matrix are also felt in the physical world. Hence, Case transcends his existence in Chiba by entering the matrix. As he was punished for stealing from his employers, his spine was damaged so that a reconnection with the matrix was not possible anymore. Although his situation is quite hopeless, Case continues to dream of finding a cure for his state. The desperate urge to leave his body behind in order to become "whole" again in a virtual world constitutes the basic paradox of Case's existence at the beginning of the novel. He thinks that his life can only become better if he is reunited again with the matrix.

In cyberspace, Case is *someone*—not just a face in the crowd. This phenomenon is also found in our everyday reality. As Daniel Punday puts it, "individuals who operate within such virtual environments play out a multitude of roles, leading to an increased fragmentation of identity and suggesting a fundamental change in the relations among individuals."[7] Case's fragmentation is not only tangible in the way he loathes his real life, but also by his use of various names throughout the course of the novel. His frequent consumption of drugs further reveals his urge to escape, to become someone else, and to again experience the disengagement from his body. Even after he has regained the ability to enter cyberspace, he tries to separate his consciousness from his body by using "derms" in real life. Following Sherry Turkle's argument, a person engaged in cyberspace can be anyone they want to be, thus creating an alter ego which can be different from the real self.[8] Thus a virtual body is created to exist next to the real one. The virtual self exceeds the real one in many ways; in the case of *Neuromancer*, the virtual projection of a hacker is fast and able to move anywhere within seconds. In *Strange Days*, the "self," which is experienced, is a creation of someone else. Thus, it is just as virtual as Case's trips to the matrix.

The strongest metamorphosis from human to hybrid in *Neuromancer* is represented by Molly Millions, a mercenary. Apart from having several aliases (Rose Kolodny, Sally Sheers in Gibson's *Mona Lisa Overdrive*), she has extensive physical modifications: surgically inset glasses in her eye sockets called "mirrorshades," "double-edged four centimeter scalpel blades"[9] under her fingernails, enhanced reflexes, and strength. She is hired alongside Case to make sure the run is successful and to fulfill her own important part of the mission. Molly's role as mercenary partly turns her into a "killing" machine; she hardly reveals any emotions, although there might have been a time when she actually loved another person.[10] It is important for the development of the novel that Molly uses her cold, cynical attitude to fend off any emotional attachment—especially towards Case. Therefore, she represents what Dani Cavallaro calls "technobodies," which are "bodies produced by the encounter of the biological and the artificial."[11] As such, Molly moves beyond being human to reject her weaker self to become a stronger, better version so she can do what she is good at: hunting and killing. However, Molly remains human in her moral make-up. Not only does she mediate between Case and her client, but she also sees that Case needs more help in surviving within the cyber-enhanced world. In order to become the mercenary she is, Molly had to work as a "meat puppet,"[12] a prostitute who is left in a blacked-out state during intercourse. This sacrifice shows the extent of the wish to be better, to be more than human. Here again, the separation from body and mind plays a decisive role.

These physical modifications directly link Molly and Case to Ezekiel Stane and Tony Stark from *Rise of Technovore*. Ezekiel supposedly injected "nanobots" into his brain to become even more intelligent; he thus supersedes his existence as mere human to become a hybrid creature, or rather a "technobody." The nanobots enhanced his mental and physical abilities, thus making it possible for him to create the techno-armor at will, due to its direct connection to his body. Ezekiel's body thus is as enhanced as Molly's, or Case's for that matter. All three share the urge to transcend their original bodies in order to become better, more intelligent, faster or bodiless altogether. In one of the scenes in Ezekiel's lair, he states, "Technology and the people who give birth to it are nothing more than false idols leading society to disaster."[13] Clearly, he does not see himself as one of "these people"; he refers to Tony Stark instead. The allusion to the act of giving birth sets him further apart, as this is an act that defines any natural being. But that is something Ezekiel rejects due to his fusion of body and Technovore.

In both, *Neuromancer* and *Rise of Technovore*, the body is conceived as something which can be (and has to be) enhanced and ultimately overcome by science, so that the original is no longer needed. It is difficult to deny the connection of this idea to the Gothic tradition. Describing contemporary Gothic's obsession with the body, Catherine Spooner suggests that, "Gothic bodies are frequently presented to us as simulations, as replacements of the real."[14] Her statement also implies a connection to the notion of bodies in Cyberpunk. Using the Gothic perspective can provide insight into the inner workings of Cyberpunk and its relationship to the body.

Connections to Gothic Fiction

The Gothic tradition is concerned with the body in key works such as Mary Shelley's *Frankenstein*, Robert Louis Stevenson's *The Strange Case of Dr Jekyll and Mr Hyde* or H.G. Wells' *The Island of Doctor Moreau*. In those texts, science is used to supposedly improve the body, but in the end only produces creatures of questionable status. Especially in Shelley's novel, the obsession with a scientifically altered body is expressed. The dream to transcend death is what drives Victor and also what brings about his downfall; the same eventually happens to the scientists in Stevenson's and Wells' novels. Gothic literature explores a fear of technological advancement and what it could create, or change, in people. The frightening aspects of what science and technology can lead to overwhelm the positive ones. However, the urge to transcend one's physical restrictions is present in both Gothic literature and Cyberpunk. Jules Law comments on this as follows: "Gothic is thus not so much about embodiment as it is about a dangerous desire for transcendence which must be articulated but held at bay. This desire for transcendence is a desire for virtuality—a life without bodies or narrative constraint."[15] The desire Law talks about is exactly what Case experiences in Gibson's narrative: he does not want to be chained to his physical life.

In both *Neuromancer* and *Rise of Technovore*, we can find traces of this fear. In *Rise of Technovore*, Ezekiel openly admits to moving across the boundaries of humanity with the help of the Technovore. Hence, he creates fear by showing what nanorobotics—which already exists to some degree nowadays[16]—could lead to a self-replicating artificial intelligence aimed at wiping out humanity. *Neuromancer* presents this fear in a different light, as human-kind has accepted and adapted to technology as part of everyday life. However, the fear of an independent artificial intelligence is so strong that any attempt of Wintermute and Neuromancer to join forces is to be prevented by any means necessary.

Another aspect of the Gothic that must be considered here is the relationship between man and body. Cavallaro points out that Gothic bodies exemplify the abject as defined by Julia Kristeva: attractive and repulsive at the same time due to their instability.[17] Cavallaro goes on to explain that "Cyberpunk's bodies are likewise fluid and permeable: their integrity is continually challenged and violated. Pollution, contagion, disease, bestiality and monstrosity are some of the most harrowing aspects of the body that recur in both the Gothic and Cyberpunk."[18] The change of the body—both from the outside and from within—is a source for horror. Images of parasites, shape-shifters, and werewolves are quite common in Gothic literature as the frequent vampire narratives show. In *Neuromancer*, Case's body changes from damaged to "normal" (as far as the world of the novel is concerned), but with a twist—slowly dissolving toxin sacs were added during his operation to make sure he does the job. Only when the run is successful will the sacs be removed. This change in the structure of his body represents the imminent danger that his body may turn on him at any moment and tear him away from his personal promised land of the matrix once and for all. Not unlike Gothic fiction, the fear is located inside the body. Case cannot escape from the toxins, thus turning him into a victim of scientific advancement.

In *Rise of Technovore*, the body is also changeable. Iron Man may put on his armor, but Ezekiel changes his body from the inside. His armor has become part of his body, therefore altering at his will. This transformation, however, is only at first presented in a positive light. At the end of the film, the Technovore betrays Ezekiel and his body starts to mutate. The mutation starts suddenly without warning when Ezekiel is, seemingly, captured on S.H.I.E.L.D.'s "helicarrier." Again, science cannot be trusted. Although the Technovore still needs Ezekiel as a host, the young adult's will has been taken over. Similar to the stories of Gothic literature, the artificial creature betrays the human and turns into the monster the audience fears. This fear is evoked by the seemingly threatening new technology, but in fact, it is not the technology itself which is threatening, it is its use by a human. Similarly, the fear evoked by Frankenstein's creature in Mary Shelley's novel can be read in a different way. In fact, the creature was more humane than its own maker as it showed compassion (e.g. the poor family in the woods). However, the circumstances of its coming to life as well as the reactions of the human world towards it, turned it into a monster. In Sue Chaplin's terms, the novel

> requests the reader's sympathy for a creature who is the product of forces beyond his control, who appears to possess an innate sensibility and capacity for intellectual advancement..., but who lacks any social and cultural reference points to help him develop a fully socialized human subjectivity.[19]

Hence, it is rather human ambition, pride and lack of understanding which turn the creature into a monster. Its identity is not formed by a parent (in this case Victor), but by the monstrous reactions of its surroundings.

When the body changes so easily and transgresses its actual form and state, the person's identity is left behind. This leads to the second focus of this chapter: *Who are we if technology takes control of our body?* How does the loss of identity affect us? We oftentimes define who we are by our outward appearance; it reflects our emotions, our attitudes and at times protects us from revealing our true selves. Interestingly, this is the very purpose of technology in *Neuromancer*. By using surgical techniques, people do not seem to age (ex: Julius) or even become an entirely different person (ex: Armitage and Corto). Furthermore, it is the implants which give meaning to the characters' lives: Molly is even better at her job due to her physical alterations, Case can only be inside the matrix due to medical progress. Everything in Gibson's world is, seemingly, made better by one technology or another. It is what the characters make of it that turns everything to the worse.

The Role of Identity

The loss of identity is also a theme in both Bigelow's *Strange Days* and Proyas' *Dark City*. Each film, however, deals with the topic differently. In Bigelow's film, identity is something you can escape, whereas in *Dark City* it is something which has been taken away from the characters by someone else (in this case: by aliens). The same element can be found in *Rise of Technovore*: Ezekiel is not just a human body anymore, but has developed an alter ego with the help of the Technovore. Iron Man is the technologically enhanced version of Tony Stark. In the world of Marvel, identity is a commodity which can be altered and twisted at will. Be it Hulk/Bruce Banner, Spiderman/Peter Parker or Silk/Cindy Moon,[20] hiding one's true self to adopt an artificially altered self is the premise of many a superhero story.

In the Marvel Universe, the idea of identity is a crucial element. It not only "comprises the codename and the costume, with the secret identity being a customary counterpart to the codename,"[21] but it also defines the superhero's actions. Peter Coogan points out that the trinity of mission-powers-identity is important for the genre, but all three elements are not always used. He explains this aspect with regard to *The Fantastic Four*:

> The secret identity is a typical, but not necessary, convention for the genre. It clearly has great importance to the genre as its stable presence in superhero stories shows. Lee and Kirby were trying to be inventive and so chose to disregard aspects of the genre that they felt held them back. But the first issue of *The Fantastic Four* is clearly a superhero comic book, as is evident from the characters' powers and mission, the superhero physics, and the supervillain Mole Man.... And it is so without costumes. Significantly, although the Fantastic Four initially wore ordinary clothes, they quickly acquired costumes.[22]

It is interesting that despite the efforts to move away from conventions, the very formula is still used, albeit in an altered form, as the "Fantastic Four" are known superheroes without secret identities. For some of these heroes, however, the changing of identity is a crucial part of their story: Batman, Iron Man, Phantom and the villains, Black Cat or Iron Fist to name a few. The same standards can be applied to *Rise of Technovore*: the archenemy has a telling name and wants to take over the world, while the hero with costume and two identities saves the day. In the Marvel Universe, some of the heroes do not obtain their superpowers at will; they are bitten by radioactive spiders or survive a gamma ray explosion. But characters like Tony Stark decide to become Iron Man and live like that.

The concept of identity is strongly connected to memory. One does not seem to be able to exist without the other. All narratives discussed here deal with memory in their own way. *Strange Days* uses experiences and the connected emotions as a drug: people "jack in" using a "squid"[23] attached to one's skull to transmit brainwaves and thus the experiences. This drug creates the illusion to "be" someone else, to take on someone's identity, for just a few moments. This is of course illegal, so the protagonist Nero (an ex-cop gone rogue) lives and works in the underworld of Los Angeles, addicted to the very tapes he sells. In a scene depicting him selling a tape to a potential customer, Nero explains, "This is not like 'TV only better.' This is like a piece of someone's life—straight from the cerebral cortex."[24] The memories are removed from the brain, recorded, and duplicated in order to be fed to another person so that they can get high on these images and emotions. The essence of what humans are made up of—the experiences—is a product to be sold to the highest bidder. For a few moments, a stranger's identity is assumed by another stranger. Although the consumption of the tapes is voluntary, the recording is mostly done in hiding. This creates a certain tension between the recorded and the recording person.

In contrast, the characters in *Dark City* do not have a choice. A group of aliens called "the Strangers" want to study human behavior in order to find out what actually makes us "human." They inject memories into the brains of their test objects to see how they react in different situations. The process of obtaining and combining the memories reveals an advanced technology. The lack of understanding for the human race, paired with science, begs the comparison with *Frankenstein*: Victor only wanted to understand, to learn, but took it too far, just like the Strangers. What neither Victor nor the Strangers realize is that the human soul cannot be dissected or removed like a specimen in medicine. Only when it is too late and their destruction is imminent do they seem to begin to understand.

Dark City is an allegory for humankind's constant search for meaning. *Who are we if our memories are fake?* None of the characters in the movie has their "original" memory; the images are constructed artificially and then injected into their brains. The identities are also products, constructs placed into the peoples' minds. In Cyberpunk, identities are fluid entities which can be altered at will with any measures possible, so it is difficult to define them. In Ollivier Dyens' terms, "the impact of technology on our perception of life is so great that it prevents the building of any archetype of the human body."[25] Dyens goes on to stress the instability of what the body constitutes to show that our definitions are not based on human grounds, but on technological ones.[26] Who we are is therefore determined by outside authorities. If we are the sum of our experiences and memories, and they form our identity, then the subjects of this analysis play with that notion in an attempt to understand the essence of our being.

In this context, Roger Ebert's comments on *Dark City* highlight Ezekiel's attitude towards his existence. According to Ebert, *Dark City* follows the lines of Hal 9000 from *2001: A Space Odyssey*: "Hal was a computer that understood everything, except what it was to be human and have emotions. '*Dark City*' considers the same theme in a film that creates a completely artificial world in which humans teach themselves to be themselves."[27] The connection to Ezekiel from *Rise of Technovore* is apparent: Ezekiel—just like Hal

9000 and the Strangers—does not fully understand why humans are who they are. He sees them as inferior as they do not appreciate the technology of the Technovore and rather believe in their hand-made technology. Ezekiel does not see himself as one of the humans and cannot understand why they behave like they do. Instead of analyzing them, however, he simply wants to destroy them.

To develop the idea of replicated memories further, it is necessary to look at the means of saving them. In an interview, William Gibson stated that in his books, computers are a metaphor for human memory.[28] It seems as if the Strangers in *Dark City* take this metaphor literally, because they treat memoires like computer programs, which are constructed, exchanged or altered. In *Rise of Technovore*, memories actually are part of Ezekiel's personality, although not in a manner that Iron Man—or any other person—understands. In one of the crucial moments of the film, Iron Man faces Ezekiel in his hiding-place, trying to talk to the boy (at that point, Iron Man sees in him just as a "boy") out of his plans. It is revealed that Iron Man killed Ezekiel's father Obadiah Stane, and thus Iron Man thinks he comprehends Ezekiel's motivation. However, the memory does not really affect Ezekiel. Instead, Ezekiel creates a larger-than-life image of his father which directly addresses Iron Man—albeit with Ezekiel's voice—thus tapping into the problem at the core of the conflict: memory affects the human in a metal shell, but not the human shell infested with nanobots. One could even go so far as to say that Zeke's memory is in fact only collected data he can access but which does not have any effect on him. Zeke's father is just an image he reproduces, but not something he values.

Imagery of Cyberpunk Literature

In the last section of this essay, I would like to go into detail with the imagery used in *Rise of Technovore* and its function as reverberation of Cyberpunk literature. The introductory sequence of the film sets the scene for the battle which is about to start. It shows an ant in close-up; this image gives way to a boy standing next to an empty road in the middle of a desert. He is watching a group of ants preying on a much bigger bug—the collective thus killing the supposedly stronger, individual adversary. This short sequence foreshadows the events of the film: physically small beings take on a bigger foe and together they prevail. At the end of *Rise of Technovore*, the AI is not defeated by a man in a metal suit, but by (physically speaking) one of the smallest entities of the planet: a computer virus. Here, the image of the beginning is repeated and stressed. In both cases, a collective mind is used to create havoc—artificial warfare is fought on a rather small physical scale. This might be a foreshadowing of the future wars in our real world.

With this vivid image of destruction right at the beginning, the remainder of the film can be seen in the grim light of a deadly entity invading vulnerable spaces. The recurring shots of cells destroying their surroundings evoke associations of sickness, disease and death. The first appearance of Ezekiel and/as the Technovore in his white armor is accompanied by these images. This coincides with what Istvan Csicsery-Ronay describes as a "sharp inward turn."[29] He thus depicts the latest preoccupation of science—and hence science fiction and Cyberpunk—with technologies enhancing the body from the inside, such as bionic prosthetics and A.I., or which focus on the smallest elements constituting the world (particle physics, microbiology).[30] This is in Csicsery-Ronay's terms implosive science fiction, which engages with the "analogies of the invasion and transformation of the body by alien entities or of our making."[31] This definition not only describes parts of *Neuromancer*, but also *Dark City*, *Strange Days* and *Rise of Technovore*. In each case, the body is invaded more or less by technology. *Rise of Technovore* makes this invasion quite literal, as Zeke has the Technovore injected into his brain; he goes on to use it to invade and ultimately kill other people and to invade objects and manipulate their design.

The strength of the Technovore is shown in the first encounter between Zeke and Iron Man. Here, it is the physical strength which throws Iron Man on the ground; during the second encounter, Zeke paralyzes him by "infecting" his suit with the Technovore. The imagery of disease is taken up again to show two things: first, Zeke and his Technovore are able to hack into the armor of Iron Man to control it, and second, human technology seems to be defenseless against this apparently omnipotent adversary.[32] Hence, the film evokes primal fears of man being attacked by an invisible enemy. The connection to Gothic fiction could not be clearer. It is also telling that the infection takes place at a moment expressing human emotion: Zeke has his back turned to Iron Man when the latter tries to convince him to stop killing people and in an affectionate gesture puts his hand on the boy's shoulder. Infecting the armor at this particular moment is a straightforward rejection of empathy, emotion and humanity. It underlines Zeke's departure from his human self, which is in itself an uncanny wish.

In this last aspect we can find another connection to Gothic fiction, as "[i]t is in the idea of the *uncanny* that the Gothic's codification of spatial and temporal instability manifests itself most blatantly, as a troubling intermingling of the ordinary and the unfamiliar."[33] Cavallaro's comment sees the uncanny at the heart of Gothic fiction, and when looking closely at Cyberpunk, we can find this same idea. The technologically enhanced body is both familiar and unfamiliar at the same time, as parts of it simply "do not belong." The body is something changeable, and thus instable, in most Cyberpunk narratives; hence, every character can develop into someone (or something) altogether different. The aspect of being uncanny within this area is important to mention. We might see a familiar person at first glance, but the inside might have changed into something threatening.

All the aforementioned aspects regarding Zeke's character are revealed in the scenes in his own lair. We see him accompanied by a young woman named Sasha.[34] They are talking about the events which have happened up until that moment. In both scenes, the ethereal surroundings stand in a harsh contrast to the content of the conversation. At the center of the room is a pond giving the setting an unnatural feel, as this scene takes place inside a building. All the walls, the furniture and ground are white; hence, the viewer is reminded of a clean room thus contradicting the scenery with the pond. Furthermore, the voices echo in this structure, underlining not only the ethereal atmosphere, but also the connection to an otherworldly existence. The partly cryptic comment by Sasha on the events initiates Zeke's manifesto explaining his actions. She states, "Even with talent you need chaos to give birth to a dancing star."[35] Sasha directly refers to Nietzsche's famous line from *Thus Spoke Zarathustra*: "I tell you: one must still have chaos in one, to give birth to a dancing star." This sentence is mentioned in context with the concept of the "super human." Furthermore, Nietzsche states some lines prior to this quotation that "Man is something that is to be surpassed."[36] When taking these lines literally, they aptly express Ezekiel's attitude towards life and the human race. He sees himself as a super human who is not part of the rest of the race. Nietzsche's theories seem to serve as an excuse to act out his (and Sasha's) plans. In this context, Ryan Litsey's observations of the Joker as "Nietzschean Superman" are of importance. Similarly to the Joker, Ezekiel strives to overcome his self; he frequently denies any connection to "them"—"them" being the human race. Litsey puts emphasis on the ideas of self-overcoming and on the will to power, which are the characteristics of the Superman and of Ezekiel: his relentless strive for perfection surpassing the "puny humans" can only be explained by his utter will to power. Litsey's reading of the Joker could also be a description of Ezekiel: "He cannot feel remorse or seek punishment because he defines himself by his deeds. He cannot look back on what he has done to define his actions as good or bad because he defines his actions as he does them, thus he is incapable of remorse or vengeance because he has nothing to refer those ideas to."[37]

Litsey furthermore argues that the dichotomy Batman/Joker is also explained by Nietzsche's concept. In *Rise of Technovore*, Ezekiel and Iron Man have a similar relationship; one character defining the other by sheer existence. Litsey states, "If Batman represents the hero society holds hear, then his inability to relate to the Joker places the Joker in a position of self-overcoming, conquering the hero of the day in his process toward becoming the Superman."[38] Iron Man can surely be seen as "the hero of the day," and it is evident that he cannot relate to Ezekiel's attitude or point of view. In a similar constellation to Batman/Joker, their relationship is determined by Ezekiel trying to overcome Iron Man in an attempt to prove his point, namely that the human race should not rely on its own technology, but embrace the power of the Technovore.

On a metaphorical level, we could say that something new and better can be created only when there has been utter chaos and destruction. The "dancing star" could be read as a metaphor for creativity. In Cyberpunk fiction, chaos is the status quo of society. In all treatments discussed in this chapter, we find chaotic circumstances. Bigelow's bleak vision of L.A. in *Strange Days* is determined by violence, corruption and crime. The metropolis in *Dark City* is a chaotic construct with crime as a trigger to test human emotions. *Neuromancer*'s entire plot is founded on a chaotic state of affairs, which allow Case to do his job effectively. One could say that in Cyberpunk, chaos is created by the decline of the society depicted; it is, as Istvan Csicsery-Ronay stated at the beginning of his essay, "pure negation: of manners, history, philosophy, politics, body, will, affect, anything mediated by cultural memory."[39] In other words: chaos presents anarchy. The constant transgressions of all the boundaries that hold society together culminate in Cyberpunk fiction. But in all these texts, "dancing stars" are created—not as a new society, but as singular occurrences or people becoming better than their initial self. In *Dark City*, Murdoch defeats the aliens and takes control of his life; in *Strange Days* the murder of Iris is avenged (although the happy ending is rather abrupt and slightly unbelievable). In *Neuromancer*, Case regains his life and Neuromancer is reunited with Wintermute to leave the human spheres and find others of their kind. *All's well that ends well*, one might think. However, the chaotic societies mentioned in these treatments are never restored to order. Anarchy looms over the protagonists as they continue to stumble through the crowds of technobodies. Even *Rise of Technovore* remains open-ended, as Ezekiel is able to flee from the S.H.I.E.L.D.'s helicarrier—another duel with Iron Man is likely imminent.

When taking all the aforementioned elements together, a mosaic of Cyberpunk is formed. The correlations between Marvel's *Rise of Technovore* on the one side, and the

Cyberpunk texts *Neuromancer*, *Dark City* and *Strange Days* on the other side, are clear. Cyberpunk can be seen as the next step in the evolution of the Gothic genre, which moves away from the traditional tropes to embrace new ones. *Rise of Technovore* uses dichotomies such as identity/memory and body/technology to establish the Technovore as a character in the Marvel Universe and simultaneously connects the film to Cyberpunk.

NOTES

1. Hereafter referred to as *Rise of Technovore*.
2. Larry McCaffery, "An Interview with William Gibson," *Storming the Reality Studio: A Casebook of Cyberpunk and Postmodern Fiction*, 263.
3. A structural similarity to Gothic fiction can be found here: the first Gothic novel as such was Horace Walpole's *The Castle of Otranto* in 1764. In the preface, the author himself described the novel as being "Gothic". Hence, he defined an entire genre with his novel.
4. "Cyberpunk," *Oxford Dictionary*, accessed February 12, 2015, http://www.oxforddictionaries.com/definition/english/cyberpunk.
5. These topics have been discussed in detail by academic theorists such as Manuel Castells (real virtuality), Donna Haraway (cyborg manifesto) as well as Anna Balsamo (disappearing body).
6. Notable discussions for example on gender can be found in Cadora (1995), Plant (1985) and Flanagan (2010).
7. Daniel Punday, "The Narrative Construction of Cyberspace: Reading *Neuromancer*, Reading Cyberspace Debates," *College English* 63, no. 2 (2000): 194–213. 197.
8. Sherry Turkle, *Life on the Screen: Identity in the Age of the Internet* (New York: Simon & Schuster, 1995), n.p., quoted in Daniel Punday, "The Narrative Construction of Cyberspace: Reading *Neuromancer*, Reading Cyberspace Debates," *College English* 63, no. 2 (2000): 197.
9. William Gibson, *Neuromancer* (New York: Penguin, 1984), 25.
10. The novel here refers to the character's first appearance in Gibson's *Johnny Mnemonic* as love interest of Johnny.
11. Dani Cavallaro, *Cyberpunk and Cyberculture* (London: The Athlone Press, 2000), 43.
12. Gibson, *Neuromancer*, 147.
13. *Rise of Technovore*, directed by Hiroshi Hamasaki (2001; Culver City, CA: Sony Pictures Home Entertainment, 2013), DVD.
14. Catherine Spooner, *Contemporary Gothic* (London: Reaktion Books, 2006), 63.
15. Jules Law, "Being There: Gothic Violence and Virtuality in *Frankenstein*, *Dracula*, and *Strange Days*," *ELH* 73, no. 4 (2006): 975–996, 976.
16. For instance, the American Chemical Society published an article on nanorobots swimming through blood to deliver drugs to the target. This new development opens up the gates for treating patients with nanorobots in the rather near future. See also http://www.acs.org/content/acs/en/pressroom/presspacs/2015/acs-presspac-june-17–2015/toward-nanorobots-that-swim-through-blood-to-deliver-drugs-video.html.
17. Julia Kristeva, *The Powers of Horror*, trans. L. Roudiez (New York: Columbia University Press, 1982), n.p., quoted in Cavallaro, *Cyberpunk and Cyberculture*, xiv.
18. Cavallaro, xiv.
19. Sue Chaplin, *Gothic Literature* (London: York Press, 2011), 76.
20. The first comic book based on the character of Silk was published February 15, 2015. Source: http://marvel.com/comics/issue/52492/silk_2015_1
21. Peter Coogan, "The Definition of the Superhero," in *A Comics Studies Reader*, ed. Jeet Heer and Kent Worcester (Jackson: University of Mississippi Press, 2009), 78.
22. Ibid., 83–84.
23. *Strange Days*, directed by Kathryn Bigelow (1995; Berlin: Studiocanal, 1998), DVD.
24. Ibid.
25. Ollivier Dyens. "Cyberpunk, Technoculture, and the Post-Biological Self," *CLCWeb: Comparative Literature and Culture* 2, no. 1 (2000), 3. http://docs.lib.purdue.edu/cgi/viewcontent.cgi?article=1061&context=clcweb&sei-redir=1&referer=https%3A%2F%2Fscholar.google.de%2Fscholar%3Fq%3Dollivier%2Bdyens%26hl%3Dde%26as_sdt%3D0%2C5#search=%22ollivier%20dyens%22.

26. Ibid., 3–4.

27. Roger Ebert. "Dark City," rogerebert.com, last modified February 27, 1998, http://www.rogerebert.com/reviews/dark-city-1998.

28. William Gibson, interview by Larry McCaffery, transcript in *Storming the Reality Studio*, ed. Larry McCaffery (Durham: Duke University Press, 1991), 270.

29. Istavan Csicsery-Ronay, "Cyberpunk and Neuromanticism," in *Storming the Reality Studio: A Casebook of Cyberpunk and Postmodern Fiction*, ed. Larry McCafferty (Durham: Duke University Press, 1991), 187.

30. Ibid.

31. Ibid., 188.

32. This feeling of defenselessness is also created by current concerns uttered on American media that a cyber-attack of destructive scale is imminent. This further stresses that the Gothic fear is not only existent in contemporary society, but still determines our actions to a certain degree. Furthermore, the idea of cyber-attacks is perpetually discussed by theorists across fields (law, literature, sociology etc.); among others Oona A. Hathaway ("The Law of Cyber Attack" 2012), James Adams ("Virtual Defense" 2001) and James A. Green (*Cyber Warfare: A Multidisciplinary Analysis* 2015) have published works on this very topic, highlighting its importance for the academic community as well.

33. Cavallaro, 167 (italics by Cavallaro).

34. Sasha Hammer: in Marvel Universe, she is the girlfriend and assistant of Ezekiel Stane; he later augments her physical power with the Technovore, too. See also http://marvel.wikia.com/Sasha_Hammer (Earth-616). She is mentioned in *Invincible Iron Man* #516 which was published May 2, 2012.

35. *Iron Man and the Rise of Technovore*.

36. Friedrich Nietzsche, *Thus Spoke Zarathustra. A Book for All and None*, trans. Thomas Common. gutenberg.org, last modified November 5, 2012, http://www.gutenberg.org/files/1998/1998-h/1998-h.htm.

37. Ryan Litsey, "The Joker, Clown Prince of Nobility. The 'Master' Criminal, Nietzsche, and the Rise of the Superman," *The Joker. A Serious Study of the Clown Prince of Crime*, ed. Robert Moses Peaslee and Robert G. Weiner (Jackson: University Press of Mississippi, 2015), 186.

38. Ibid., 184.

39. ICsicsery-Ronay, 182.

On Your Stupid Earth
The De-Gerberized Duck

Rick Hudson

The principal failure of the 1986 movie adaptation of Marvel's *Howard the Duck* was that it was so asinine that it could well have featured as an object of humor and derision in an issue of the very comic book from whence it came. Indeed, like the *Judge Dredd* (1995) movie, it served as a fine example of exactly the sort of thing the original source text sought to lampoon and satirize. Unlike Raimi's *Spider-Man* films and the more recent cinematic versions of Marvel characters that are faithful to the comic books in plot, style and spirit, *Howard the Duck* missed the point by a country mile.

It is the purpose of this collection to interrogate Marvel comic characters as they have been interpreted in films, not as they appeared in the original comic books. However, a discussion of the *Howard the Duck* film requires an outline of the features that characterized the comic book from which it claimed to be adapted. To put it bluntly: it needs to be established what the comic book *was*, if *what is was not* is to be fully understood.

Howard the Duck, as a comic book, was a means by which Marvel not only satirized contemporary American society and media output—such as Kung-Fu movies and *Star Wars*—but also Marvel itself. Its success was due to the fact that it allowed writer Steve Gerber to unleash his anarchic and chaotic imagination, unchecked, on the comic-reading public, but the movie is just an example of a bad studio product. Utilizing Bakhtinian critical theory, this chapter assesses the differences between comic book and cinematic adaptation to investigate why one was a creative (if not commercial) success and the other a dismal, humorless disaster. It seeks to explore the work of Steve Gerber and his contribution to comic books and argues that it is the lack of "Gerberishness" in the *Howard the Duck* movie more than anything that resulted in the film being such a momentous failure. To do this, I first give an overview of the comic book on which the film was allegedly based, and the work of the comic book's author, Steve Gerber (1947–2008).

Gerber established himself as something of a maverick writer for Marvel Comics in the early 1970s and soon garnered a reputation for producing comic strips that were somewhat unusual in plot, characterization and manner of presentation. Gerber not only worked on conventional superhero strips, such as *Daredevil*, *The Incredible Hulk* and *Iron Man*, but also liminal narratives which featured Marvel's more *outré* heroes and anti-heroes (e.g., *The Guardians of the Galaxy*, *Son of Satan* and *The Defenders*). Gerber also created some of Marvel's most off-beat characters, such as *Man-Thing, Omega the Unknown* and, of course, *Howard the Duck*.

It was during his tenure on *The Defenders* that Gerber perhaps established himself and his reputation for more experimental stories and story-telling styles in the eyes of the general comic book reading public. First appearing in 1969, *The Defenders* were conceived and presented as a team of outsider heroes in contrast to Marvel's more "cleancut" Avengers. Whereas the Avengers were an establishment approved team of Marvel's more comfortable heroes—epitomized by "Captain America"—the Defenders were a loose coalition of anti-heroes (for example, the monstrous "Hulk," the misanthropic "Submariner" and the former super-villain "Nighthawk") who not only were viewed with hostility by both the establishment and the public they sought to protect, but were also a singularly dysfunctional unit prone to squabbling and in-fighting. The Defenders were not only comprised of unlikely and unusual members, but the adventures they undertook were equally strange: the plots centered upon a dark, cosmic mysticism informed by psychedelia and the horror fiction of H.P. Lovecraft.

Although *The Defenders* was penned by writers with existing reputations within the comic book industry, these writers had often established their credentials in fields outside of the "regular" superhero comic book. The initial issues of this title were written by Roy Thomas, who was noted for his work on Marvel's "sword and sorcery" comics such as *Savage Sword of Conan*. Thomas was then superseded by Steve Englehart (long term writer of *Dr Strange*—Marvel's occult superhero), who then passed the title onto one of the highest regarded horror comic writers of the 1970s, Len Wein. From its onset, under the authorship of these writers, *The Defenders* was a different, darker, stranger breed of superhero comic compared to Marvel's other titles. However, *The Defenders* became odder still on the appointment of its fourth writer, Steve Gerber in 1975.

Importantly, Gerber's writing not only made *The Defenders* more bizarre in terms of plot and not only introduced even weirder characters, but the manner in which the comic book was written challenged the industry's accepted protocols. During his tenure on *The Defenders* (1975–1976), Gerber utilized many of the devices that were to be employed by Alan Moore and Frank Miller ten years later in comic books like *Dark Knight Returns* (1986), *Watchmen* (1987) and *Killing Joke* (1988). Gerber introduced *faux* magazine and newspaper articles and other documents, such as a family photo album, in the body of the comic strip to provide textual alternatives to the "normal" comic strip layout of the narrative.[1] That is to say, pages would not always be presented in the conventional format of sequential panels, but would sometimes be printed as a page of a newspaper, or take the form of a single illustration of a page from a book or other document. Gerber would also, on occasion, produce comic book pages that were presented in prose form.[2] Nevertheless, Gerber's writing challenged comic book protocols even further when he took to writing *Howard the Duck* (1976–1979).

Howard the Duck featured an anthropomorphic duck that was a cynical and cantankerous revision of Disney's "Donald Duck." Howard first appeared as an ancillary character in the "Man-Thing" strip, which was published in *Adventure into Fear* 19 (1973); he then featured in his own comic, which ran for twenty-seven issues between 1976 and 1979, all of which were written by Gerber. Although billed as a humorous comic book that openly spoofed mainstream media output and other comics produced by Marvel, the events of *Howard the Duck* were still understood to take place within the "Marvel Universe" (the shared diegetic world populated by all Marvel characters).

Consequently, *Howard the Duck* was a medium through which Marvel parodied itself, its characters and overall product line and Howard could—and frequently did—run into other Marvel characters such as Spider-Man and the Defenders. In *Howard the Duck* Gerber took even greater liberties with storytelling technique; readers were first introduced to Howard by means of a direct address from character to reader that refers to his existence as a comic book character and his own creators:

> With typically anthropomorphic disregard for my personal safety and for the state of exhaustion so clearly delineated on my face, Gerber, Mayerick [Val Mayerick, illustrator], and Marvel Comics transported me by means unknown back here to the Florida Everglades, where I first appeared on your stupid Earth. I'm supposed to bare my soul and confess all I know about that ridiculous incident. Unfortunately, I refuse.[3]

The following page is mainly taken up with an argument between Howard and a disembodied "Voice from on High" who orders Howard to "cut the whining and get on with your synopsis." From this point on, Howard—in his own and other titles—would not only satirize other comic book characters, but also feature in stories that undermined conventional notions about the very nature of the comic book. Issue 16 of *Howard the Duck* (1977) perhaps illustrates this best of all. The issue starts off as a direct follow-on from the previous issue on the first page, however Gerber then interjects directly and apologizes to the reader—explaining that he will be continuing the ongoing story in issue 17—and launches into a prose essay on writing (among other things) for the remainder of the comic book. Part of this essay takes the form of a conversation between Gerber and Howard in which the character chastises his creator, and halfway through the issue we are presented with a prose section entitled "Obligatory Comic Book Fight Scene" which runs as follows:

> There is one rule of comic book writing that cannot be violated, even by a writer in search of something as impalpable as his soul or Las Vegas. Being a visual medium, comics theoretically require at least a modicum of action to engage and sustain reader interest. Thus, in the interest of sustaining your interest, we reluctantly present this BRAIN-BLASTING BATTLE SCENE, pitching an ostrich and a Las Vegas chorus girl against the MIND-NUMBING MENACE of a KILLER lampshade in a DUEL TO THE DEATH!! Since we only get one picture of this CLASH OF THE TITANS, though, we'll have to tell you the outcome. The ostrich sticks its head in a manhole, shrugging off all that's happened and returning to his secret identity as a roadblock. The chorus girl finds herself in the thrill of battle, becomes one with her head-dress, and is elevated to goddesshood. The lampshade dies. Basically it's like most every other comic mag.[4]

The essay concludes with a letter from a comic fan (called Steve Gerber) commenting on the issue. The letter opens:

> Dear Steve,
> Just finished reading HTD #16, and I'm afraid my reaction to your noble experiment is somewhat ambivalent. I admire your daring, your dedication, and your determination to innovate. But frankly, I don't care much for your writing. If Edison's experiments had worked out as badly as this one, I'd be penning this letter by gaslight. Still, since I am a HOWARD THE DUCK fan, and since I realize that you'd never be insane enough to attempt this sad sort of charade again, let me enumerate some of the high points of the issue.[5]

The letter from Gerber to Gerber then proceeds to de-construct, criticize and analyze the very issue of the comic book of which it is, itself, a component.

Even when *Howard the Duck* appeared as a more conventional comic strip in other issues, it always took an ironic and satirical stance. In *Howard the Duck* 1, the banking sector and financial services are mocked in the form of "Pro-Rata," the financial wizard who dwells in a mystic tower made from credit cards where he plots to bring about the Astral Audit that will make him Chief Accountant of the Universe. In issue 2, Marvel's own *Killraven* comic book is spoofed by casting Howard as the science fiction hero "Killmallard." The "Moonies" and religious cults in general are lampooned in issue 6, which sees Howard confronting the "Reverend Joon Moon Yuc" and his disciples, "The Yuccies." Issues 8–9 see Howard running for the U.S. presidency and taking on Gerald Ford, Jimmy Carter, the news media, political assassins and the entire American political system as they satirize the role of marketing, public relations and electioneering in the 1976 election. Among the goof-ball tomfoolery in these issues, Gerber gives voice to his own dissatisfaction with the political system and America as a whole in Howard's comments at press conference:

> You meat brains willingly subject yourselves to more abuse, physical and psychological, than any other nation in history! You allow your eyes and lungs to be eaten away by pollution. You fill your digestive tracts with chemicals. Your ears are barraged by the sounds of jackhammer progress. All the while politicians and Madison Avenue bang away at your minds. You all wanna be happy and secure, yet you open yourselves to the constant tension an' pressure of a society that claims to be free, but refuses to let you make a move without filling in forms in triplicate. You wonder why you get violence? Why your young are either dissident, empty-headed or drugged into a stupor? It's because you've fashioned an emotionally and intellectually sterile culture, that's why! If an individual is unwilling to spend his life in the plodding pursuit of possessions, there's nothing for 'em to do. The United States is one big dateless Saturday night![6]

Importantly, although we can see Gerber as a particularly revolutionary figure within comic book writing, we can argue that this medium—even at its most conservative—has had a tendency to subvert and parody itself and other forms of writing. Indeed we can see humor based upon subversion and lampooning of existing texts being something of a staple of U.S. comic magazines as a whole, rather than this being specific to superhero comic books—*Mad* magazine being the exemplar instance of this. The superhero comic book has always been a shameful raider of other literary and cultural sources, drawing upon and exploiting *film noir*, horror, science fiction, fantasy, mythology and surrealism. Masked crime-fighters, alien creatures, sorcerers and androids co-exist in the same fictional world. Their adventures are as likely to take them to a mystical past or a technologically advanced future, just as much as they are to take them to downtown New York. Such a cavalier attitude to story-telling and genre conventions is never rationalized or justified in the comic book; it's just assumed to be how the stories work. Likewise, narrative techniques and illustrative styles are "open" for comic strip creatives, as Scott McLoud claims in *Understanding Comics* (1994). The comic book utilizes a fusion of influences that include Dada, horror, folk-tales, erotica, blank verse, epic, stream of consciousness writing, satire: "no genres are listed ... no schools of art are banished ... no philosophies, no movements, no ways of seeing are out of bounds."[7] If the comic book can be argued to be a ludic blending and subverting of genres and distinctions, then it may constitute a form of Menippean satire.

As discussed earlier, Bakhtinian thought as a means of evaluating the comic strip in terms of the carnivalesque, dialogism and the Menippea is significant, however it would be useful to detail the fundamentals of the Menippean satire here, as it is crucial to understanding Gerber's work.[8] Mikhail Bakhtin was famously interested in the phenomena of the novel and what constituted "novelness." He stressed that the novel—as opposed to the epic—was perpetually in a state of reinvention and that all novels were in dialogue with the novels that precede them and those that will follow. The novel is essentially "plastic" and evolves and engages with all other texts. As he states in *The Dialogic Imagination*:

> The novel, after all, has no canon of its own. It is, by its very nature, non canonic. It is plasticity itself. It is a genre that is ever questioning, ever examining itself and subjecting its established forms to review. Such, indeed, is the only possibility open to a genre that structures itself in a zone of direct contact with developing reality.[9]

In *Problems of Dostoevsky's Poetics,* Bakhtin compares the novel to the Roman Menippean satire—works that fused, troubled, and played with literary form and convention, and indicated by

> a wide use of inserted genres: novellas, letters, oratical speeches, symposia and so on; also characteristic is a mixture of prose and poetic speech. The inserted genres are presented at various distances from the ultimate authorial position, that is, with varying degree of parodying and objectification. Verse portions are almost always given with a certain degree of parodying.[10]

Indeed, we must note that "satire" in this instance means "a mixture"—derived from the Latin for "salad"—and is not employed in its contemporary sense. As such, Bakhtin's claims regarding the Menippea would appear to be in sympathy with those made by McLoud regarding the comic strip. This point can be pressed further; not only can we claim that the comic book as a form is intrinsically Menippean, but the work of Gerber in particular is an *exemplar* case of the Menippean satire. This is exemplified by the *Howard the Duck* comic book pushing the comic strip's free-for-all relationship with genre(s) further: a central feature of the ongoing narrative, after all, is that various universes which follow the "rules" of various genres are spilling over into each other, and realities are conflicting as worlds collapse into each other in a "Congress of Realities" (established with Howard's first appearance in *Adventure into Fear* 19).

In this book, Gerber took satirical swipes at various aspects of American culture, including advertising, political parties, the press and consumerism, and established himself as a voice of dissent within a mainstream commercial media. However, when the *Howard the Duck* movie appeared in 1986 (directed by Willard Huyck and produced by Gloria Katz and George Lucas) it was a completely different beast. Indeed, the film met with appalling reviews on its release and many film fan-sites have decreed it the worst film of all time. The failure of the film in both aesthetic and commercial terms is difficult to rationalize and quantify other than to state that it is an astonishingly bad movie; however, this is what this chapter seeks to explore.

One of the failings could be that the film was made as a live-action movie rather than an animated cartoon, which would have allowed the filmmakers to portray the more surreal and anarchic aspects of the comic strip that would not be reproducible using film-making technology available in the 1980s. Nevertheless, it is probably true to say that the principal failings of the film lie in the writing of the script rather than the medium in which it was produced.

In the movie, the story begins with Howard being transported from his home world (populated by anthropomorphic ducks) to our world. As soon as he arrives on Earth, he utilizes his "Quack-Fu" skills to rescue "Beverly Switzer" from muggers. The script then follows a fairly pedestrian, mad scientist oriented adventure plot, alongside a sub-plot revolving around Beverly's career as a rock star. A derivative science fiction villain named "The Dark Overlord" makes an appearance and is finally defeated in an equally derivative manner. The film ends with Howard taking on the role of manager for Beverly's band Cherry Bomb. As such, the *Howard the Duck* movie conforms to the standard template of the 1980s sci-fi comedy plot, and is only remarkable to the degree that it conforms to conventionality. But even so, the movie *could* have worked had it embraced the ironic "knowingness" of the *Howard the Duck* comic book. After all, many of the editions of the comic book utilize clichéd plot lines, albeit for comic effect. For example, the story "Hellcow" that appeared in *Giant-Sized Man-Thing 5* (1975) is a generic vampire story; "Howard the Barbarian" which features in the premier issue of the character's own title (1975) is in essence a typical sword and sorcery tale, and in *Marvel Treasury Edition 12* (1976) Howard joins the Defenders to embark on what is—if we ignore the humorous and satirical aspects of the story—a conventional superhero tale. There is no reason at all why the movie could not have embraced the humor of the comic strip source material; the writers/directors chose, however, to replace the ironic satirical tone of the comic book in favor of 1980s frat-boy humor (and not particularly funny 1980s frat-boy humor, at that) and a special-effects driven science fiction movie plot (and not a particularly good special-effects driven science fiction movie plot, either). Indeed, the *Howard the Duck* film redraws the character of Howard himself. In the comic book he is irascible, irritable and often unpleasant, juxtaposing him against other cartoon ducks. The film portrays Howard as a far nicer, conventional anthropomorphic character and thus the fundamental "gag" of Howard is lost.

We should not get distracted by considering too much whether the film was authentic to the comic book or not, or how funny it was. We need to, nonetheless, address the issue of its failings and we can claim that the film's failings are due in part to it straying so significantly from the comic book. What is most important of all here is the fact that the movie lacks the "Steve Gerber" qualities of the comic book. Without trying to over-intellectualize Gerber's work (after all, in the comic-book itself the jokes are as often wise-cracks and goof-ball antics as much as they are moments of scathing satire) the comic book succeeds as much as anything due to its Menippean elements while the film fails due to its abject conventionality. Put bluntly: the *Howard the Duck* comic book had its flaws—and was not always the avant-garde self-reflexive masterwork some readers claim it to be. It was at its best an interesting, funny and brave attempt to expand the parameters of what the comic book could be. The film, on the other-hand, lampoons elements of action hero narratives, in that it sends up certain aspects of such texts and plays them for laughs, but it does nothing to question or trouble our notion of the action movie or comic book. The *Howard the Duck* movie aims to be a comic adventure movie in the style of *Ghostbusters* (1984) rather than a text that deconstructs and interrogates the conventions of its own genre(s). The key issue here is that while the movie satirizes features and elements of adventure fiction, it never becomes a true satire in that the comic scenes are enacted for their immediate comic effect, but never extend to embrace broader issues or make more nuanced observations about culture, media or the society as a whole. An example of this would be the scene where Howard rescues Beverly using his martial arts skills. A duck practicing Kung Fu is funny, but it is only a funny scene in a movie; it does not then move on to engage with anything deeper or more complex, but rather just invites us to laugh at something silly. Likewise, the Dark Overlord is a stereotypical villain who is presented to us as a humorous figure in that he is an exaggeration of a cliché, but again: the joke stops there. There is no extension of the gag beyond itself; the satire serves no satirical purpose. Moreover, the movie does nothing to problematize the medium of film itself. Had it done so, and done so while remaining entertaining and comic, it would have been more in keeping with the comic book on which it was based, but also a braver more challenging and, essentially, more "Gerberesque" text.

Finally, however, in fairness to the makers of the *Howard the Duck* movie, it should be pointed out that until *X-Men* (2000) and *Spider-Man* (2002), all screen adaptations of Marvel comic characters had failed to some degree. Irrespective of their inherent quality as movies or TV shows, there was an ongoing problem of bringing Marvel heroes to the screen. Curiously, film adaptations of DC comic heroes never seemed to suffer quite so badly and made the transition from page to screen less painfully. It may well be that this is due to DC heroes being more recognizably "heroic" in the traditional sense, whereas Marvel heroes have generally been more ambivalent and ambiguous.[11] Hollywood in the 1970s and 1980s could well have been comfortable with DC's conventional characters, but it wasn't until the 2000s that the Hollywood movie industry could handle more paradoxical heroes. It is perhaps possible to suggest that the current wave of Marvel films has not just been made possible by CGI technology, but also by maturity within the film industry, which has now come to acknowledge that audiences of popular action films are grown-up enough to understand and admire complex characters within a popular, action-narrative framework.

It is perhaps then valid to suggest that it was the climate that the *Howard the Duck* movie was produced in, rather than a failing of those involved in its production, that doomed this film. In the 1980s the movie industry was still struggling to acknowledge that there were comic books and comic book characters that were of sufficient sophistication and complexity to form the basis of a solid narrative. Even so, its early successes were limited to adaptations of DC rather than Marvel Comics, as mentioned above. Considering that it would take the movie industry another twenty years to come to terms with the ambiguity of even the more conventional Marvel heroes, it is perhaps asking too much of that industry to expect them to be able to successfully translate something as unconventional as *Howard the Duck* from comic book to screen. Even now, when Hollywood has embraced Marvel characters with enthusiasm, we must ask ourselves: *How reasonable is it to expect the film industry to make a success of a hero who lives within, yet questions and problematizes, a fictional universe that it has only just learned to accept?*

NOTES

1. Steve Gerber, Len Wein, et al., *The Essential Defenders Vols 1, 2, 3* (New York: Marvel, 2006, 2007), n.p.
2. Ibid.
3. Steve Gerber, Frank Brunner, Gene Colan, et al., *The Essential Howard the Duck Vol 1* (New York: Marvel, 2002), n.p.
4. Ibid.
5. Ibid.
6. Ibid.
7. Scott McLoud, *Understanding Comics* (London: HarperCollins, 1994), 22.
8. Rick Hudson, "The Derelict Fairground: A Bakhtinian Analysis of the Graphic Novel Medium," *CEA Critic* 72.3 (2010), 33–47.
9. Mikhail Bakhtin, *The Dialogic Imagination* (Austin: University of Texas Press, 1981), 39.
10. Mikhail Bakhtin, *Problems of Dostoevsky's Poetics* (Minneapolis: University of Minnesota Press, 1984), 118.
11. Rick Hudson, "Sinister Six: Anti-Villains in an Anti-Heroic Narrative," in *Web-Spinning Heroics: Critical Essays on the History and Meaning of Spider-Man*, ed. Robert M. Peaslee and Robert G. Weiner (Jefferson, NC: McFarland, 2012), 128–133.

PART 7
The Anti-Hero

Punishing the Punisher
Can Hollywood Ever Capture the Essence of the Character?

CORD A. SCOTT

"Who Punishes You? Who Punishes the Punisher?"
—Jigsaw in *Punisher: War Zone* (2008)

One of the most violent and popular characters in the Marvel universe is Frank Castle, commonly known as "the Punisher." Since his debut in 1974, the vigilante has served as an anti-hero willing to use his combat skills honed in Vietnam as a way to right the wrongs that he saw within society. His appearance was coincident with the release of *Death Wish* (1974), when many citizens of the U.S. felt either rightly or wrongly that crime was rampant, the police were a symbol of corruption or ineffectiveness, and little was being done to stop those responsible.

Since then, adapting the Punisher to the big screen has been problematic and commercially damaging. There have been three attempts to depict him on film, beginning with the Golan-Globus *Punisher* from 1989, starring Dolph Lundgren. This movie failed for a variety of reasons. The most glaring of these reasons was the lack of the trademark Punisher skull logo on Castle's shirt, which left many established readers unimpressed even by the mere appearance of the character. While the film was based on the comic books and even had Stan Lee listed as an executive producer, it was nonetheless a tepid version of the story.

The second and third movies came out from Marvel studios or were affiliated with Marvel in the more direct sense. The 2004 version, in which Marvel Productions took control of not just merchandising rights, but production of the character, featured the marquee name of John Travolta as the main villain, Howard Saint, and Thomas Jane as the Punisher.[1] While it was an interesting take on the character, it still fared poorly at the box office, compared to other Marvel movies of the era, such as *Spider-Man 2* (2004), or *Fantastic Four* (2005). The third movie, over which Marvel had control, featured Ray Stevenson as the Punisher and was in theatres for only a week in some locations. *What made a popular character such a failure when adapted to the screen?*

One could argue that the very nature of the Punisher, especially in recent years, has become violent to the extent that any proper movie adaptation would need an R rating. While this rating would be appropriate for the material, it often goes against the wishes of movie studios, which prefer "PG-13" for box office maximization. Critics and fans alike noted that the scripts were problematic. This article analyzes the three movies, the critiques of each, and how the Marvel name served to boost neither interest nor sales. The article also looks at two significant fan-fiction movies available online, which some readers have stated are actually better than the studio films and closer to the "feel" of the Punisher.

The Comic Book Origins

To effectively understand the Punisher, one has to look at the time frame in American history when he was introduced. Originally a villain in the *Amazing Spider-Man* #129 (1974), The Punisher was a Vietnam War vet and former candidate for the priesthood who witnessed his family killed in a mob shootout in Central Park in New York.[2] Castle was working for a villain called "the Jackal," and was led to believe that Spider-Man could have done something to stop the assault by the mafia. Those two events became part and parcel of how the Punisher was depicted in the comics, as it gave Castle his *raison d'être* to kill, as well as his hatred of those who do not use their abilities to help those weaker or in need.

The Punisher's training in military weapons and tactics is another important aspect of the character, as it blended into the war in the streets against an enemy that was elusive and deadly. However, the rage against the military and authority in the early to mid–1970s may not translate with readers of the Punisher now, who see the professional armed services as that—professional, not conscripted. The need for Castle to punish those who were seemingly untouchable by the law and society was another important factor in his backstory, as it tied directly into aspects of real-life crime and punishment within major American cities in the 1970s. A current adaptation of the Punisher might concentrate on corrupt officials or even police, especially given the news reports in 2015 concerning excessive force and brutality. Given the fact that the Comic Book Code was still partially adhered to by companies like Marvel, the limitations on the police as corrupt may have been too extreme.[3] These factors still play a part in the movie story lines.

Another part of the character is his appearance. While the uniform has an overall black appearance as well as white accents and boots, his trademark is the stylized skull logo displayed prominently on his chest (known as a Death's Head). Castle is distinguished by his ability to kill through a variety of weapons and unarmed combat styles, and he has a moral compass that allows execution of the guilty through a form of moral judgment of the wicked of society. He has no superpowers *per se*; he is simply a man on a mission to eliminate the evils of the world as he sees them. From a character development standpoint, this struggle with good and evil played both into Castle's backstory as a would-be priest, as well as the black and white color scheme of his wardrobe. Like his world-view, one is "good" or "evil": there is no middle ground.

The Punisher *(1989)*

The first foray into the live action version of the Punisher series was released in 1989 by New World (Australia) Pictures. Written by Boaz Yakin and directed by Mark

Goldblatt, *The Punisher* was supposed to be a gritty version taken from the comics. As Frank Castle/Punisher, the studio cast Lundgren, who had first gained notoriety as the Russian boxing opponent Ivan Drago in *Rocky IV* as well as the live-action adaptation of the *He-Man* cartoon, *Masters of the Universe* (1987). To look more like the Punisher, Lundgren had his hair dyed black. His "uniform" was simply a black biker jacket, black t-shirt, jeans, and black biker boots with shin guards, so the only use of the skull logo was on the stiletto style knives that the Punisher used as his calling card.

The common complaint used by critics of the movie was that Marvel held some sort of "final say" on any of the movies released. This led to the argument that the 1989 movie failed because it didn't have the look of the comic book. The reality was a bit different, however, as Marvel had leased the rights to other studios for production. The first problem was that the producers of the movie were trying to go for an action movie rather than a comic book adaptation. To that end the trademark Punisher skull logo was dropped from the costume as it looked "too comic-booky."[4]

At that time only the DC franchise movies had shown any real commercial success at the box office. Marvel movies had shown the opposite effect. They took a general "hands off" approach, and many of the Marvel movies were commercial failures, starting with *Howard the Duck* (1986). The Marvel-based television shows had better success. The key element for this failure of the movies was the lack of an idea as to what the movies should be: action or adaptation.[5]

Another substantial change to the story of Castle/Punisher was that his military training was eliminated from the story. Rather than being a military veteran with substantial experience and ability to counter threats, the character was presented as a cop (but Castle's family being killed by the mafia was kept as a plot device). Louis Gossett, Jr., was cast as a police detective named Jake Berkowitz, whose career and life were saved by Castle prior to the mob hit on the family. The script had the mafia merge families to control all aspects of crime, as well as a threat from the "Yakuza" (Japanese mafia) to boot.

As the story progresses in this movie, the Yakuza kidnap mobsters' children to hold as a leverage point. It is only after many of the Mafiosi are killed that Castle decides to intervene, as the children are innocent and need some sort of protection. As with the comic books, the Punisher also relies on intelligence gathering. In this movie, the info is often gathered from a drunken actor, who delivers information in iambic pentameter, drawing from Shakespeare. The traditional enemies of the Punisher from the books are not used, except in general terms like the various crime families.

In the final showdown, Castle takes on the Yakuza, and rescues the remaining children. When this is accomplished, the mob boss who remains tries to kill the Punisher. In the end, when the mob bosses are killed, and all is wrapped up, Castle goes back to killing those who wronged society. The movie ends in an open style of sorts to allow for a sequel. Overall, the movie took in $30 million in receipts, while being made on a budget of $9 million.[6]

While many criticized Lundgren's "dead shark like eyes, and wooden acting," a few expressed their appreciation of the actor and his campy performance of the Punisher. Regardless, the movie did not do well enough, and in the end a sequel was not made. As with the other Punisher (and for that matter all comic book-inspired films) there was a comic book adaptation that attempted to bring new readers to the comic books from which the character originated.

The Punisher *(2004)*

The 2004 re-boot of the Punisher story was meant to be a stronger showing than the 1989 version. In this version, Castle is an undercover agent for the DEA, who has prior military experience in counter-terrorism. In the opening scenes, he operates undercover as a gun dealer, and as the deal goes awry, the buyer is killed. That man is the son of Tampa mob king Howard Saint (John Travolta) and from there, the movie is set. It was hoped that between the actions of Punisher, the marquee name of Travolta, and the Marvel tie-ins, there would be a boost in marketing. The movie did not lack Hollywood stars: Rebecca Romijn-Stamos is the female interest, Roy Schneider plays the part of Frank Castle's dad, and character actors Laura Harring and Will Patten have pivotal roles in the film. After the mob kills off Castle's entire extended family, he eventually recovers and takes to wearing a shirt with the Punisher skull logo on it as a reminder of his dead son.

Castle uses his usual violence to get the job done, which includes considerable psychological torture. This came at the same time as the Abu Grahib scandal[7] and was topical. The concept of torture may have made audiences uncomfortable due to the assumption that American combatants did not "stoop" to the act of obtaining information though what Donald Rumsfeld called "enhanced interrogation" techniques. In the end, many viewers did not necessarily complain about the torture or the violence, but rather about the slow pace of the movie.

While Jane did play the Punisher well, there was a certain disconnect with the movie. Some characters felt forced, such as Castle's neighbors in Tampa. To audiences, the very idea of having the movie set in Tampa was a poor one, since the Punisher's traditional hunting grounds were, and are, in New York.

What the director did do well was the incorporation of certain elements from the comic books into the film. One scene noted that Castle was going to use a blowtorch on a mob informant to gain information. What he did was describe what would happen—the torch searing nerves and all the person would feel would be cold—then place a popsicle on his back to simulate the intense pain. While the scene seemed improbable, it was taken directly from the comics, and it provided a sense of dark humor to the scenes.

Also, in the movie, the idea that the Punisher could not be seriously injured was stressed. In one scene, the Punisher takes three direct blasts to the chest from a shotgun but is unfazed. The idea from the comics was that he could be, and was often, uninjured due in part to wearing body armor, but also because of his military training.

In the credits, many of the Marvel teams that worked on the Punisher comic book series were recognized. Stan Lee again served as an executive producer, and special thanks were extended to Garth Ennis, Jimmy Palmiotti, and Steven Dillon for inspiration. These three served as creators of some of the more successful *Punisher* comics and graphic novels from that same time frame. In fact, the 2004 release also had an official comic book tie in—a four issue mini-series, as well as the critical and commercial success of *Punisher: Born*, which was written by Ennis, and looked into Castle's combat experiences in Vietnam.[8]

This version of the Punisher was written and directed by Jonathan Hensleigh with co-writer Michael France, who also worked on the 2005 *Fantastic Four* movie as a writer. The story was timeless, but the movie came out at an awkward time as post–Iraq War violence was on the upswing. From a commercial standpoint, this particular Punisher movie was the most successful. It had a budget of $34 million, and grossed $54 million worldwide, with $33 million of that from the U.S. market.[9]

Punisher: War Zone (2008)

The most recent studio addition to the Punisher series was the 2008 film *Punisher: War Zone* which was created by Marvel Knights Studio. In this version Ray Stephenson was cast as the Punisher, the script written by Nick Santora, Art Marcum, and Matt Holloway. The latter two wrote the script for the Marvel endorsed *Iron Man* movie of the same year. Santora had previous success writing for *Prison Break* as well as *Vegas*. Finally, former kick boxing champion Lexi Alexander was tapped to direct the movie. With this formula, it was thought that the movie would have commercial success.

With the script, it was readily apparent that the writers had tapped into the comic book series. New York and the mob were essential choices, as these elements were part of the original storyline in the comic book, but had been altered for the 2004 film. Another aspect of the film that relied on the comic book was the incorporation of some of the main secondary characters in the movie. For example Microchip, Castle's intelligence gatherer and arms dealer, was used as a key character in the film. This was augmented by the use of many of the villains that readers had liked from the comics: Jigsaw, Pitsy, and McGinty. While seeming to be a solid basis for the script, aside from Jigsaw, the others were minimized or changed for the worse and came off as corny.

For the Punisher, the basic story line was maintained. Castle was again a Special Forces instructor (a slight change, but true to the military origin), and the basic story of his family being killed in a mob hit was maintained. What did change was the premise involving an undercover cop's death by the Punisher, by which he was wracked with guilt.

From a film standpoint, the plot dragged at times. The basic idea of the comic book was kept, but for many viewers the plot had a lot of holes or at least lags, due in part to character development (or lack thereof) as well as a comic being able to fill in plot shifts. From a commercial standpoint, the movie was a failure. It had been budgeted at $35 million, but only grossed $10 million worldwide.[10] In some locations, the movie only lasted a week in theatres. Again the usual arguments of poor writing, deviation from the comic book, and a lack of continuity were all noted in the Internet chat rooms. From the critics, the comments ranged from "a guilty pleasure (but still not great)" to comments of "horrible, uber-violent mayhem."

Punisher '79–'82 (2012)

It stands to reason that in this Internet era, when a film is not done to the satisfaction of the audiences, others try to create their own version. The Punisher has been no exception. In 2008, the first of four fan fiction films surrounding the Punisher were created by Blinky Productions. While not as slick as a Hollywood style film, the fan fic films tried to capture the essence of the Punisher. The four films were small vignettes taken from the Punisher's war journal from 1979 to 1982.[11]

The Punisher was played by Shawn Parr and his appearance stayed more in line with the depiction of the Punisher from the late '70s: thinner and a bit haggard, but still incredibly agile and violent. The films were more in tune with the Punisher as envisioned by the writer of the series at the time the fan fic films came out: Garth Ennis. This shift in production, combined with the Marvel Max line which offered readers more swearing and violence, was in tune with the target audience of the comics, males in their 20s with disposable income.

In these movies, old nemeses were brought into story lines, along with music from the era. For example, in *Punisher '79*, Jigsaw lip-syncs the words to the Sex Pistol's version of *My Way* sung by Sid Vicious. He also quotes Shakespeare, apparently in an attempt to show his sophistication. In the *Punisher '82* movie, different characters including Typhoid Mary, Bullseye and Crossbones appear as well. In an interesting note, a comic book creator, Graig Weich also appeared in a cameo. His comic book *Civilian Justice*, which features a character referred to by the same name, was produced soon after the September 11, 2001, attacks on the World Trade Center and Pentagon. Civilian Justice was meant to be a patriotically inspired hero similar to Captain America.

Punisher: Dirty Laundry *(2012)*

One of the more recent additions to the Punisher live action series was the Internet film *Punisher: Dirty Laundry* (2012). The film, shot professionally and aired free to viewers, was a ten-minute vignette in which Thomas Jane returns as Castle/Punisher. For fans, this film was considered the best of the Punisher films, as it certainly captured the feel of the comics. In the story, Castle is living out of his van and steps into a Laundromat to wash his clothes. During that time, he witnesses the actions of a neighborhood gang boss terrorizing his prostitutes as well as a young boy walking through the neighborhood. Castle tries to ignore the scenes while he grabs a shirt and notices a bullet hole. He reaches to get change for the dryer, and it's revealed he has a shell casing in his pocket as well. As he walks through the "gang bangers," Castle is threatened by the gang leader.

As the movie progresses, Castle steps in to a liquor store to buy a "Yoo-hoo" and speaks with the clerk, a veteran played by Ron Perlman. Though the script writing was sparse, it was indicative of the Punisher scripts. "There's always a war somewhere" notes Perlman's character, "I get a front row seat to watch it all burn." When Castle, who doesn't drink, asks for a bottle of Jack Daniels, the audience thinks he is trying to quell his internal demons.

The last few minutes turn into what has made the Punisher such a success: that same bottle is used to kill, quite creatively, five gang members, before Castle further uses the bottle to kill two more members with their own pistols. As the leader gets a shot off against the Punisher, the beaten boy bites the leader's leg. This allows Castle to gain the upper hand, shoot the leader, and then proceed to break three limbs. He then soaks the leader in the same bottle of Jack while asking him if he knows the difference between "justice and punishment." In the end, it is not Castle who immolates the gang leader but the prostitute who was beaten up earlier.[12]

This "short" is indicative of the promise of the movie adaptations of the Punisher as a whole. In the comments surrounding the movie, many people who posted Internet comments stated that they liked Jane in a return to the role. Others noted that perhaps the scripts would make for a better movie down the road.

Fan fic films have run into issues with Marvel, however. One such film, the *Dead*

Can't Be Distracted, was produced by Pecci and McFarland; the film's creator was hit with legal action from Marvel demanding that a "cease and desist" order be placed upon the film. While Pecci was distraught that the film would not be aired, and even cited *Punisher: Dirty Laundry* as an example of how there is hypocrisy towards which films will be aired and which ones will not, Marvel claimed that the film was far too similar to a Punisher comic book series that came out around the same time. Marvel attorneys felt that the look of *The Dead Can't Be Distracted* was too close to the story from the book. Arguably, the characters do resemble their depiction in the Punisher comics from that same time.[13]

As of this writing, there is a TV show in development using the Punisher as a character for an ABC/Disney/Marvel production tentatively slated for 2015 airing. However, the premise that has been posted on IMDB.com makes the character appear more in line with the television show version of the Punisher from the late 1980s, in which the main character was a police officer moonlighting as a vigilante. This may not translate well for the small screen.[14] To make the situation more complicated, the television adaptation had been reported three years earlier, and based on the Fox television network. Therefore, the likelihood of the show actually airing on any television network may be hindered if not halted.

Conclusions: Why Aren't the Movies More Successful?

There are a variety of reasons as to why the movies have not been commercially successful. One reason is the variance in casting. While all three actors have brought certain strengths to the films, and been lauded for their interpretation of the Punisher, overall the movies have not been commercially viable. Some comments on post boards such as on IMDB.com—one of which was simply entitled "how to fix the Punisher"—have noted that Dolph Lundgren has wooden actions and dead eyes, and was therefore what the Punisher should be; others have countered that Thomas Jane brought a nuance to the character. While some felt that Jane or Ray Stephenson would work well with a better script, others have suggested Chris Meloni from *Oz* and *Law & Order: SVU* fame to play the role, as he would bring to light issues such as morality and religion with which Castle struggled. Others have suggested Jon Hamm or Jeffrey Dean Morgan, who starred in the comic book adaptations of *Watchman* and *The Losers*. Ultimately, as with many versions of the same character, it falls into personal preference.

Another reason the movies have not worked is that the scripts have deviated from the comics to the point of offending the "purist" readers. One of the similarities of all the movies is that Castle's backstory has been changed from that of a battle-scarred veteran to that of a character with military experience, but who now works for the FBI or DEA. This takes away a critical part of the character's development. Again, the comments on the post boards note that perhaps the Punisher should be a member of the Marine Recon community who has been scarred by the excessive violence he has seen. This would be more in line with the skills and reasoning for the violence: a need to right the wrongs of an enemy without remorse. Garth Ennis captured a lot of this in the comic books: Castle is trying to forget the images and demons of Vietnam and in the end he only feels alive by re-visiting that violence. In one regard, he becomes a sociopath.

The last reason for the lack of success of the films can be attributed to the time in which they were released. For Marvel, the character's interpretation fell during the time of the second Gulf War. As with any form of popular culture, sometimes it is hard to present material that contains torture and revenge killing when the nightly news seems to have a deluge of the same type of material. The audience can become burned out or desensitized to such news if it becomes a constant. In sum, although the various directors tried to make the character their own, their attempts ultimately failed.

One suggestion towards successfully revamping the Punisher films would be to bring in some of the more famous writers from the original comic books. Perhaps the most successful of these writers is Garth Ennis, whose tenure as writer on the Punisher comic book lasted ten years. His work creating the conditions of Castle's war experiences fed directly into the actions—and it works. Another option for the studio would be to bring in some of the more memorable characters such as Barracuda. This would allow for more of a connection to the audience, including the "purist" readers.

The last part of the equation to potentially create a better film would be choosing the *right* kind of director. Again, there have been some interesting suggestions on the Internet. One option that's widely mentioned in the conversations would be to have Pierre Morel, the director of the highly successful film *Taken* (2008), come aboard the franchise. Others have mentioned that Sylvester Stallone should write and direct, given his recent time and success behind the camera on the *Expendables* franchise. Again, it would not, solely, be the right director, but the right ensemble that would make a positive difference.[15]

Regardless of the directors, actors and writers, the biggest problem with bringing the Punisher to the screen is that, at its core, the story is inherently violent. However, it has instant recognition with audiences. Even within the military community, the Punisher skull has found its way into unit "patches." The skull has even been used on a hat worn by Navy SEAL Chris Kyle, both for his company as well as in the movie based on his life, *American Sniper* directed by Clint Eastwood.[16] The likelihood of an R rating is high, and that in turn cuts away from the core audience for the film: teenage boys. So, to find any sort of balance, the creators of the film have to sacrifice certain creative elements, but that may take away interest from the readers of the comics: adults who expect a certain level of wit in the story lines, as well as more of a plot.

With any movie based on a comic book or book that is popular with a wide audience, there is bound to be criticism. For any character that has developed a following, there will be purists who will not like the finished product, regardless of the outcome. For Marvel studios and Disney, the need to make money on a winning formula for a movie adaptation of the character, especially one that is so violent, may preclude any further serious cinematic attempts. The recent success of *Deadpool* (2016) may be relevant. Perhaps if the Punisher were to be developed into another movie, the script should be written by a writer of the Punisher comics—this would give it a more original but true feel, as previously mentioned. Until that time, fans may have to make do with the older versions, attempt to make their own versions, or simply use their own imagination in regards to the comic and the Punisher. Then again, they may be simply punishing themselves in the hope of bringing an accurate and likeable portrayal of the character of the Punisher to the big screen.

NOTES

1. http://variety.com/2004/scene/news/heroic-marvel-gain-1117904309/ (accessed July 8, 2015).
2. Mike Baron, et al., *Essential Punisher, vol. 1* (New York: Marvel Comics, 2004).

3. The comic book code of 1954, and updated in 1971, noted in part that comic books should not depict acts against authority figures such as police officers or judges. While Marvel comics often had stories that went against the code, the traditions may have been too much for comic writers to deviate.

4. Superherocomicuniverse.com/punisher (retrieved January 15, 2015).

5. http://www.thestar.com/entertainment/movies/2008/05/11/howards_end_for_now.html.

6. IMDB.com/Punisher1989, http://www.imdb.com/title/tt0098141/?ref_=fn_al_tt_2 (retrieved January 7, 2015).

7. Abu Grahib was used as the central prison for interrogating suspected terrorists or Saddam sympathizers. However, by late 2004, National Guard units used to guard the prisoners had been exposed for violating human rights as well as conducting forms of torture against prisoners. This was further compounded by the 2005 release of documents that noted in official U.S. government memos concerning the use of torture on "enemy combatants." These issues made the use of torture in movies and television controversial, to say the least.

8. Garth Ennis, *Punisher: Born* (New York: Marvel Comics, 2003).

9. IMDB.com/Punisher2004, http://www.imdb.com/title/tt0330793/?ref_=fn_al_tt_1 (retrieved January 7, 2015).

10. IMDB.com/Punisher:WarZone(2008) statistics, http://www.imdb.com/title/tt0450314/?ref_=fn_al_tt_4 (retrieved January 10, 2015).

11. BlinkyProductions:Punisher'79-'82 (www.blinkyproductions/ https://vimeo.com/album/3068769/video/107964075) (retrieved January 29, 2015).

12. https://www.youtube.com/watch?v=bWpK0wsnitc.

13. http://www.comicbookresources.com/?page=article&id=48344 (retrieved Jan 16, 2015) and digitalspy.com/comics/news/a522230/punisher-fan-film-gets-cease-and-desist-order-from-marvel-studios.html#~phRb4xd2I4tWSr (accessed July 8, 2015).

14. Imdb.com/punisher2015, http://www.imdb.com/title/tt2358753/?ref_=tt_rec_tti. Retrieved Jan. 15, 2015

15. www.mattsmoviereviews.net/spotlight-in-development-make-punisher-work.html (retrieved January 28, 2015).

16. http://nothingbutcomics.net/2014/07/22/the-military-skull-art-inspired-by-the-punisher/ (accessed July 10, 2015).

Hulk Smash Binaries

D. Stokes Piercy *and*
Ron Von Burg

The Hulk is a unique figure in the Marvel Universe. Even as other superheroes struggle with an ontological identity inflected by unworldly powers and the attending responsibilities of such powers, these superheroes largely embrace a commitment to social order, protecting a fragile society from villains who possess similar powers, but lack the humility and drive for communal tranquility. The recent uptick in superhero films, especially after the terrorist attacks of September 11, 2001, highlight anxieties and morality plays that engage concerns of democratic social order.[1] The Hulk, however, defies such clean categories. Born out of an experiment gone awry, the brilliant and mild-mannered scientist Bruce Banner is transformed into the Hulk when sufficiently enraged. Hulk, a gargantuan figure that possesses a penchant for destruction, has few, if any, physical vulnerabilities. His physical abilities are proportionate to his anger, wreaking havoc on all that stands in his way. Despite his appetite for rage and destruction, Hulk is largely aligned with the "good guys"—The Avengers—who find his power to be a welcome asset in confronting an assortment of evildoers. *The Avengers* (2012) and *The Avengers: Age of Ultron* (2015) depict a tortured Banner who does his best to keep Hulk under wraps, until the heroes require Hulk's services. But Hulk's presence comes at a price; expressions of his rage defy containment. Hulk is equally comfortable exacting his wrath on Thor as he is on Loki.

The story of Bruce Banner and Hulk is largely cast within a Dr. Jekyll and Mr. Hyde narrative, reflecting on the anxieties of technological advancements.[2] Even though Banner harbors a Jekyll-esque shame regarding the creature he can become, Hulk is no Mr. Hyde. Hulk is not a morally unrestrained being. His fury may be unbridled, but Hulk does not lack pity or even compassion. Hulk often risks himself to save the people who are persecuting him, only to be hunted down and persecuted again.[3] This persecution does not end with the military who wishes to neutralize the threat or the villains who see Hulk as a violent alter ego to be overcome. The superheroes who utilize his abilities in performing their heroic deeds are often the quickest to seek control or expunge the threat when he slips beyond their control.

Planet Hulk (2010), a Marvel animated feature based on the 2008 graphic novel by Greg Pak, highlights how Hulk defies simple boundaries between good and evil. Hulk is no anti-hero, a flawed figure that audiences cheer on despite his penchant for destruction, although that is often the case. Rather, Hulk is a character that problematizes the clean boundaries between good and evil, and the respective commitments to social democratic order or fascistic chaos. Although the heroes of the Marvel Universe possess numerous character flaws and moral ambiguities, they remain committed to protecting the presumed democratic order. Their exploitative relationship to Hulk, however, troubles the normative adherence to social democratic order. In *Planet Hulk*, the heroes characterized by their efforts to combat oppressive antagonists are all too comfortable with exiling the intransigent Hulk when he becomes unmanageable, and his instrumentality functions as a liability to the heroes' sense of order. To that end, this chapter examines the Hulk narrative, with particular attention to *Planet Hulk*, to problematize the boundaries between good and evil within the Marvel universe, especially as they relate to particular political imaginaries. In the following chapter, we first explore the broader narrative contours that position Hulk as an uncontrollable heroic figure used as a foil for other superheroes within the Marvel Cinematic Universe. Specifically, this section attends to the tropes that assign normative dimensions to superheroes and villains within the moral universe. Second, we present an extended analysis of *Planet Hulk*, examining how Hulk troubles rigid moral categories. We argue that non-mainstream Marvel films, such as *Planet Hulk*, require us to reconsider the common articulations of the "good guys" as defenders of democratic order. In fact, we argue the *Planet Hulk* identifies how the celebrated superheroes operate in tension with their stated goals, leaving Hulk as the true inheritor of the democratic imaginary.

Hulk Tool

The Marvel Cinematic Universe boasts heroes and villains with a myriad of backstories that animate their choices and goals. The superheroes come about their powers in an assortment of ways: divine or alien gifts, technological enhancements, or science experiments gone awry. As these individuals come to grips with their abilities, they are guided by a moral compass according to which they use their powers for either putatively good or harmful ends. While the lines of demarcation are often porous, Hulk presents an anomalous condition: Banner's transition into Hulk is the realization of a superpower that presumably lacks rationalization. He is the embodiment of rage, indiscriminately destroying everything in his path. Even though the humble and stoic Banner seeks anonymity, fearful of the damage his uncontrollable alter ego can unleash, he clearly aligns himself with the tropes that mark the "good guys": social order, democratic stability, and selfless acts of justice. Conscious, moral decisions, we assume, escape Hulk, eclipsing Banner's mild-mannered commitment to thoughtful, moral action.

Hulk is a patient beyond Freud's wildest dreams. The Banner/Hulk relationship is largely, and productively, understood within a psychoanalytic lens.[4] The gamma radiation that fundamentally changes Banner's biological composition also alters his mental framework. The superego that suppresses the ID steps aside when Banner becomes angered, unleashing the personification of rage. Banner is fully aware of Hulk's existence, even though he loses consciousness when Hulk appears, and does his best to limit his transformations into Hulk. Be it from guilt or shame, Banner goes to great lengths to repress Hulk's presence, retreating from civil society and performing altruistic deeds as compensation for the destruction left in Hulk's wake. Banner, a rational scientist with the noblest intentions, fears the chaotic potential of Hulk. Even in effort to perform acts of justice, the indiscriminate damage levied by Hulk unsettles the stoic Banner. The Banner/Hulk psychoanalytic dynamic presents an engaging dilemma when we consider the superheroes' putative attempts to protect democracy against fascistic or chaotic villains.

Traditionally, superheroes serve as protectorates of a democratic social order: defending truth, justice, and the American way. The proliferation of more cynical superhero films, such as *The Dark Knight* (2008) and *Hancock* (2008), demonstrate how such tropes are deployed ironically, calling attention to the excesses of vigilantism and superpowers that cannot be contained within a democratic space. Such films emerge from the fear that gripped Americans after September 11, which ushered in a slew of security measures that are realizations of a political ID, legislating security at the expense of individual liberty. For example, Veloso and Bateman highlight how the Civil War between Iron Man and Captain America over the ethicality of the Superhero Registration Act problematize the democratic ethos of these defenses of freedom.[5]

To be sure, superheroes, even the "good guys," are positioned uncomfortably within self-defined democratic spaces, as they possess powers that largely cannot be contained by the State. The bioconservative indictments of posthumanism, for example, echo a similar concern, whereby these super-human entities destabilize democratic assumptions of equality among State controlled subjects and trouble their ability to be governed.[6] The posthuman subjects, the argument goes, will not only outstrip the power of the governed human subjects, but the State's very ability to govern these subjects.[7] The cleavages of control and democratic legitimacy of both the State and the governed illuminate a tension central to democracy itself. The struggles between the centralized state and the people it governs, the two factors empowered under the purview of democracy, reveal what Tocqueville cautions in *Democracy in America* as "limitless social power," which in actuality constitutes the greatest threat to democratic order.[8] Donald Pease, in discussing Tocqueville, presents the concept of the "democratic thing," the animating fantasy that seeks to resolve such tensions through a policy of "dual containment," which reveals a particular democratic essence.[9] Pease notes:

> Citizens who believe themselves empowered to act on the democratic norms and assumptions sedimented within the dual containment policy also believe themselves to be the authors and agents of the norms through which they "manage" U.S. democracy. These enactments materialize the fantasy spaces they inhabit and of which they recognize themselves to be a crucial part.[10]

Such fantasies position subjects as assumed agents of democratic authorship, individuals well positioned to defend the fabric of the democratic political imaginary. Pease suggests that such a fantasy gains efficacy when there is a projected threat to the presumed democratic ethos. He contends, "The threat to the survival of the democratic thing triggers a generalized process of transference whereby the citizenry cathect their fear over the loss of the 'thing' into the need to rescue and protect the national uniqueness."[11] For rhetorical scholars, such a process is reminiscent of Burkean scapegoating, perfecting the threat to the established order as a scapegoat to be expunged, leaving the order and its animating assumptions intact.[12] However, as Pease cautions, "the desire to resolve or disavow the articulation of liberalism's logic of differences to democracy's logic of equivalences can only lead to the destruction of democracy."[13] The story of Hulk, and why he constitutes a threat to the Illuminati and their effort to defend the planet against antidemocratic forces, reflects how the democratic fantasy is further problematized within superhero narratives.[14]

Even though Hulk first emerges as a critique of our relationship with technological advancements, the character assumes distinct symbolic value with the newer, big budget films: *Hulk* (2003), *The Incredible Hulk* (2008), and *The Avengers* (2012). That Bruce Banner is played by three different actors, in a series of "reboots," speaks to broader uncertainties as to how Hulk as an individual character resonates with post–9/11 audiences steeped in defenses of democracy from external threats. It is particularly noteworthy that the most successful incarnation of Hulk, played by Mark Ruffalo in *The Avengers*, is with a cadre of other superheroes who band together to thwart Loki's fascistic plan to rule Earth. When Hulk is featured alongside these other heroes, he is often treated as the *deus ex machina*, a plot device, often leveraged by heroes to fight in service of the pro-democratic forces. Within this context, Hulk assumes an identity as a beast in need of control. He is depicted as one of the most powerful characters in the film, yet is consistently coached to harness or curtail the uncertainty associated with Banner's transformation into the raging Hulk. When questioned on how to control his beastly alter ego, the low-key Banner responds: "I'm always angry."

Such an admission is telling, especially in relation to the controllability of not only Hulk's rage, but also Hulk himself. Anger binds Banner to Hulk, and it is only through a constant state of anger that Banner is able to "control," albeit sporadically, the presence of Hulk. This ability, however, does not extend to those who wish to control Hulk and channel his rage to their ends. Hence, Hulk is a continual threat to the superheroes' democratic fantasy of maintaining order. *Planet Hulk* puts this tension into sharp relief. In the next section, we explore how *Planet Hulk* problematizes the Illuminati's assumed commitment to democratic order, demonstrating how the Hulk unearths inherent tensions in the democratic fantasy.

Hulk Saves

Planet Hulk, one of the many Marvel animated feature films, positions Hulk as the main character with only a cursory but revealing reference to other superheroes. We never witness Bruce Banner or his transformation into the Hulk; instead, we follow Hulk as the main character. He is not a raging monster incapable of rational thought, but a deliberative, even if angry, character who uses his power discriminately. *Planet Hulk* is driven by the decision of the Illuminati to exile Hulk to a distant planet, Sakaar, where he will not disrupt the social order on Earth. The Illuminati, a secret group of the Marvel superhero intelligentsia that includes Iron Man, Black Bolt, Professor Charles Xavier, Dr. Reed Richards, Dr. Strange, and Namor, determine that Hulk is more of a liability than an asset, and therefore he must be exiled from Earth.[15]

The Illuminati first appeared in 2005 in Brian Michael Brendis' *New Avengers* storyline as a response to the *Kree-Skrull War*, written by Roy Thomas. The Illuminati attempt to restore faith in superheroes by creating a new sense of order. Tony Stark, better known as Iron Man, founds the Illuminati on the grounds that a small cadre of intellectually and monetarily elite super-humans banding together could best protect the interests of planet Earth. The group functions as the directors of a quasi-militarized superhuman United Nations that provide both regulation and oversight to the superhero community. Fearful that a young, inexperienced superhero, even with the best intentions, could sow unspeakable destruction and turn humans against the heroes, the Illuminati seek order among their ilk. The Illuminati's commitment to order helps redefine, or in fact reinforce, a notion of being a "hero" as one acting in accordance with the new world order. Hulk, however, challenges the conceit that oligarchical governance in the hands of intellectually gifted superheroes is a preferred method of social order. Hulk, in other words, is an existential threat to the Illuminati and its assumed relationship to protecting "order" itself.

The opening sequence to *Planet Hulk* finds Hulk waking up in chains aboard a spaceship hurling toward a distant planet. A hologram of the Illuminati appears to inform Hulk of their machinations (on Earth, the Illuminati convince Banner that he needs to head into space to deal with an object emitting gamma radiation). Iron Man reveals the ruse to the understandably perturbed Hulk, noting that he is "truly sorry for what we've done, but we had no choice. When you get angry, when you're overcome by rage—you are a force of destruction." In this conversation, Iron Man repeatedly refers to Hulk as "Bruce," appealing to the presumably more reasonable half of the Banner/Hulk binary to articulate the obvious rationality of his exile. Iron Man argues that because Hulk's rage is all-consuming, no superhero on the Earth can contain his power or curtail his threat to order; he further explains to Hulk that they are sending him to a plant full of vegetation but lacking in intelligent life, ensuring that he will not be a harm to himself or others. He notes that Banner always wanted to be alone, and so the Illuminati are merely granting his wish, acting in a reasonable manner that is receptive to the desires of a rational subject. The animating assumption, therefore, is that Hulk only belongs in a space that lacks intelligent life, articulating a connection between intelligence and a commitment to order. For the Illuminati, this relationship is instrumental to their identity as a faction of intelligent superheroes committed to a sense of democratic order.

Iron Man's speech is spliced together with images of Hulk's ship barreling through space and Hiroim, a Shadow Priest of Sakaar, kneeling on the ground praying for a savior. The Shadow Priest chants, "Oh most divine creator, I seek thy hand and pray for the health of Sakaar. For we are a divided and dying world. Through the ancient prophets you have promised us a warrior savior." The dialogue in this opening montage strikes an important juxtaposition between the Iron Man's warrant for exiling Hulk and Hiroim's prayer for a possible savior. To wit, Iron Man notes, "You fear nothing. And even the mightiest heroes of earth cannot deter you." The following cut highlights the Priest's call for "a warrior who looks into the face of death and stands his ground." At the conclusion of the sequence, Hiroim sees the ship crash onto Sakaar, a divine sign that his prayers have been answered.

The exile of Hulk highlights some key themes that frame the subsequent narrative. First, the Hulk functions as a threat to the order imposed by the Illuminati because he cannot be controlled, rupturing the democratic fantasy promoted by the superheroes. In fact, Hulk becomes a literal Burkean scapegoat, expunged into the outer reaches of space so as to not reveal the more oppressive tendencies of the Illuminati. Second, Iron Man repeatedly attempts to interpolate Hulk as Bruce, referring to a subjectivity that Iron Man considers more reasonable and legislated. Even though Hulk is the character Iron Man addresses, the subject of his discourse is the unseen Banner. Such discursive dynamics are a literal manifestation of Iron Man's democratic fantasy. The rational subject that is necessary for a functioning democratic imaginary must, in this sense, be created, if nothing else to justify the actions for defending the illusionary order. While the interactions with the Illuminati highlight a variety of tensions in their treatment of Hulk in the spirit of democratic order, the rest of the narrative throws into sharp relief the importance of Hulk and his presumably irrational rage in problematizing the democratic fantasy.

Third, the juxtaposition of the Illuminati and the Shadow Priest demonstrate the limited scope of the former's moral and democratic imagination. If Hulk was "created" to deliver the Sakaarian people from bondage, then Hulk functions as a "Moses" type figure clearly placing Hulk within the moral universe of liberation from oppressive forces. Moreover, the Priest's prayer both highlights the shortcomings in the Illuminati's essentially pragmatic and consequentialist moral landscape and demonstrates a much broader rational and moral commitment beyond the purview of the Earth's mightiest heroes.

Hulk crash-lands on Sakaar, contrary to the assumption of the Illuminati, a planet teeming with intelligent life. The surrounding landscape could easily be mistaken for a location in the Middle East, and the clothing worn by the planet's inhabitants confirm the symbolic importance of the setting. As Hulk leaves the wreckage of his ship, he is immediately attacked by a hive of insect-like creatures. Imperial Guards enter the scene and proclaim the Hulk to be "imperial property" by virtue of a decree from the Lord Emperor of Sakaar, essentially taking Hulk away from the insect creatures and taking him as the Red King's prisoner. Hulk is subsequently tagged with an "obedience disk" that limits his ability to resist the authority. Weakened by his journey through the wormhole, Hulk is unable to overcome the Imperial Guards and collapses, accepting the temporary status of his enslavement. This marks a notable departure from traditional Hulk narratives. Typically when the Hulk loses consciousness, he reverts back into his human form, assuming the role of the rational Banner. In *Planet Hulk*, no such transformation materializes. Rather, Hulk awakens to find himself a prisoner of the Red King, the supposed savior of the Sakaarian people.

Prior to the Hulk's arrival, the Red King "liberated" the Sakaarian people from the menace of "the spikes," a biotechnological parasite that turns hosts into ravenous zombie-like creatures, attacking the uninfected. The backstory suggests that the Red King descended upon Sakaar to rid the planet of this torment, only to be welcomed as a new ruler. The Red King uses the spikes to leverage religious prophecy into institutional power. He created a story in which he is the obvious inheritor of a divine claim, delivering the inhabitants of Sakaar from the plague-like menace, which is later revealed to have been unleashed by the Red King himself. The spikes, which rain from the sky like many other biblical plagues, control the infected and could only be defeated by the Red King's army. He brings devastation in order to restore peace, and he does so under false pretenses, utilizing religious appeals to validate his claim to authority. The fulfillment of the prophecy, however artificial, secures numerous loyal followers, who treat the Red King as an unquestioned leader who only acts in the best interest of Sakaar. However, the Red King's rule is far from an equitable, democratic order.

Hulk, along with an assortment of other Red King prisoners, finds himself as the unwitting entertainment of the Red King. In a very *Gladiator*-esque storyline, Hulk and the other prisoner battle an increasingly difficult set of opponents, and like Maximus, Hulk and his cohort begin to win the crowd. Hulk is initially reluctant to join forces with the other warriors, instead electing to escape the arena and later attack his jailer, the Red King. Both attempts fail.

Ultimately, Hulk aligns himself with the others prisoners, rebuffing the advances of Cairea, the dutiful bodyguard of the Red King, who wish to strike a deal with Hulk for his freedom at the expense of the other prisoners. Wise to the machinations of power, Hulk has little faith in the sincerity of the offer, refusing to fall into another trap based on the promise of freedom and liberty. With a cohesive team, Hulk and the others defeat some the most menacing opponents offered by the Red King. The final showdown pits Hulk and company against Beta Ray Bill, a divinely commissioned warrior of Asgard and cherished prisoner of the Red King. If victorious, they are promised their freedom by the Red King. A dramatic skirmish ensues, and Hulk defeats Beta Ray Bill. Instead of yielding, Hulk continues to pummel Beta Ray Bill, unleashing his wrath on the vanquished opponent. His fellow gladiators look on in horror as Hulk pounds away, only for the sagely Hiroham to plead: "Hulk it's over. You've won—you don't need to kill him." As his rage subsides, Hulk demonstrates his mercy, releasing Beta Ray Bill, who also lost his obedience disk in the fight.

With that victory, Hulk looks to the Red King to grant them freedom, but in yet another act of authoritarian betrayal, the Red King requires Hulk to kill fellow prisoner Eloia, a leader of a Sakaarian rebel movement. Hulk refuses, and is subsequently sentenced to death. Hulk, once understood as a selfish being animated purely by rage, exercises agency that fractures the political imaginary. Although Hulk is often characterizes as an irrational being, unhinged from a sense of reason and order, he is actually quite reasonable, and his exercising of choice highlights the absurdity of the Red King's rule. With the crowd in support of Hulk, the Red King's actions belie his purported benevolence, revealing that his rule is based on a falsehood, an exercise of authority not grounded on a legitimate foundation.

Before the Red King is able to exact his brand of callow justice, a revived Beta Ray Bill, unencumbered by an obedience disk, destroys all obedience disks, declaring, "No more slaves! Only free people tied only by the bounds they have chosen. Claim your freedom!" Beta Ray Bill's characterization of enslavement is quite telling; his announcement of no more slaves suggests that shackles are inevitable, and the only difference lies in which bonds one chooses. Beta Ray Bill offers Hulk passage back to Earth, but recognizing such a journey would only return him to his previous enslaved state as tool of the Illuminati's commitment to democratic order, Hulk elects to stay in his existing state of enslavement and ultimately inspires an insurgency, overthrowing the Red King and establishing peace and a new world order. It is telling that Hulk was exiled from Earth on the grounds of keeping the peace, only to find refuge on a violent world where his supposed curse ushers in a new era of peace.

Hulk Concludes

Planet Hulk depicts Hulk as a fully empowered and rational figure, able to consciously make the decision to overthrow his jailor, and as a result, liberate those imprisoned by a religious mythos that created a collective delusion. Much like the constructed salvation offered by the Red King, the Illuminati operate under the assumption of a democratic imaginary, believing that they are responsible protectorates of democratic order. Unelected saviors who presume their reasonability offers the best conduit for order. Such a responsibility requires them, they believe, to exile the "uncontrollable" Hulk, who threatens that supposed order. But Hulk is not the irrational creature his tormenters believe; rather, he is a character whose unruly anger escapes legislation and fractures the democratic imaginary of equal subjects who can limit the power of the State. The subsequent comic book storyline, *World War Hulk*, depicts a vengeful Hulk returning to Earth, exacting revenge against his banishers, but demonstrating discriminating mercy toward those who resisted betrayal. Hulk's rage, in other words, is not simply aimless violence leaving destruction in its wake, but a presumed tool that is rendered problematic once it defies control of those who wish to use it.[16]

The treatment of Hulk by both the Red King and Iron Man reveal similarities that demonstrate the inherent contradictions of the Illuminati's commitment to democratic order. Like Iron Man, the Red King uses manipulation and subterfuge as central conceits. Pretense and objectification are portrayed as villainous acts within the story, yet the Illuminati employ the same tactics on Hulk. When such acts are propagated under the auspicious of the democratic fantasy, however, they are not considered villainous—they are necessary and heroic. To that end, *Planet Hulk* ultimately vindicates the persona of Hulk over the person of Bruce Banner. Hulk is oppressed and exploited by both and fascist and "democratic" leaders. His will and power present a threat to both institutional fantasies. The logos of Hulk compromises the integrity of the hero myth propagated by Iron Man and the Illuminati. Systems of government, democratic or otherwise, are structures to cage our baser instincts. Hulk smashes structures and, according to *Planet Hulk*, smashing is good.

Notes

1. For further discussion of how superhero narratives ruminate on challenges to democratic order, see Shaun Treat, "How American Learned to Stop Worrying and Cynically ENJOY! The Post-9/11 Superhero Zeitgeist," *Communication & Critical/Cultural Studies* 6, no. 1 (2009): 103–109, and Rebecca Wanzo, "The Superhero: Meditations on Surveillance, Salvation, and Desire," *Communication & Critical/Cultural Studies* 6, no. 1 (2009): 93–97.

2. Adam Capitanio, "'The Jekyll and Hyde of the Atomic Age': The Incredible Hulk and the Ambiguous Embodiment of Nuclear Power," *Journal of Popular Culture* 43, no. 2 (2010): 249–270.

3. This is a common plot line in Hulk narratives, including the comic books and the television show. Hulk often saves McKee in the TV show and General Ross in the cartoon series. Both are chief antagonists for the Hulk.

4. Freud describes the psyche, thusly: "The ego's relation to the id might be compared with that of a rider to his horse. The horse supplies the locomotive energy, while the rider has the privilege of deciding on the goal and of guiding the powerful animal's movement. But only too often there arises between the ego and the id the not precisely ideal situation of the rider obliged to guide the horse along the path by which itself wants to go." Sigmund Freud, *New Introductory Lectures on Psycho-analysis*. (New York: W. W. Norton, 1989), 96.

5. Francisco Veloso and John Bateman, "The Multimodal Construction of Acceptability: Marvel's Civil War Comic Books and the PATRIOT Act," *Critical Discourse Studies* 10, no. 4 (2013): 427–443.

6. For further discussion of the critique of posthumanism, see Francis Fukuyama, *Our Posthuman Future: Consequences of the Biotechnology Revolution* (New York: Farrar, Straus and Giroux, 2002).

7. This is particularly salient in the *X-Men* film narratives, where human fears of mutants lead to numerous political and military measures, such as the Mutant Registration Acts of *X-Men* (2001) and the Sentinel program of *X-Men: Days of Future Past* (2013), respectively.

8. Alexis de Tocqueville, *Democracy in America* (New York: Penguin Classics, 2003).

9. Donald Pease, "Tocqueville's Democratic Thing; or, Aristocracy in America," in *Materializing Democracy*, ed. Russ Castronovo and Dana Nelson (Durham: Duke University Press, 2002), 22–52.

10. Pease, 30.

11. Pease, 31.

12. Kenneth Burke, *The Philosophy of Literary Form* (Berkeley: University of California Press, 1973): 191–220.

13. Pease, 48.

14. Peaslee advances a similar argument, noting that "as characters who act variously toward (in tandem with, outside of, in opposition to) explicit expressions of social cohesion (police and government are prevalent examples), superheroes evoke a correspondent implicit goodness, a common-

sense approach to doing right that often operates outside the acceptable parameters of bureaucratic authority." Robert M. Peaslee, "Superheroes, 'Moral Economy,' and the 'Iron Cage'": Morality, ed. Wendy Haslem, Angela Ndalianis, and Chris Mackie (Washington, D.C.: New Academia, 2007), 38.

15. The decision to exile Hulk, however, was not unanimous among the Illuminati. Namor dissents on principle, arguing that they have no right to exile their ally and that Hulk will return to Earth to exact revenge, a prediction that comes true in the World War Hulk storyline. Namor ultimately leaves the Illuminati because of their decision to exile Hulk.

16. The subsequent *World War Hulk* storyline further complicates this understanding of the Illuminati's relationship to Hulk. Although Hulk returns to Earth to exact revenge for the Illuminati's betrayal, it was not the initial exile that precipitated Hulk's revenge, but the assumption that the Illuminati were responsible for the death of his wife and child.

From Comic Book Anti-Hero to Cinematic Supervillain
The Transmedia Extension of Magneto

Joshua Wucher

Unlike cinematic adaptations of novels, superhero comic book movies exist in a unique realm. The films are not simply relying on one text, but rather a series of works that can span hundreds of issues over years, or in some cases, even decades. Screenwriters "cherry-pick" issues and use comic arcs as loose frameworks for the films, rather than follow a specific sequential and chronological order. Much like classic adaptation theorists' fidelity arguments that privilege novels over cinematic adaptations, ardent fans of the comics often judge superhero films based on faithfulness to the source. This trend is inherently limiting because of its biased, and circumscribed, perspective that prioritizes the literary text over the cinematic adaptation. Rather than focusing critical attention on how true the superhero film remains to the original—which is a loaded term in relation to comic book adaptations, since any given series has a multitude of authors—centering discussion on the relationships between texts could be more productive. It can be contended that an intertextual perspective is better suited for critically engaging the superhero film, and is important for advancing the study of cinematic adaptations of comic books. The focus of this writing is not to determine the unique features of each medium, but to explore the aims of particular artists and how they emphasize or exploit aspects of each medium to serve their purposes. This essay is concerned with tracing the nature of "good" and "evil" in storytelling, particularly focusing on the complex anti–hero/super villain dichotomy within the character Magneto, the militant, terrorist leader of the Brotherhood of Evil Mutants in the long-running X-Men franchise. While several comic book franchises, from DC's *The Dark Knight* trilogy to Marvel's *The Avengers*, provide illustrations of complicated villains, the five *X-Men*[1] films are significant for their portrayal of Magneto as a tragic, Jewish figure and Holocaust survivor. By basing his motivations on the noble task of preventing future extermination, writers provide a level of depth that is lacking in many comic book movie villains, which challenges the audience's conception of what a "super villain" is. This narrative marker is important for investigating the way Magneto is transformed and adapted from the expansive realm of the comic book to the more limited space of film.

To ask questions about the adaptive process such as: *how representations of Magneto are affected, how limited is the transfer from text to screen, and what/how comic book concepts change or stay the same*, this essay borrows arguments from visual rhetorical analysis, comics studies, and adaptation theories. This analysis starts by contextualizing Magneto's status as an "anti-hero" in the comic book series *The Uncanny X-Men* from 1978 to 1991 under Chris Claremont's authorship, then moves to a close reading of the X-Men franchise by examining variations and continuities in the content and forms of both media, and finally addresses notions of seriality and interiority. While it is not the focus of this essay, some attention is devoted to the Fox animated X-Men series, which is significant for also illustrating Magneto's oscillation between "villain" and "anti-hero."

I seek to reveal how the Claremont comics portray Magneto as a nuanced and morally ambiguous antihero, whereas the X-Men films attempt a similar depiction but ultimately present a more simplified super villain, due to specific narrative and stylistic decisions intended to make the films more appealing to a mass audience. The purpose of highlighting these variations is not to declare that the comics medium is inherently superior to cinema in depicting psychologically rich characters, or that one medium is incapable of portraying the nature of good and evil, but rather to examine how the Claremont comics explore the dialectical opposition of these forces within Magneto's psyche—while the X-Men films externalize this philosophical debate by staging it between Magneto and Professor Xavier (X). By acknowledging that such variation in the depiction of evil exists in media, we can better investigate and explore the cultural and philosophical implications of a more simplistic portrayal of these themes.

Complex Anti-Hero

Emerging from the Silver Age of comics (1956–70), "with its righteous superheroes, its diabolical super villains, and nothing in between,"[2] the Bronze Age (1970–85) introduced fictional worlds where right and wrong were not absolute; instead, shades of grey existed. During this period, publishers were less scrutinized by the Comics Code Authority[3] and no longer felt the pressure to present a clearly defined "good vs. evil" dichotomy. Complicated villains like Magneto added depth and complexity to storylines where characters were often portrayed as flat and one-dimensional. His tragic origin revealed that forces outside his control shaped his transformation into a villain. Similar to Harvey Dent's (*Batman*) split-personality, unleashed from a jar of acid thrown at his face, and the Lizard's (*Amazing Spider-Man*) failed experiment to regenerate his amputated arm, Magneto and these villains are presented as victims of circumstance. This distinctive sympathetic element served as context for the audience to infer that Magneto viewed his cause of ensuring mutant survival as noble, in spite of his questionable means to achieve that end.

In Arie Kaplan's *From Krakow to Krypton: Jews and Comic Books*, Claremont explains that adding a backstory to Magneto changed him from a two-dimensional villain:

> I was trying to figure out what made Magneto tick. And I thought, "What was the most transfiguring event of our century.... It has to be the Holocaust!... It allowed me to turn him into a tragic figure, in that his goals were totally admirable.... When I can start from the premise that he was a good and decent man at heart, I then have the opportunity over the course of 200 issues to attempt to redeem him."[4]

This characterization is by no means unique to comics; Magneto does not represent the first complicated villain/anti-hero, but rather he is a descendent of hundreds of years of creative production from literature, theatre, and film. Arguably, these characters are endearing because their fears and frustrations often reflect our own, therefore, their actions weigh heavily on their consciences, which encourages the audience to confront its morality.

Similarities and Variations of Magneto

The prologue of *X-Men* (2000), typically space designated for a superhero's origin, is from Magneto's perspective and details the tragic loss of his parents in a Polish concentration camp in 1944. As the Nazis tear young Erik Lehnsherr away from his parents, he resists and reaches to them as they are being herded through a metal gate, surrounded by barbed wire. Suddenly, his powers manifest, causing the gate to bend. Amidst the family's cries, several Nazis fail to move the boy, who appears connected to the gate. A soldier knocks Erik out, and the gate ceases bending. Several Nazis bewilderingly look at the damaged gate, and then at Erik; ostensibly, their astonished stare suggests their assumption that this is no ordinary child.

Just as *X-Men* opens from Magneto's perspective in a Polish concentration camp, *X-Men: First Class* retells the story and further develops Erik's origin. Although neither films' prologue is directly adapted from a comic book story, Magneto's Holocaust past is essential to the X-Men canon and foregrounds the films in an attempt to add complexity and depth to his character and create a sense of conflict that affects how viewers will perceive him. Following the separation from his family, Erik is introduced to Dr. Klaus Schmidt (Kevin Bacon), a Nazi scientist whose experimentation on Jewish mutants parallels the work of the real-life Josef Mengele. When Erik is unable to move a coin on Schmidt's desk, the Nazi orders Erik's mother in and threatens to shoot her unless Erik completes the test. Again, Erik fails, and Schmidt murders the woman. In grief, the boy's magnetic powers are unleashed, destroying the room and killing two Nazis by caving in their metal helmets. Schmidt, appearing amused by the situation, gives Erik the coin and says, "So we unlock your gift with anger. Anger and pain."

A similar sympathetic framing of Magneto exists in the comics, in which he is haunted by the past. In *The Uncanny X-Men* #161, the story plays out in Charles Xavier's memory 20 years in the past in the Israeli seaport city of Haifa. Charles meets Magnus (an alias for Magneto/Eric) for the first time. We see Magnus' tattoo from Auschwitz— his number is 214782. Xavier says, "That tattoo, Magnus, were you—" to which Magnus replies, "Auschwitz. I grew up there." Xavier responds, "And your family—?" Magnus answers, "I have no family, Dr. Xavier. Anymore."[5]

These panels serve as strong visual and verbal cues to Magneto's past that clearly parallels the experience of millions of Jews and countless survivors living in Israel and abroad. The image of Magneto's tattoo is emblematic of what Martin Medhurst and Michael Desousa refer to as an "enthymematic form,"[6] which allows the reader to construct or evoke meanings from that image. An "enthymeme" is simply an argument with a missing part that the audience has prior knowledge of and then fills in. The word "Holocaust" is not mentioned in the panel, nor is an explanation given to what Auschwitz is, or why Magnus' family is gone. The authors assume that the audience already knows what the tattoo represents, that Auschwitz was a death camp in World War II, and that more than a million Jews died there. The image and text do not explicitly state the creators' rhetorical argument; rather, the audience draws its own enthymematic conclusions. In other words, the creators provide some context for viewing Magneto sympathetically, but it is the reader who realizes the significance in the panel and constructs his/her own argument about Magneto as a Holocaust victim/survivor worthy of sympathy.

The use of Magneto's Auschwitz tattoo as signifier of multiple concepts also appears in the X-Men films. In *First Class*, Erik encounters a pair of fugitive Nazis at a bar in 1960s Argentina. After one of them reveals his father was from Dusseldorf, Erik retorts that his parents also lived there. The Nazi asks for their names, to which Eric responds, "They didn't have a name." As he slowly reveals his tattooed arm, he continues, "It was taken away from them," and then he proceeds to execute them. Here, the tattoo denotes the branded mark of concentration camp prisoners and serves as a historical cue to provoke the Nazis. It also connotes the dehumanization and degradation of Jews who were stripped of their names and reduced to being identified simply by numbers. Showing the tattoo to the Nazis further symbolizes Erik's implicit need to justify his actions to himself. A close-up of the tattoo, however, represents the filmmakers' mediated attempt to justify to the audience Erik's imminent, retributive justice against the two fugitive Nazis. The scene sets the foundation for Erik's transformation into an "anti-hero"—a killer who can garner audience support because the people he attacks are viewed as deserving extreme punishment.

While the Holocaust is not directly invoked in the animated X-Men series, there is still an introduction of a tragic element to Magneto's past. In the season 1 episode "Deadly Reunions," Magneto gives an explanation for his declaration of war on humanity: "When I was a child, my people talked while others prepared for war. They used reason, while others used tanks, and they were destroyed for their trouble. I won't stand by and let it happen again." Before Magneto can complete his mission Professor Xavier uses his telepathic powers to stop Magneto's attack on a chemical plant. Xavier unlocks Magneto's childhood memories and forces him to confront the murder of his parents. The sensory overload causes Magneto to flee. The scene is significant for showing that Magneto suffers from survivor's guilt and uses the emotions of regret, sadness, and anger as motivation and justification for his violent actions to prevent further mutant deaths.

That nightmare scenario becomes a reality in the franchise's fifth film *X-Men: Days of Future Past*, which opens in an apocalyptic New York City circa 2023. The setting is a dystopian future where government-sponsored identification of and experimentation on mutants has led to their near-extinction. Most of the X-Men, the mutant population, and humans have been hunted down and murdered by robotic overlords called Sentinels. The remaining survivors are either imprisoned in concentration camps or in hiding. The Sentinels, designed by the scientist Bolivar Trask in the 1970s to serve as mankind's protectors by identifying mutants and herding them into internment camps, ostensibly modified their own protocols and started hunting down, capturing, and killing both humans and mutants. Just as Erik predicted in *First Class*, the elimination of mutants—and subsequently the human race—began with Trask's team taking mutants, experimenting on their bodies, and using the results to advance the Sentinels program.

The remaining X-Men in 2023 deduce their future could have been averted by the prevention of a single event in 1973: Mystique's assassination of Trask at the Paris Peace Accords, which precipitates the Sentinel program's widespread adoption. To ensure Mystique's plan fails, Kitty Pryde uses her abilities to send Wolverine/Logan's consciousness back into his younger self 50 years earlier. The future Professor Xavier and Magneto task him with finding them and convincing them to work together at their most divisive time. In 1973, Charles is addicted to a serum that restores the use of his legs, but simultaneously blocks his telekinetic powers. Erik is incarcerated in the Pentagon, charged with the assassination of President Kennedy. After Logan persuades Xavier to help, they break Erik out of prison and head for Paris. The team stops the assassination attempt, however Erik declares that Mystique must die to secure mutant survival. Just before shooting her, Erik apologizes and says, "Forgive me, Mystique. As long as you're out there we'll never be safe." Beast saves Mystique, though Erik's attempt inadvertently sets the dystopian future in motion by providing Trask with a sample of her blood for use in creating Sentinels with adaptable powers. Erik's rationalization is noteworthy because it provides the audience with a deeper insight into the character—one that shows his action is not grounded in pure malevolence, but rather a necessary step in stopping the cyclical nature of violence between mutants and humans. Where the super villain displaces the antihero though, is in Magneto's disregard for the potential collateral damage in his pursuit to remake the world.

Traversing the Moral Spectrum

A more altruistic Magneto emerges in issue #150 where his motives behind forcing the disarmament of all global powers is revealed—aside from acquiring a dictatorship—to be less selfish: "The nations of the world spend over a trillion dollars a year on armaments. I intend to deny them that indulgence. The money and energy devoted now to war will be turned instead to the eradication of hunger, disease, poverty."[7] Magneto as "pacifist" appears in the fourth season of the animated series in episode "Sanctuary Part 1"; fatigued from battling for mutant supremacy, the master of magnetism desires to relocate mutants to Asteroid M where they can live peacefully and separated from humans. In an effort to free mutants from human cruelty, Magneto declares, "I come to rescue my people, not to avenge them." Magneto forgoes his usual plan of seeking mutant liberation through human subjugation and instead promises that no further aggression will occur if mutants are allowed a mass exodus to their own homeland.

A stark contrast to this "benevolence" emerges in *X2* when he modifies a replica of Cerebro—a machine that locates mutants by centralizing Professor Xavier's telekinetic powers—into a weapon of mass destruction against humans. The device was designed by the film's villainous Colonel William Stryker (Brian Cox) to eradicate the mutant race, but Magneto alters the target from mutants to humans. Magneto proffers his justification to Professor X: "How does it look from there Charles? Still fighting the good fight? From here it doesn't look like they're playing by your rules. Maybe it's time to play by theirs." With a nefarious grin, Magneto appears delighted at the prospect of his plan unfolding. Magneto's decision reflects decades-long changes in the depiction of the character, from Stan Lee's two-dimensional villain who, in issue #1, Professor X suggests "hate[s] the human race, and wish[es] to destroy it," to Claremont's more ambivalent version that *X-Men* comics writer Fabian Nicieza claims became "…recognized as a good guy."[8] *X2*'s Magneto evokes sympathy for his views while reverting to a megalomaniacal plan to wipe out the human race. There is a relative balance, though, within Claremont's Magneto, who oscillates between hero and super villain, with most portrayals lying somewhere in the middle. However, *X2*'s Magneto takes an unprecedented leap, setting into motion a plan to wipe out humanity when he alters Cerebro. *What is more villainous than the total destruction of the human race?*

This is exactly what Magneto warns humanity of in *Days of Future Past* after uprooting a baseball stadium and enclosing the White House within it. He declares, "Today I give you a glimpse of the devastation my race can unleash upon yours." An interesting dialectic emerges here through the temporal and spatial juxtaposition of Magneto fighting on two fronts. The 1973 Magneto is visually and thematically presented as a super villain—thrusting metal pipes into Wolverine and terrorizing the people of Washington, D.C., while cross cuts reveal a 2023 Magneto in a more heroic role battling Sentinels alongside the surviving X-Men. Although both iterations of the character are working toward the same end, which is mutant survival, their methods are diametrically opposed. These oppositions illustrate an attempt to depict Magneto in a complex way that shows his vacillating between super villain and anti-hero.

Super villains such as Marvel's planet-consuming Galactus or DC's Joker are evil incarnate and lack any remorse for their actions. Claremont and his artistic collaborators' Magneto, however, often ruminates over the implications of his actions. This level of introspection is virtually absent in the films save for a few lines of dialogue. When Charles Xavier—Erik's closest friend—dies in *X-Men: The Last Stand*, Magneto laments, "My single greatest regret is that he had to die for our dream to live." While Charles' death emotionally affects Erik, he still views it as collateral damage, i.e., an unfortunate but necessary outcome that will ensure his version of the greater good with mutants as rulers over humans. Magneto's most reflective moment in the film trilogy appears in *X-Men: The Last Stand* when he realizes the consequences of unleashing Phoenix—an unstable reborn version of the X-Men's Jean Grey—onto the world. After the uncontrollable Phoenix begins killing mutants and humans alike, Magneto admits culpability for his actions, rhetorically asking, "What have I done?" This afterthought either represents Magneto's recognition of his grave error in pursuing mutant superiority, or his disappointment in his plan backfiring and resulting in mutant deaths. Here, much of the audience's understanding of Magneto's character is shaped by McKellan's poignant portrayal of Magneto being briefly reflective. Magneto offers a more concrete notion of regret in *Days of Future Past* upon realizing he and Charles are near death in the dystopian 2023 future: "All those years wasted fighting each other, Charles. To have a precious few of them back." While these admissions are fleeting they are noteworthy for the film's effort to portray Magneto as reflexive and questioning of his actions.

A similar revelation of remorse is more thoroughly explored in the comics. Magneto's path toward redemption begins in *The Uncanny X-Men* #150 after he comes to believe he killed the X-Men's Kitty Pryde by sending an electric charge through her body during a fight. Unbeknownst to him, Kitty is not actually dead; however, this event triggers a major psychological transformation within Magneto. While holding what he believes to be her lifeless body, Magneto explains his philosophy on humanity and then admits his plan was misguided:

> I remember my own childhood—the gas chambers at Auschwitz, the guards joking as they herded my family to their death. As our lives were nothing to them, so human lives became nothing to me.... I believed so much in my own personal vision that I was prepared to pay any price, make any sacrifice to achieve it. But I forgot the innocents who would suffer in the process.... In my zeal to remake the world, I have become much like those I have always hated and despised.[9]

The visual topos of Magneto holding Kitty's, presumably, lifeless body close to him and resting his head against her forehead is a recognizable image that conveys deep sadness. His lamentation over her death reinforces his remorse and provides the audience with an explicit reference to Magneto's reflection and realization of the consequences of his transgressions. This moral transformation as illustrated through the comic book's content reinforces the artist and writer's goal of developing the archetype of a tragic figure worthy of audience sympathy.

In *First Class* a similar transformative moment mirrors the visual topos of Magneto holding Kitty Pryde from issue #150. After Erik re-directs a barrage of missiles meant for the X-Men toward the naval ships that released them, Charles tackles him in an attempt to break his magnetic control over the weapons. Moira MacTaggert (Rose Byrne), a CIA operative aiding the X-Men, starts shooting at Magneto, who deflects each bullet. However, one misdirected swipe of his hand inadvertently sends a bullet into Xavier's spine, paralyzing him. Magneto drops to his knees, grasps Charles' body and cries, "I'm so sorry.… Us turning on each other, it's what they want. I tried to warn you Charles. I want you by my side." In a moment of radical intertextuality, Michael Fassbender's Erik echoes Ian McKellan's Magneto, who in turn reproduces Stan Lee's Magneto saying, "This society won't accept us. We form our own. The humans have played their hand. Now we get ready to play ours. Who's with me? No more hiding."[10]

Still cradling Charles' paralyzed body, Magneto says, "We're brothers, you and I. All of us together, protecting each other. We want the same thing." Charles replies, "My friend. I'm sorry, but we do not." This motivates Erik not toward a redemptive path like Claremont's Magneto, but to a destructive one. When Magneto holds Kitty's seemingly dead body in issue #150, he realizes that, in his fervor, he was mimicking the genocidal actions of those he hated, and this prompts the redemptive journey on which his character embarks in the following issues. This demonstrates Claremont's attempt to create sympathy for Magneto, to force readers to reexamine their conceptions of what a true "super villain" is and consider the context of Magneto's motivations for survival.

Hollywood Superhero Blockbusters vs. Serialized Comic Books

What makes it more likely that evil will be "thinned" out and "simplified" in comic book films rather than in comic books themselves? The short answer is the inevitability of Hollywood building a franchise where economics and commercial viability dictate a majority of decisions. Disney and Marvel's budget for *The Avengers* was roughly $220 million. Arguably, when that much money is invested into a single project there is less room for experimentation; because production costs for comic books pale in comparison, artists often feel less creative constraint.

Another answer is that the serial nature of comics allows for more room to experiment compared to films, which have a limited time for character development. In *Comic Book Nation*, Bradford W. Wright notes that Stan Lee's editorial strategy at Marvel during the '60s was to "…weave his characters and plot references into a coherent modern mythology that invited an unusual degree of reader involvement."[11] The serialized structure of the Marvel comics universe facilitated the unfolding of interconnected storylines across hundreds of issues, with new stories appearing every week. Since the cost of comic production was relatively low, substantially below that of a typical studio film's budget, writers and artists did not face the same pressures of delivering a success with every issue (or even series of issues) as filmmakers had with a movie. This in turn, allowed creators the freedom to present reinterpreted variations of characters throughout their titles, often introducing complicated heroes and villains that revel in ambiguous motives.

While the X-Men films portray Magneto as a persecuted victim who metabolizes his rage into the pursuit of mutant survival, five, two-hour-long films have limited space to unravel the mystery of Magneto—particularly in comparison to Claremont's sixteen-year run as writer of the series where Magneto's journey toward redemption took place within 200 issues. But, Magneto's sympathetic portrayal became a contentious issue for the subsequent writers who felt that he was seemingly adopting Professor X's ideals, which left little room for dramatic conflict. Fabian Nicieza notes that he and fellow X-Men writers "…had to find a way to bring tension back between them because they were both starting to go too close together on the same philosophical road."[12] This tension constitutes the core of the X-Men films, where Magneto is explicitly depicted as the villain.[13] While many of the comics have instances of Magneto's introspection,[14] the cinematic version is more streamlined and reflects Nicieza's claim that too much similarity between Xavier and Magneto would leave no conflict to dramatize. Instead, Marvel Studios proved this formula worked, as its experiment of introducing an expansive cinematic universe with *X-Men* led to several successful blockbuster superhero franchises.[15]

Interiority in Comics and Films

The comic book's primary tool for showing Magneto's innermost feelings is what Scott McCloud and Will Eisner call a "thought balloon": a cloud shape with a tail consisting of a series of bubbles that indicate the character is not speaking, but thinking.[16] The panel in issue #113 illustrates David Carrier's explanation of the function of word balloons: "by externalizing thoughts, [they] make visible the inner world of represented figures, externalizing their inner lives, making them transparent to readers."[17] There are instances in the films where the audience can infer that Magneto is contemplating his actions, however no words are uttered. In *X-Men*, after Magneto examines the numbers on Wolverine's dog tag, the camera tilts down, revealing a close-up of his faded concentration camp tattoo. A similar scene unfolds in *X-Men: First Class*, where Erik rolls the coin given to him by Dr. Klaus Schmidt earlier in the film through his fingers. Again, through subjective visuals—the camera zooms onto Erik's tattoo, the shot then cuts to pictures of Nazis including Schmidt, then back to Erik—rather than through dialogue or voice-overs, enough visual context is given to suggest the filmmakers are alluding to Erik's past and are directing the audience to reflect on his experience at Auschwitz.

As Catherine Khordoc notes, "in film or theater, the use of voice-overs are often relied upon in order to create the illusion that a character is not actually uttering his thoughts," whereas in comics, thought "is made clear immediately through the use of a particular type of balloon."[18] In the case of the *X-Men* films: would Magneto's voice-over seem awkward and out of place, particularly if his was the only voice used in this manner? Conveying these emotions is entirely possible in cinema but as Noël Carrol observes, "clearly the existing output of any medium will only consist of objects designed to serve uses that it is logically and physically possible for the medium to perform."[19] In other words, the cinema is completely capable of conveying inner thought on screen through the use of voice-overs, dramatic music, or subjective visuals such as the *X-Men* films' illustrates by showcasing Magneto's implicit need to justify his actions to himself through a series of close-ups and subsequent camera tilts, which visualizes Magneto looking down at his tattoo.

Richard Berger makes an applicable assertion regarding the relationship between texts in his discussion of how the five *Superman* films are not adaptations in the traditional definition, but rather, "they are heteroglossic in that they are 'shot through' with the voices of the many artists, writers and adaptors of the comic books."[20] The cinematic Magneto is, similarly, an amalgamation of his creators Stan Lee and Jack Kirby, subsequent artists and writers from Len Wein and Chris Claremont to Dave Cockrum and Jim Lee, and various screenwriters such as Zak Penn and David Hayter. Magneto does not have one author, but many. In other words, the multitude of authorship in the various incarnations of Magneto certainly dialogically influenced the cinematic Magneto, and can partly account for variations in the character. There is no privileged text that the Marvel films solely relied on; rather they contained "elements or utterances" of previous versions of Magneto, such as Stan Lee's arrogant and antagonistic super villain and Claremont's compassionate anti-hero. Although each film problematizes issues of restraint with Magneto and simplifies the debate between good and evil, they all represent Marvel's attempt at depicting the multi-faceted nature of the master of magnetism to build expansive stories, transmedially, that offer consumers multiple entry points to the *X-Men* franchise.

NOTES

1. *X-Men*, directed by Bryan Singer (2000; Beverly Hills: 20th Century–Fox Home Entertainment, 2000), DVD; *X2*, directed by Bryan Singer (2003; Beverly Hills: 20th Century–Fox Home Entertainment, 2003), DVD; *X-Men: The Last Stand*, directed by Brett Ratner (2006; Beverly Hills: 20th Century–Fox Home Entertainment, 2006), DVD; *X-Men: First Class*, (2011; Beverly Hills: 20th Century–Fox Home Entertainment, 2011), Blu-ray; *X-Men: Days of Future Past*, directed by Bryan Singer (2014; Beverly Hills: 20th Century–Fox Home Entertainment, 2014), Blu-ray.

2. Christopher Robichaud, "Bright Colors, Dark Times," in *Supervillains and Philosophy: Sometimes, Evil Is Its Own Reward*, ed. Ben Dyer (Chicago: Open Court, 2009), 61–70.

3. The CCA was a self-regulated organization established in 1954 in response to accusations by psychologist Fredric Wertham, who wrote in *Seduction of the Innocent* that comic books were a leading contributor to juvenile delinquency.

4. Arie Kaplan, *From Krakow to Krypton: Jews and Comic Books* (Philadelphia: The Jewish Publication Society, 2008), 120.

5. Chris Claremont and Dave Cockrum, *The Uncanny X-Men* #161, September 1982 (New York: Marvel), 7.

6. Martin J. Medhurst and Michael A. Desousa, "Political Cartoons as Rhetorical Form: A Taxonomy of Graphic Discourse," *Communication Monographs* 48.3 (1981): 197–236.

7. Chris Claremont, Dave Cockrum, Joseph Rubinstein, and Bob Wiacek, *The Uncanny X-Men* #150, August 1981 (New York: Marvel), n.p.

8. Thomas J. McLean, *Mutant Cinema: The X-Men Trilogy from Comics to Screen* (Edwardsville, IL: Sequart Research & Literacy Organization, 2008), 184.

9. Claremont, Cockrum, Rubinstein, and Wiacek, *X-Men* #150, n.p.

10. See *X-Men* #4, March 1964 (New York: Marvel). Magneto is given some ideological justification for his hatred of humans when he recounts how he saved a fellow mutant from an angry human mob: "Have you forgotten that day, not long ago, when I first came to your village in the heart of Europe? Have you forgotten how the superstitious villagers called you a witch because of your mutant powers? It was I who saved you, keeping the maddened crowd back by means of my magnetic power! You must never forget that! Never!"

11. Bradford W. Wright, *Comic Book Nation: The Transformation of Youth Culture in America* (Baltimore: Johns Hopkins University Press, 2003), 218.

12. McLean, *Mutant Cinema,* 184.

13. In *X2*, a new member of the Brotherhood of Mutants says to Magneto, "So, they say you're the bad guy."

14. At one point, Magneto abandons his crusade to ensure mutant superiority; he aligns himself with Xavier's ideals and begins training the X-Men at Xavier's mutant academy.

15. In the article "*X-Men* as J Men: The Jewish Subtext of a Comic Book Movie," Lawrence Baron convincingly argues that part of *X-Men*'s success lies in its positioning of the *Holocaust* "as a metaphor for the vulnerability of any minority group" which is revealed through the ideological conflict between Magneto and Professor X (51).

16. Will Eisner, *Comics and Sequential Art by Will Eisner* (Tamarac, FL: Poorhouse, 1985); and Scott McCloud, *Understanding Comics: The Invisible Art* (New York: HarperCollins, 1993).

17. David Carrier, *The Aesthetics of Comics* (University Park: Pennsylvania State University Press, 2000), 73.

18. Catherine Khordoc, "The Comic's Soundtrack: Visual Sound Effects in *Asterix*," in *The Language of Comics: Where Word and Image Intersect*, ed. Robin Varnum and Christina T. Gibbons (Jackson: University of Mississippi Press, 2002), 170.

19. Noël Carroll, *Theorizing the Moving Image* (Cambridge: Cambridge UP, 1996), 29.

20. Richard Berger, "Are There Any More at Home Like You?': Rewiring *Superman*," *Journal of Adaptation in Film & Performance* 1.2 (2008): 90.

About the Contributors

Jason **Bainbridge** is chair of Media and Communication at Swinburne University of Technology, Australia. He has published widely on screen culture, comic books and popular culture more generally.

Daniel **Binns** is a film producer, teacher and researcher with a strong interest in genre studies, Hollywood cinema and storytelling across platforms both digital and real-world. He lectures in film and media studies at the Royal Melbourne Institute of Technology.

Arnold T. **Blumberg** is a comics historian and the "the MCU guru," a world-renowned authority on the Marvel Cinematic Universe and professor of the world's first college course specifically focused on the MCU and offered at the University of Baltimore.

Liam **Burke** is a media studies lecturer at Swinburne University of Technology, Australia. His publications include *The Comic Book Film Adaptation: Exploring Modern Hollywood's Leading Genre*, *Fan Phenomena Batman*, and *Superhero Movies*.

Jef **Burnham** has taught film genre courses on Marvel movies at Columbia College Chicago and DePaul University. He teaches in DePaul's College of Communication and College of Computing and Digital Media.

David Ray **Carter** is the author of *Conspiracy Cinema: Propaganda, Politics, and Paranoia*. He has written on multiple comic book and pop culture topics.

Julian C. **Chambliss** is an associate professor of U.S. history at Rollins College. His research examines cultural perceptions linked to real and imagined urban spaces.

Brian **Cogan** is an associate professor at Molloy College in the Communications Department. He is the author, co-author and co-editor of numerous books, articles and anthologies on popular culture, music and the media.

Rodney **Donahue** is the drama program coordinator at Clarendon College and adjunct instructor in integrative studies at Texas Tech University. He has published on theatre, film and higher education.

Jeremiah **Favara** is a doctoral candidate in the School of Journalism and Communication and a graduate teaching fellow in the Women's and Gender Studies Department at the University of Oregon. His research focuses on intersections of gender, media, technology and popular culture.

Eric **Garneau** is the comics manager at Pastimes in Niles, Illinois, one of the Midwest's largest gaming and collectible stores. He also writes and produces shows, podcasts and games for the sketch comedy group the Nerdologues.

Jacob **Garner** is the electronic reserves specialist at the Mary Kintz Bevevino Library, Misericordia University.

Vanessa **Gerhards** is a lecturer the University of Siegen (Germany). Her research interests are adaptation studies (mainly Shakespeare adaptations) as well as Gothic literature and culture and Cyberpunk culture.

About the Contributors

Rick **Hudson** is a novelist and academic specializing in the study of fantasy/sf and horror narratives. He is a research fellow at Manchester Metropolitan University.

Jesus **Jimenez-Varea** is an associate professor in the Department of Media & Advertising in the University of Seville, Spain. His area of expertise is the intersection of popular culture, narratives and image theory, particularly comics, along with genres like horror and superheroes across media.

Miriam **Kent** is a Ph.D. candidate in film studies at the University of East Anglia, UK. Her research combines the theoretical approaches of feminist film theory, comics studies, gender studies, queer theory and postcolonial studies.

Naja **Later** lectures in genre media and pop culture studies at the University of Melbourne, Australia. Her work explores post–9/11 theory in popular horror cinema, television, journalism and transmedia.

Jeff **Massey** is a professor of English language and literature (medieval-classical-linguistical) at Molloy College, where he periodically teaches courses on comic history and scriptwriting.

Matthew J. **McEniry** is an assistant librarian at Texas Tech University Libraries specializing in creating descriptive metadata for digital manuscripts and archive collections. His research interests focus on video game preservation.

Stephen **Miller** earned a BA in Japanese language and literature from Boston University. He is a full-time Japanese/English interpreter and translator.

Robert Moses **Peaslee** is an associate professor and chair of Journalism & Electronic Media in the College of Media & Communication at Texas Tech University. He has published books and articles on a variety of comic book subjects.

Miguel Ángel **Pérez-Gómez** is a member of the Department of Media & Advertising in the University of Seville, Spain, where he researches fandom and participatory cultures, specifically fans' audiovisual creations.

D. Stokes **Piercy** is a filmmaker and media studies scholar who explores the intersections of popular culture, philosophy and religion. His primary research and creative work explore myth, storytelling and historical memory and identity.

Cord A. **Scott** is a member of the traveling collegiate faculty for UMUC–Asia. He has written and published on a variety of comics topics and cultural history.

Thomas **Simko** is an MFA student at Wilkes University and a writer and musician. He has written and/or published work in poetry, nonfiction and critical essays.

Ron **Von Burg** is a rhetoric of science scholar who explores intersections of popular culture and public discussions of science. His primary research explores how science fiction films provide a series of tropes and discourses that shape public scientific discourse.

Joseph **Walderzak** studies media and cinema at DePaul University. His research investigates how narratives involving teen status have shaped and shifted the discourse on class in American teen films from 1978 to the present.

Liam T. **Webb** is a freelance writer and editor of online content, film scripts, news articles, blogs, comic books and short story books. He interned at Marvel Comics and for the past two years has been building his own publishing company, Red Branch Publications.

Robert G. **Weiner** is a popular culture/humanities librarian at Texas Tech University. He has published on a wide variety of popular culture topics including comics, librarianship, film and music.

Joshua **Wucher** is a Ph.D. candidate in the English Department at Michigan State University, where he specializes in film and comics studies. His research interests include popular culture, film genre theory, specifically horror and superhero films, and the Jewish influence on comic books.

Index

Abby 98
ABC 107, 118, 125
Abimelech 74
Academy Award 110, 125
Achilles 18
Action Force 61
Adam and Eve 15
Adventures of Captain Marvel 94, 130, 131
Aegisthus 40
Aenied 15
Affleck, Ben 169
Africa 189, 193
Agamemnon 40
Agent Carter (2015 series) 2, 118, 161, 173
Agent Maria Hill 39
Agent Zero 101
Agents of S.H.I.E.L.D. (2013 series) 2, 17, 118
Akira (1988) 110
Alfred Hitchcock Presents 125
Alien 60, 64-65, 69
Aliens 65, 69
The Amazing Spider-Man (1978 series) 3, 107, 133-134, 141, 191, 233
Amazoness 87
America Toons In 108
Ancient Greece 41
Anderson, Craig 80
Anderson, J.L. 205
Angel 11
Ant Man (2015) 6, 35, 39, 196
Antigone 41
Apollo 40
Apple (company) 57
Aquaman 13
Arad, Avi 1, 3, 34, 111, 113, 189
Arashikage, Thomas 99
Arcee 28, 32, 57
Arctic 90
Armada 57
Army 132
"Arnold at the Gates: Subverting Star Persona in *Conan the Barbarian*" 77
Asgard 44
Assassin's Guild 42
Athena 15
Athens 41
Atom Man vs. Superman 131

Atomic Age 11
Attack of the Killer Tomatoes (animated series 1990-1991) 2
Atwell, Lionel 130
Aum Shinrikyo 97
Aunt May 13
Autobot 27-28, 30, 53, 55
Autobot City 53, 57
Autobot Matrix of Leadership 54
The A.V. Club 53
The Avengers 11-12, 16-18, 34, 87, 108, 121, 123, 138, 177-187, 241, 250
The Avengers (2012 film) 1, 5, 10, 39, 48, 106, 129, 156, 173, 177, 182-186, 196, 241, 244
Avengers Assemble 34
The Avengers: United They Stand 111
Axis Powers 130
Azoth 80

Bainbridge, Jason 27
Banner, David Bruce (character) 14, 37, 118, 120-126, 140, 159, 217, 241-245
Banshee 145
Barnes, Bucky (character) 130-131, 161
Baron Zemo 35
Bat Cave 96, 131
Bat-Mania 85
Batman 12, 14, 17, 19, 85, 94-96, 102, 113, 119, 124, 131-132, 217, 221
Batman (1943 comic) 130-131
Batman (1989 film) 2, 95-96, 106, 110-111, 125, 135-136
Batman and Robin 131
Batman Begins (2006 film) 2, 163
Batman: The Animated Series (1992-1994) 110-111
Battle Fever J (1979) 2, 87-88
Bauer 45
Baxter Building 18
Bay, Michael 30, 36
Bazin, Andre 112
Beast 110, 113
Beauty and the Beast (1992) 110
Beetlejuice 110
Bella 87
Bendis, Brian Michael 34

Bible 15, 18
Big Hero 6 (2014 film) 2, 95, 101-102
Bigelow, Kathryn 212-213, 217
Binns, Daniel 4, 39
The Bionic Woman 119
Bixby, Bill 119-127
Black Entertainment Television (BET) 195
Black Panther 5, 189-199
Black Panther: Cry the Accursed Country 193
Black Sabbath 55
The Black Scorpion 64, 66
Black Widow 17, 39, 43, 48, 125, 161, 177-180, 183
Blackheart 21, 24
Blacula (1972) 192, 206
Blade 89, 97-99, 101-102, 115
Blade (1998 film) 2, 95-96, 114, 200-211
Blade: Trinity (2004) 98, 201
Blade II (2002 film) 98, 201
Blake, Don (character) 14, 122
Blast from the Past (website) 108, 110
Blaxploitation 204-207, 210
Blaze, Johnny (character) 20-25
Blazing Saddles 135
Bloody Lips 42
Blue Oyster Cult 55
Bluestreak 29
Blumberg, Arnold T. 5, 118
Blundell 41
Blunt, Emily 158
Blurr 32-33, 57
Bollywood 4
Bowman, Rob 39-40, 42-44, 47-48, 98
Brackett, Lou 140-143
Brawn 29
Brevoort, Tom 84
Broadcast Energy Transmitter (BET) 66
Broadway 134-135
Brooks, Eric (character) 200, 207
Brother Guido 23
Brown, Jeffery A. 190
Brown, Reb 120, 127
Budiansky, Bob 30
Buffy the Vampire Slayer 11, 39
Buffyverse 11

Index

"Bullet Man Joe" 62
Burg, Ron Von 5, 241
Burke, Liam 1, 3, 5, 106
Burnham, Jeff 5, 138
Burton, Tim 95, 110–111, 125, 135–136
Buscema, John 1
Buza, George 113

Cadence Industries 85, 108
California 133
Callahan, Harry (character) 204–205
Camera Fiend 132
Cameron, James 65
Campbell, Joseph 44
Cannon Group 135
Cape Crow 42
Capli, Sue 216
Captain America 1–2, 4–5, 12, 17, 34–37, 39, 48, 86, 107–108, 111, 119–121, 129–143, 146, 177–188, 225, 243
Captain America (1979 animated series) 3, 107, 126–127, 134
Captain America (1990) 3, 129–137
Captain America and Santo vs. Spider-Man 132
Captain America and the Falcon 134
Captain America Comics 131–132
Captain America Death II Soon (1979) 3, 134
Captain America: The First Avenger (2011) 11–12, 129, 136–137, 151, 196
Captain America: The Winter Soldier (2014) 12, 16, 17, 129, 136, 178, 182, 196, 209
Captain Marissa Fairborne 68
Captain Marvel 130, 173
Captain Tendelli 124
Car Robots 29
Caribbean 126
Carter, David Ray 3, 5, 129
Carter, Jimmy 139–143
Carter, Peggy (character) 43, 48, 160–162
Case 214–217
Castaneda, Carlos 64
Castle, Frank 95–96, 232–240
Cave of Horrors 96
CBS 107, 119–121, 126–127, 133–134, 138
Celtic heroes 12
Cerebro 255
CGI 98, 113, 230
Challenge of the Gobots 30
"Chamber of the Gods" 64
Chambliss, Julian C. 5, 189
Chaste 42, 44, 46, 98, 100
China 42, 97
Christ 12
Christmas Eve 89
The Chronicles of Conan 76
Chu, John M. 99
Chung, Jamie 101
Church of the Damned 89

Citizen Kane 57
Clark, Eric 31
Closer Than We Think 64
Clover, Carol 207
Clytemnestra 40
Cobb, Ron 64–65
Cobra 61–66
Cobra Commander 61–66
Cobra Emperor 62–64
Cobra-La 64–67, 69
Cogan, Brian 4, 10, 115
Colan, Gene 88–90
Cold War 66, 193
Collins, Jim 200–201
Colon, Gene 206–208
Columbia 3, 95
Colvin, Jack 120
Combat Joe 29
The Comic Book Film Adaption 114
Comics Code of the Comics Magazine Association of America 88
Commissioner Gordon 124
ComsoContak Lamborghini 29
Conan 2, 72–81
Conan (1982) 4
Conan, King of Thieves 80
Conan Meets the Academy 77, 81
Conan the Barbarian 72–77, 79–81
Conan the Barbarian in The Horn of Azoth 72, 79–81
Conan the Destroyer 4, 72–73, 76–81
"Conan the Screenplay" 79–80
Conway, Gerry 72, 80
Copperhead 131
Corea, Nicholas 121
Corman, Roger 3
Crocodile Dundee 109
Crom 74
Crypt of Shadows 80
Cullen, Peter 27
Cyberpunk 212–222
Cybertron 28, 54, 56
Cyborg 009 (1964) 86
Cyclops 110, 112

Dagoth 76–77
daikaiju 85–87
Dante 23
"Dare to Be Stupid" 35, 53, 55
Daredevil 3, 42, 47, 115, 118, 123–126, 167, 224
Daredevil (2003 film) 98, 165
Daredevil (2015 series) 2, 123–124
Daredevil # 168 39
Daredevil: The Man Without Fear 123
Daria Dil (1988) 4
Dark City (1998) 212, 217–221
Dark Knight 19, 98, 125
The Dark Knight (2008) 10, 16–17, 163, 243
The Dark Knight Rises (2012) 17
Dawes, Rachel 163
Daywalker 200–201, 207–210
DC Comics 5, 10, 12–16, 90, 94, 99, 108, 119, 124, 130–131, 163, 190, 193, 230, 250
de rigueur 11

Deadpool 2
"The Death of Optimus Prime" 56
The Death of the Incredible Hulk (1990) 118, 125–126
Death Wish 135, 144, 232
Decepticon 27–28, 30, 53, 56
Defenders 121, 224–225
Defenders of the Earth 108, 111
DeLaurentiis, Dino 79
Del Toro, Guillermo 98
DeMarco 45–47
Denison, Rayna 3
Denshi Sentai Denziman 88
DePatie-Freleng Enterprises (DFE) 28, 107–108
Dery, Floro 32–33
Dev Adam 132
Devo 53, 55
Diabolik 4
Diaclone 29, 33
Diamond Direct 35
DiCola, Vince 54
Dille, Flint 28–30, 37, 63–64, 68
Dille, John F. 63
Dinobots 56–57
Di Pego, Gerald 123, 125
Dire Straights 58
Dirty Harry 204
Disney (film studio) 1–2, 5–6, 118, 256
Disney, Walt 107
Disney Renaissance 110
Disney XD 34
The Disuniting of America: Reflections on a Multicultural Society (1992) 193
Ditko, Steve 2, 11, 13
Dixon, Buzz 62, 64–66, 68
Doc Ock 13, 155
Dr. Araki 85
Dr. Cyrus Maldor 130
Dr. Daka 95–96, 101
Dr. Doom 15
Dr. Mills 133–134, 143
Dr. Mindbender 63, 65
Doctor Strange 3, 120–121, 133, 141, 146, 225
Doctor Strange (1978 animated series) 107, 126–127
Dr. Vaselli 135
Domini 89–90
Donahue, Rodney 4, 72
Donner, Jill Sherman 126
D'Onofrio, Vincent 124
Doomed: The Untold Story of Roger Corman's Fantastic Four 3
Douglas, Susan 152
Downey, Robert, Jr. 119, 180
Dracula 88–90, 98, 212
Dracula: Sovereign of the Dead 89
Drago, Ivan 234
Drake, Bobby 108
Drake, Frank 89–90
Dreamworks 36
DuBois Marta 123
Duke 29, 68
Dungeons & Dragons 108
Dunsay, George 29
DVD 52, 54, 106, 132

East Asia 97, 101
Easter 11
Eastwood, Clint 46, 239
Ebert, Robert 218
Eddas 18
Edge of Tomorrow 158
El Santo 132
The Electric Company (1971) 2
Elektra 39–48, 98, 100, 102
Elektra (2005) 4–5, 10, 95, 98, 165–174
Ellie 123
Emad 43
Emperor of Darkness: Vampire Dracula 98
Empire State University 108
Equality Now 39
Eternals 64
Evans, Chris 35, 177–185
Evel Knievel 133
Eye of Ibis 80

Falkof, Nicky 77
Famous Studioes 94
Fanfilms.net 4
Fang 132
Fantastic Four 2, 11, 13–15, 34, 107–109, 115, 191, 217
Fantastic Four (1994) 3
Fantastic Four (2005) 3, 6, 232
Fantastic Four (2015 film) 1
Fantastic Four Annual #3 108
Fantastic Four #1 66
Fantastic Four #6 108
Fantastic Four: The Rise of The Silver Surfer (2007) 15
"Fat Man" 100
Faust 20–25
Faustus 20
Favara, Jeremiah 5, 177
Fawcett Comics 130
Feige, Kevin 1, 11, 126–127
Ferrigno, Lou 120–122, 126–127
Fin Fang Foom 66
Fingeroth, Daniel 183
Finland 3
Firefly 39
Firestar 108–109
Fisk, Wilson 123–124
A Fistful of Dollars 205
Flash 13, 87
Flash Gordon 108
Fleischer, Richard 72, 81
Fleischer Studios 94
Fleming, Dan 32
"Flint" 68
The Flintstones 107
Force 44
Ford, Gerald 227
Ford, John 202
Foster, Jane 159
Four Heavenly Kings 97
Fox (film studio) 1–2, 34, 99, 101, 109, 251
Fox, Garner 88
Fox Kids 5, 108, 110–116
France 3, 88
Frankenstein 88, 90, 212, 215, 218

Fred and Barney Meet the Thing (1979) 2, 107
Friedman, Ron 65
Friedrich, Gary 90–91
Friends of Old Marvel (FOOM) 17
From Dusk Till Dawn 203
Frost, Deacon (character) 97, 200–210
The Fugitive 120
Fukushima, Rila 100
Full Latent Ability Gain (FLAG) 133, 140
Furman, Simon 30–32, 58, 131
Fury, Nick (character) 11, 16–17, 61, 139–146, 177–178, 183
"Fury Force" 61

Galactus the World-Devourer 15, 31
Gallagher, Tad 203
Galvatron 28, 30–33, 53, 56–58
Gambinus 79
Gambit 112
Gardner, Grant 130–133
Garia 86
Garneau, Eric 4, 52
Garner, Jacob 4, 20
Garner, Jennifer 40, 167–173
Geis, Richard E. 64–65
General Miguel 134
Generation X 140–146
Genesis 15
Genette, Gerard 32, 106
Gerbner, Steve 5, 64, 224–229
Gerhards, Vanessa 5, 212
German Shepherd 89
Ghost Rider (character) 20–25
Ghost Rider (2007) 20–21, 25
Ghost Rider (2007, 2011) 4, 155
Ghost Rider #9 24
Ghost Rider: Spirit of Vengeance (2011) 21, 24–25
Ghostbusters (1984) 229
G.I. Joe 29–30, 33–34, 60–68, 99, 102
G.I. Joe and the Transformers (1987 miniseries) 69
G.I. Joe: Retaliation (2013) 95, 99
G.I. Joe: The Movie (1987) 4, 60–69, 91, 99
G.I. Joe: The Rise of the Cobra (2013) 61, 95, 99
Giambrone, Sean 27
Gibson, William 212–219
Giger, H.R. 64
Gilgamesh 18
Giraud, Jean 64
The Girl with the Dragon Tattoo (2011) 162
Globus, Yorum 135
Glut, Donald 4, 131
Gobots 34
God 13, 21–22, 90, 123
Godzilla 87
Godzilla (1954) 85
Goethe, Johann Wolfgang 20–23
Golan, Menahem 135
Goldberg, Adam (character) 27–29

The Goldbergs (2013 series) 27–29, 35
Goldblatt, Mark 95, 234
Golden Age of Comic Book Filmmaking 113–115
Golden Gate Bridge 101
Golobulus 65–67
Good Soldier 11
Goodman, Martin 85
Goodwin, Archie 61, 88
Gorgolla 66
Gotham City 16–17
Goyer, David 98
Gracen, Elizabeth 125
Grantray-Lawrence 107–108
Gray, Jonathen 27, 33–34, 165
Gray, Richard J., II 138, 144
Great Dane 89
Greco-Roman demigods 12
Greek Civil War 42
Green Goblin 154
The Green Goblin's Last Stand (1992) 4
Green Goliath 119, 121
Green Lantern (2011) 6, 10, 16
Gretchen 23–25
Grey, Jean 112, 153, 255
Griffin-Bacal Advertising 28–29
Grimlock 55, 56
Grimm, Ben (character) 14–15, 107
Gross, Edward 107–108
Guardians of the Galaxy (2014) 2, 34, 196, 209, 224

Hagar, Sammy 55
Hal 9000 218
Hall, Don 101
Hama, Larry 30, 60–64, 99
Hamada, Hiro 101–102
Hamada, Tadashi 101–102
Hamasaki, Hiroshi 212
Hammond, Nicholas 107, 120, 125, 127
Hancock (2008) 243
The Hand 44–47, 98, 100, 102
Hangman 132
Hannah Barbera 30, 107–108
Hannibal King 89
Harada 100–102
Hard Master 99
Harker, Quincy 89–90
Harnel, Joe 120
Harras, Bob 107
Harrold, Harold H. 89
Harry Potter 73
Harvey, Robert C. 112
Hasbro 28–30, 32, 34–35, 57, 60–69, 91, 99, 108
"Hasbroverse" 68
Hassenfeld Brothers 28
Hawkeye 200–203
Hawkman 13
The Headmasters 36
Hearst, Patty 139
Heavy Metal 52–55, 58
Hell 21–22, 24
Hell Cycle 25
Hellcat 35
Hell's Kitchen 124–125

266 Index

Hemsworth, Chris 122–123, 177, 180–181, 185
Henney, Daniel 101
Henshin Cyborg 29
henshin hero 85–86
Hephaestus 15
Hera 15
Hercules 15, 18, 122
Hesiod 15–16
Hijab 43
Hillyer, Lambert 95
Hilton, James 64
Himalayas 67
Himitsu Sentai Gorenger 86
Hindi 89, 97
His Majesty Hirohito 95
The Hobbit 73
Hoberg, Rick 110
Hohauser, Ron 189
Hollywood 2–4, 10, 14, 17, 35, 73–75, 77, 80, 111, 123, 150, 165, 207, 230
Holocaust 252
Holograms 68
Homer 15–16
Honda, Ishiro 85
Hood, Gavin 101
Hooton, Peter 120, 127
Hot Rod 32–33, 53–57
"House of Ideas" 87
House of 1000 Corpses 75
Houston, Larry 110
How to Adapt Anything into a Screenplay 72
How to Draw Comics the Marvel Way (book) 1
Howard, Robert E. 73, 75, 78–80
Howard the Duck (1986) 3, 5, 99, 119, 224–230, 234
Howe, Sean 3
Hu, Kelly 101
Hubristic Warrior 11
Hudlin, Reginald 195
Hudson, Rick 3, 5, 224
Hugo 42
Hugo, Victor 120
Hulk 2, 5, 10, 14, 18, 37, 61, 85, 107–108, 118–127, 132, 178–179, 207, 217, 225, 241–249
Hulk (2003 film) 120, 159, 244
The Human Torch 3–4, 14, 107–108, 132
"Hunger" 55
Hunt, Leon 205
Huyck, William 99
Hydra 61, 145

Iceman 108–109
Idle, Eric 28, 34, 55
Iger, Roger 6
IGN 129
Iliad 10, 16
Illuminati 246–248
Imada, Jeff 97
In the Heat of the Night 125
The Incredible Hulk 3, 107, 118, 121, 126, 133–134, 224
The Incredible Hulk (1977 TV movie) 138, 146
Incredible Hulk (1988–1989) 5, 111, 140
The Incredible Hulk (2008 film) 120, 159, 244
The Incredible Hulk and She-Hulk 111
The Incredible Hulk Returns (1988) 118, 121–123, 125
Infinity Wars 37
InHumanoids: The Movie (1986) 2, 68–69, 139
Internet Movie Database (IMDB) 2, 238
Interpol 87
Iron Cross Army 86–87
Iron Man 1, 10, 12, 17, 34, 37, 107–108, 111, 125, 132, 178–188, 212–224, 243–245
Iron Man (2008) 1, 11–12, 17, 34, 39, 152, 156, 177
Iron Man: Rise of Technovore (2013) 5, 212–222
Iron Man II (2010) 11–12, 17, 151, 156, 177, 196
Iron Man III (2013) 12, 156, 160, 177, 190
Ironhead 56
Ironside 29
Ishinomori 86
Italian Spiderman (2007) 4
Italy 4, 41
Ivanhoe 127
The Invisible Girl 14
Iwanter, Sidney 109–110

Jackman, Hugh 109
Jackson, Samuel L. 177, 182
Jade Giant 119, 121
J.A.K.Q. Dengekitai 86
Janus 89
Japan 3, 84–86, 88–91, 94–102, 110
Japan Action Club (JAC) 87
Japoteurs 94
Jasmin 125
Jason and the Argonauts 11
Jedi Knight 32
Jehnna 79
Jekyll-and-Hyde 13, 120, 122, 207
Jem 68–69
Jenkins, Henry 32, 114
Jenson, Karen (character) 200–204, 207
Jesus 24
Jewett, Robert 139, 144
The Jim Henson Company 108
Jimenez-Varea, Jesus 3, 5, 84
Joen, Michael 99
Johansson, Scarlet 39, 125, 177–179, 182
Johnson, Derek 108
Johnson, Kenneth 119–121, 127
Johnson, Mark Steven 98
Joker 96, 221
Jones, Angelica 108
Jones, Grace 77
Jones, James Earl 75
Joshua Lambert Institute 122
Journey into Mystery #83 14
Jubilee 109, 112

Judge Dredd (1995) 224
Judges 9 74
Jungle Action Featuring the Black Panther 191–194
Junk 55
Junkions 34–35
Jurassic World (2015 film) 2
Jurwich, Don 99

kaizo ningen 85
Kaklimanidou, Betty 138, 144, 153
Kamen Rider 86–87
Kapture 126
Karloff, Boris 90
Keaton, Michael 96
Kenji 97
Kent, Clark (character) 13, 94
Kent, Miriam 5, 165
Kento 42
Kenya 88
Kick-Ass (2010) 155
Kill Bill: Vol. 2 (2004) 13, 19
kimagure 44, 47, 98
King, Geoff 202
King, Martin Luther, Jr. 135
King Conan 73
King Features 108
King Osric 74–75, 77
Kirby, Jack 2, 4, 11–13, 18, 64–65, 69, 131, 189–195
Kirigi 45–47, 98
Klein, Christa 124
Knight Rider 28
Kodansha 85
Koh, Wilson 113
Kohara, Shohei 32
Komori, Yu 85
Kona 64
Konami 109
Kramer, Eric Allan 122–124, 127
Krevolin, Richard 72–73, 75, 79–80
Kryptonite 131
Kubrick, Stanley 78
Kung Fu 60
"kunoichi" 98
Kup 32, 54–57
kuzuri 100
kyodai hero 85, 87
kyrios 41

La Magra 97
Lady Tanaka 95–97
"laissez-faire" 62
Landay, Lori 43
Lassie 28
Later, Naja 2, 5, 200
Laughton, Charles 65
Law, Jude 215
Lee, Ang 120
Lee, Christopher 134
Lee, Stan 1–4, 11–13, 31, 66, 78, 87, 108, 110–111, 118, 127, 135, 189–191, 195, 235, 256
Lee, Will Yun 98, 100
Lefevre, Pascal 112
The Legacy of Unicron 31, 36
The Legend of Conan 72, 80–81
Lehnsherr, Erik (character) 252–259

Lennie 55
"Leopardon" 87, 91
Levitt, Steve 122
Lichtenfeld, Eric 204
Lt. Falcon 68, 178, 182
Lilith 89
Lions Gate 3, 189
"Lithone" 52
Little, Cleavon (character) 135
Little Tokyo 96–97
Liufau, Sidney 97
Loesch, Margaret 108–112, 114
Loesch, Will 110
Logan 100, 253–254
Loki 10
Lolita 78
"The Lonely Man" 120
Lord of Vampires 89–90
Lost Horizon 64
Lucas, George 3, 228
LucasFilm 3
Lupeski, Anton 89

Machine Robo 30
Mackie, Anthony 182–183
Mad Max 109
Mad Max: Fury Road (2015) 158
Madhouse 98
Magneto 5, 109, 250–259
Mahabharata 18
Maisel, David 34
Malik 78
Mamiya, Juzo 87
Man of Steel (2013) 17
Man Thing 2, 3
mandaka 85
Mandrake the Magician 108
Mangold, James 100
Manovich, Lev 113
"Margarete" 23
Mariko 100–102
Marines 133
Marlowe, Christopher 20
The Marvel Action Hour 111
Marvel Anime 98
Marvel Cinematic Universe (MCU) 1–5, 11–17, 34–37, 39, 43, 84, 106, 111, 116–127, 129–162, 177–186, 190, 196, 210, 242
Marvel Entertainment Group (MEG) 110–111
Marvel Graphic Novel #59 72
Marvel Illustrated Book 76
Marvel Infinity 35
Marvel Knights (2010) 5
Marvel Legends 35
Marvel Productions 28, 30, 52, 91, 108–111
Marvel Spotlight #6 24
The Marvel Super Heroes 106–108, 114, 132
Marvel Television Universe (MTU) 5, 118–127
Marvel TV 138–145
Marvel UK 58
Marveller 87
Massey, Jeff 4, 10, 115
Master Roshi 98
Masters of the Universe (1987) 234

The Matrix (1999) 44, 74, 144
Mazinger Z 85
McEniry, Matthew J. 1
McFeely, Chris 29
McGee, Jack (character) 120
McGregor, Don 192–194
McNiven, Steve 34
mecha 85–87, 91
Medea 41
Megatron 30, 53, 56–58
Meizumi 98
Men in Black (1997) 2
Men's Fitness 180
Mephistopheles 21–25
The Merry Marvel Messenger 107
Metis 15
"Metroplex" 57
Metropolis 13, 17
Meugnoit, Will 109–110
Mexico 132
Microchange 29
Microman 29
Midgard 14
The Mighty Avengers 209
Mighty Morphin Power Rangers 88, 91, 110–111
Milius, John 75
Miller, Abby 44, 46–47
Miller, Frank 39, 123
Miller, Mark 44–46
Miller, Stephen 5, 94
Ming the Merciless 108
Les Miserables 120
Miss America 88
Mr. America 120
Mr. Fantastic 14–15
Mr. Foster 95
Mr. Ito 96
Mittell, Jason 110
Miyazaki, Hayao 64
Mjolnir 14
Mockingjay 73
Moebius 64
Monarch of Monster Isle 64
"Money for Nothing" 58
The Monster of Frankenstein 90
Monte Carlo 45
Monty Python 34, 55
Moreau 22
Morph 110
Morrison, Grant 12, 16, 18
Mount Doom 75
Ms. Marvel 119
MTV 53, 58
Mummy 88
Muppet Babies 108
Muppet Babies (1984–1991) 2
Murdock, Matt (character) 42, 123–124
My Little Pony (1986) 2, 68, 91, 99
The Mysterious Dr. Satan 131

Nagasaki 100
Naked City 125
Nama, Adilifu 190
Natari 80
Natchios, Christina (character) 42
Nausicaa of the Valley of the Wind 64

Nazi 5, 130, 135, 189, 252–255
NBC 108, 119, 121, 125–127
Nelson, Foggy (character) 124
Nelson, Judd 28
Nemesis Enforcer 65
Neo 44, 74
Nero 65
Netflix 118, 123, 173
Neuromancer (1984) 212–222
The New Fantastic Four 107
New Leaders 31
New Line Cinema 2, 96, 99
New World Entertainment 109, 121, 126–127
New York City 13, 42
"Ni Ten Ichi Ryuu" 97
Night of the Living Dead (1968) 208
"Night of the Sentinels" 110
Nihon Doga (studio) 88
Nimoy, Leonard 28, 32
Ninders 87
"ninja" 94
Nippon 86
Noble Peace Prize 139
Noboru 100–101
Norse God of Thunder 12, 14
Norrington, Stephen 96
Norton Antivirus 11
"Nothing's Going to Stand in Our Way" 55

Odin 14, 122
Odyssey 10, 16
Of Mice and Men 55
oikoi 41
Okamoto, Tao 100
Okamura, Gerald 97, 99
"Om" 97
"Once Upon a Joe" 68
"One Jem at a Time" 68
Optimus Prime 27–35, 37, 53, 56, 68
Orestes 40–41
Orient 85
Orwell 57
Osborn, Harry 115
Osborn, Norman 115
Otomo, Katsuhiro 110

Page, Karen (character) 124
Page, Linda (character) 96
Pahoo-Ka-Ta-Wah 61
Palimpsests 106
Paltrow, Gwyneth 39, 158
"Pandora's Box" 15
Panther vs. the Klan 192
Panther's Prey (1991) 194
Paramount 36, 94, 129, 131
Parker, Peter (character) 13, 87, 107–108, 112, 114–115, 154, 158, 217
Pasko, Martin 111
Peaslee, Robert Moses 1
Pelc, Gene 85–88
Perceptor 57
Pérez-Gómez, Miguel Ángel 3, 5, 84
Perlmutter, David 108–109, 114

268 Index

Perlmutter, Isaac 111
Perry Mason 125
Pettiman, Al 124
The Phantom 108, 217
Phoenix 255
"The Phoenix Saga" 114
Piaget, Jean 35
Piercy, D. Stokes 5, 241
Pink Floyd—The Wall 52
The Pink Panther 108
Pizza Hut 113
Planet Hulk (2010) 5, 241–247
Ploog 90–91
Poole, Dan 4
Portland 134
The Poseidon Adventure 125
Potts, Pepper (character) 39, 150–162
Power Man 3
Power Pack (1991) 2
President Kimball 136
Price, Frank 119
Primus 31
Prince, Diane 21
Prince Daka 95–97
Princess Leia 79
Professor Monster 87
Professor Xavier 109, 244, 251–259
Prowl 29
Proyas, Alex 212, 217
Prupish, Bob 30
Pryde, Kitty (character) 109, 255–256
"Pryde of X-Men" 109–110
Psylocke 101
Punday, Daniel 214
The Punisher 4–5, 95–98, 100, 115, 213, 232–240
The Punisher (1989) 3, 95, 102, 232–233
The Punisher (2004) 235
Punisher: Dirty Laundry (2012) 236
Punisher: War Zone (2008) 236
Purcell, Lee 122
The Purple Death 130
Pustz, Matthew 138–142
Pythona 66
Pyun, Albert 135

Queen Taramis 76, 79
Quicksilver 2, 16
Quintesson 28, 54–56

Rabin, Nathan 53, 57
Raeburn 41
Ramirez, Hector (character) 68
Rammon 80
Rapping, Elayne 142
Ratchet 29
Ratner, Brett 101
Real and Robo 29
Red King 245–247
"Red Nails" 76
Red Skull 132, 135–136
Reece, Gabrielle 126–127
Reese, Dondi (character) 196
Republic Pictures 94, 130–133
The Return of Captain America: The Avenging Corpse 131

Return of the Captain America (1944) 3
Return of the Jedi 79
Rhys-Davies, John 123–124
Rice, Condoleeza 196
Richards, Gail (character) 130–132
Richards, Reed (character) 14–15
Richardson, Bob 111, 113
Rip Hunter 64
Rita 87
Rivera, Geraldo 68
Roadblock 67
Roarke 21
Rocket Racoon 34, 35
Rocky IV 234
Rodan 64, 66
Rodimus Prime 28, 32, 54, 58
Rogers, Buck 63–64
Rogers, Steve (character) 130–136, 140–141, 146, 161, 184
Rogue 109, 153
Roots 133
Ross, Betty 132, 159–162
Rotten Tomatoes 72
Roxanne 24, 25
Russia 88

sai 46, 47
Saint 89
Saint, Howard (character) 235
Samson 18
San Francisco 101
Sanada, Hiroyuki 100
Santo 4
Satan 24, 25, 89
Savage Sword of Conan 73, 225
Scarab 130–132
Scarlet Witch 16
Scarlett 67
Schlesinger, Arthur 193
Schwarzenegger, Arnold 76–77, 80–81
Scognamillo, Giovanni 133
"Scorpio" 204–205
Scott, Cord A. 3, 5, 232
Scotti Bros. 55
Sea Devil 87
The Searchers 202
Secret Wars (2015 comic book) 2
Segal, George 27
Selfish Intellect 11
Selleck, Tom 3
Semper, John 111, 114–115
Senator Stern 17
Sensation Comics #1 19
September 11 43, 241
Serenity 39
Sgt. Slaughter 65
Serpentor 62–66, 69
Shadow Priest 244–245
Shaft (1972) 192, 202, 206
Shakespeare, William 40
Shandling, Gary 17
Shane 203–206
Sharkticon 56
Shaw, Margaret 122
Shazam 13
"She-Hulk" 121, 126–127
Shelley, Mary 90, 212, 215–216

Shelton, John 139
Shephard, Harvey 121
S.H.I.E.L.D. 17, 61, 143–145, 156–157, 160, 178, 213, 216, 221
Shin, Nelson 57, 99
Shingen 100–101
Shingri-La 63, 67
SHOCKER 86
Shoko Asahara 97
Shooter, Jim 61
Shueisha 85
Silk, James R. 135, 217
Silliphant, Stirling 125
Silver Surfer 2, 111
Simko, Thomas 4, 20
Simonson, Walt 14
The Simpsons 110
Singer, Bryan 99, 101, 106, 166
Sitwell, Jasper 17
The Six Million Dollar Man 119
Skywalker, Luke 74
Slade, Carter (character) 21
Smith, Barry Windsor 73
Smith, Rex 123–126
Smulders, Cobie 39
Smythe, Spencer 115
Snake Eyes 99
Snipes, Wesley 205–206
Solar Man (1986) 2
Solomon, Albert (character) 27
Sommer, Stephen 99
Son of Satan 224
Sony (film studio) 1, 15, 34, 113
Sophocles 39–40
Sound of Music 57
Soviet Russia 66
Soylent Green 72
spectatorship 33
Spectre 65
Spectre General 55
Spider-Bracelet 86–87
"Spider-Extract" 86
Spider-Machine GP7 87
Spider-Man 1–4, 11, 13–15, 30, 34, 84–86, 88, 100, 107–108, 111–113, 119–121, 132–134, 153, 210, 217, 224, 226
Spider-Man (animated series) 106, 111–115, 120, 125–127
Spider-Man (2002 film) 2, 106, 154, 230
Spider-Man (2012 film) 106
Spider-Man 2 (2004 film) 154, 232
Spider-Man 3 (2007 film) 155
Spider-Man and His Amazing Friends (animated series) 108–110, 115
Spider-Man: Confidential 107
Spider-Man the Dragon's Challenge (1981 series) 3
Spider Planet 86
"Spider-Protector" 86
Spider-Woman 4
Spirit of Truth 43
Springer 32, 57
Spy Smasher 130–131
Stack, Robert 28, 33
Stacy, Gwen 112
Stam, Robert 106

Index   269

Stan Lee Presents: The Mighty Marvel Strength and Fitness Book 181
Stander, Lionel 28
Stane, Ezekiel (character) 213–215, 218–221
Star Trek: The Motion Picture (1979) 53, 57, 144
Star Wars 30, 33, 35, 44, 60, 61, 68, 224
Stark, Tony (character) 10–11, 17, 37, 156–159, 162, 180, 184, 213–222
Starscream 29, 53, 56
Stevenson, Robert Louis 15
Stick 42, 98
Stoker, Bram 89, 212
Storm 153
Storm, Johnny (character) 14
Storm, Sue (character) 14
Storm Shadow 99
Strange Days (1995) 212–213, 216–218, 221
The Stranger Case of Dr. Jekyll and Mr. Hyde 215
Strucker, Baron 16
Stryker 101, 254
Subatoi 75
Submariner 2, 107–108, 132
Sumerians 20
Sun God 12
Sunbow Productions 28, 30, 32, 52, 54, 91, 99
Supaidaman 86–88, 91
Supaidaman (1978) 3, 87
Super Friends 108
Super-God Masterforce 36
super sentai 88, 91
Superboy 64
Supergods 12, 16
Superheroes: A Modern Mythology 190
Superman 4, 12–14, 16–17, 28, 64, 94, 102, 113, 119, 130–131, 221
Superman (1978 film) 3
Superman IV: The Quest for Peace 135
Superman Returns (2006) 163

Tagawa, Cary-Hiroyuki 98
Taiyo Sentai Sun Vulcan 88
TajNital 89
Takaku, Susumu 87
Takara 29, 32
Takemoto, Koichi 87
Taken (2008) 239
Tarantino, Quentin 13
Target: 2006 30–31, 33
T'Challa 191–194
Tee, Brian 100
Teen Titans 139
Teenage Mutant Ninja Turtles (1990) 144
Terminator 77, 80
Terminator: Genisys 80
Terminator 2 77
Tesseract 17
Theogony 15, 18
Theron, Charlize 158

The Thing 14, 107
Thomas, Rob 4
Thomas, Roy 72–73, 75–81, 244
Thompson, Derek 11
Thor 1, 12–14, 44, 61, 107, 111, 122–124, 127, 132, 161, 177–187
Thor (2011) 11–12, 17, 44, 152, 159, 196
Thor: The Dark World (2013) 12, 159–160, 196
Three Angry Men (1973) 4
3 Dev Adam 132–133
Thrush 65
Thulsa Doom 74–76
Thunder God 122
Time Master 64
Time Wars 36
Toei (film studio) 5, 84–88, 90–91, 98–99
Toei Animation 28, 32, 88
Toei Doga 88
Toei Manga Matsuri 87
Toho Studios 85
tokusatsu 3, 85, 87
Tokyo 101
Tokyo Toy Fair 29
Tolkien, J.R.R. 18
Tomb of Dracula (1980) 3, 90, 207
The Tomb of Dracula (#1–70) 88–90, 98–99, 114, 206
Tombs, Pete 133
Tonka 30
Tora! Tora! Tora! 72
Torgo 89–90
The Towering Inferno 125
Toy Biz 34, 110–111
toyetic 32–33
The Trail of the Incredible Hulk (1989) 118, 123–127
"The Traitor" 68
Transformers 2, 27–37, 68, 99, 108
Transformers Animated 36
Transformers Armada 36
Transformers: Beast Wars (1996) 36
Transformers Collector's Club 36
Transformers: Headmasters 28
Transformers #61 30
Transformers: The Movie (TTM, 1986) 2, 4, 27–37, 52–58, 68, 91, 99
Travolta, John 235
Tree of Woe 74
Trinity 74
Tunnel Rat 67
Turkey (country) 132–133
Turkle, Sherry 214
20th Century-Fox 113, 135
The 21st Century Superhero 138
"Twenty Questions" 68
Twilight 73
Twilight Zone 67
2001: A Space Odyssey 218
Typhoid Mary 169

Ultimate Avengers 2 (2004) 5
Ultimate Avengers 2: Rise of the Black Panther (2006) 189, 196
Ultra Magnus 28, 30–33, 35, 53, 57
Ultraforce (1995) 2

Ultraman 87
Ulysses Klaw 191, 196
The Uncanny X-Men 109
Uncle Ben 87
Unicron 28, 31, 34–35, 37, 52–58
United States Military 99
Universal Studios 3, 88, 119, 126
Upbin, Shari 135
UPN 111
Uslan, Michael E. 106

Valeria 74–75, 77, 80
Van Halen 53
Vancouver, Canada 124
Van Helsing, Rachel 89
Vanko, Ivan (character) 156
Variety 135
Venizelos, Dennis 111
Vimeo 4
Viper 100
Virgil 15, 22
Von Strucker, Baron Wolfgang (character) 16

Walderzak, Joseph 5, 150
Walters, Jennifer 126
Warner, Marina 208
Wasp 35
Watson, Mary Jane 112, 153–161
Wayne, Bruce (character) 21
Wayne, John 202
Weathers, Carl 3
Webb, Liam T. 4, 60
Weiner, Robert G. 1, 154
Welles, Orson 28, 55
Werewolf 88
West Germany 95
West Side Story 57
Whale, James 90
Whedon, Josh 11, 15, 39, 173
Wheelie 55–56
Wheeljack 29
Whiplash 17
Whistler 200
White House 135, 255
Williams, Chris 101
Wilson, Lewis 95
Winner, Michael 135
Wintermute 216
Wise, Robert 53, 57
Wolfman, Marv 88–90, 206
Wolverine 99–102, 109–110, 210, 253–255
The Wolverine (2013) 95, 100–102
Wonder Woman 13, 15, 21, 43, 47, 119, 132
"Working in a Coal Mine" 55
Works and Days 15
World War II 11–12, 37, 43, 102, 130, 132, 135, 252
Wreck-Gar 32, 34
Wright, Bradford 190
Wucher, Joshua 250

X-Mansion 18
X-Men 2–3, 14, 34, 100–101, 107–115, 153, 250–259
X-Men (animated series, 1992–1997) 106, 113–114

Index

X-Men (2000 film) 2, 5, 99, 106, 166, 230, 252
X-Men: Days of Future Past (2014) 114, 253–255
X-Men: First Class 252–259
X-Men Origins: Wolverine (2009) 101
X-Men: The Last Stand (2006) 101, 153, 255
X2 (2003) 101, 254
Xemnu the Titan 66
Xena 15

Yakama, Kosuke 86
"yakuza" 94, 234
Yamamura, Ken 100
Yamanouchi, Haruhiko 100
Yamashiro, Takuya 86–87
Yami no Teiou: Kyuuketsuki Dorakyura 98
Yankovic, Weird Al 35, 53, 55
Yashida 100–101
"Yellow Peril" 95
Yojimbo (1961) 205
Yokai 102

Yokohama 94
YouTube 4
Yukio 100–102

Zago 35
Zartan 99
Zombie, Rob 75
Zues 13, 15
"Zukala's Daughter" 73
Zula 77

www.ingramcontent.com/pod-product-compliance
Ingram Content Group UK Ltd.
Pitfield, Milton Keynes, MK11 3LW, UK
UKHW050539150426
5217IPUK00026B/1994